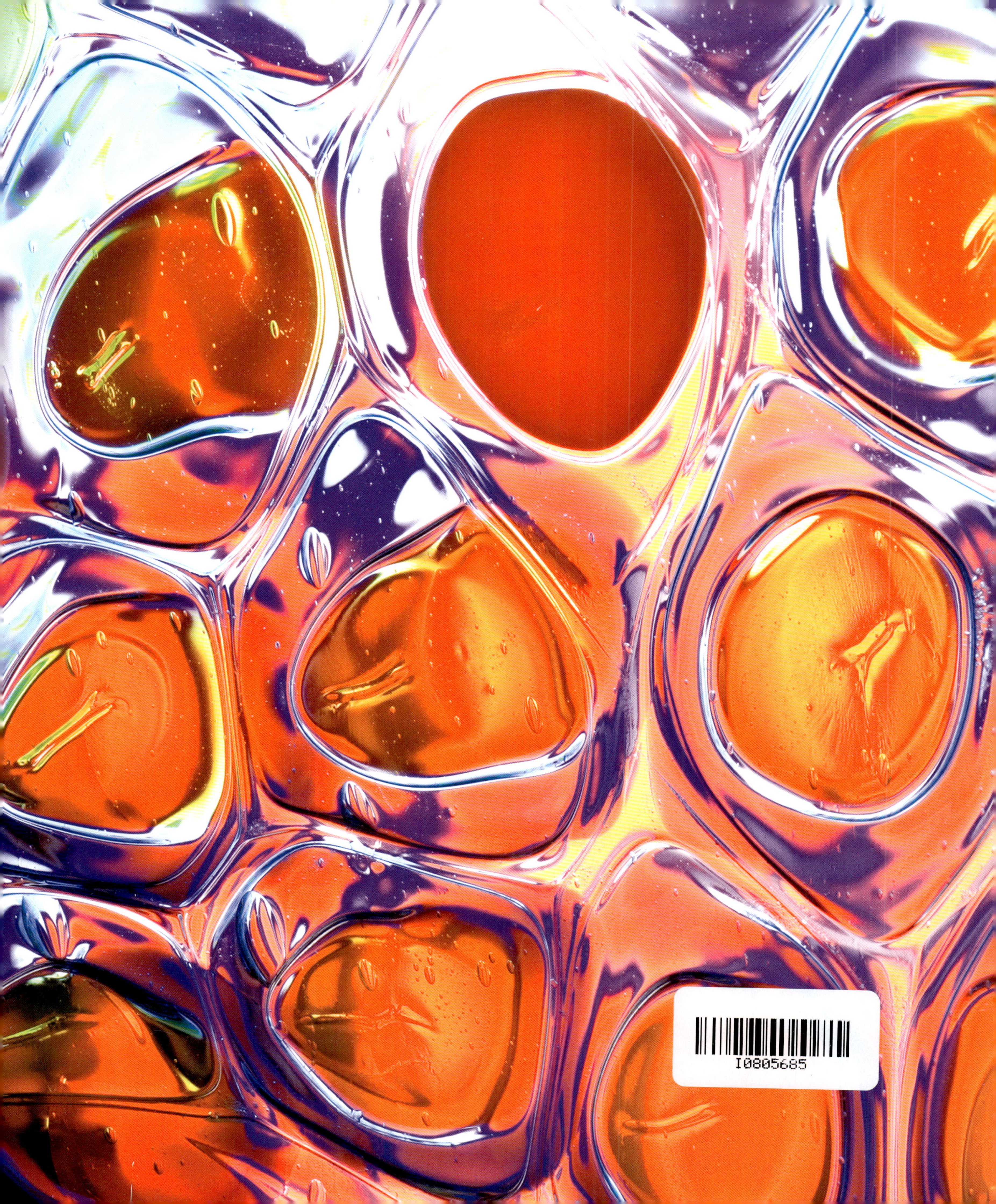

STEPHEN ROLFE POWELL

GLASSMAKER

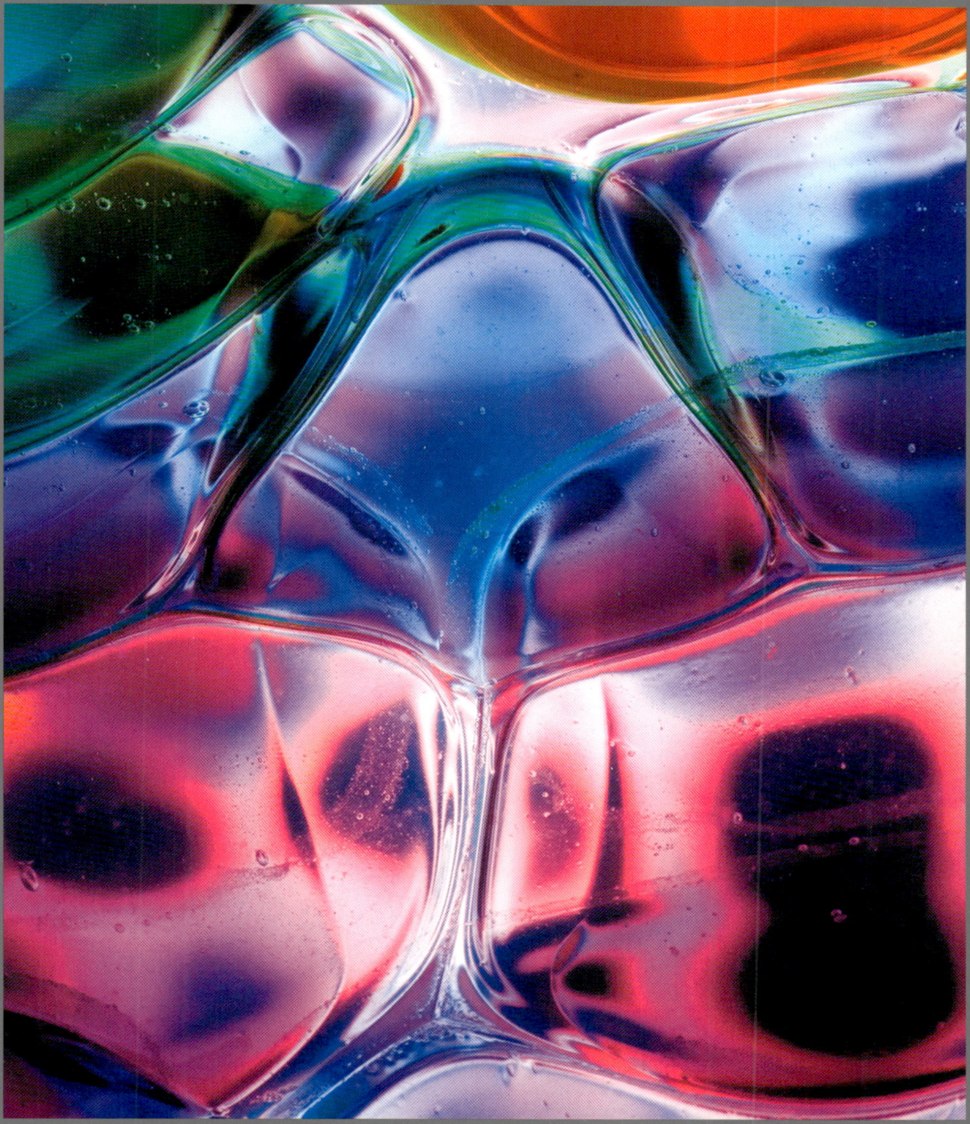

THE UNIVERSITY PRESS OF KENTUCKY

The University Press of Kentucky
Scholarly publisher for the Commonwealth, serving
Bellarmine University, Berea College, Centre College of
Kentucky, Eastern Kentucky University, The Filson Historical
Society, Georgetown College, Kentucky Historical Society,
Kentucky State University, Morehead State University,
Murray State University, Northern Kentucky University,
Transylvania University, University of Kentucky,
University of Louisville, and Western Kentucky University.

Editorial and Sales Offices:
The University Press of Kentucky
663 South Limestone Street,
Lexington, Kentucky 40508-4008
www.kentuckypress.com

11 10 09 08 07   5 4 3 2 1

Concept and design:
Images
Julius Friedman and Carol E. Johnson
Louisville, Kentucky

Photographs copyright © 2007
by David Harpe, Louisville, Kentucky

Teaser process photographs by Kate Philips
Myrtle Beach, South Carolina

Library of Congress Cataloging-in-Publication Data:
Stephen Rolfe Powell : Glassmaker.
p. cm.
ISBN 978-0-8131-2464-3 (hardcover : alk. paper)
1. Powell, Stephen Rolfe, 1951– 2. Glass art—United States.
I. Powell, Stephen Rolfe, 1951–
NK5198.P69S74 2007
748.092—dc22   2007014312

This book is printed on acid-free paper meeting the
requirements of the American National Standard for
Permanence in Paper for Printed Library Materials.

Manufactured in China

Member of the Association of American University Presses

For my family—

my mother, Anne, for her social grace;
my father, Arnie, for his passion to create;
my sister, Pam, and her husband, John,
for their enduring friendship;
and, most of all, to my wife, Shelly,
and sons, Zachary Hawk and Oliver Blue,
who keep my life in balance
and give me inspiration.

Photo by M. R. Spoonamore

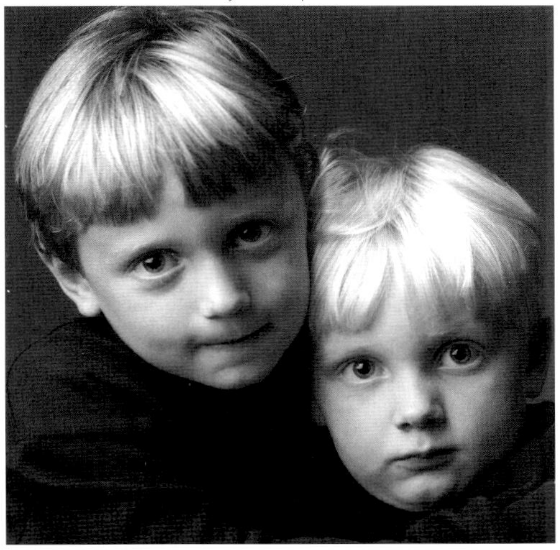

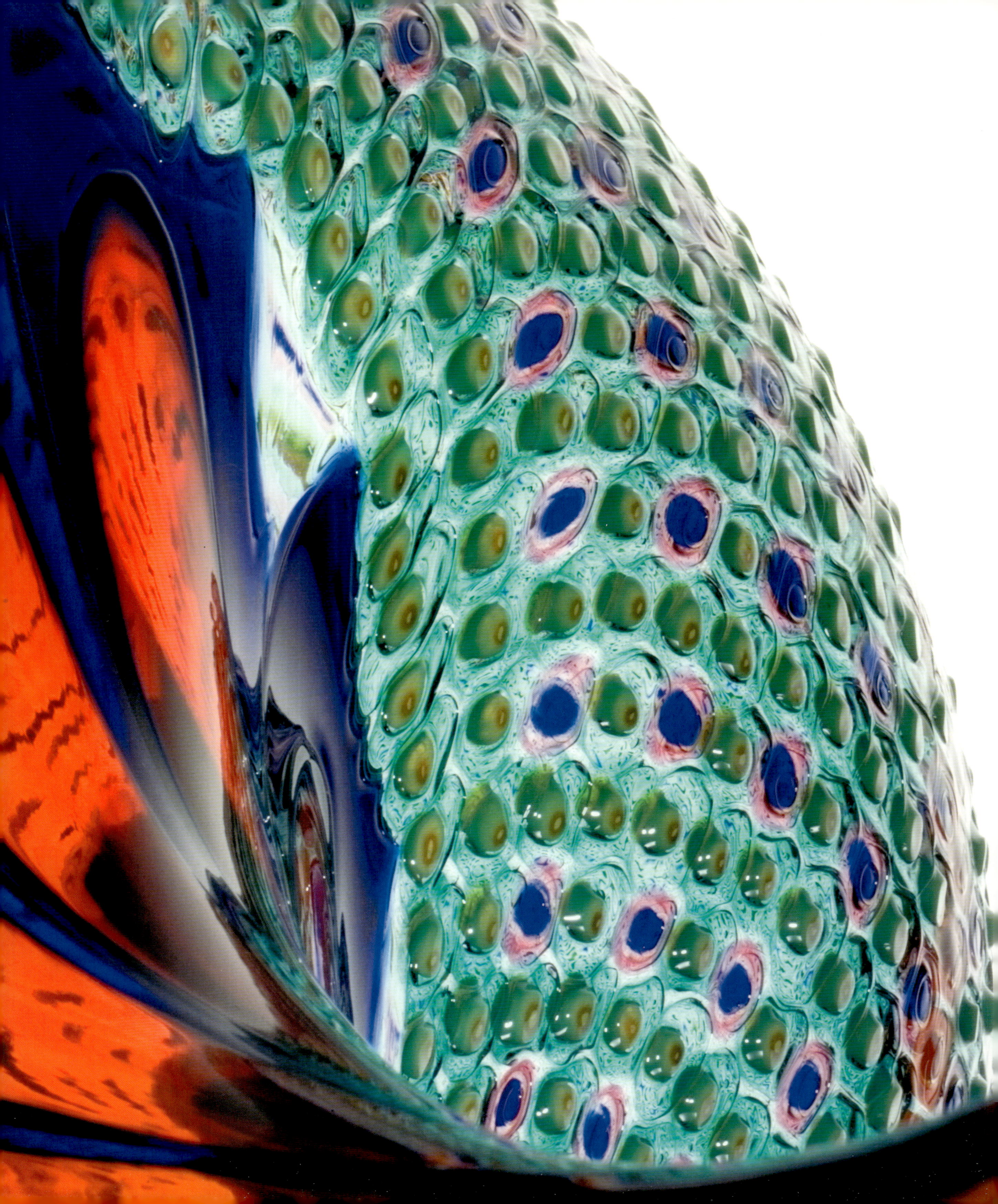

CONTENTS

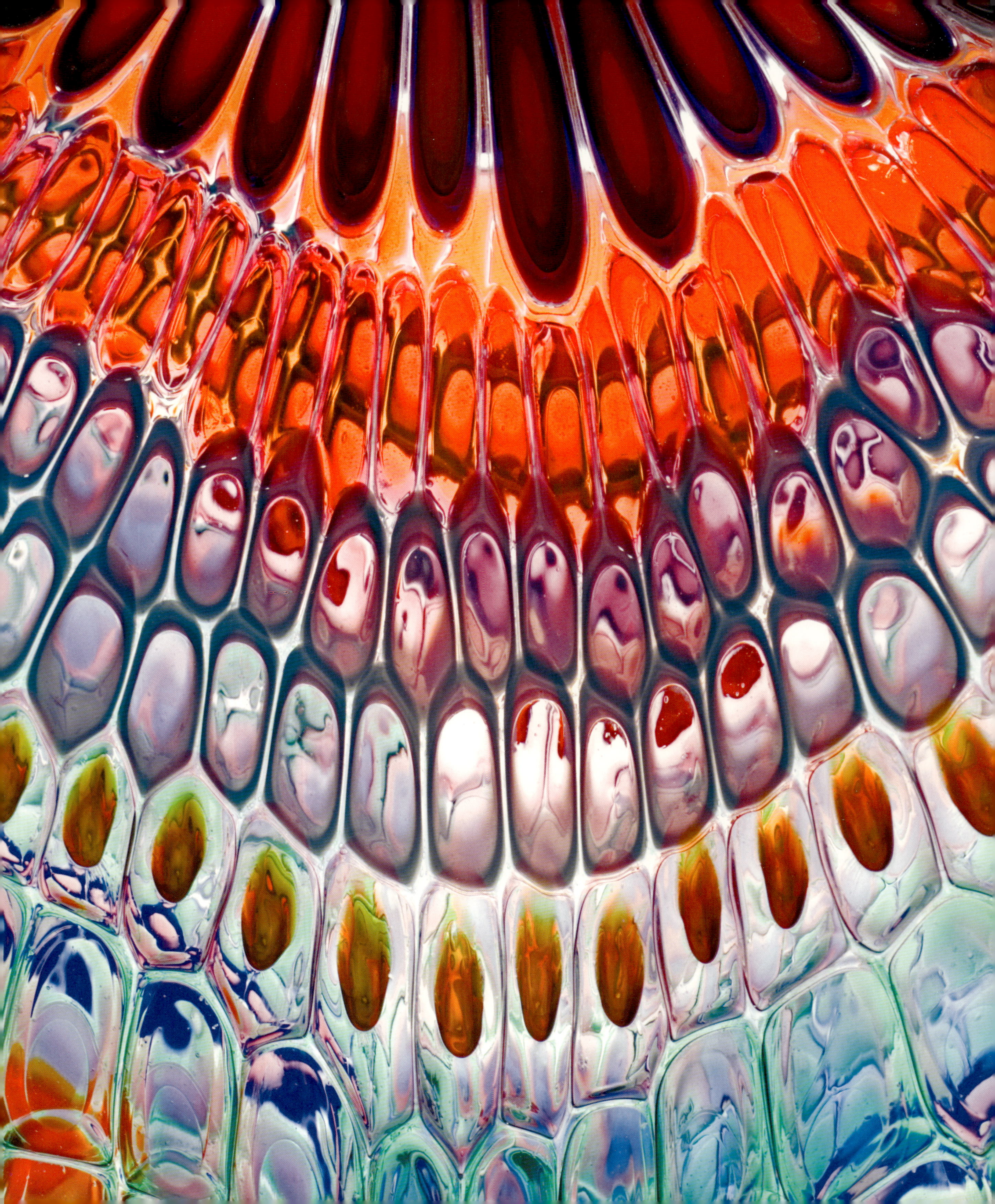

ACKNOWLEDGMENTS

First, this book would not have been possible without my old friend Julius Friedman, who brought confidence and integrity to the creation of the book, and my long-time best friend Mark "Looney" Lucas, who has experienced the ups and downs of life with me and has tied the book together with sincerity and humor.

Special thanks to David Harpe for his hard work and outstanding photographic vision. Also, thanks to William Butler for the impetus to make the book in the first place. In addition, thanks to Kate Philips for her photographic contributions.

I would like to thank James Yood and Laurie Winters for their interest in my work and their ability to put into words what it is I do and why I do it. I am deeply indebted to Kenn Holsten, Marvin Lipofsky, Dante Marioni, Bonnie Marx, John Roush, and Lino Tagliapietra for the generous reflections they have contributed to this book. I sometimes wondered whom they were talking about.

I would like to acknowledge the terrific relationship that I have with Centre College. I owe much as a teacher and artist to the support of David and Marlene Grissom, John and Susie Roush, Richard Trollinger, John Ward, Michael Adams, Leonard DiLillo, Karin Ciholas, Milton Reigelman, Richard Morrill, and Rick Nahm.

Since starting the Centre College glass program in 1985, I have had generous support from Corning Glassworks in Harrodsburg, Kentucky; Philips Lighting in Danville, Kentucky; Corhart Refractories in Louisville, Kentucky; and General Electric in Somerset, Kentucky.

Special support for the Centre facilities and visiting artist programs has come from John Schiff and the Skyler Foundation, Ray Hazard, Jim and Laurie Seabury, Rob and Kim Rosenstein, Adele and Leonard Leight, Robert and Judy Ayotte, George and Nawanna Privett, Chuck and Carol Campbell, Ken Enos, Steve Tucker, Mike Geralds, Chuck Tyler, and David Smith.

A warm thank you to Lino Tagliapietra for enhancing my academic, professional, and personal life.

Also, a special thank you to Morton Kasdan and Mack Jackson for putting my arm back together and for their friendship.

The greatest thank you goes to my assistants over the years, with particular note of the enduring presence of Chris Bohach, Richard Garvey, Brook White, Paul Hugues, Ché Rhodes, and Patrick Martin. It has been truly a team effort, and I hope all my crew members past and present realize how much I appreciate their loyalty and hard work.

ASSISTANTS

Billy Anderson
Lauren Arnold
Perry Biddle
Chris Bohach
Jon Capps
Matthew Cummings
Jennifer Carswell Daniel
Mitzi Elliott
Stephen Finney
Alysia Fischer
Richard Garvey
Josh Harris
Paul Hugues
Ted Jeckering
Adam Kenney
Patrick Martin
D. H. McNabb
Ryan Montgomery
McKinley Moore
Paul Nelson
Peter Palmqvist
Brian Pavloff
Duncan Pitchford
Ché Rhodes
Amy Roush
Anne Rushing
Harry Schwartzrock
Brent Sommerhauser
Tommy Spake
John Stokes
Naomi Stuecker
Jonathon Swanz
Shane Urquart
Kurt Waechter
Laura Ward
David Watkins
Nathan Watson
Brook White
Stuart Worobetz
Ying Wu

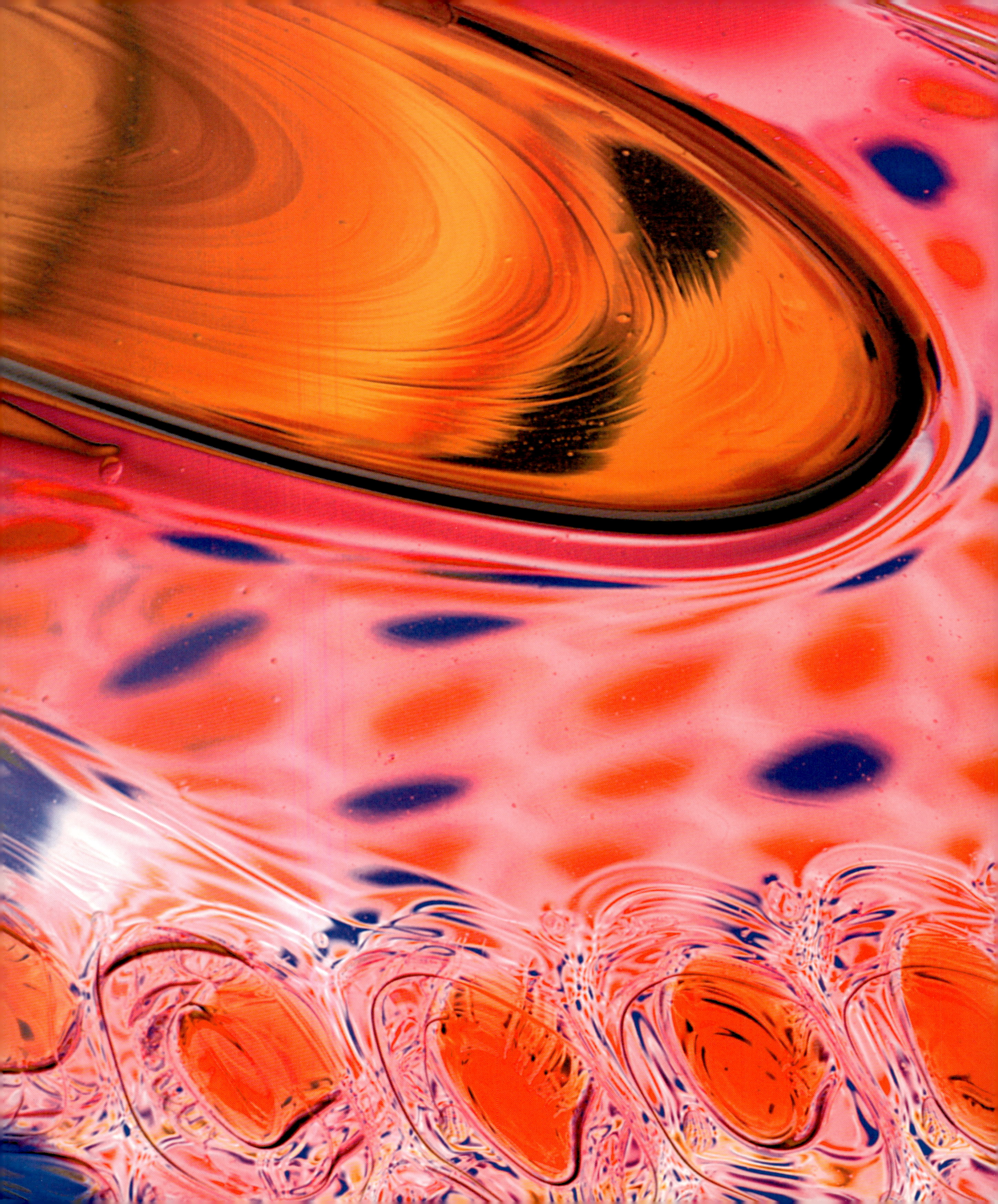

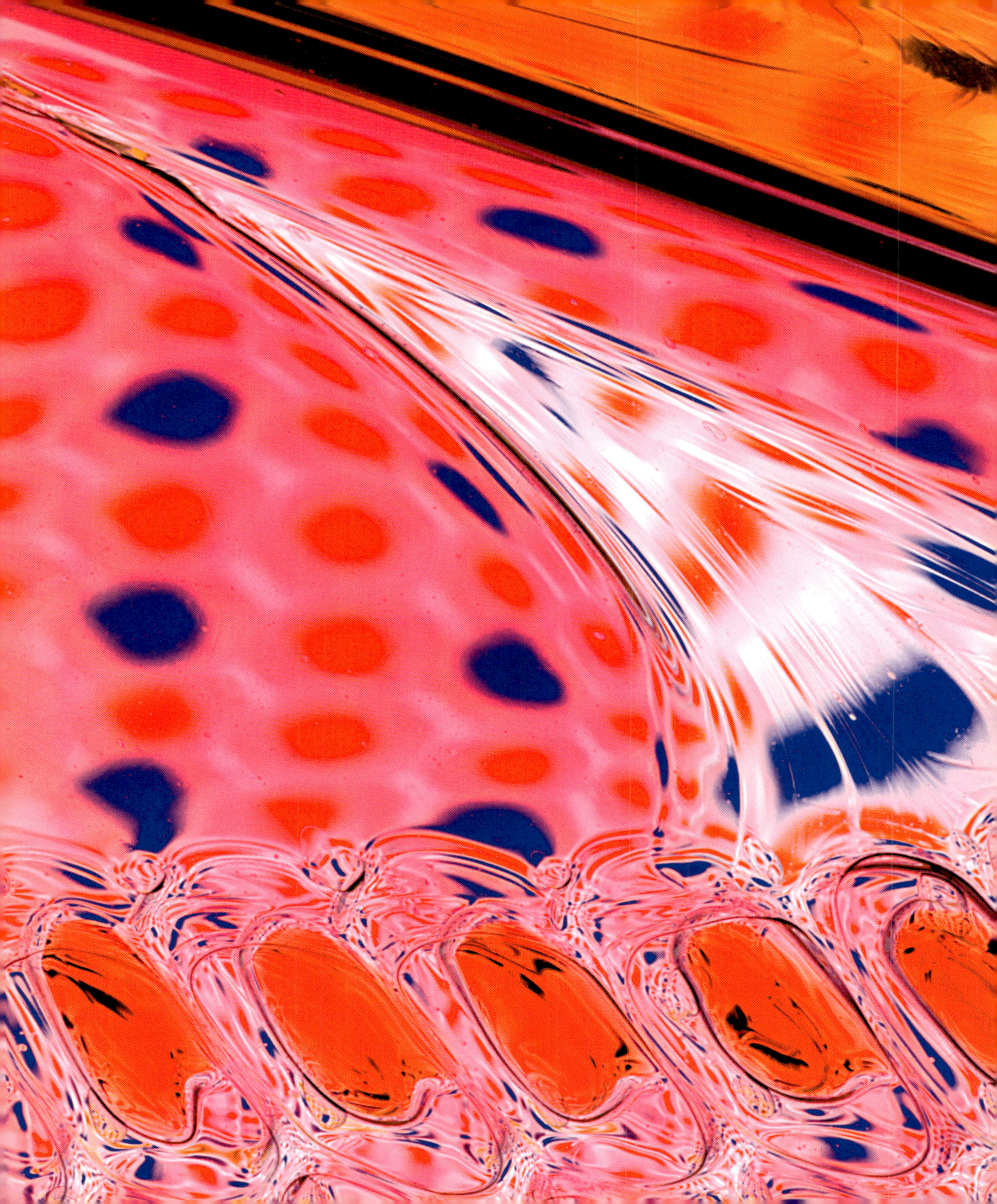

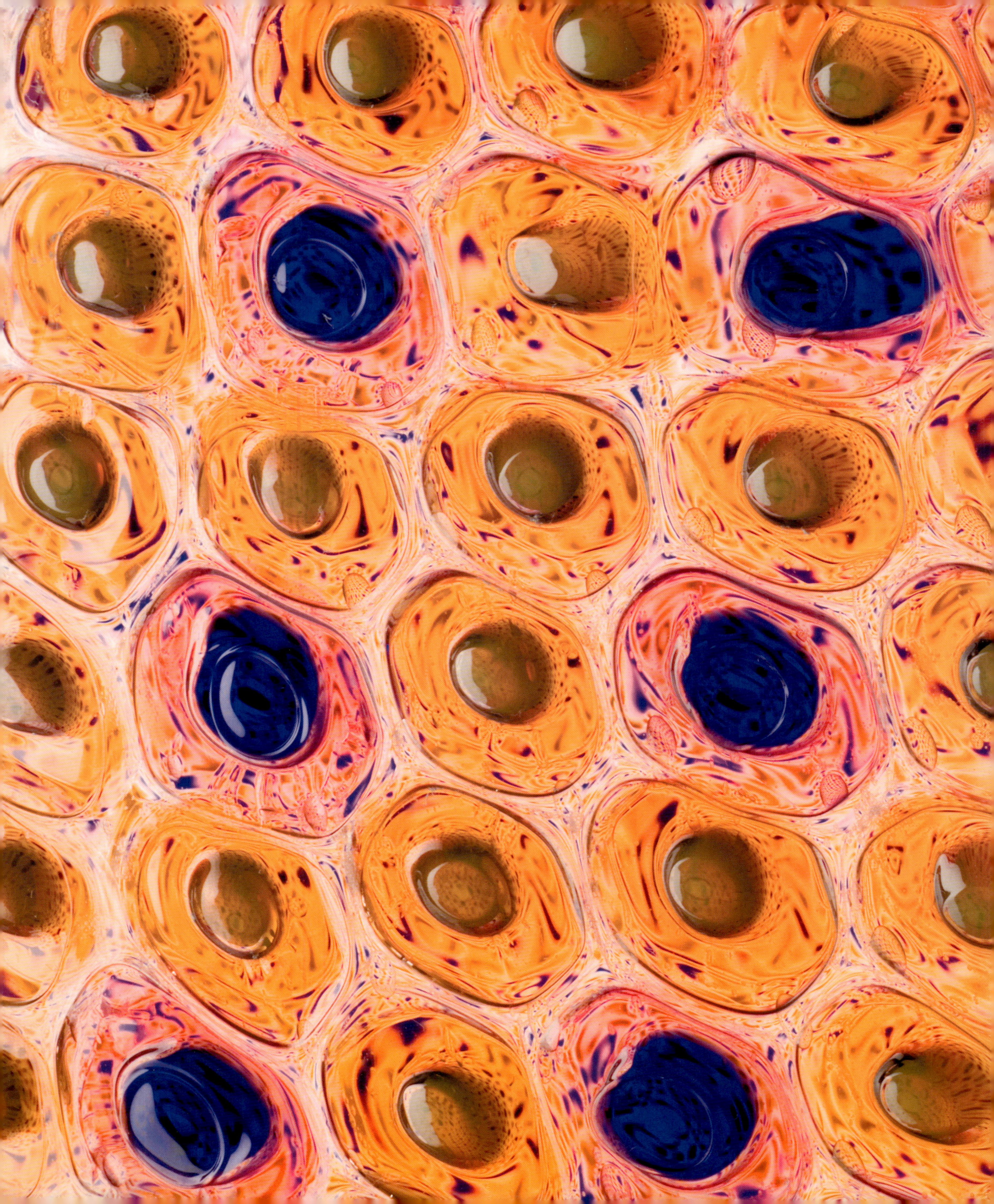

ARABESQUES OF COLOR

Reader, turn the page. It's not that I don't admire my prose; I'm as vain as the next writer. But if there ever was an art book where text might be superfluous, this could be it. If there ever was an artist whose work so completely and wonderfully said, "Enjoy me, drink deep with your eyes, immerse yourself in the sheer pleasure of looking, let color flow over you," that artist is Stephen Rolfe Powell.

Van Gogh once noted that "color expresses something by itself," and in discussing another painting, wrote that he had "tried to express the terrible passions of humanity by means of red and green." While Powell is too joyous an artist to believe that humanity's passions are limited to being "terrible," we could otherwise position him in full sympathy with Van Gogh's thoughts. Many creatures on Earth have eyesight, and some have eyesight more precise and powerful than that of humans, but no other species looks about so regularly for some kind of psychological and/or emotional sustenance. To take the most obvious examples, there's something coded deep within us that has us look with interest toward a sunset, mark the colors of autumn, take pleasure in flowers, garb our bodies with dyed garments. Color delights us from cradle to grave, it grooves some optical pleasure zone that seems almost beyond language, and it is everywhere celebrated in the almost irrepressibly vivacious glass sculpture of Stephen Rolfe Powell.

Other art mediums concern themselves with color and light, but at the end of the day these are, in fact, glass's special trump cards. Within it color and light can suggestively interweave in and around each other, real color, real light, real interpenetration, shifting, changing, and endlessly cross-pollinating. Powell is clearly among modern glass's most nuanced seekers after the eternally sensual and elusive mysteries of light and color, whose upbeat and energetic pieces have for over two decades bubbled and blistered and popped and erupted in fugues of chromatic suggestion. Powell, I would argue, is one of the most accomplished color field painters at work today, despite the fact that he neither paints nor makes color fields. Instead, Powell is one of those extremely rare individuals, an artist who thinks in hues, who makes the eye dance, and whose work provides globular prismatic bursts and an almost giddy tintinnabulation of tincture. I'll confess—there are moments when Powell's work actually makes my pulse quicken, when I get caught up in abstract rhythms that seem relentless and surprising, when he makes color hover right at the fissure between order and chaos, when rows of color start to wobble and meander, as if they want to break free of the vessel they adorn (they never quite do, though!), both of and not of their form.

Yes, the vessel, the form. The pointillist play of Powell's arabesques of color is always energized and reinforced by the shapes they come to sheathe and define. This publication is terrific, but you will not have experienced Powell's work until you see it in three dimensions, move around it, look at it from different angles. Generally speaking, one could divide Powell's mature career into two major phases. Symmetrically shaped vessels that stood upright with a straight and vertical neck at their top marked the first period, from the 1990s until around 2002. Beginning in 2003 Powell began to delve into asymmetrical pieces, often bringing the neck down to the level of the base, having it support the vessel itself. More recently he has been moving the neck out into space at an angle, sacrificing symmetry for something more visually compelling. But we can employ the word "vessel" to describe them all, some vestigial connection to the shape and function of a vase, with a neck, body, and base. Powell's objects retain a hint of functionality while literally getting tugged into another zone, both acknowledging a tradition and stretching its limits. All of his approaches employ a similar procedural strategy to get color to pool upon his surfaces, and it is Powell's consummate command of that strategy that is his signature skill.

Heat causes this inspired congealing of color and form—heat and the materiality of glass. Powell's vehicle for this pageant of wonder is his very individual employment of a murrini technique. Murrini are small bits of glass, almost like beads, sometimes as tiny as a seed, sometimes (but pretty rarely in Powell's work) as large as an inch or so. He and his crew in Kentucky make their murrini by hand, melting larger bars of colored glass, usually overlaying that with another color, and then heating it and stretching it out like taffy for some 30 feet or more, until the glass is no more than 1/8 to 1/2 inch thick. This is cooled and chopped into thousands of murrini, the raw material from which Powell will cull his color. Powell then lays the murrini in carefully composed rows on a smallish steel plate, around 10 x 20 inches in size. This now somewhat mosaicized plate is simultaneously his palette and his composition in a very raw form, and the chromatic sequencing of rows will comprise his final piece in ways that he can only approximately anticipate.

Powell lays out up to 2,500 murrini or more for a single piece, little pastilles of color that literally fulfill the title of Wasily Kandinsky's book *Point and Line to Plane*. The points of condensed color are set into lines and soon become volumetric and planar on his vessels. Powell gathers a great deal of clear molten glass on his pipe (his pieces can weigh around 30 pounds), blows a smallish bubble within it, and then rolls his hot glass over the murrini, which themselves have been heated, though at a lower temperature. The murrini are instantly picked up by the hot glass and begin to "melt," to expand, sometimes from the size of a pea to the size of a pear. Color that had been no more than a dot now becomes a dollop, a little orb of tone clustered among its brethren in very wavy and somewhat cellular rows, making tesserae in space. For the symmetrical and vertical vessels, Powell then would rush over to a platform about five feet off the ground, and holding his pipe absolutely vertically, let the glob of glass pull downward, creating the thin neck and the vessel's swelling body simultaneously. He concurrently blew air through the pipe into the vessel, causing its exterior to swell, providing pressure to expand outward at the same time that gravity was providing downward pressure. In most instances he had his hot vessel drape between two or sometimes three vertical metal bars, themselves heated to 750 degrees, that pinched his glass into the lobes that so much demarcated that body of work. Even at their heightened temperatures, these metal bars cooled the glass (which remained somewhere around 2,000 degrees) they touched, freezing the murrini in tighter diameter and denser coloration than those in the outer lobes. When all worked well (and like many artists who work glass at this scale—up to five feet—and in multiple temperatures, Powell has a failure rate of around 50 percent), the process, from picking up the murrini to ending up in the annealing oven, could take as little as 20 minutes of extremely frenetic activity. (And here's a bit of advice at how one might look at a piece by Powell—look at the neck, particularly where it meets the body of the vessel: see how he often treats it like a shoulder, some element that needs to be stretched like a tendon, that transitions the form from bulbous and volumetric to a gossamer thinness, how he makes the murrini link them both, making them sing, making color coloratura.)

That's the process; the product is another thing altogether. In liquefying his little beads, in having them go from a solid state to a liquid state and then back to a now diffused and disseminated solid state, Powell creates an effect not unlike that of watercolor. And, of course, his aim is somehow to make color spin out some kind of psychedelic lyric from the 1970s—there's a wonderful retro feel to this work, a kind of groovy tie-dye rhythm and color scheme that is instantly vigorous and carefree. Setting up the murrini in parallel rows tethers the final piece, giving it a structure it sometimes dutifully echoes, and sometimes wildly violates. While he'll employ many different colors, certain tones dominate—cranberry reds and plum purples and kiwi greens and apricot orange/browns and berry blues and lemon yellows—a fruity palette of pleasure, splayed out across these surfaces in infinite variety, no two lines of murrini ever precisely the same. Issues such as transparency, translucency, and opacity are critical for him, and his long practice has led him, particularly in the arena of translucency, to crystallize color as few others can. There is much of this that Powell can firmly control, but some crucial little bits that he can only influence, the power of heat and gravity seeming to have a will of its own.

The shapes and profiles of his vessels reinforce their loopy insouciance. His symmetrical vases ended up round and bulbous, curvaceous and ribald, replete with generous intimations of the sensuality of the human body. The lobes and swellings inevitably suggested buttocks or breasts or testicles, the soft and vulnerable zones of sexuality, in a warm cleavage and eroticism always heightened by their fantastic color scheme. The weight of these lobes, the sense of them being pulled down by gravity, was countered by the exquisite tension of Powell's very attenuated and elongated narrow necks, which strained upwards in some mannerist rhythm, as if these vessels are both bulb and sprout simultaneously. The asymmetrical vases of recent years have been a great breakthrough for this artist, freeing him to cavort in space. Instead of using gravity as the central organizational device, Powell and his crew usually swing these vessels horizontally, blowing and torching them into shape in some crazy dance of heat and motion that causes the glass and color to undulate in new ways. These pieces from the last few years suggest animals or organs, like birds or anteaters or stomachs. The swelling of the cavity and their "plumage" of the color give these vessels a kind of ebullient life essence that is very palpable and rhythmic.

And then there are Powell's titles. Powell (me too!) is a product of late 1960s and 1970s counterculture, with a kind of whimsical keep-on-truckin' sensibility and a spoofy sense of humor and generous collegiality that mark him both as man and artist. Titles like *Tangerine Cheeks Smith, Purple Zippy Mania, Gulping Poochy Fervor, Nudging Manic Scooter, Undulating Groan Jones, Lurking Solar Cleavage,* and *Pushy Tropical Puffer* are intriguing to Powell in their playful free-and-easy patter. A word or two within them (almost always three words in length) can describe some aspect of the piece, a shape or color or feeling, but shouldn't be divorced from the sensibility in which this artist was formed.

And it continues. There's something vaguely miraculous that some of the finest work in contemporary color in any medium is being wrought right now by Stephen Rolfe Powell at Centre College in Danville, Kentucky. There's no reason why that shouldn't be true, of course; Paris and New York and Tokyo and Chicago have no patent on artistic creativity. Colorists, it has been observed, are born, not made, and their pursuit of subtlety and beauty, their search for that special kind of optical exhilaration that begins where language ends and taste begins, can happen anywhere. Our role is to appreciate that it is happening at all, that something quickens the attention of an artist like Stephen Rolfe Powell, making him lay out endless rows of murrini, manipulate molten glass, and twirl and coax it into form, creating sumptuous vortices of tone and color that astound and delight, and that celebrate the infinite and affirmative pleasures of human vision. Reader, turn the page.

James Yood

James Yood teaches art history at the School of the Art Institute of Chicago and writes regularly for ARTFORM, GLASS, *and* AMERICAN CRAFT *magazines.*

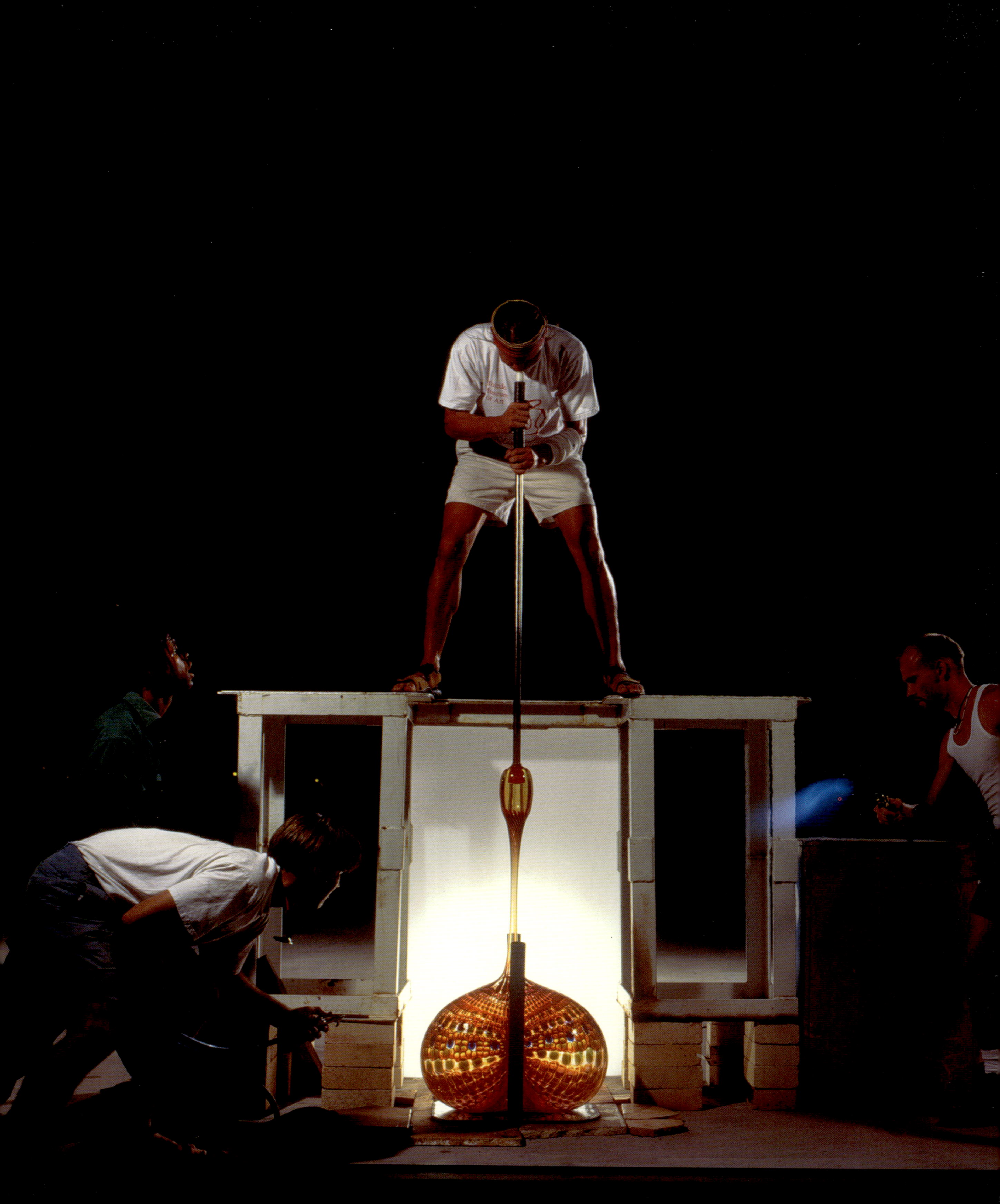

TEASERS

"Intensity—that's what drew me to glassblowing. Intensity and immediacy and fire. I admit I'm a pyromaniac. Even my background in ceramics was mostly raku firing. I build my entire glassworking process around the climax moment of the blowout."

Stephen Rolfe Powell, 2003

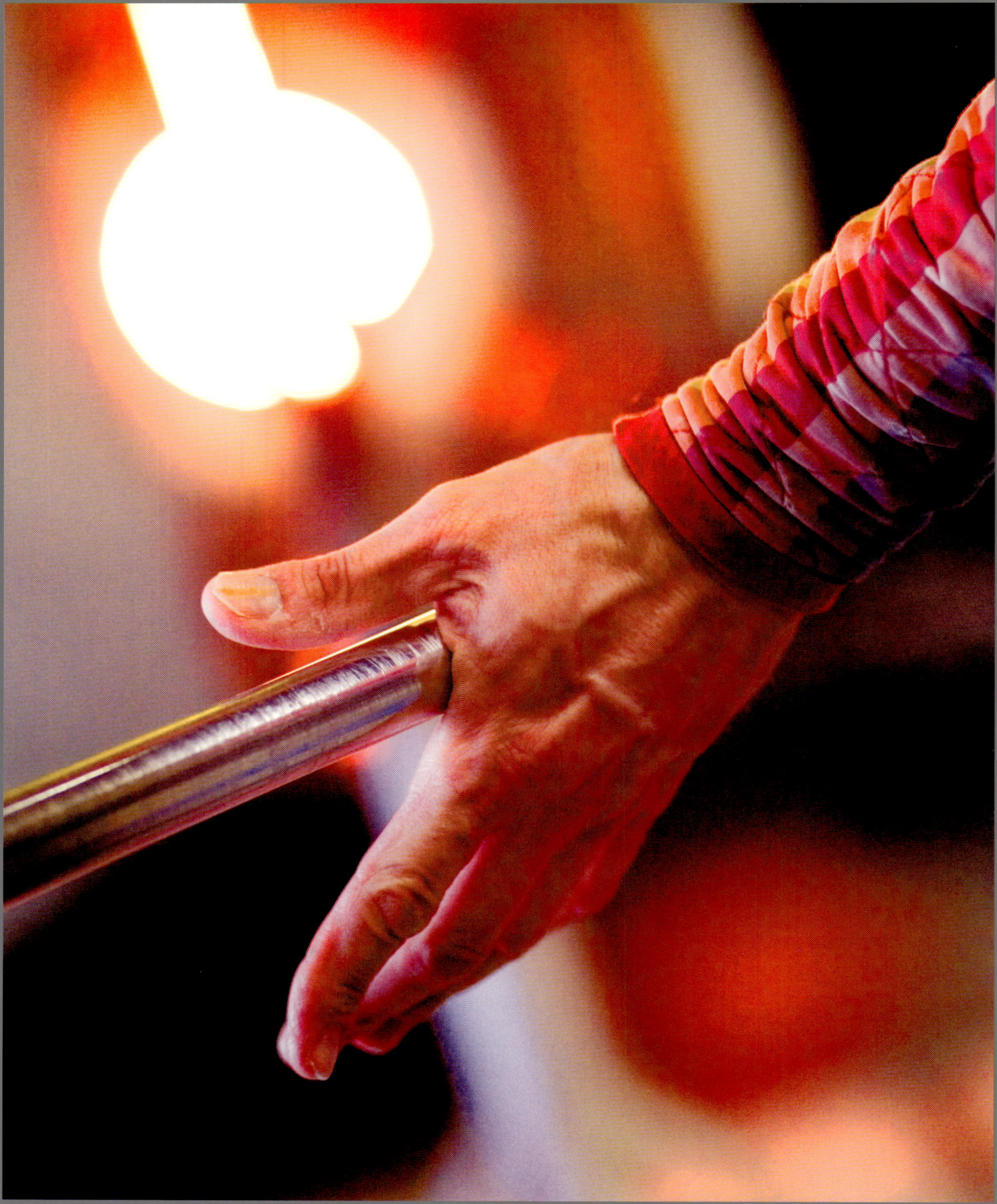

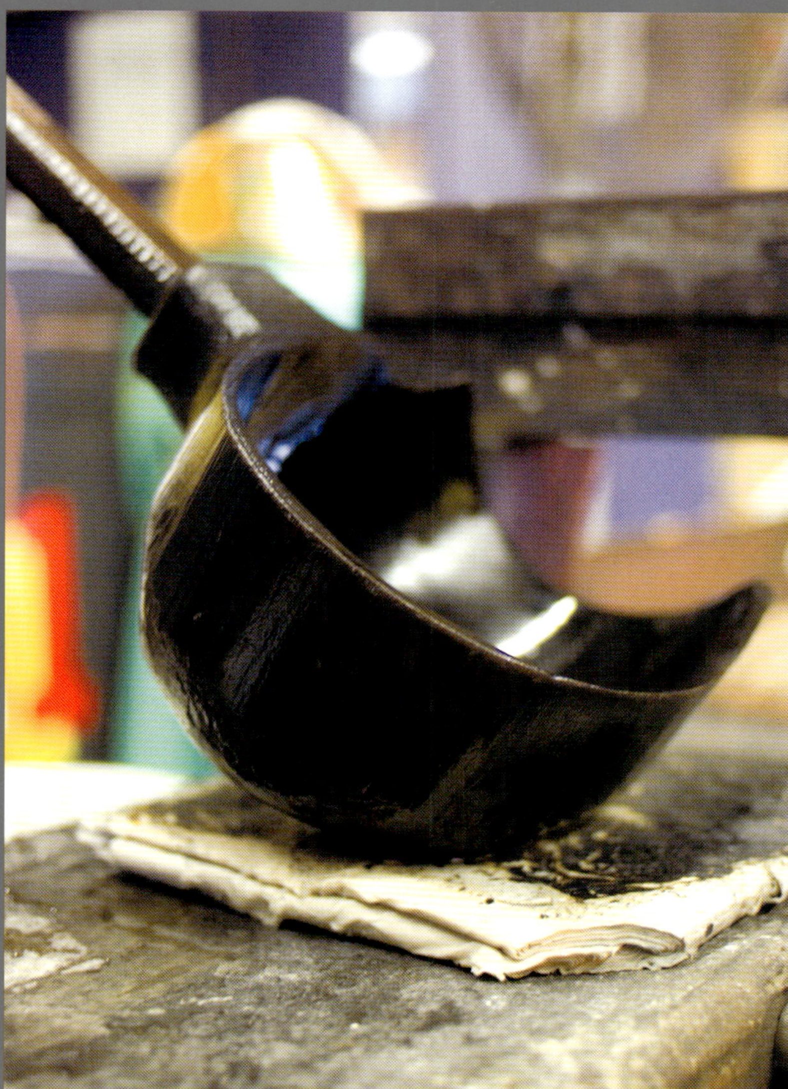

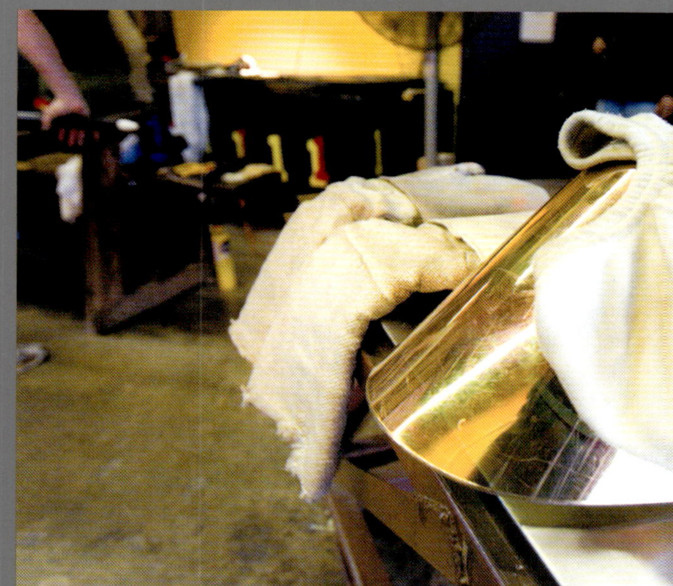

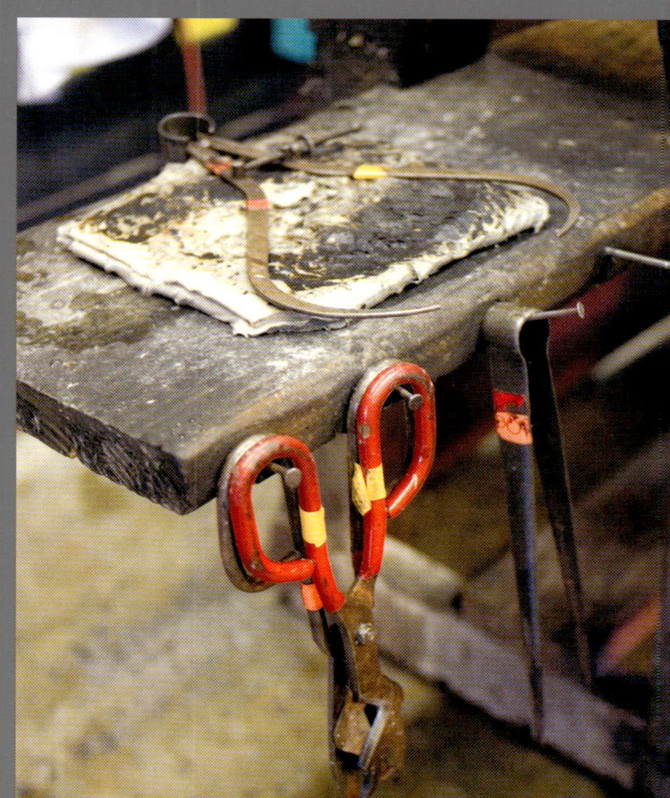

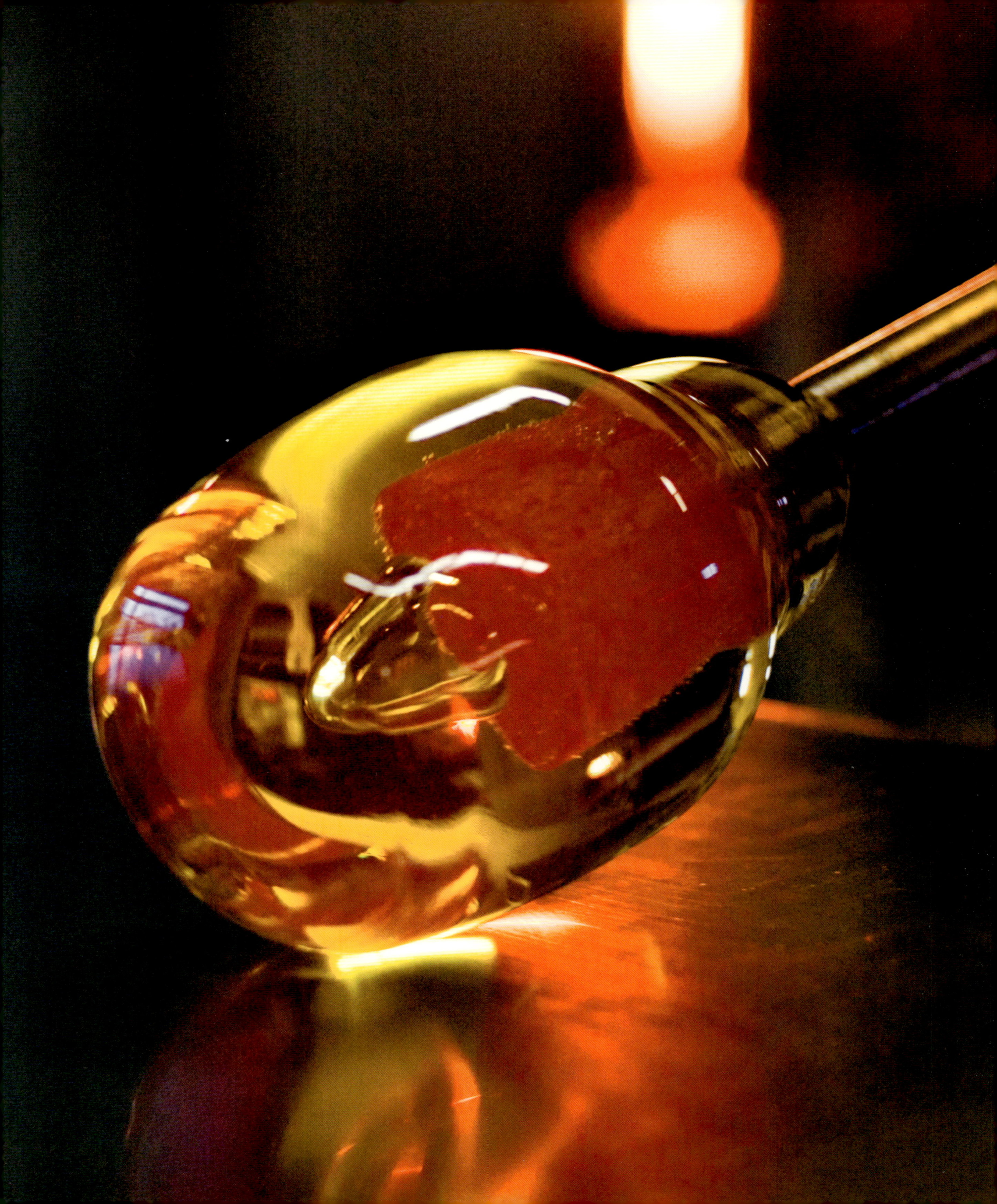

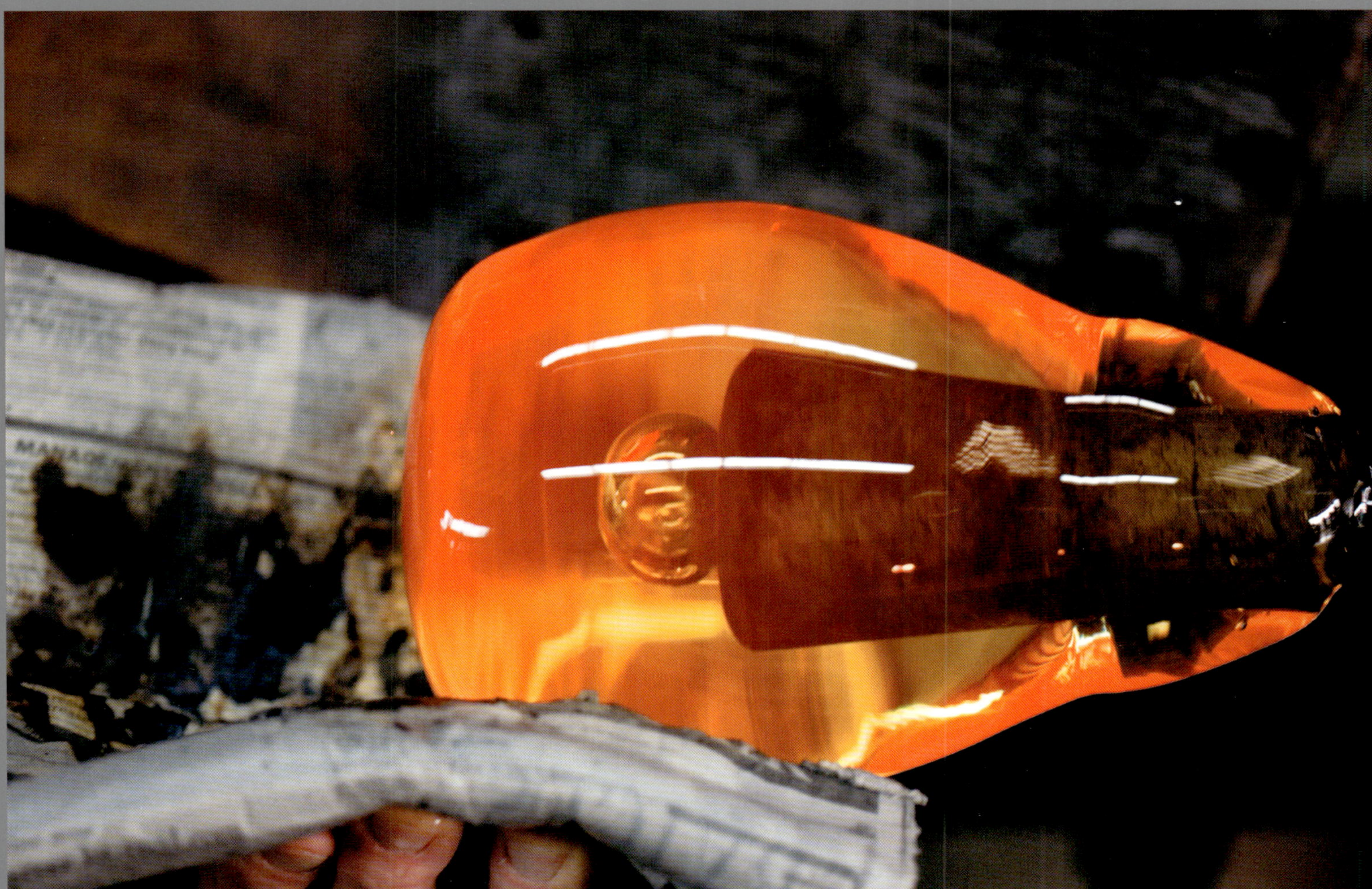

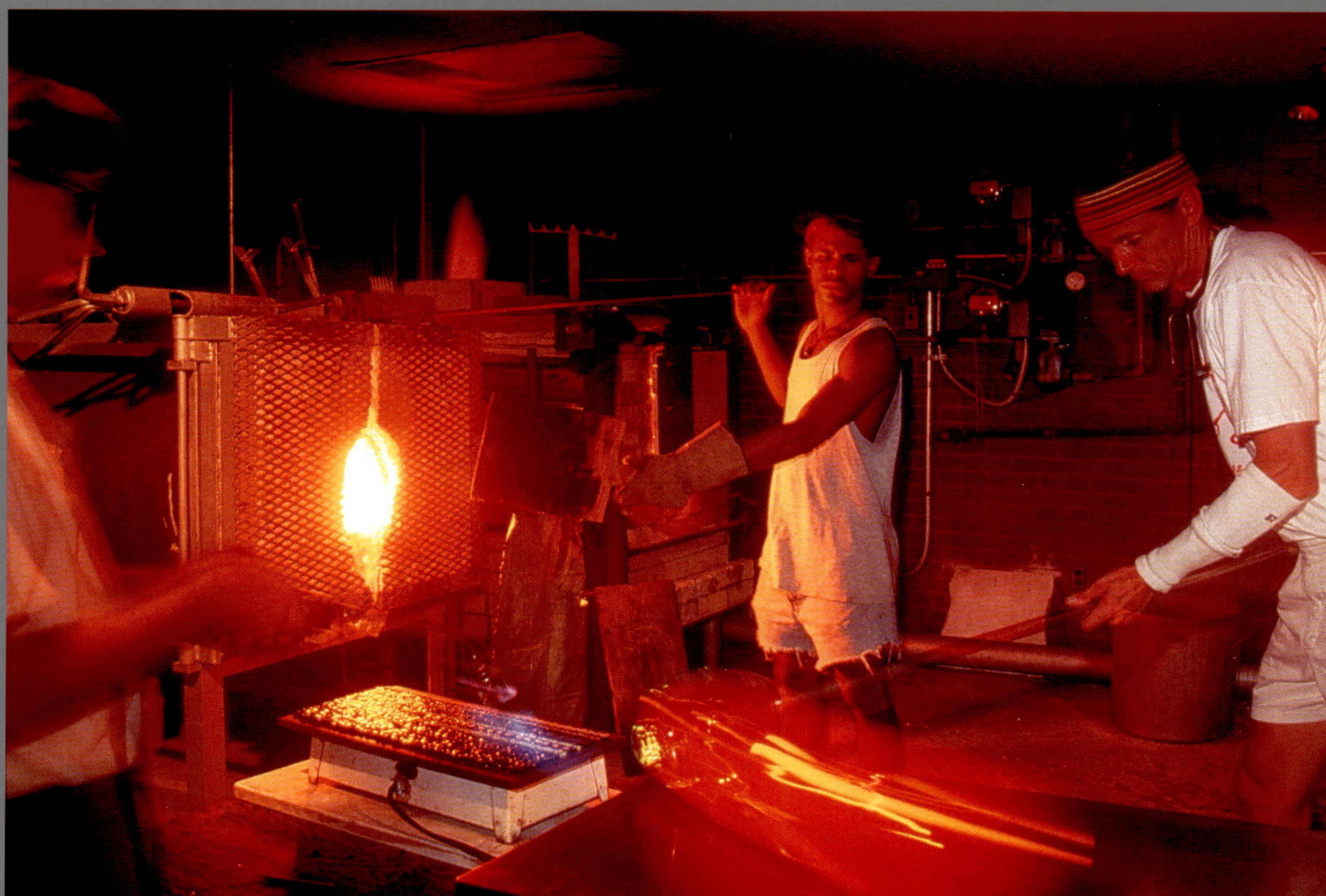

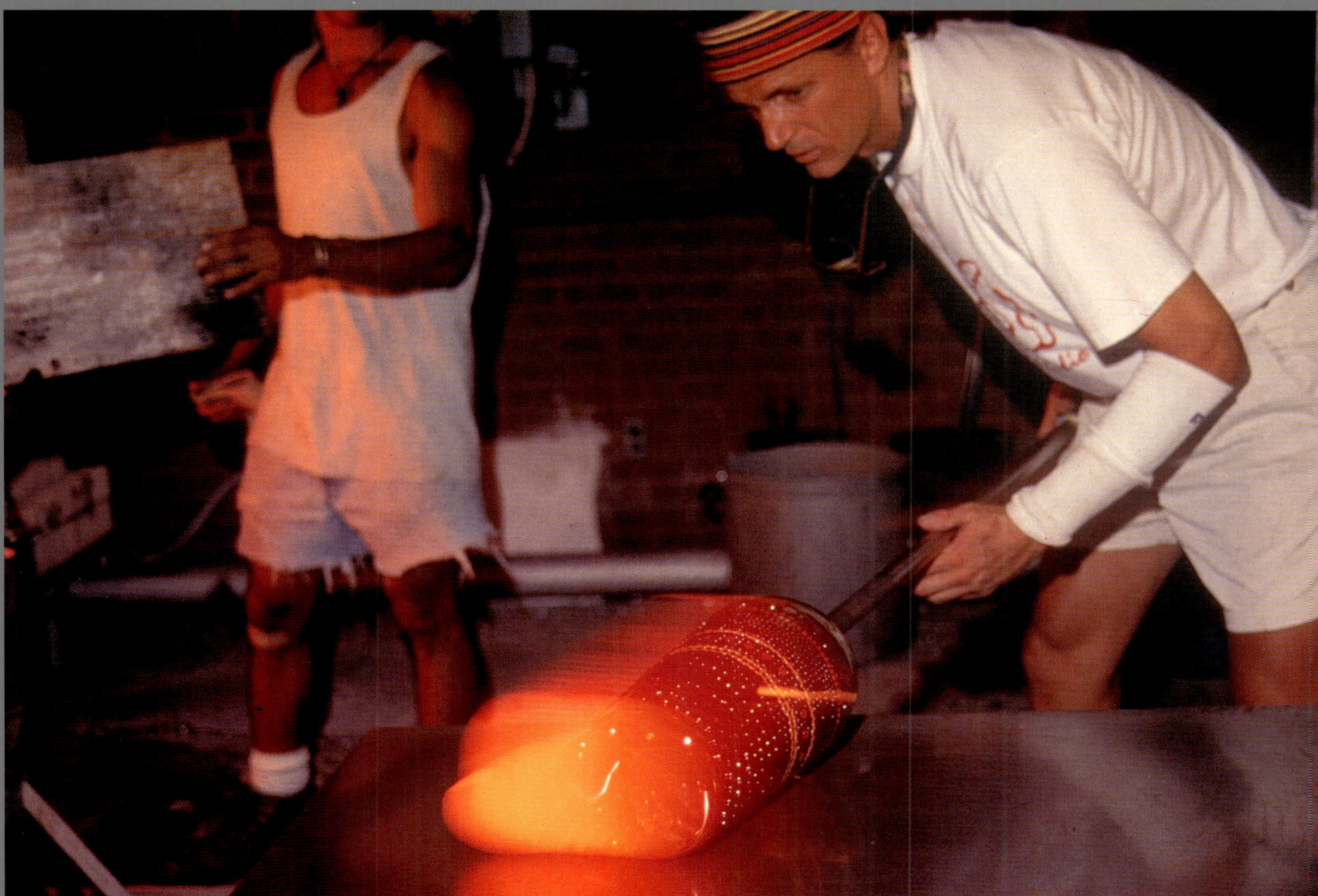

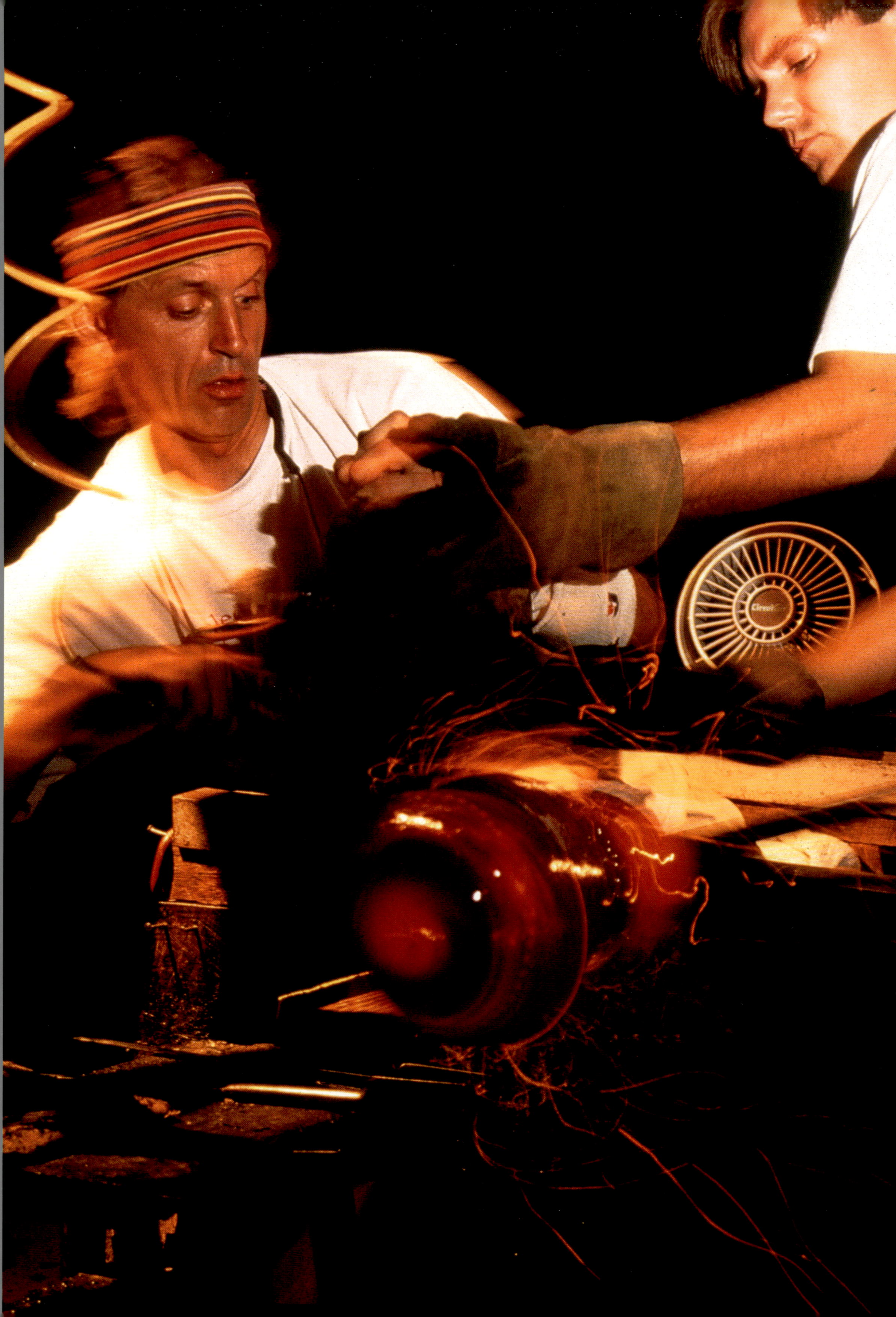

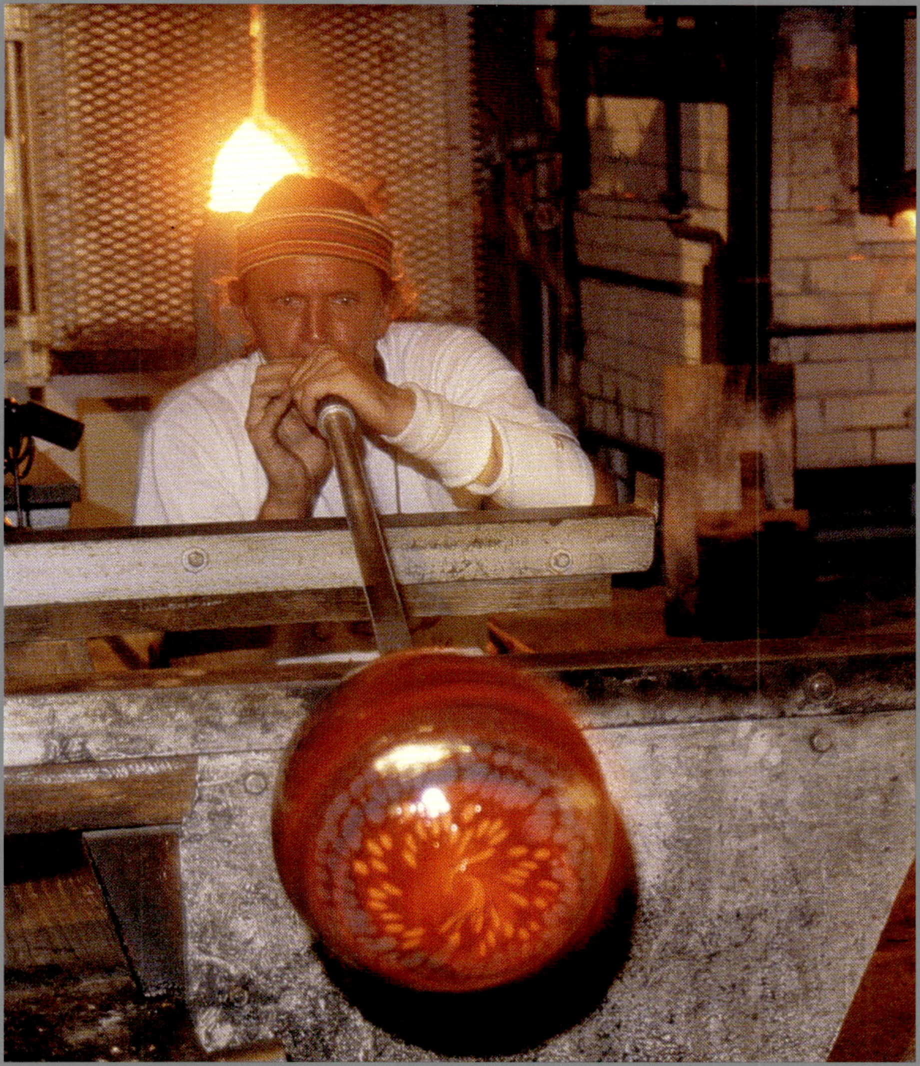

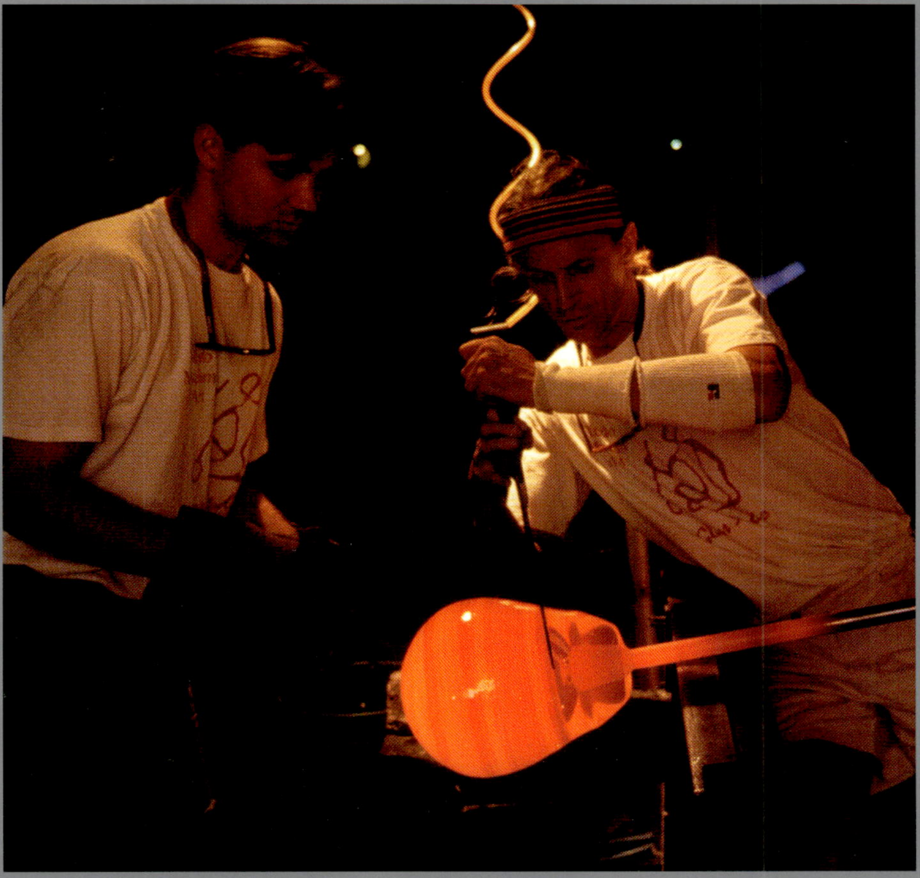

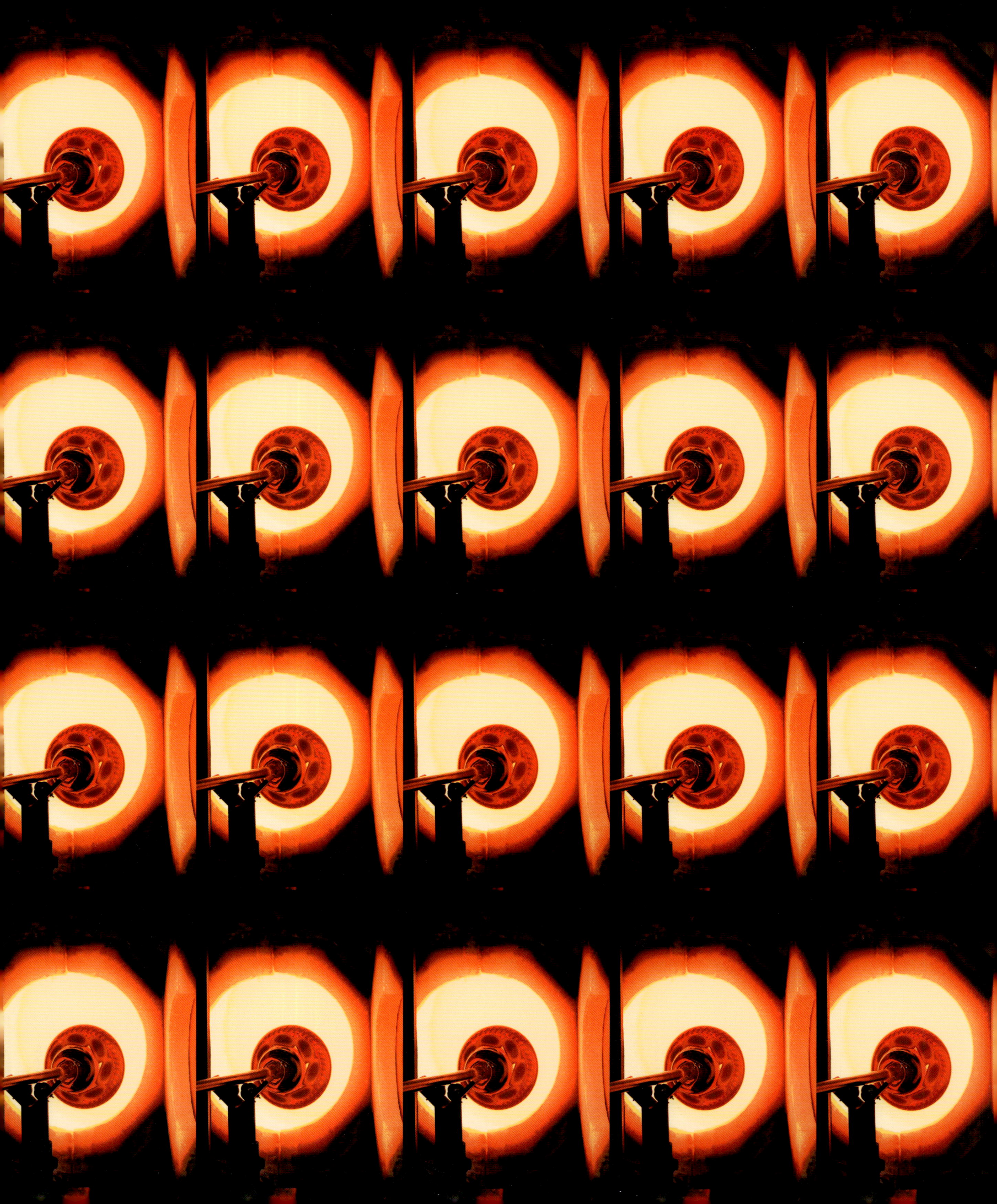

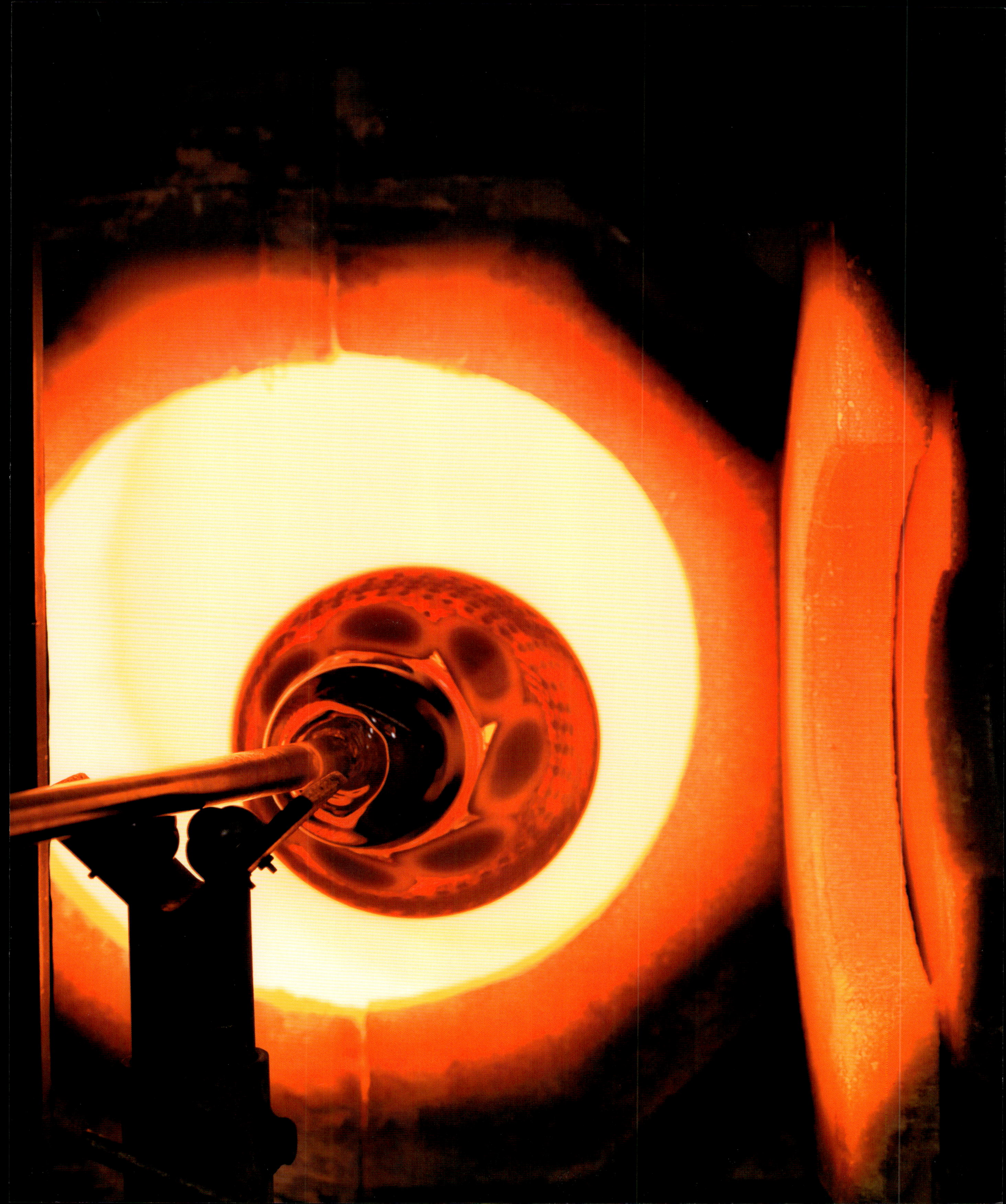

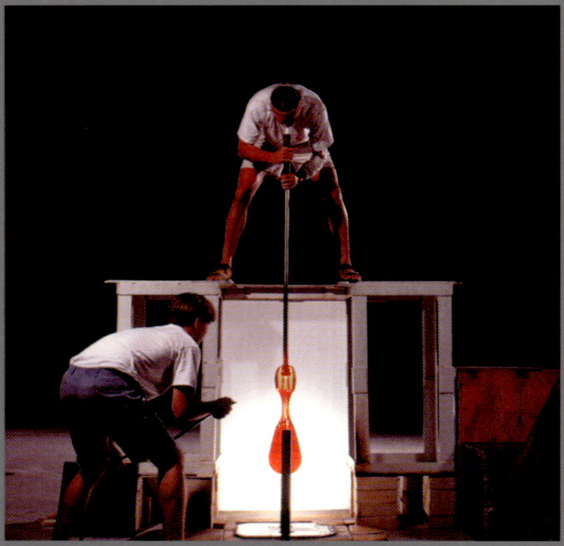
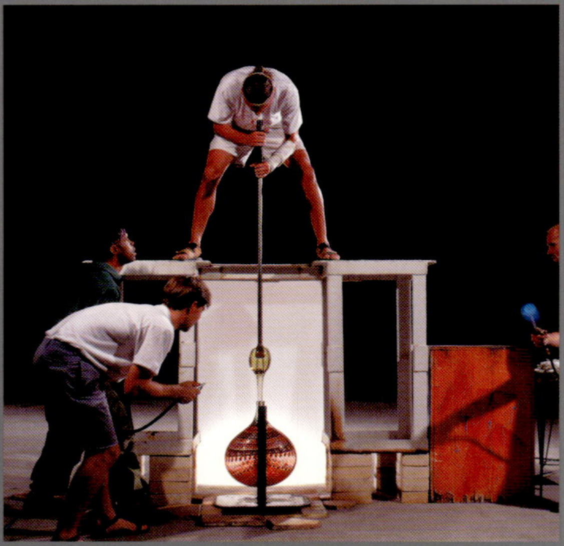
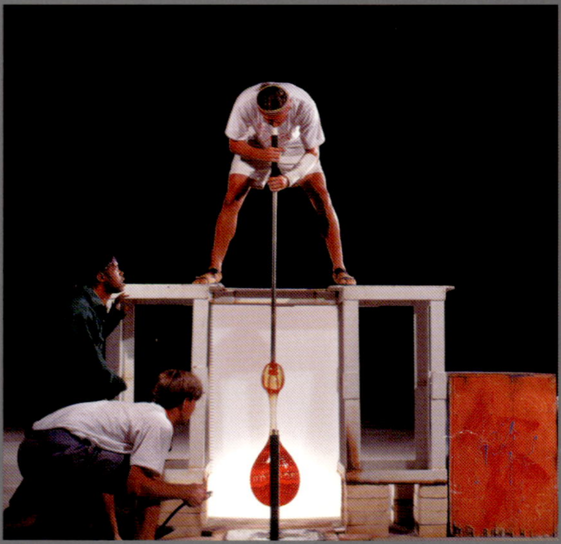
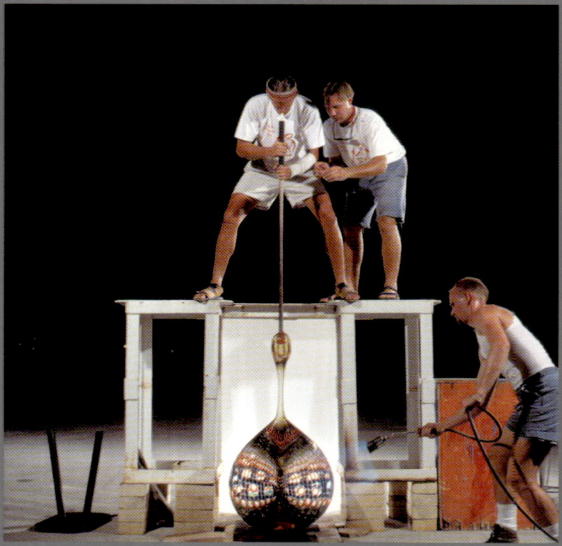
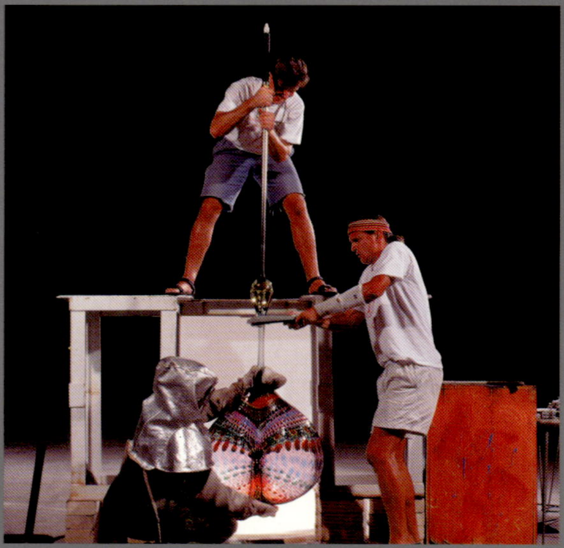

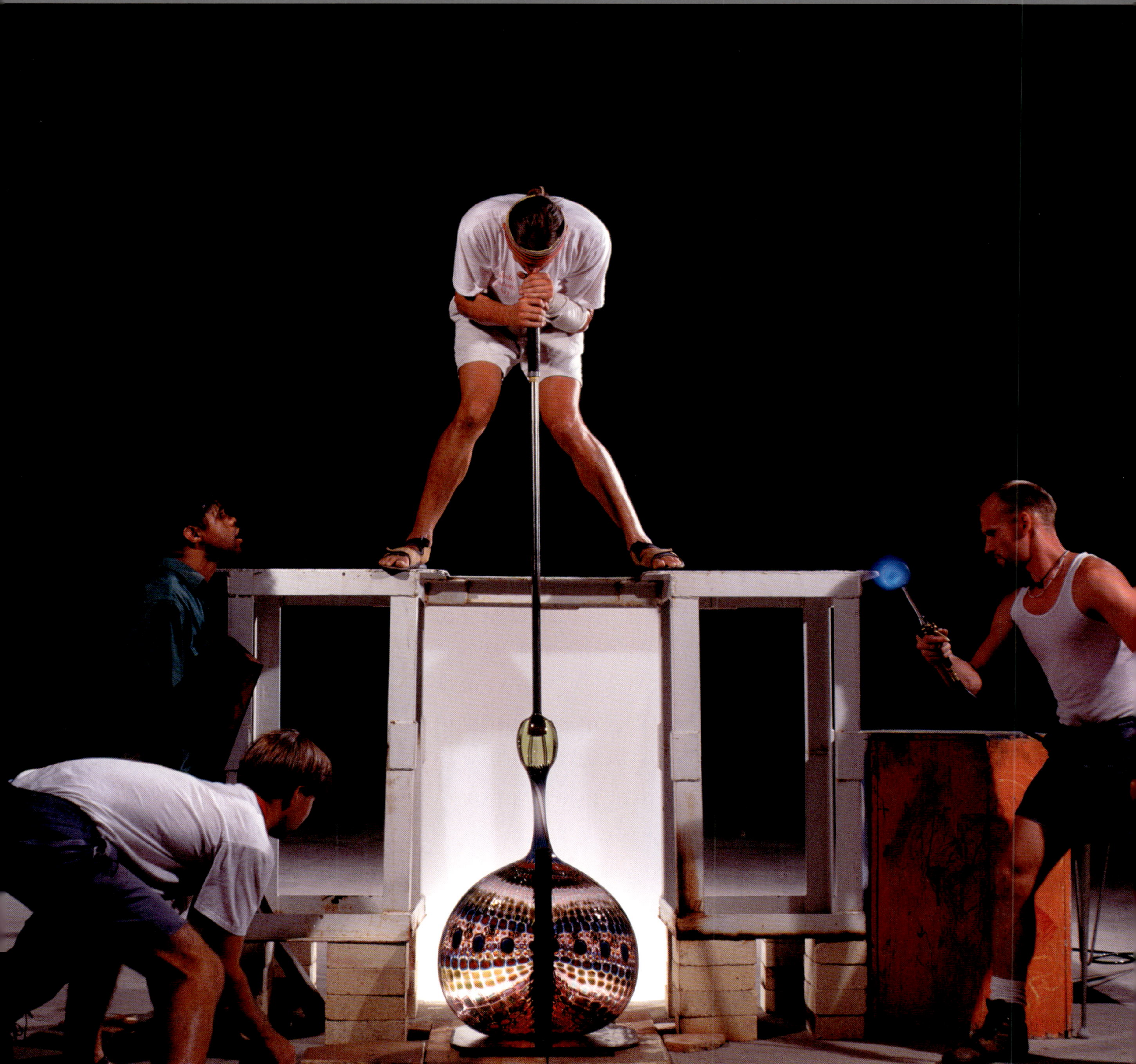

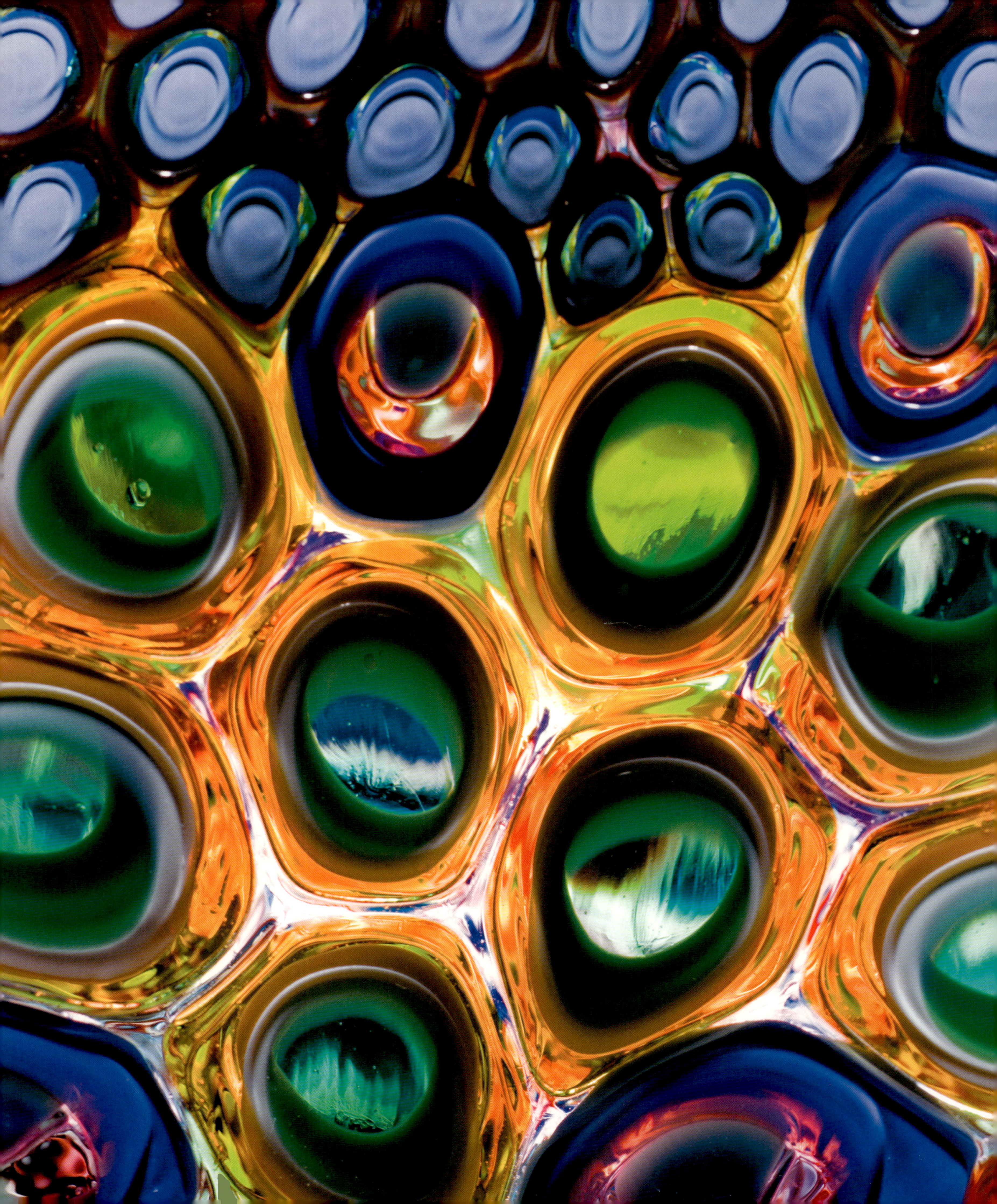

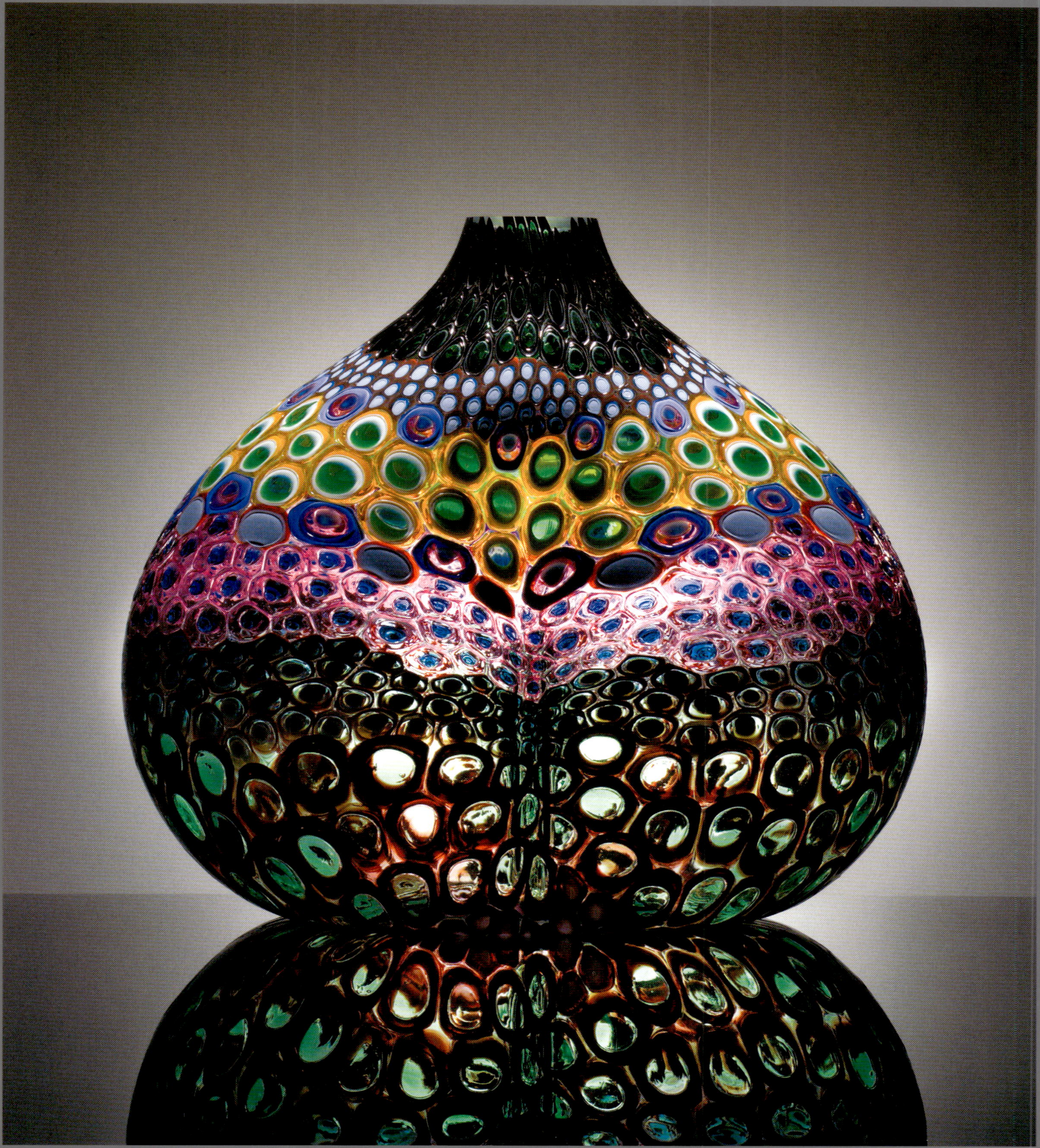

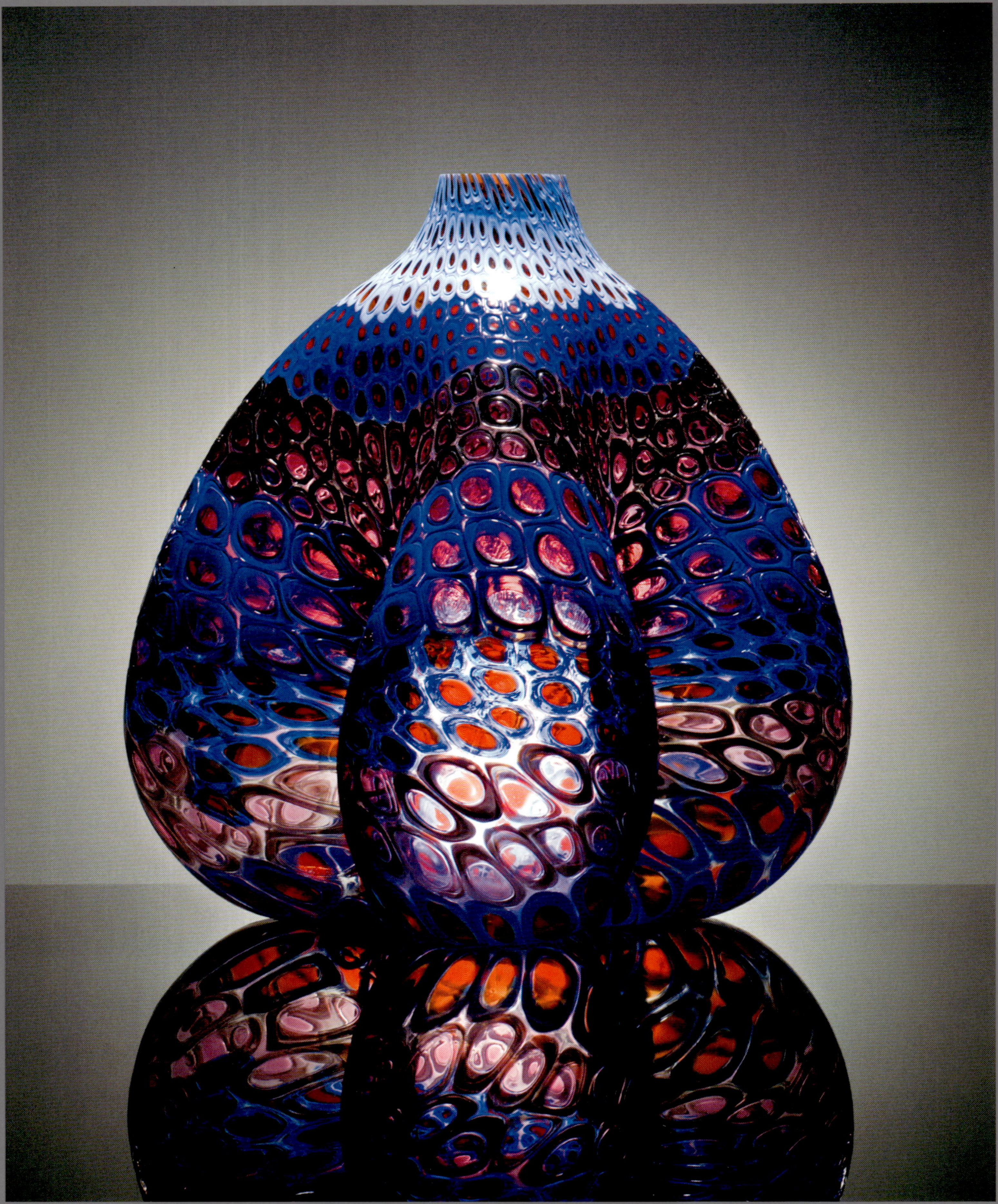

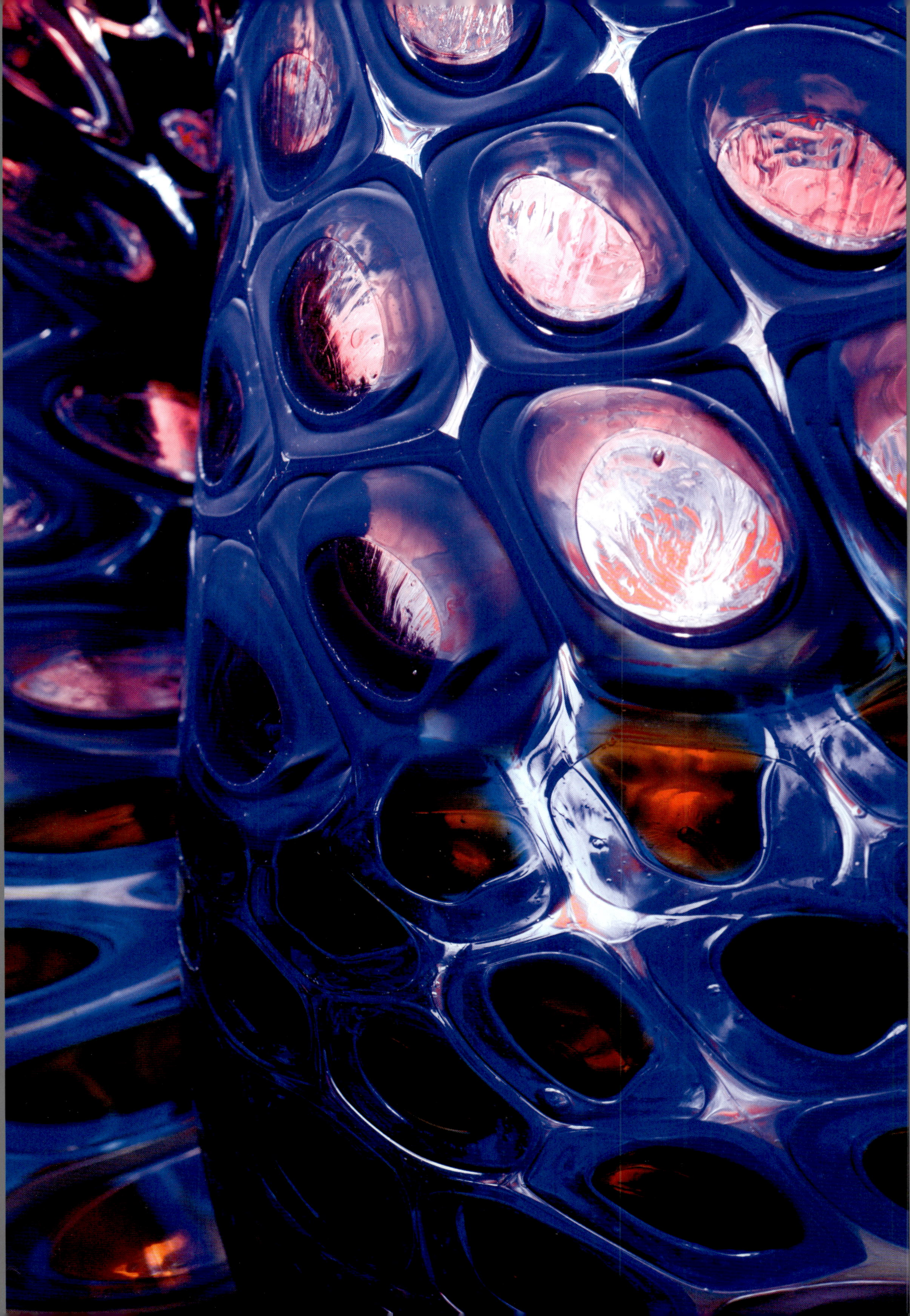

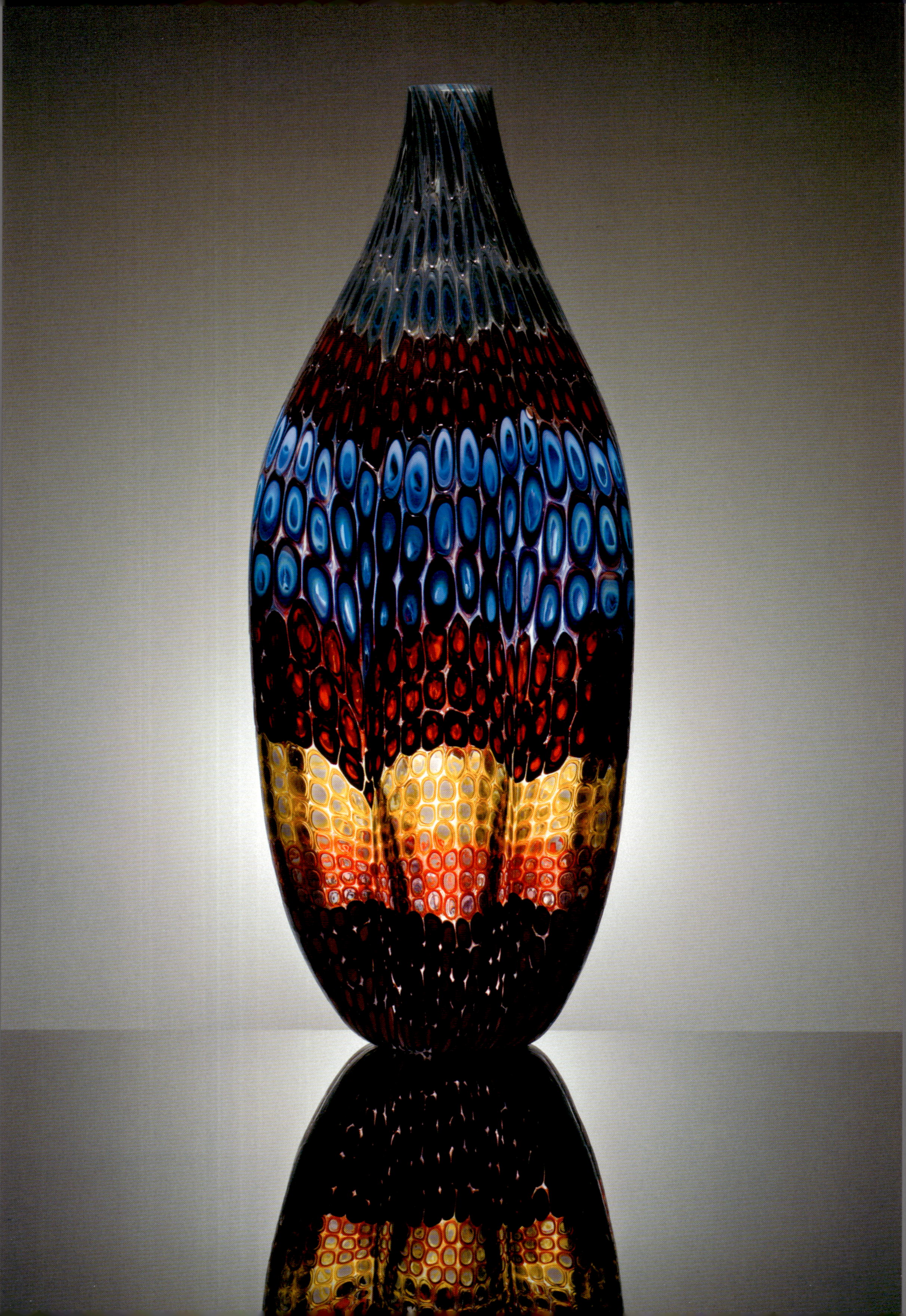

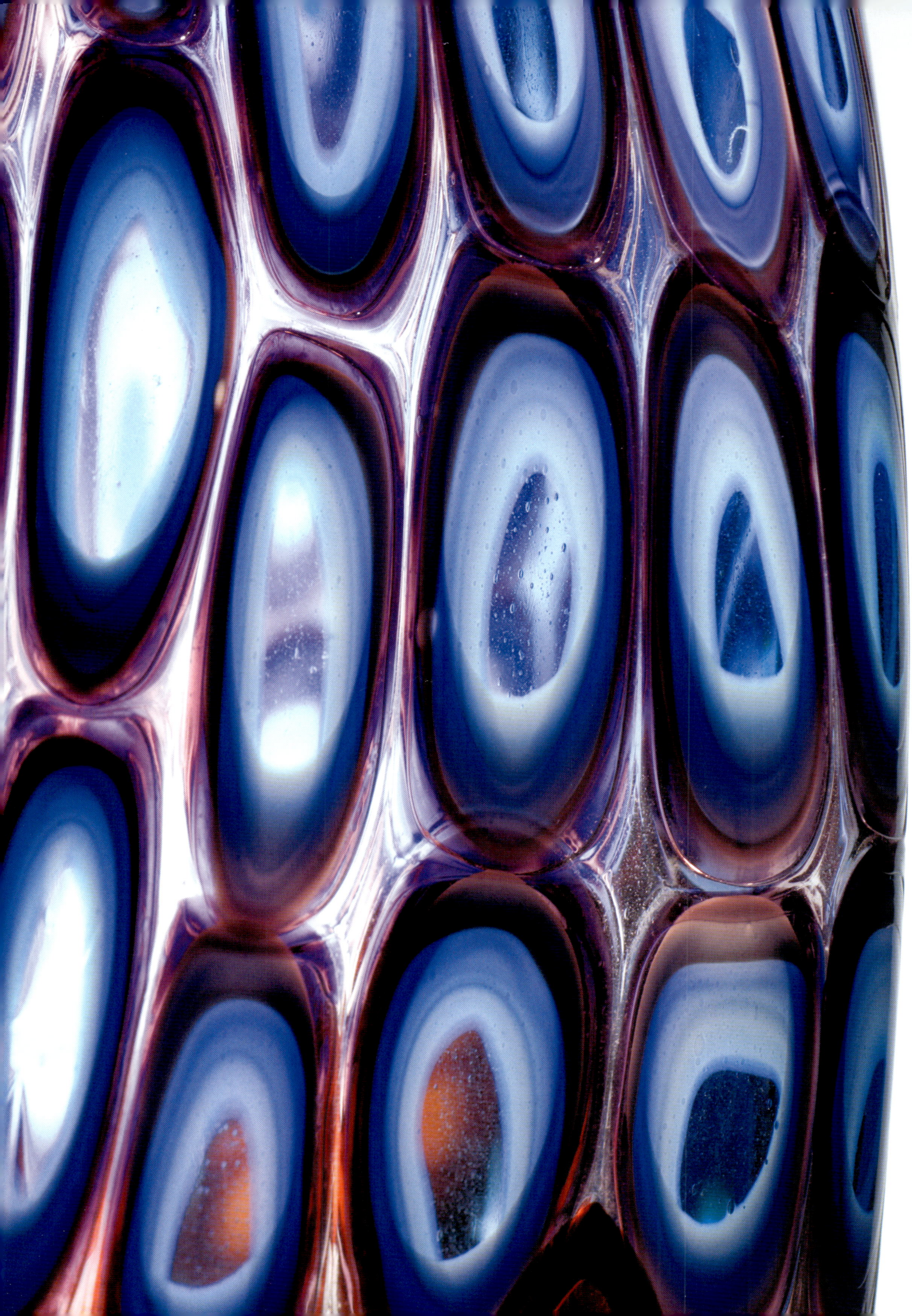

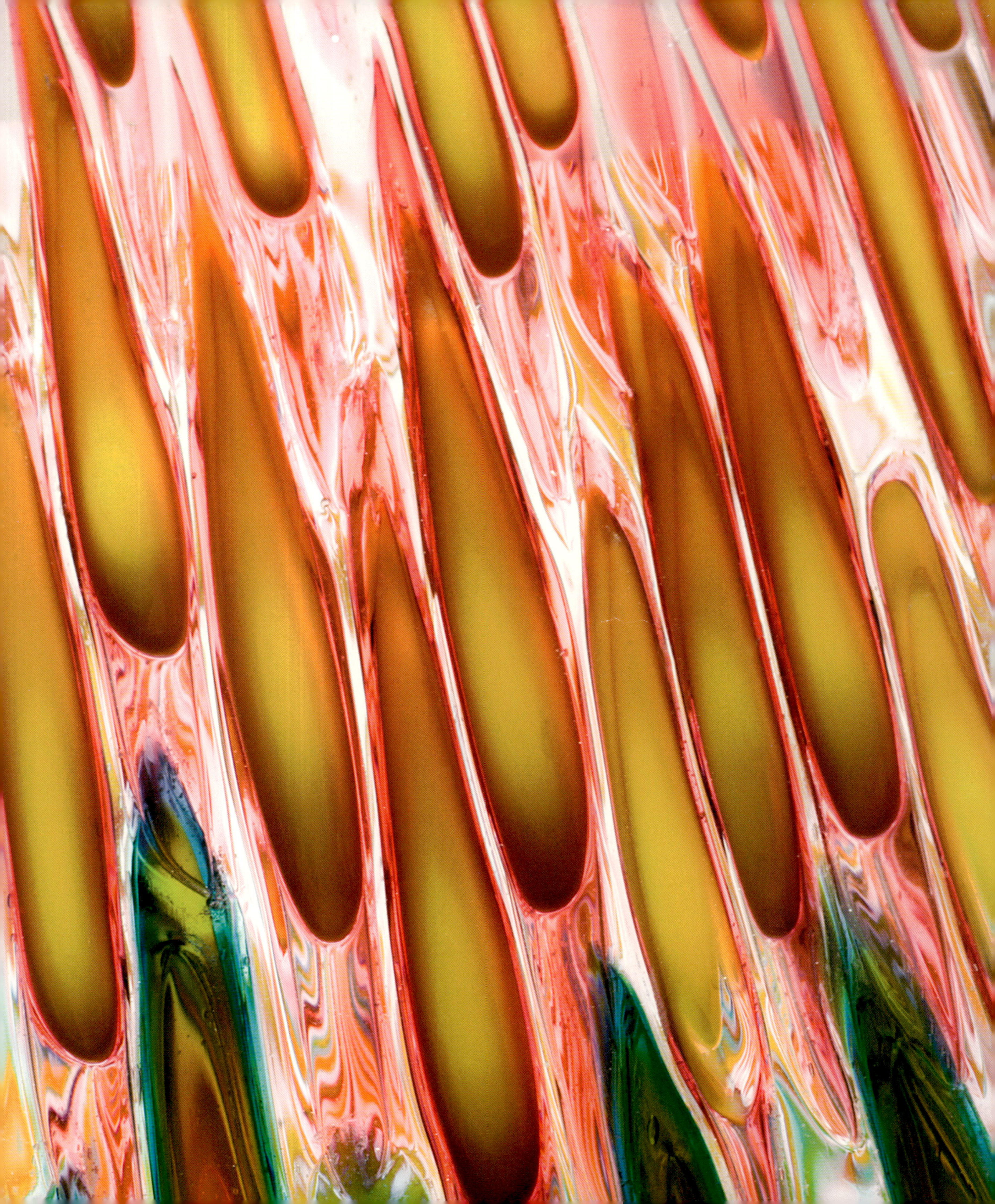

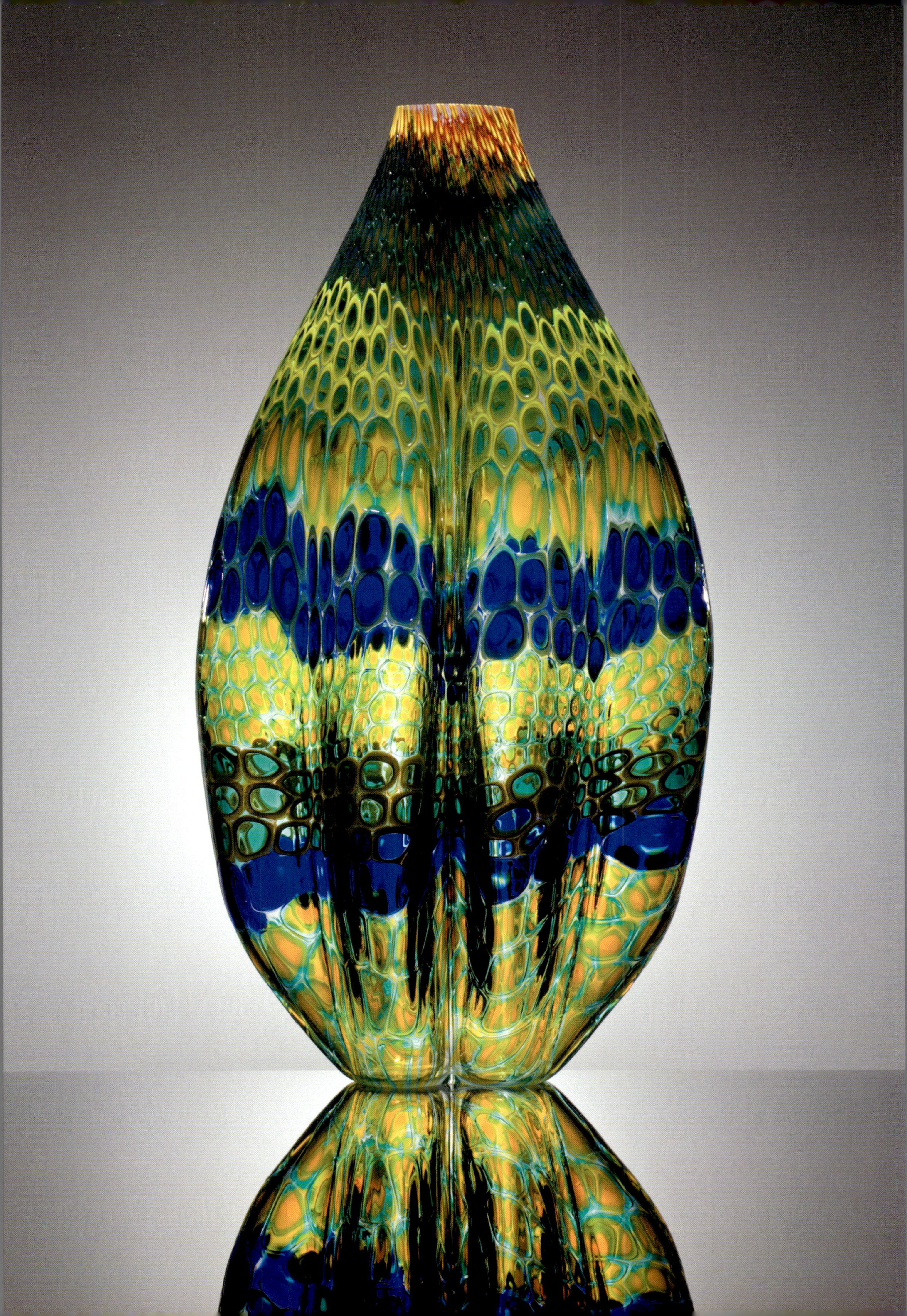

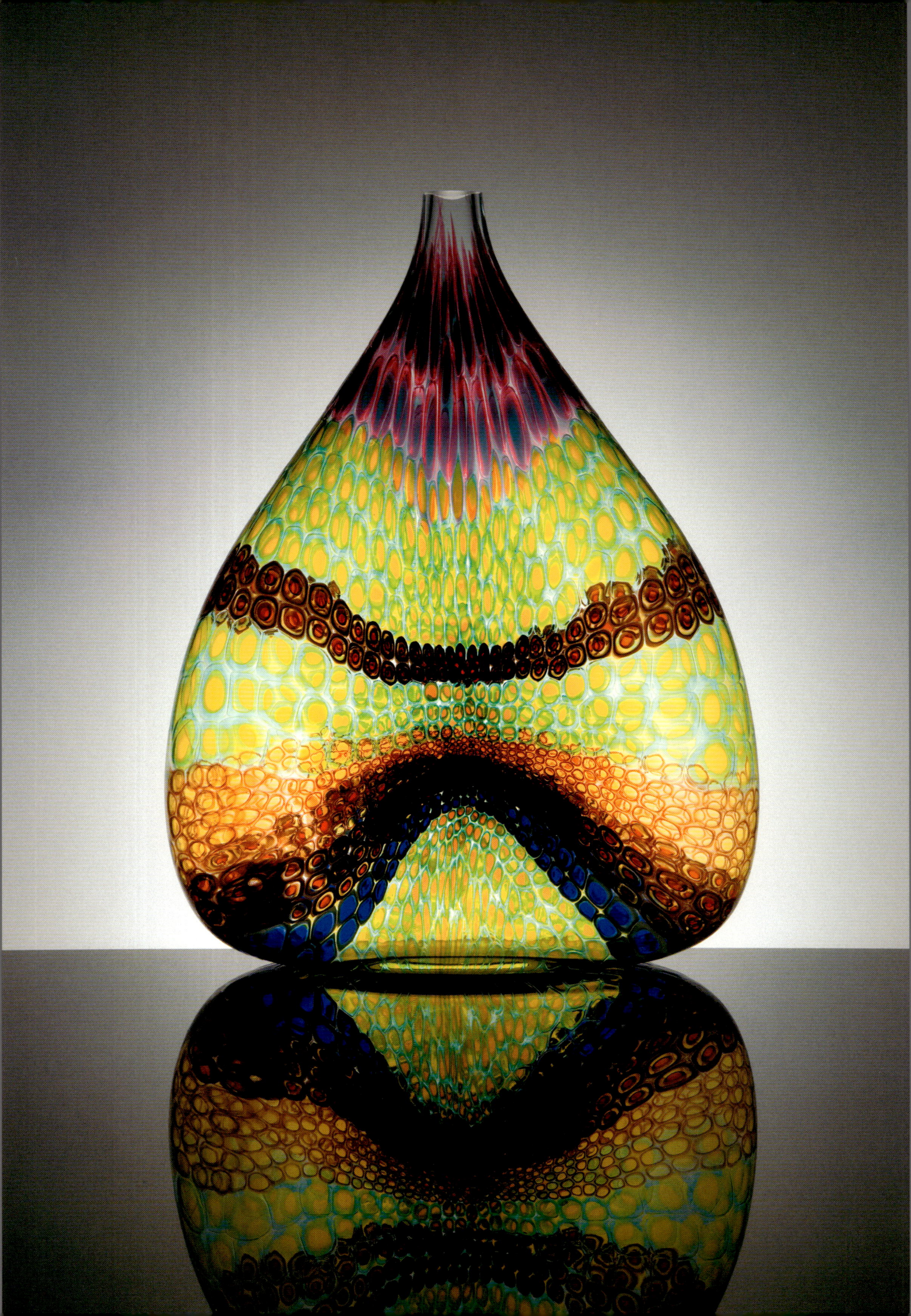

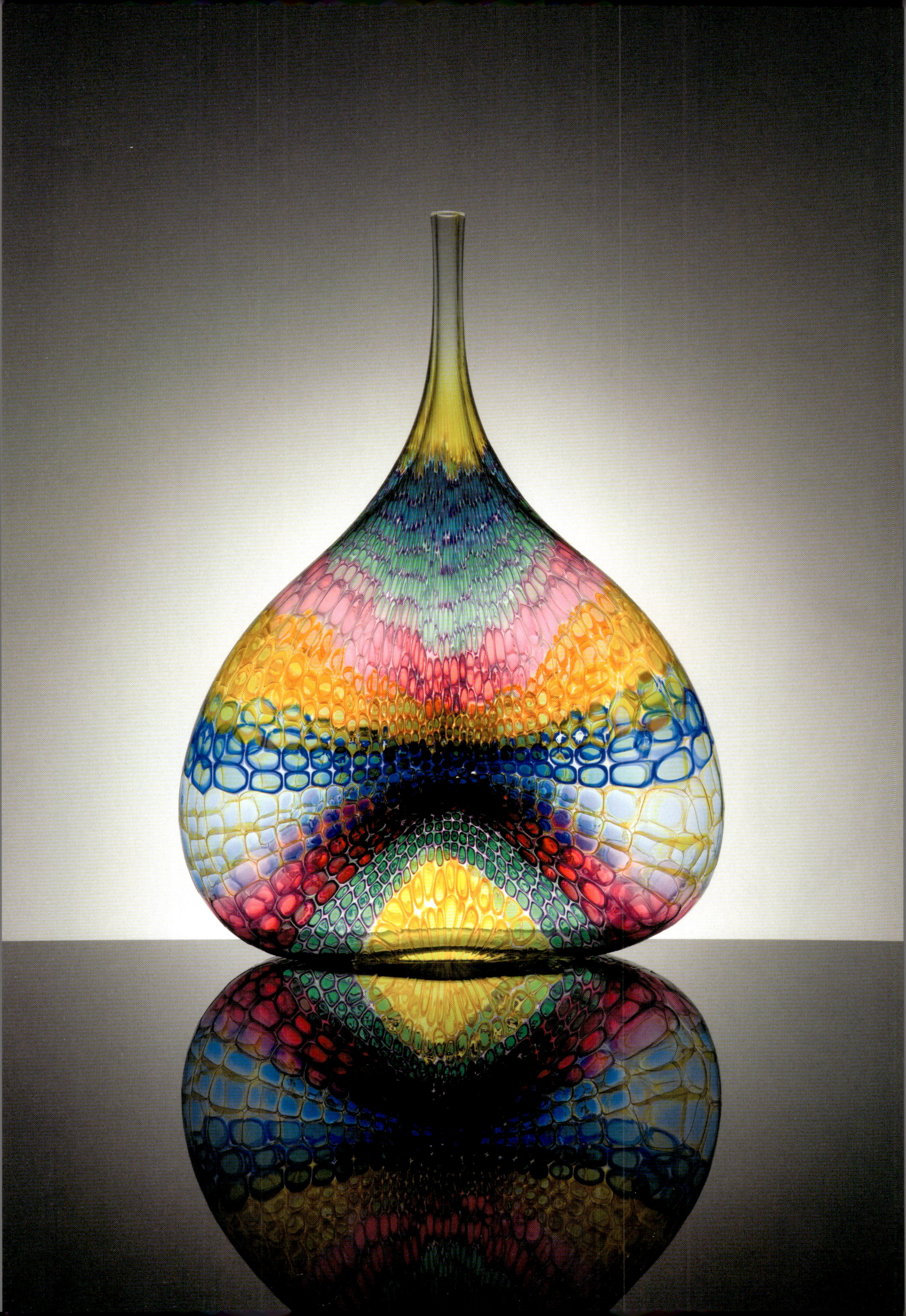

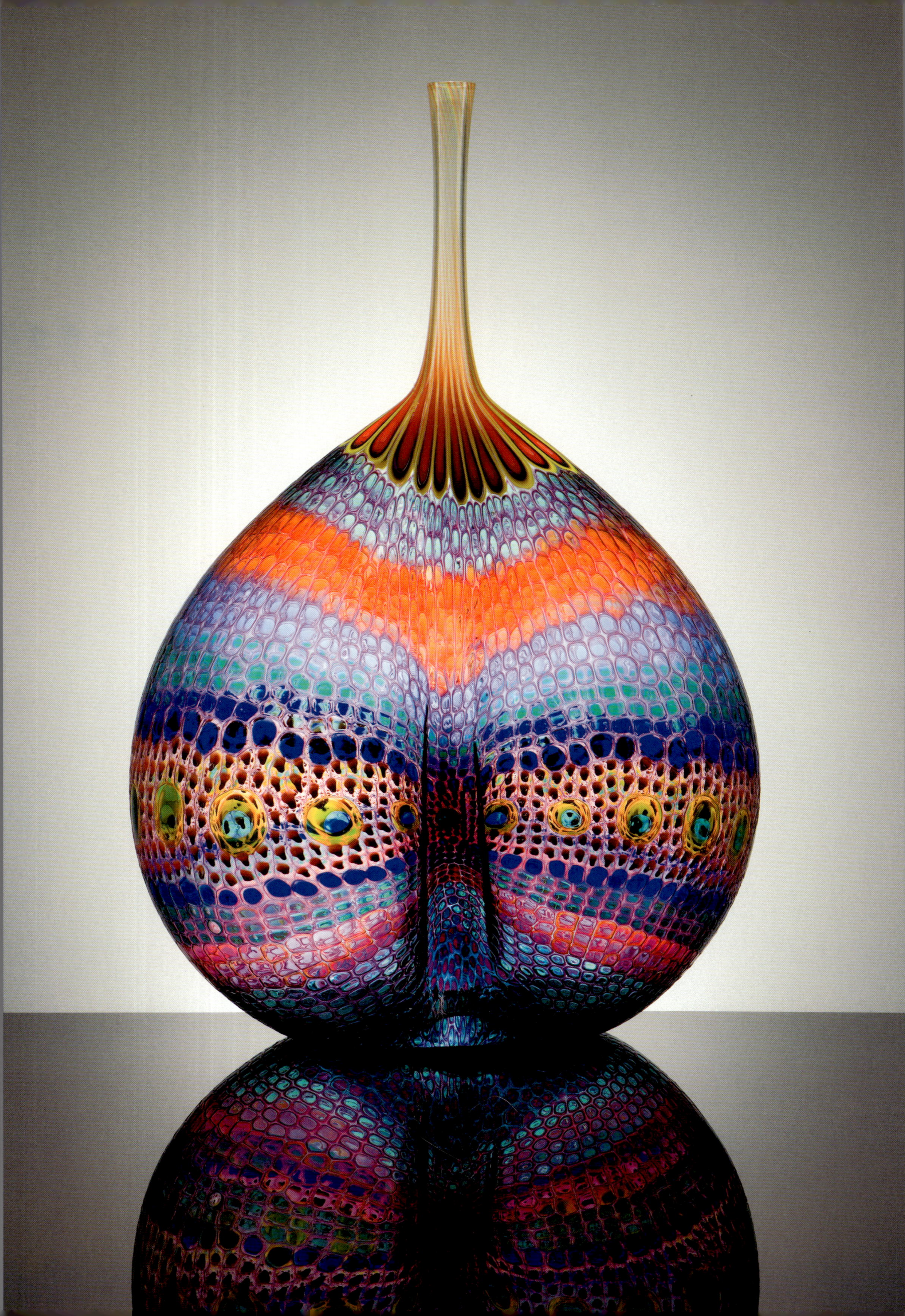

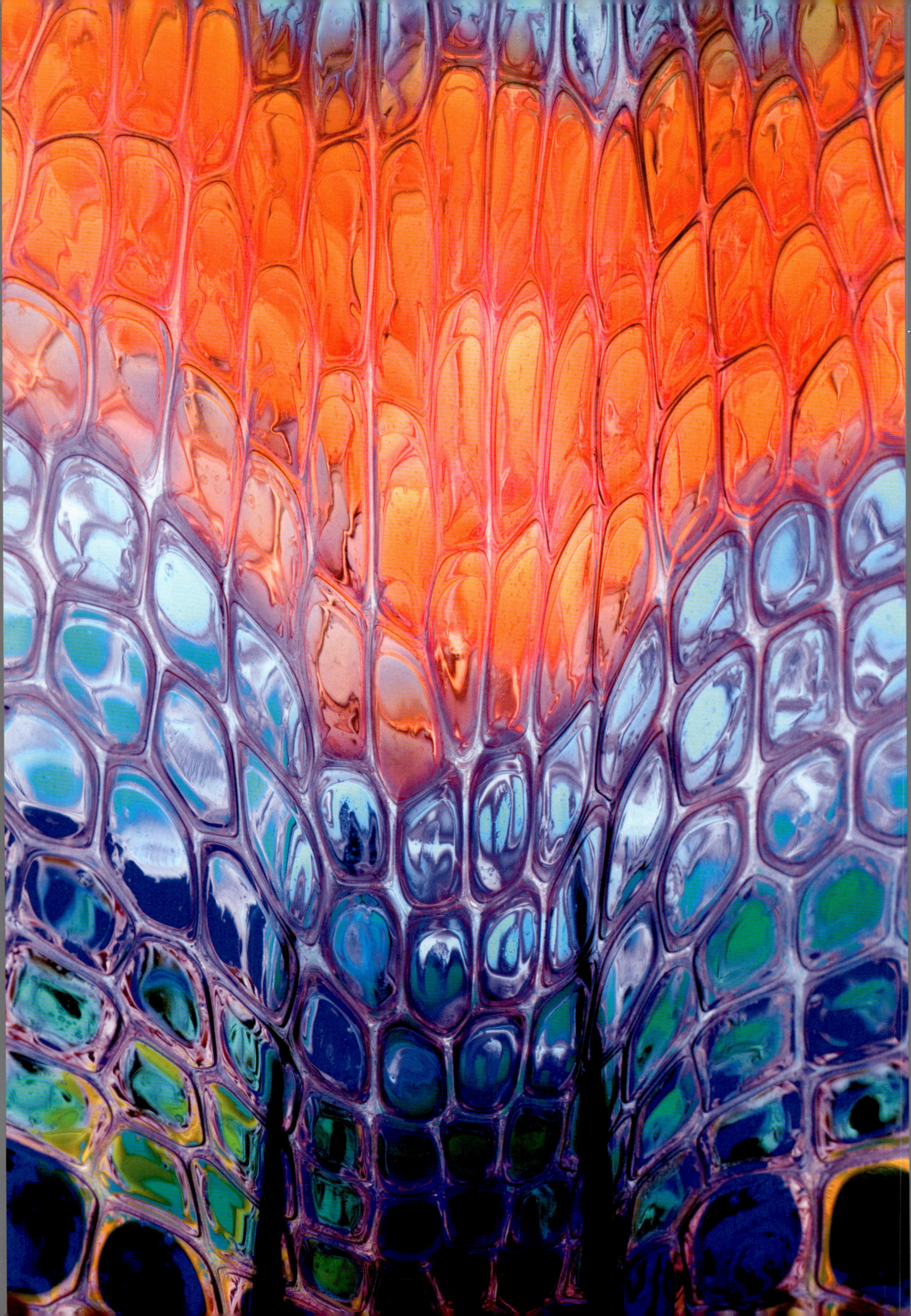

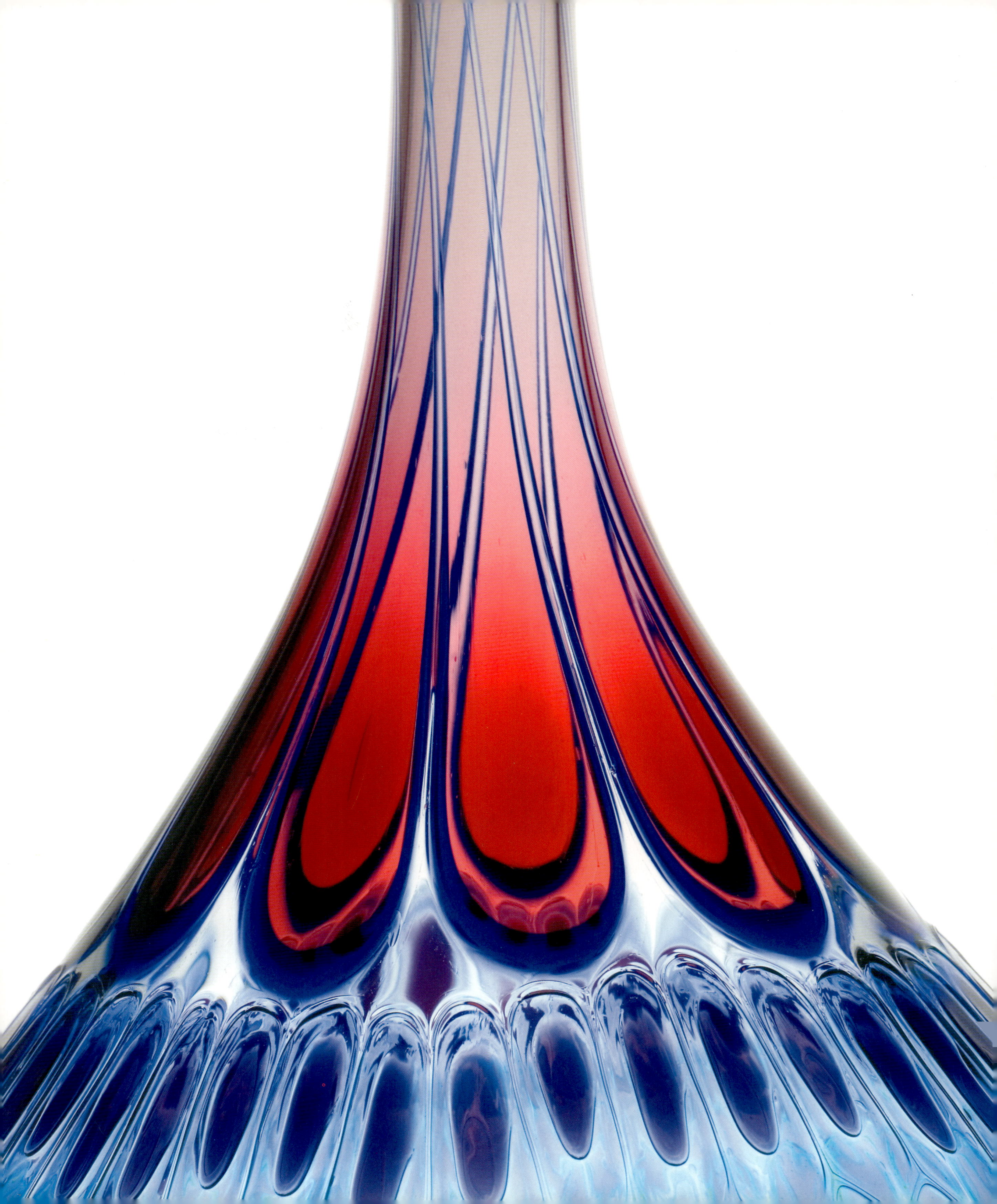

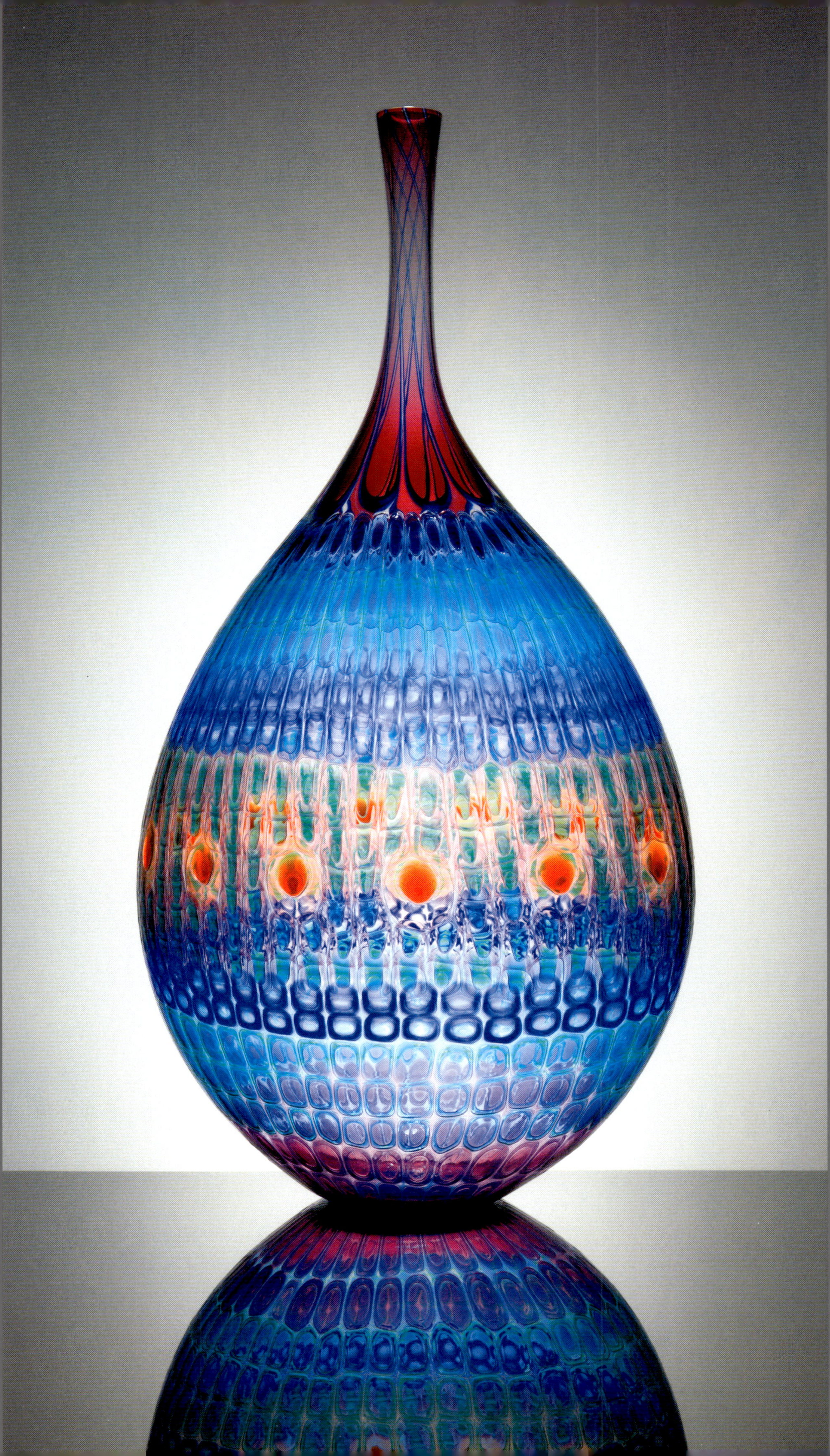

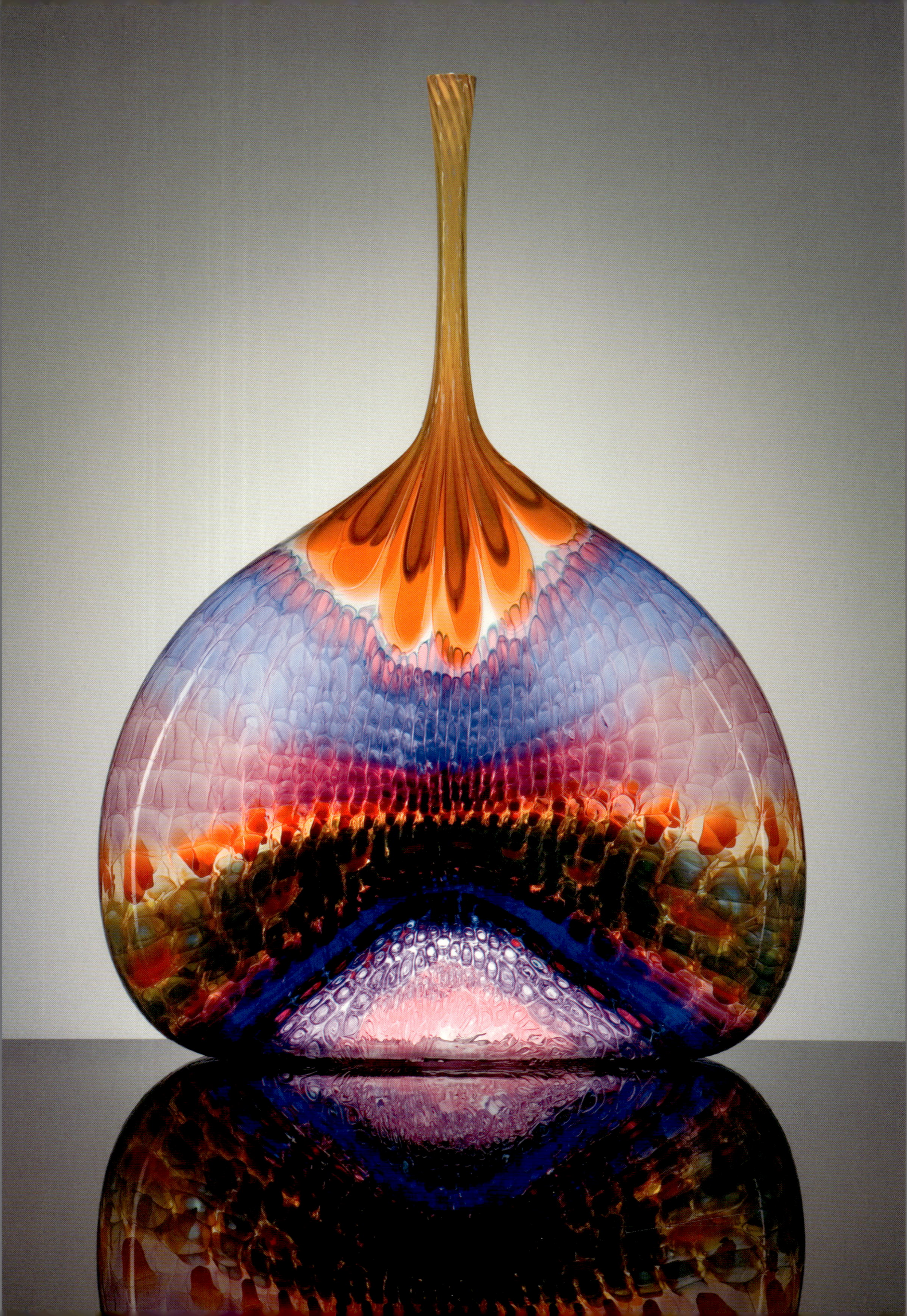

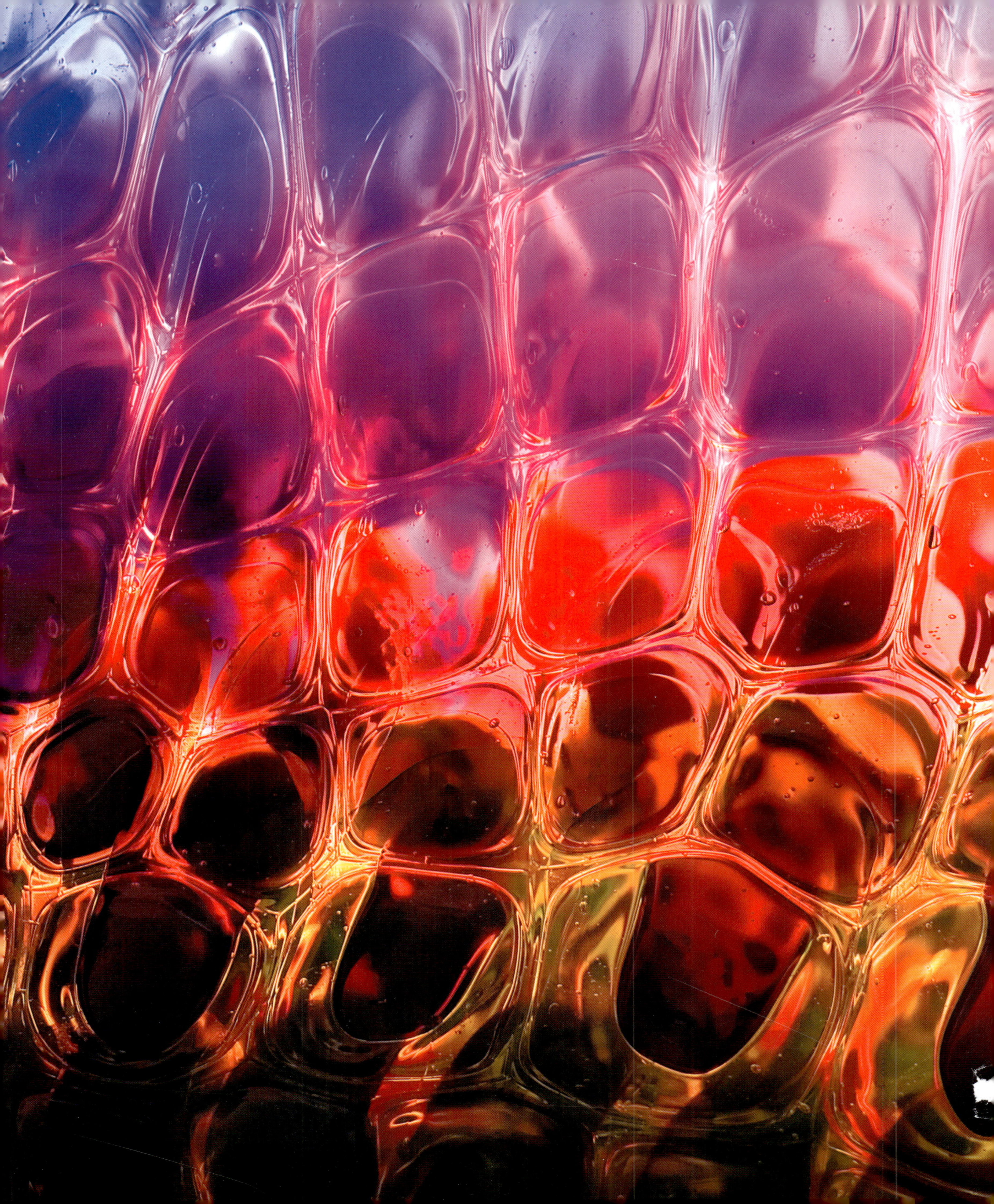

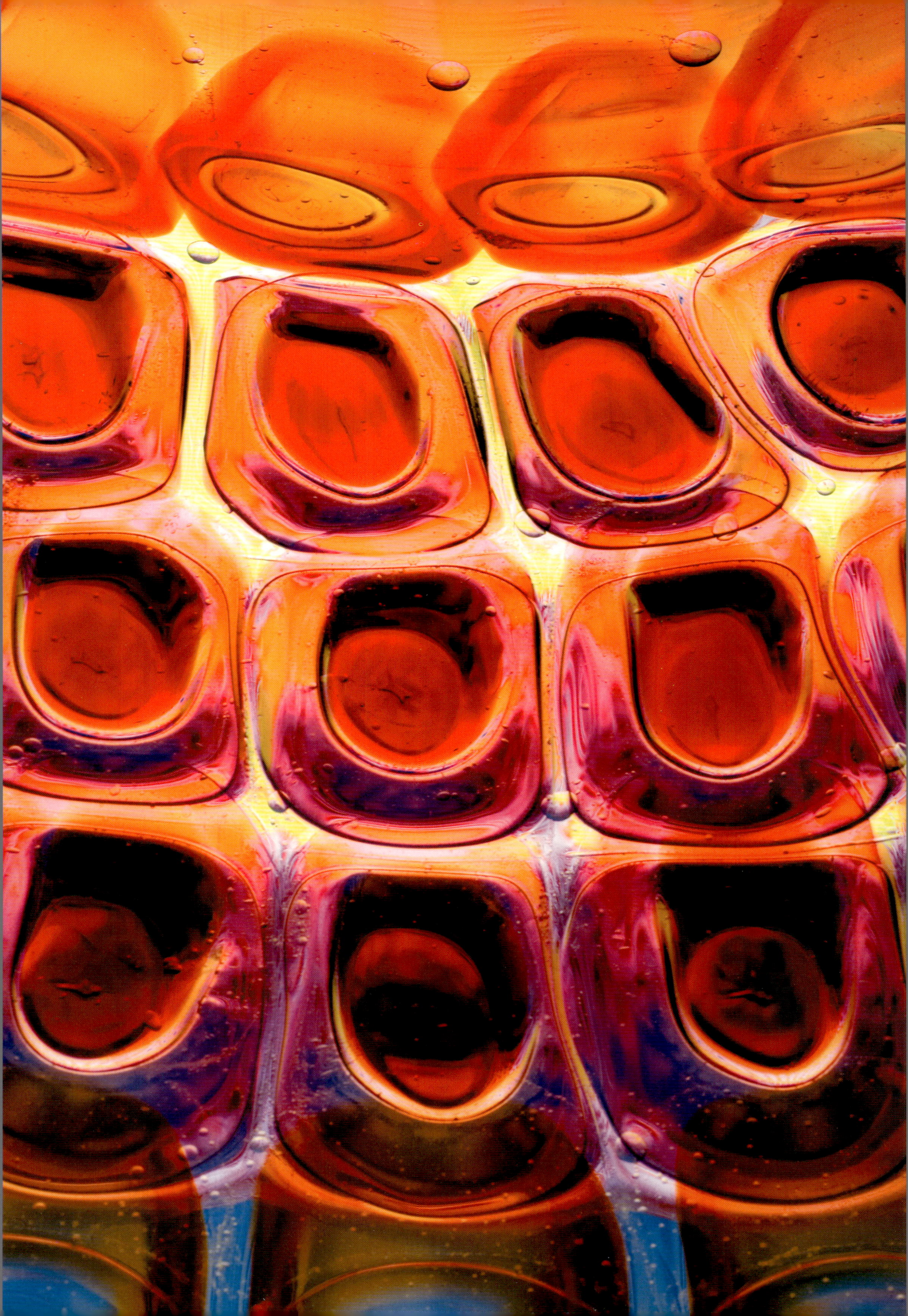

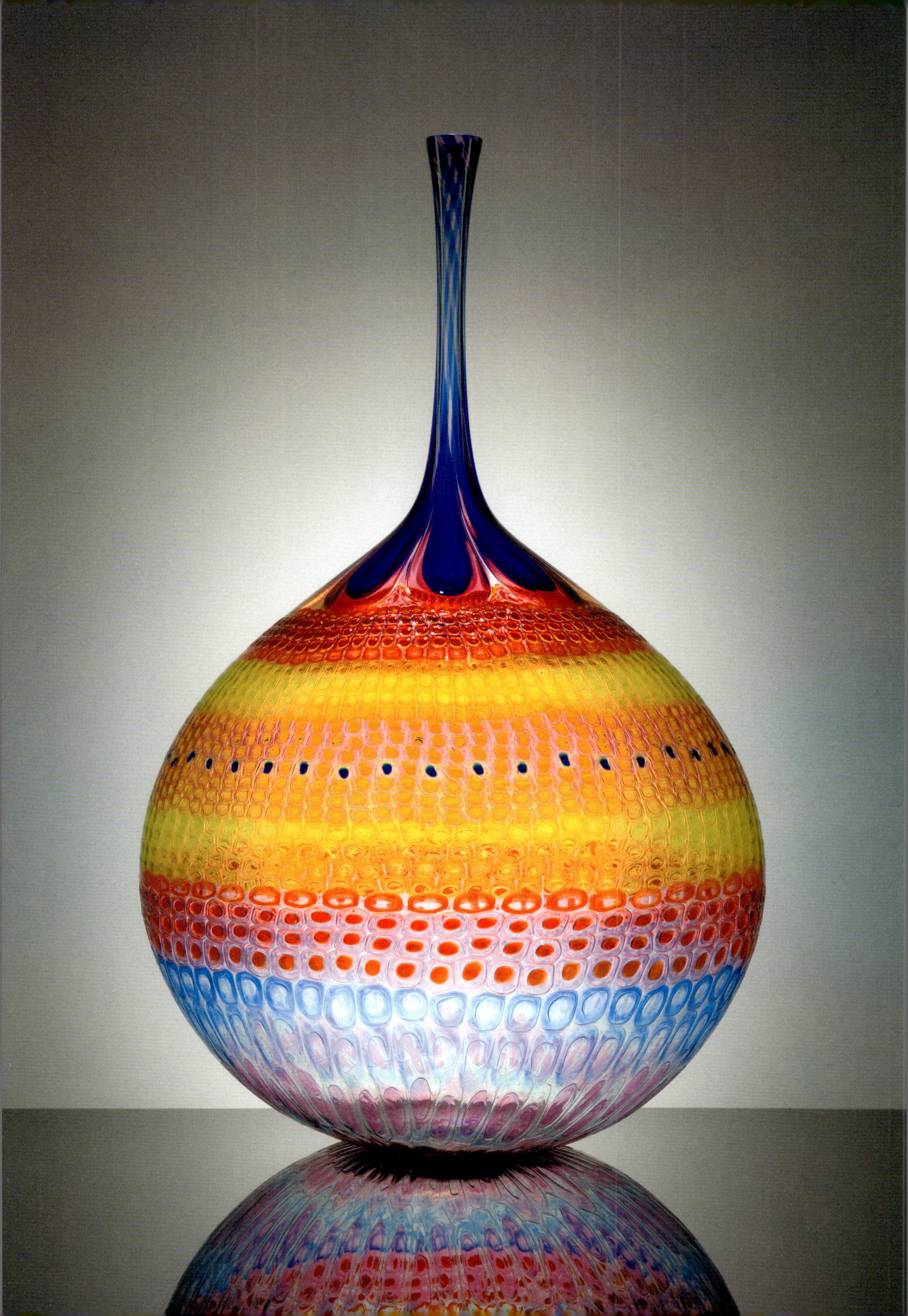

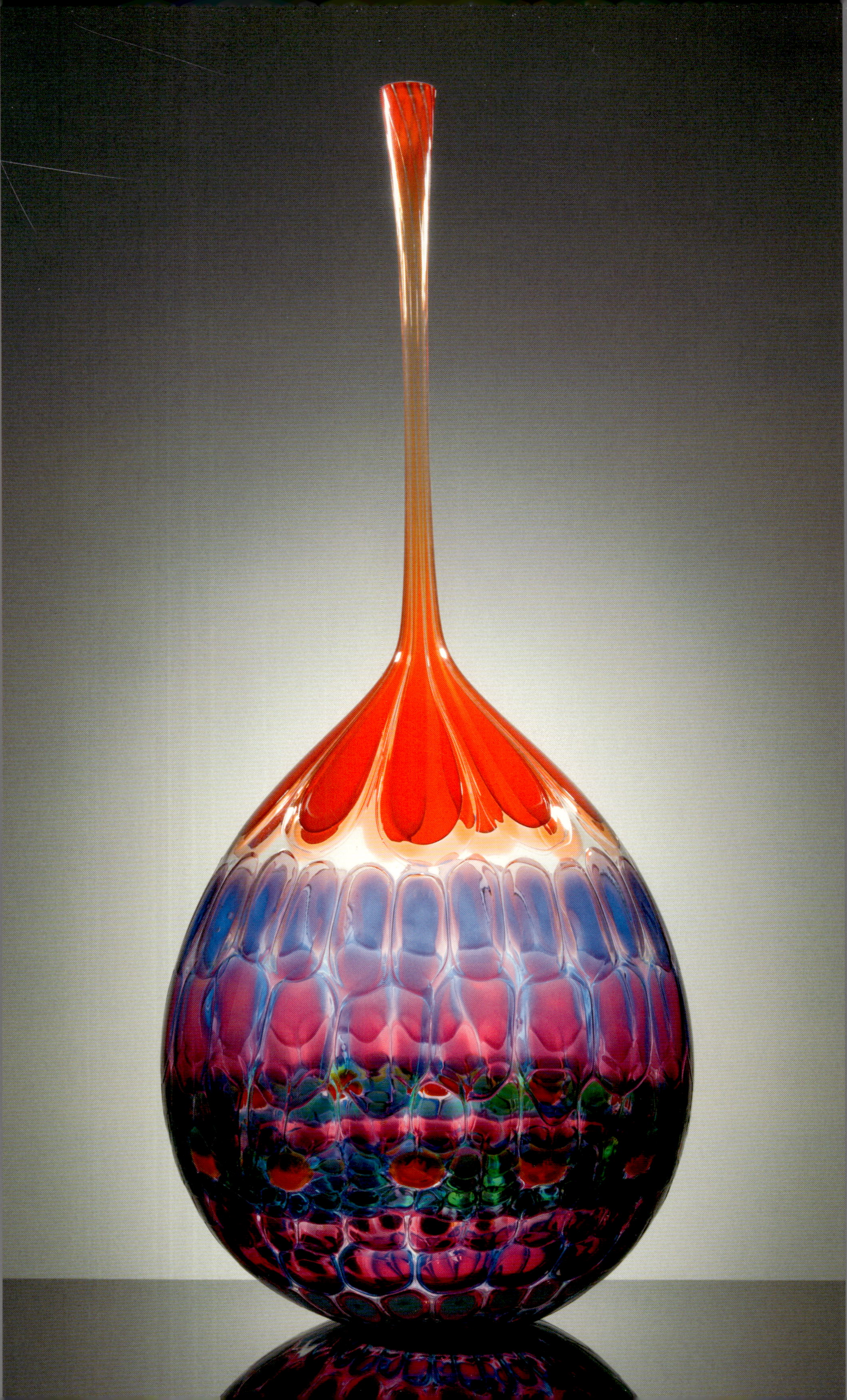

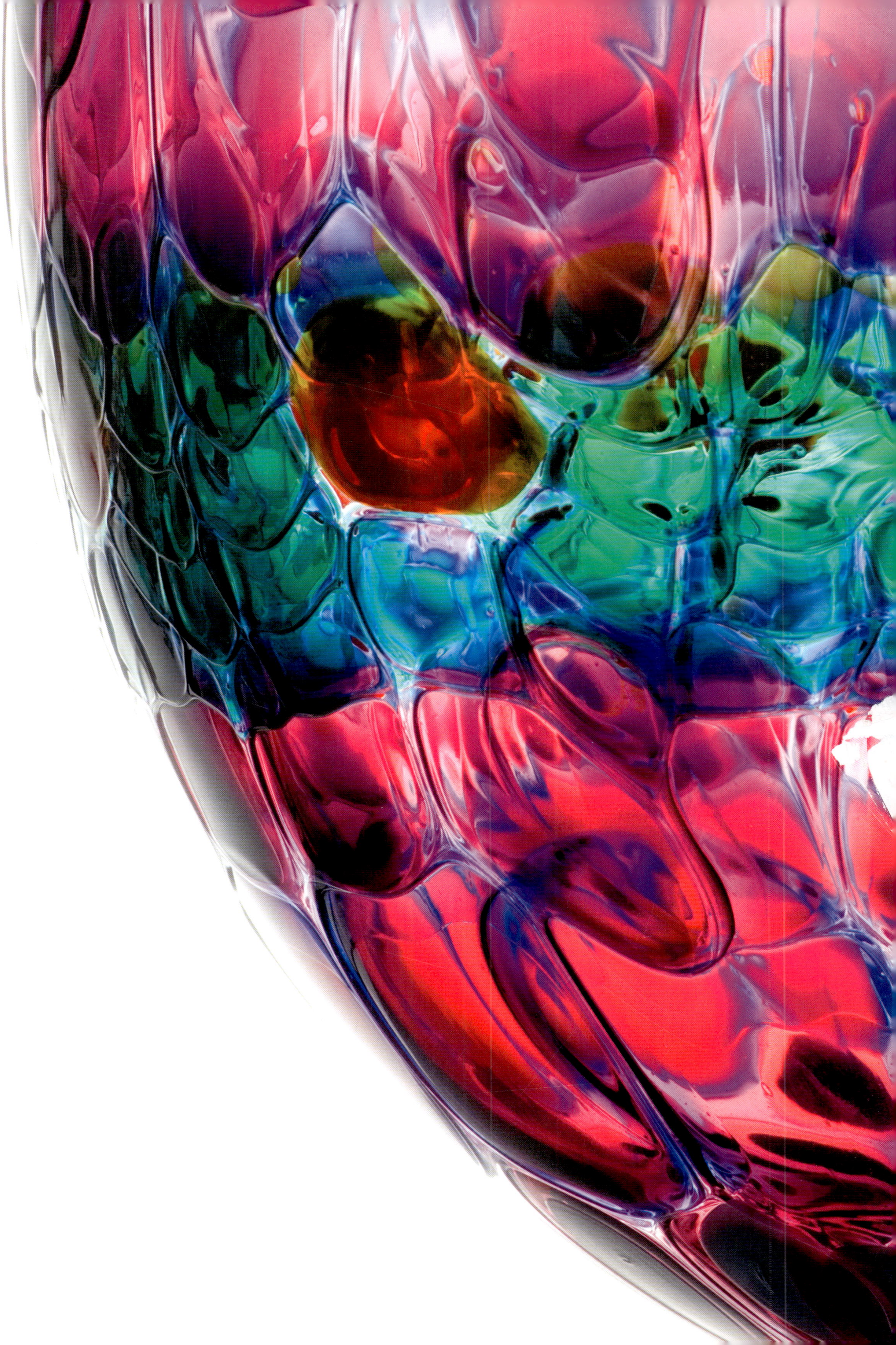

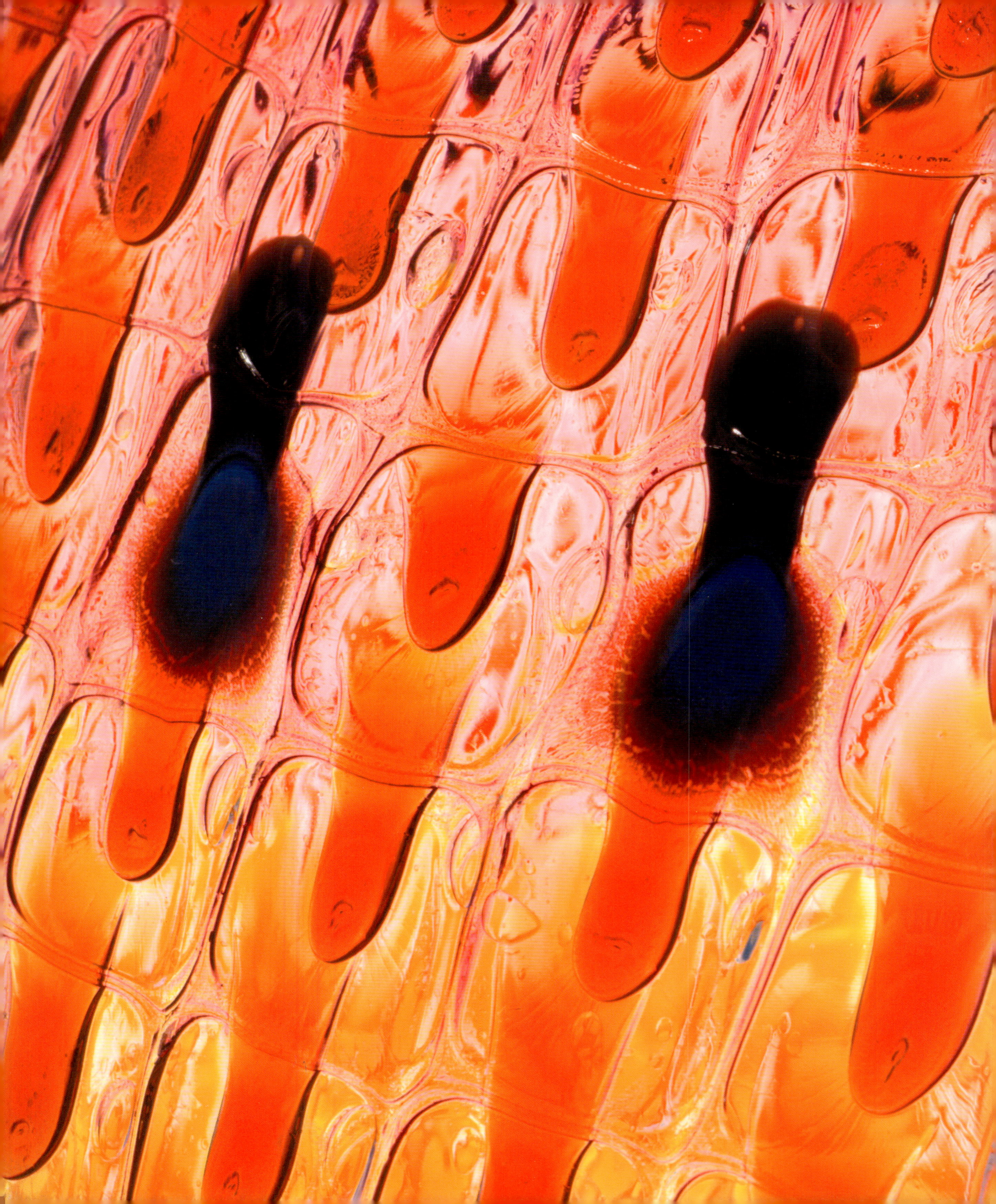

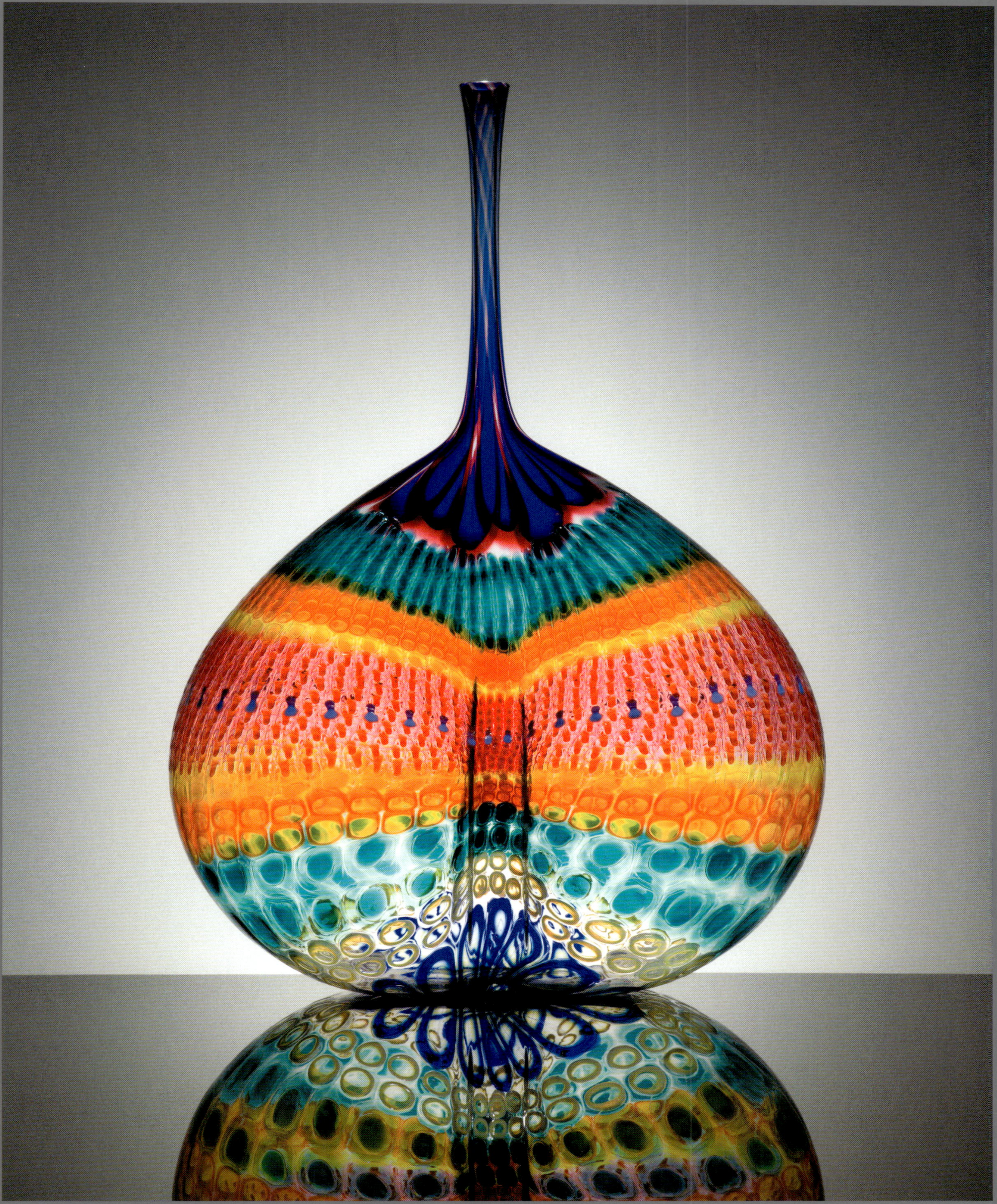

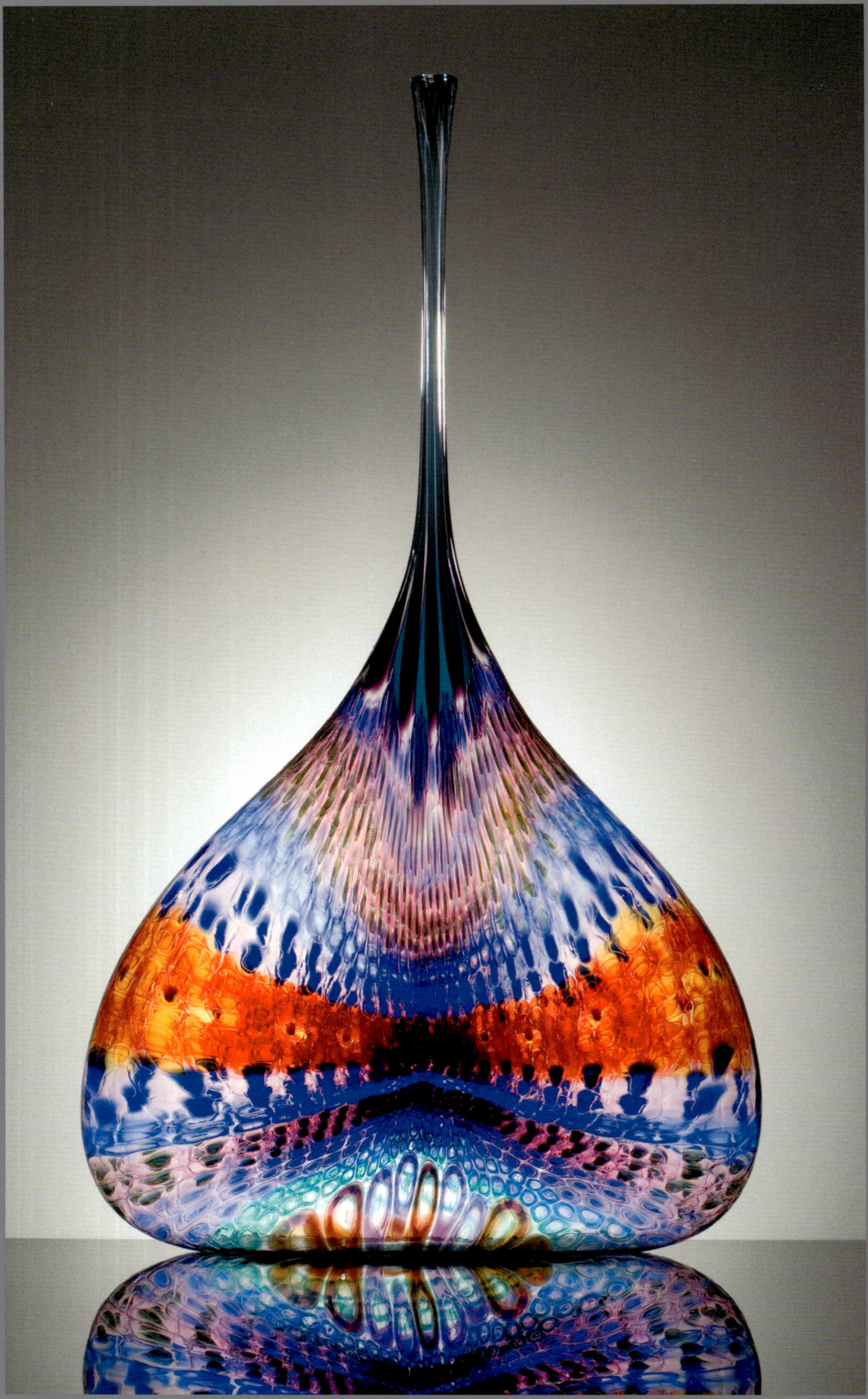

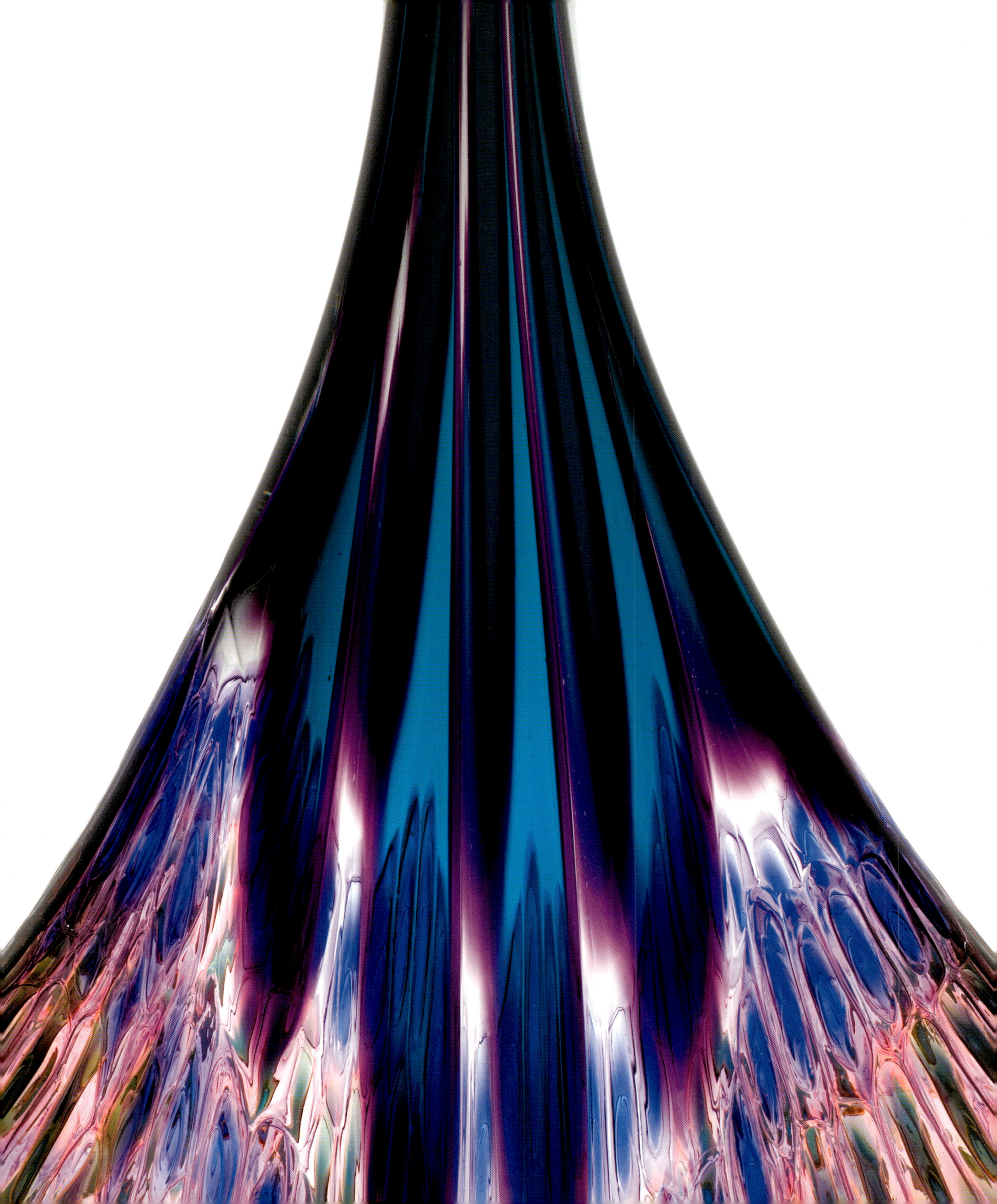

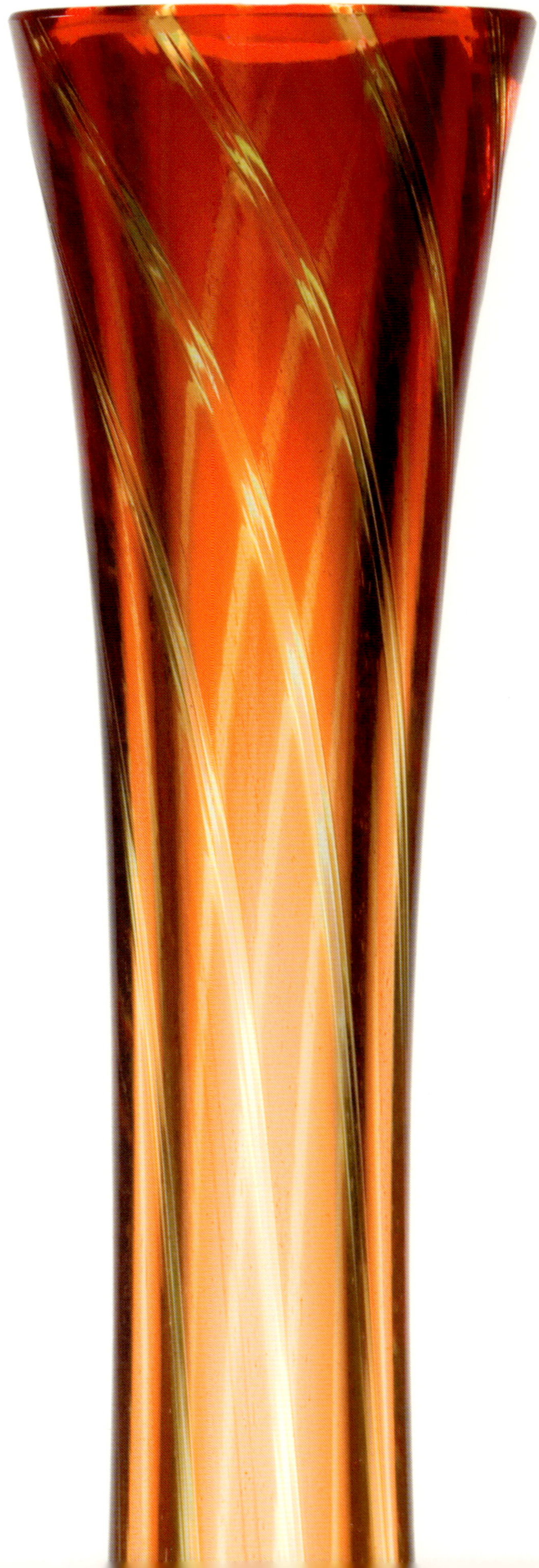

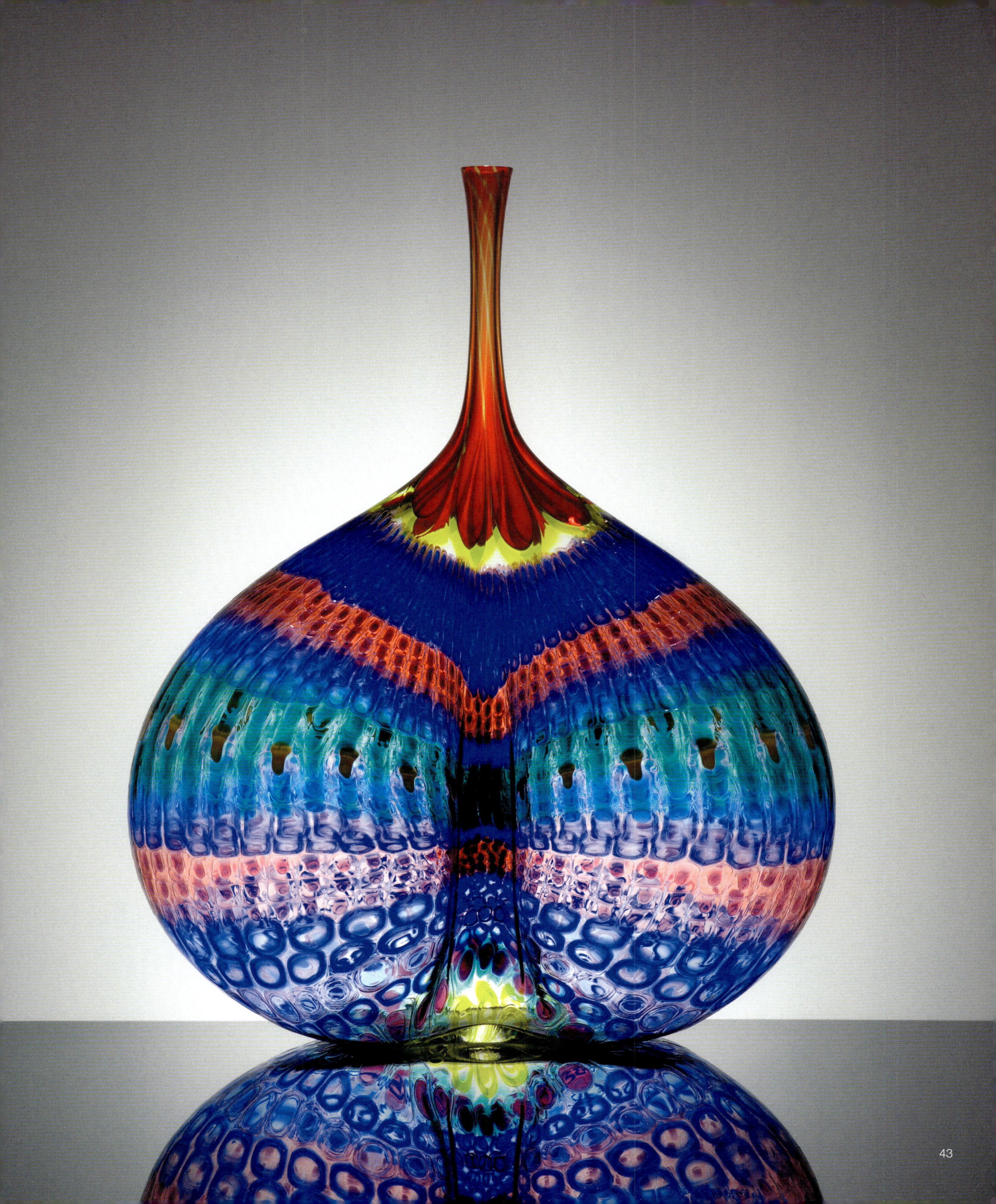

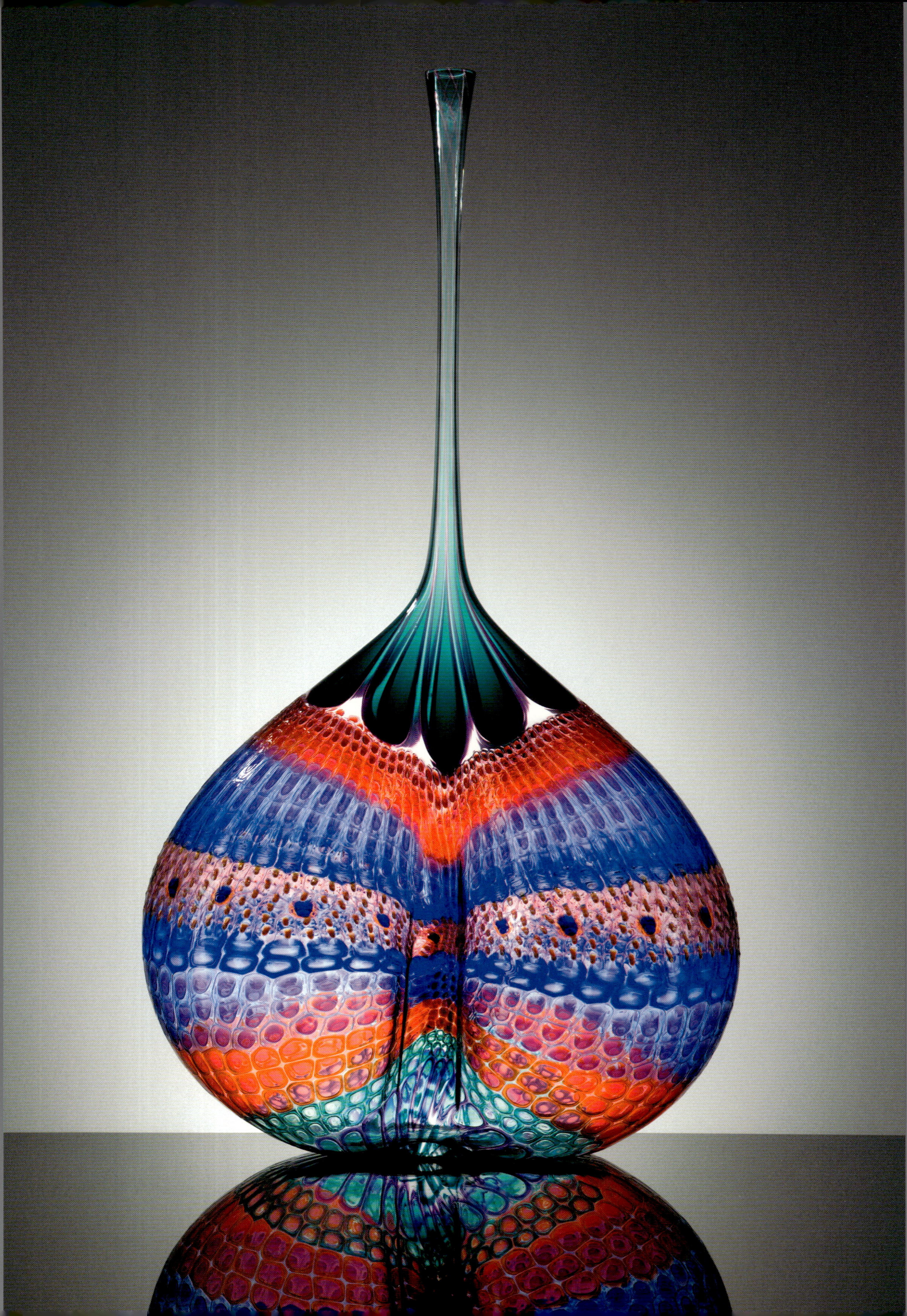

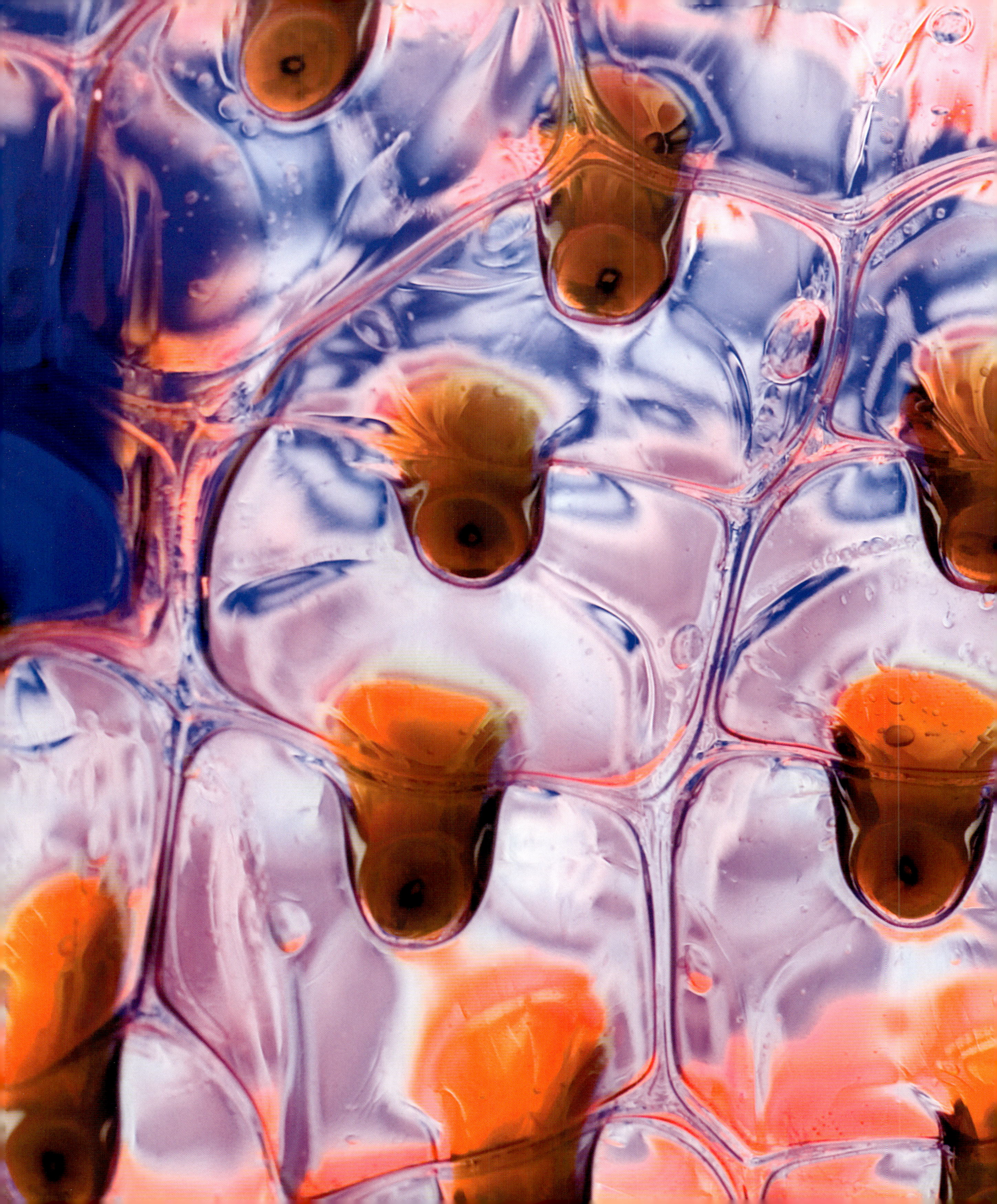

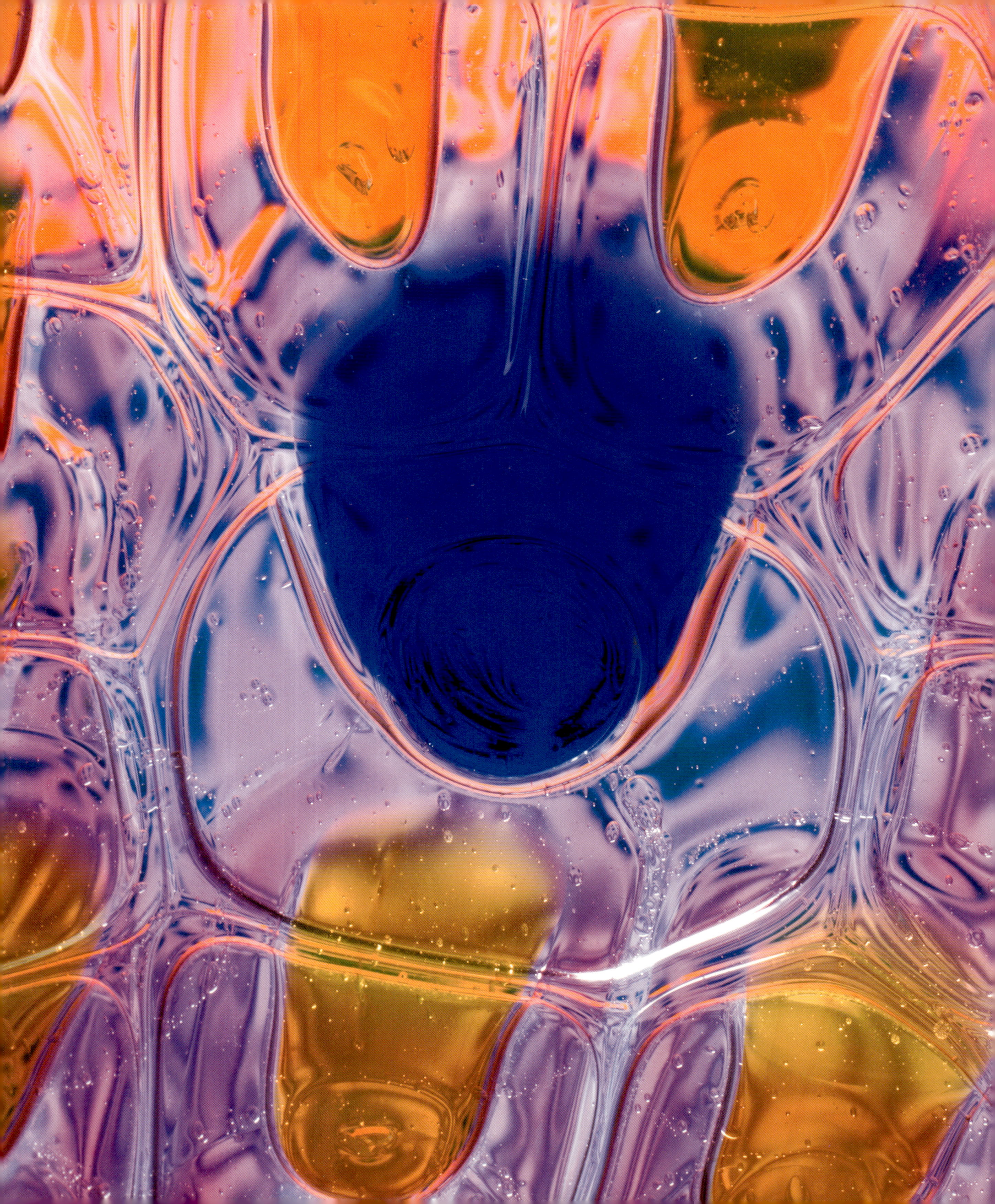

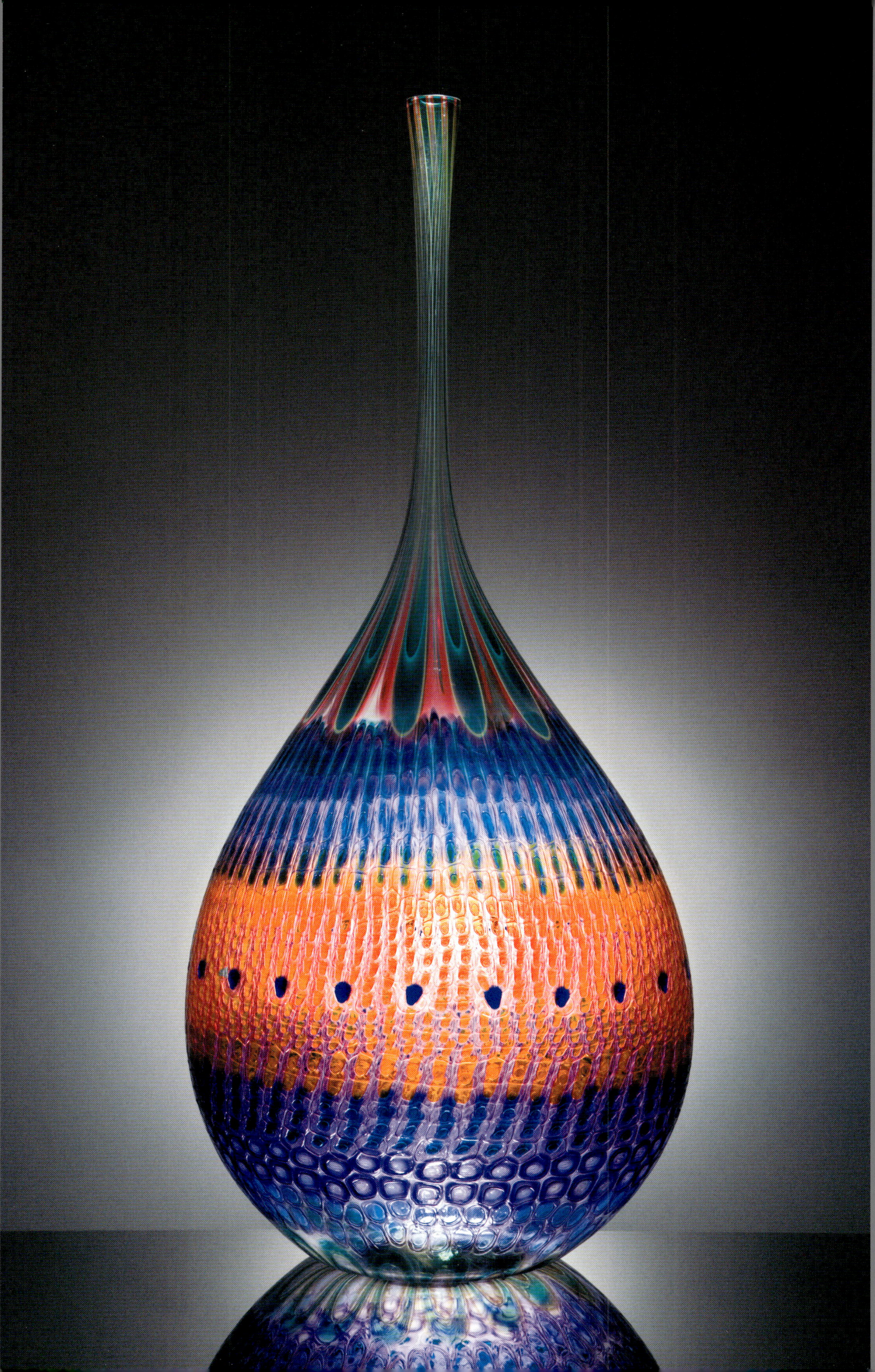

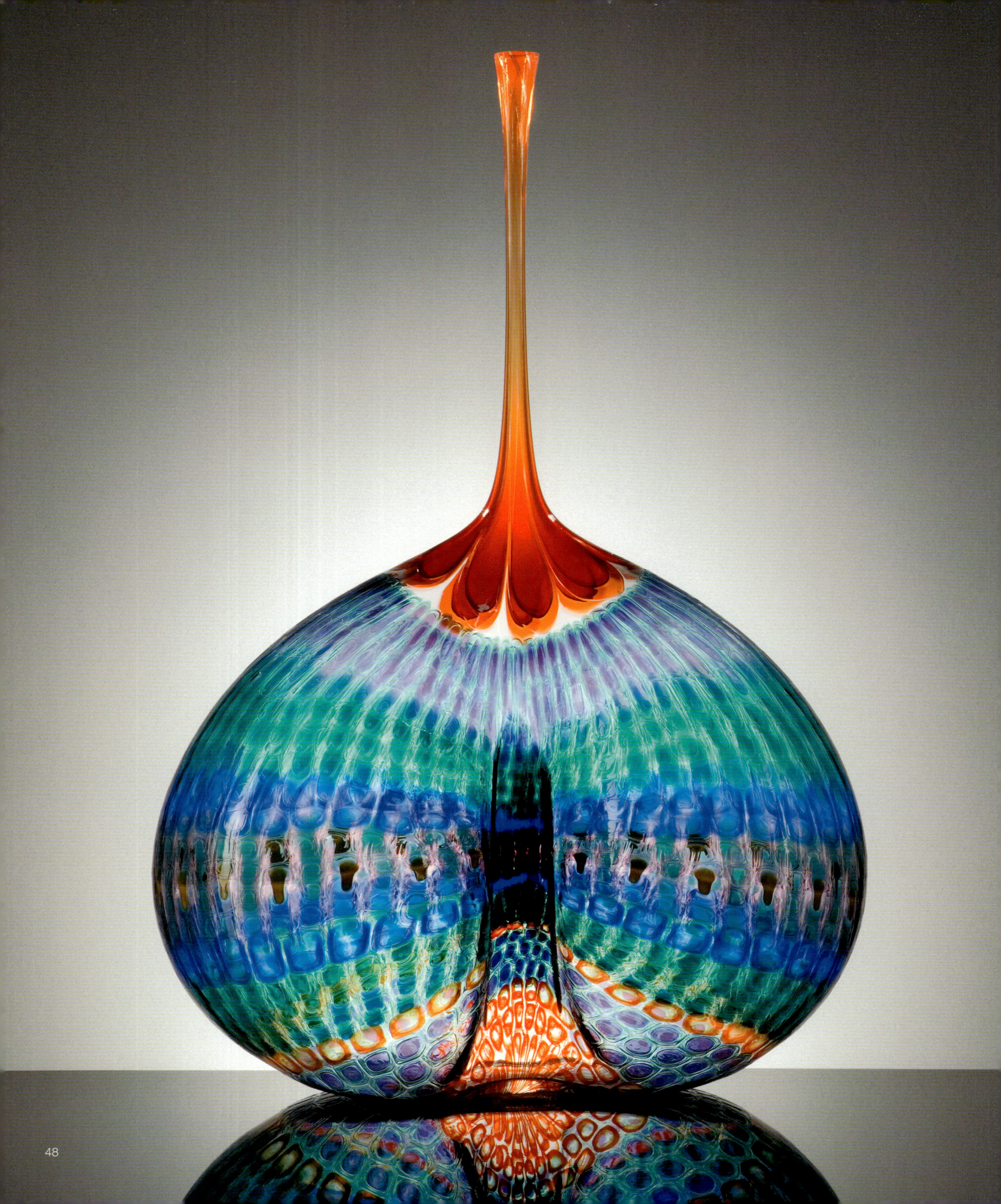

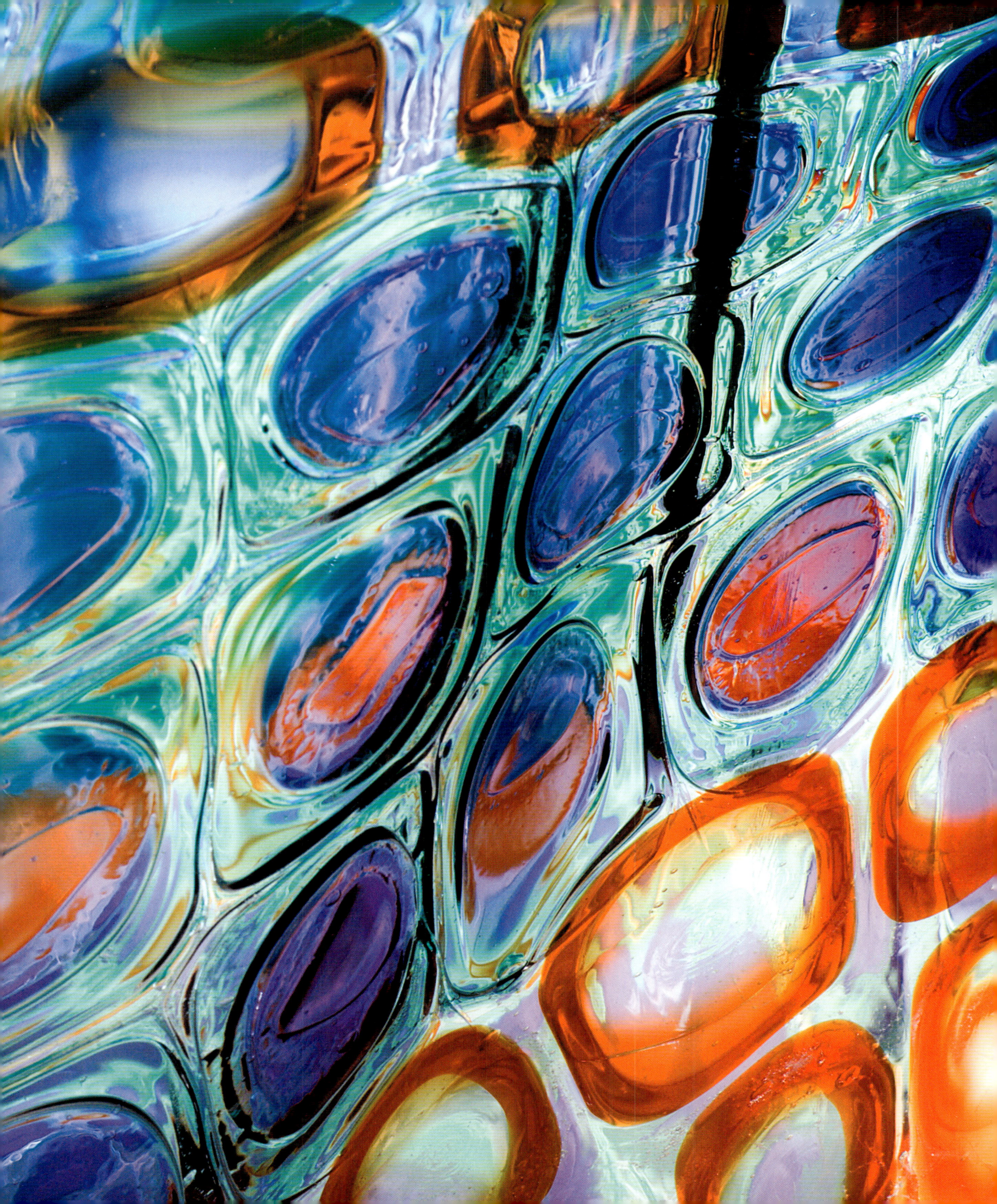

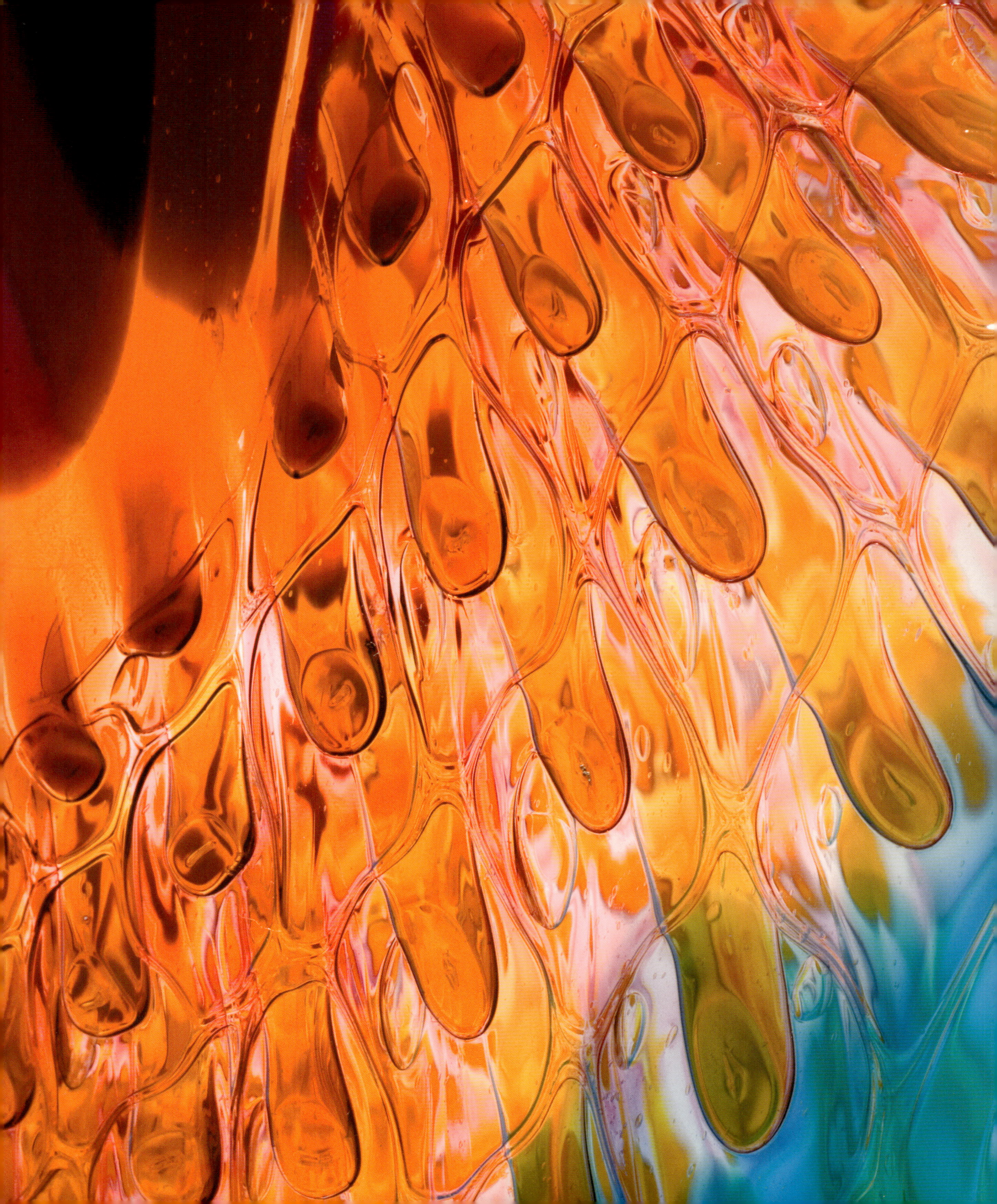

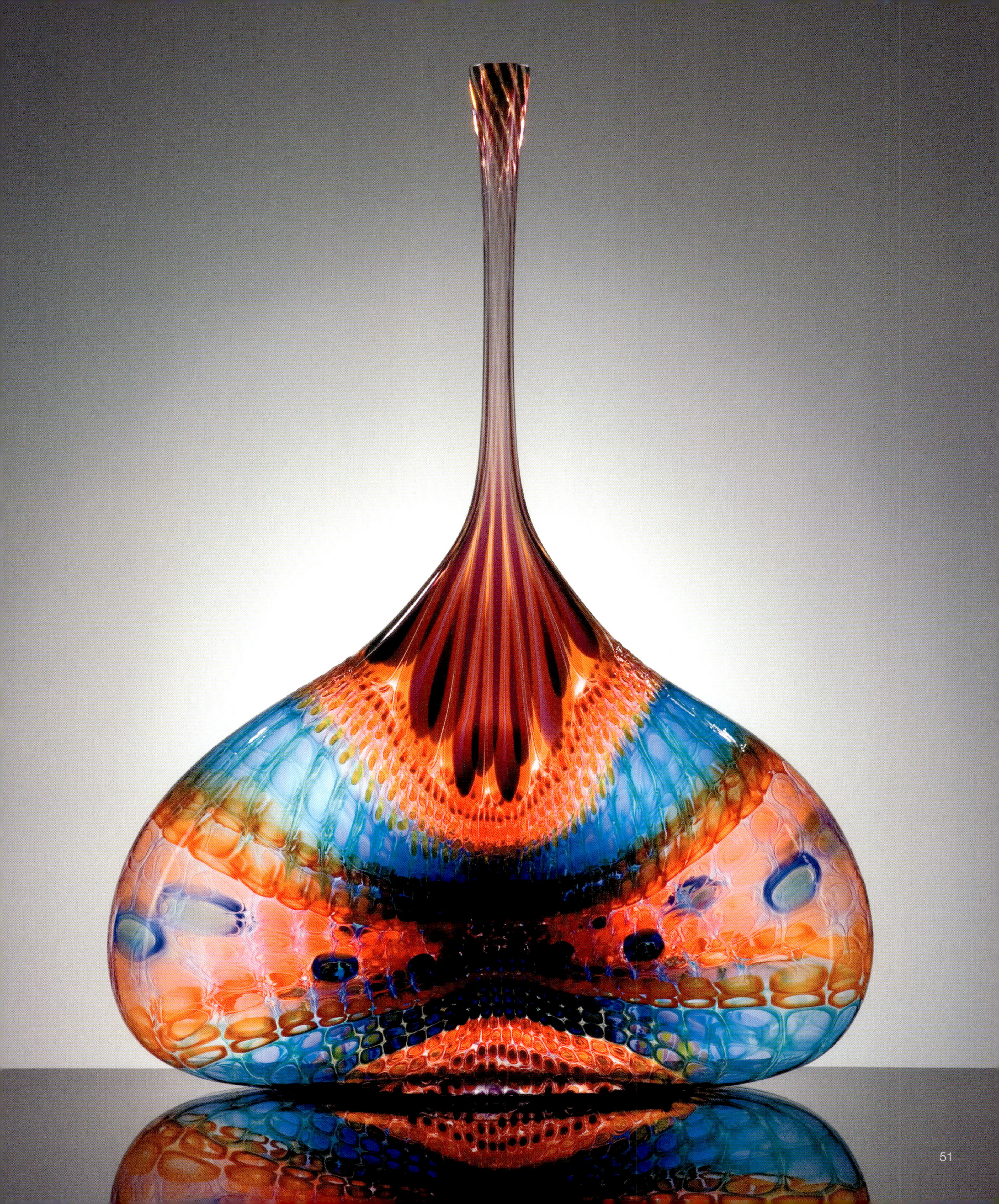

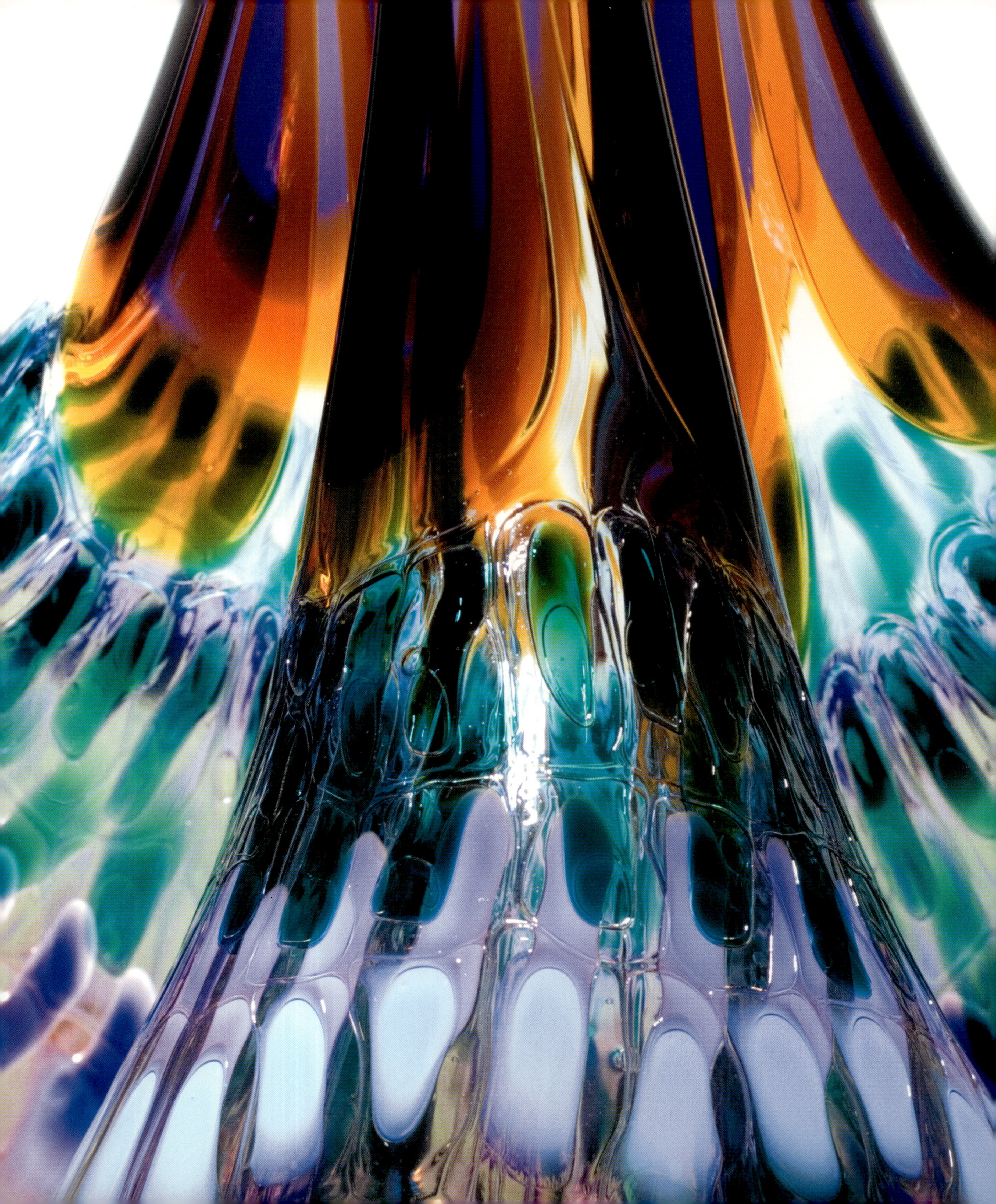

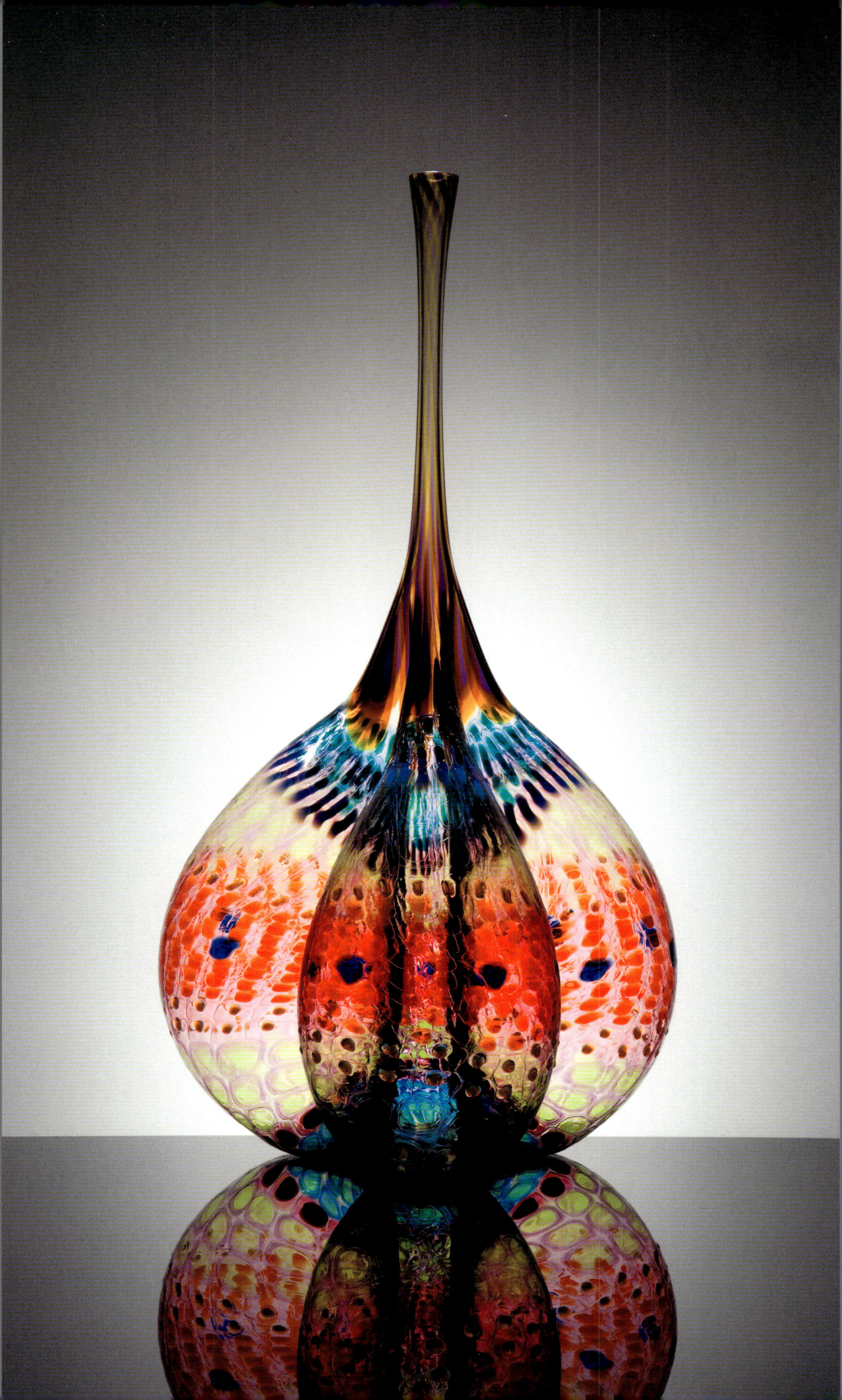

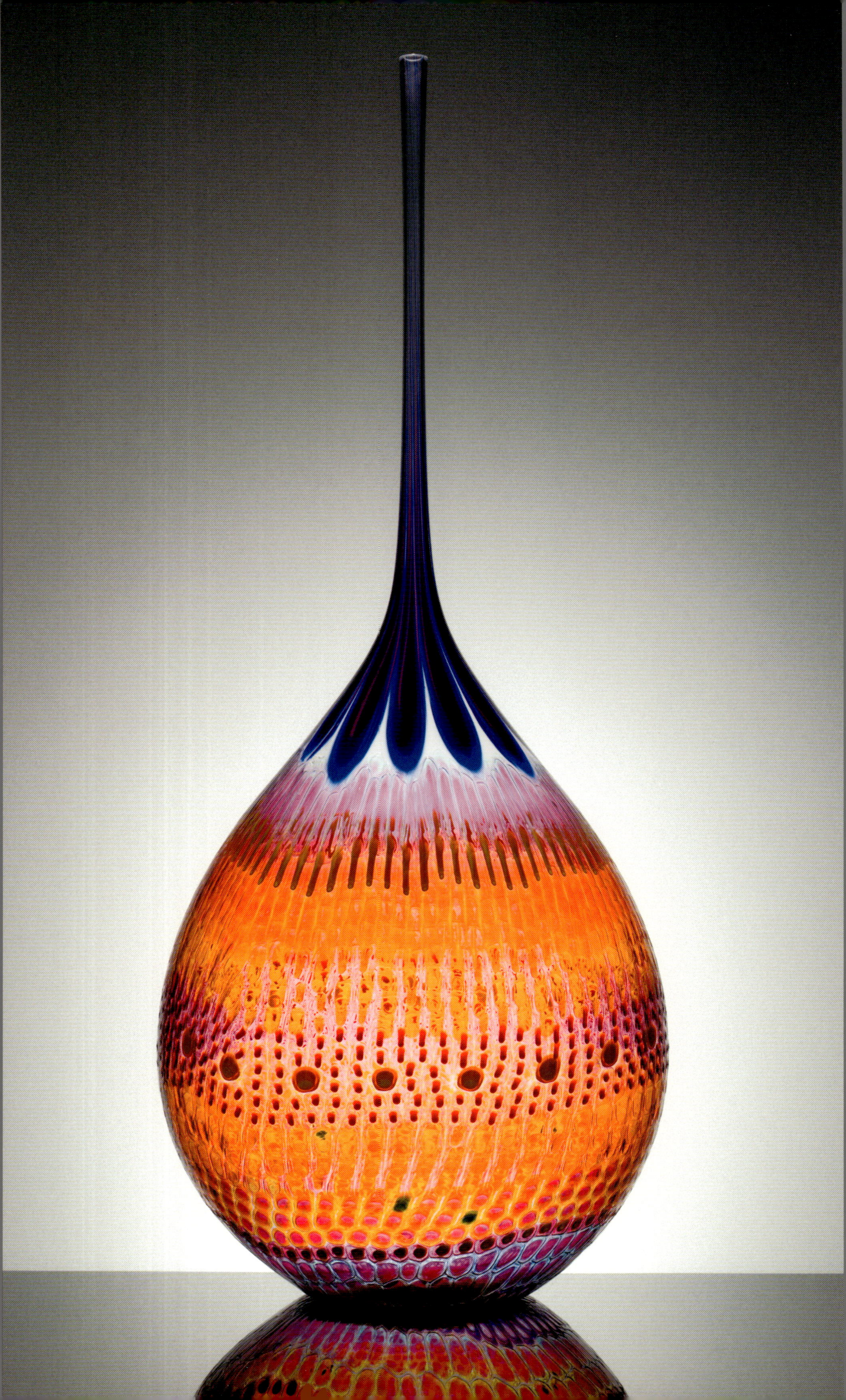

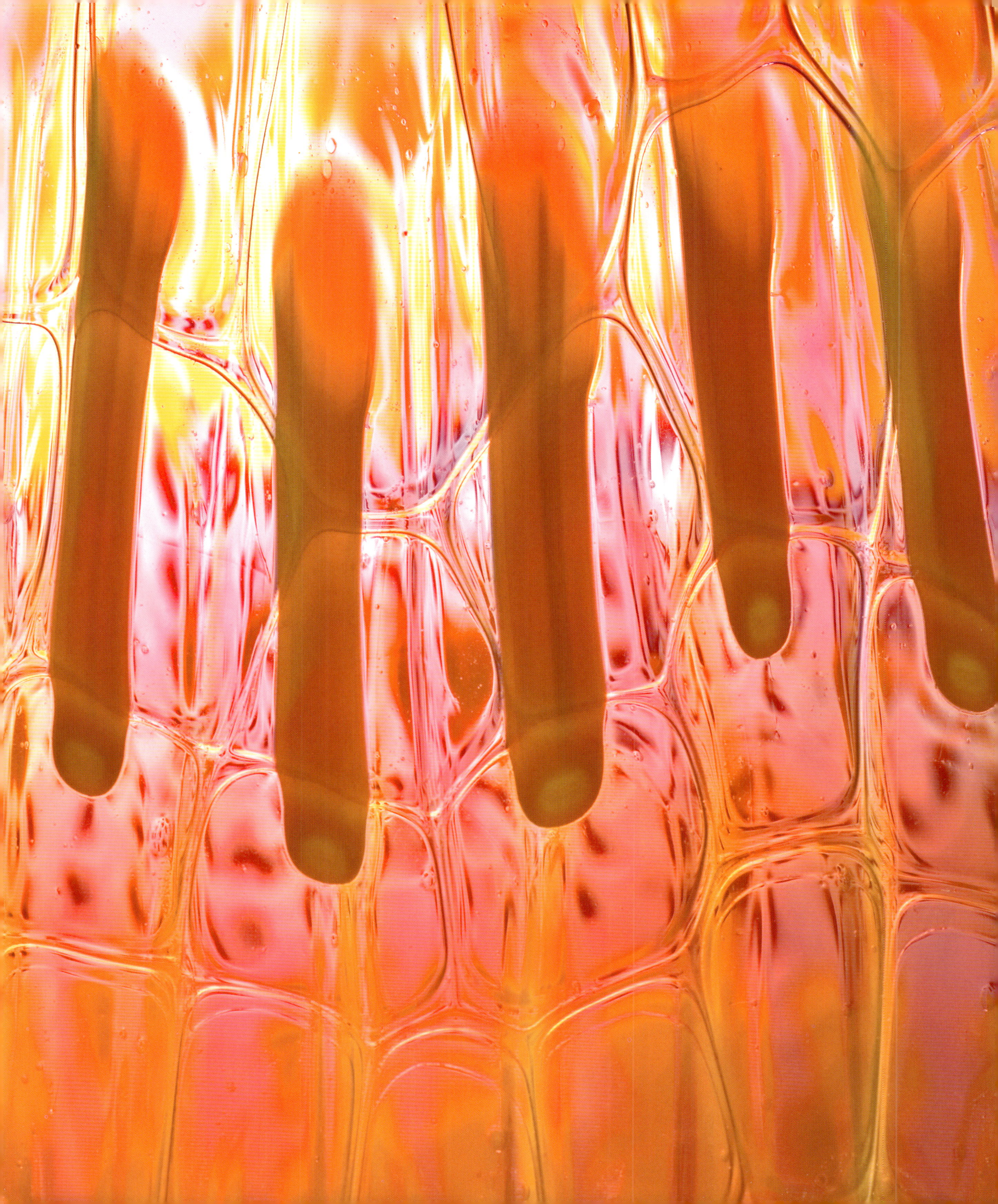

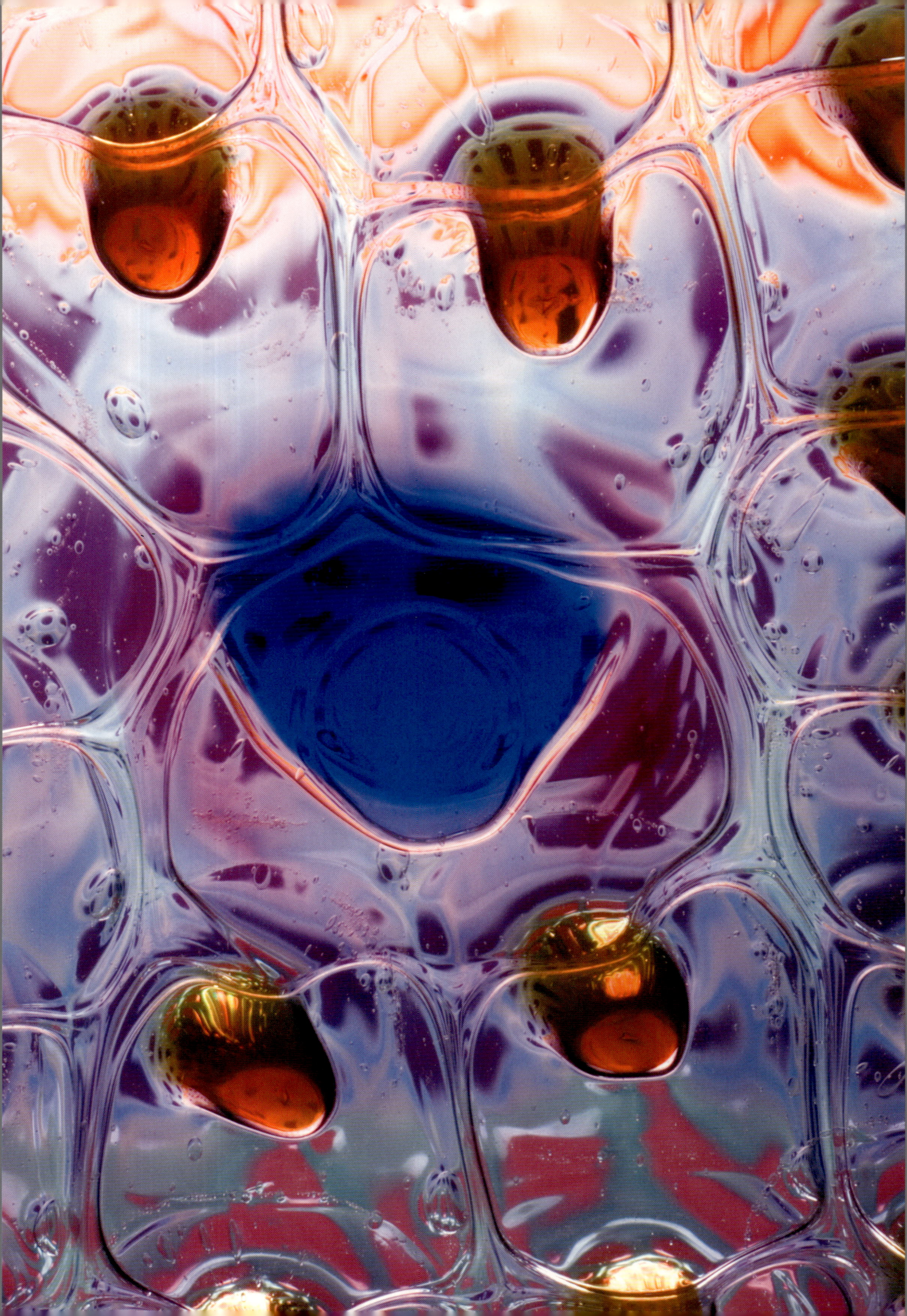

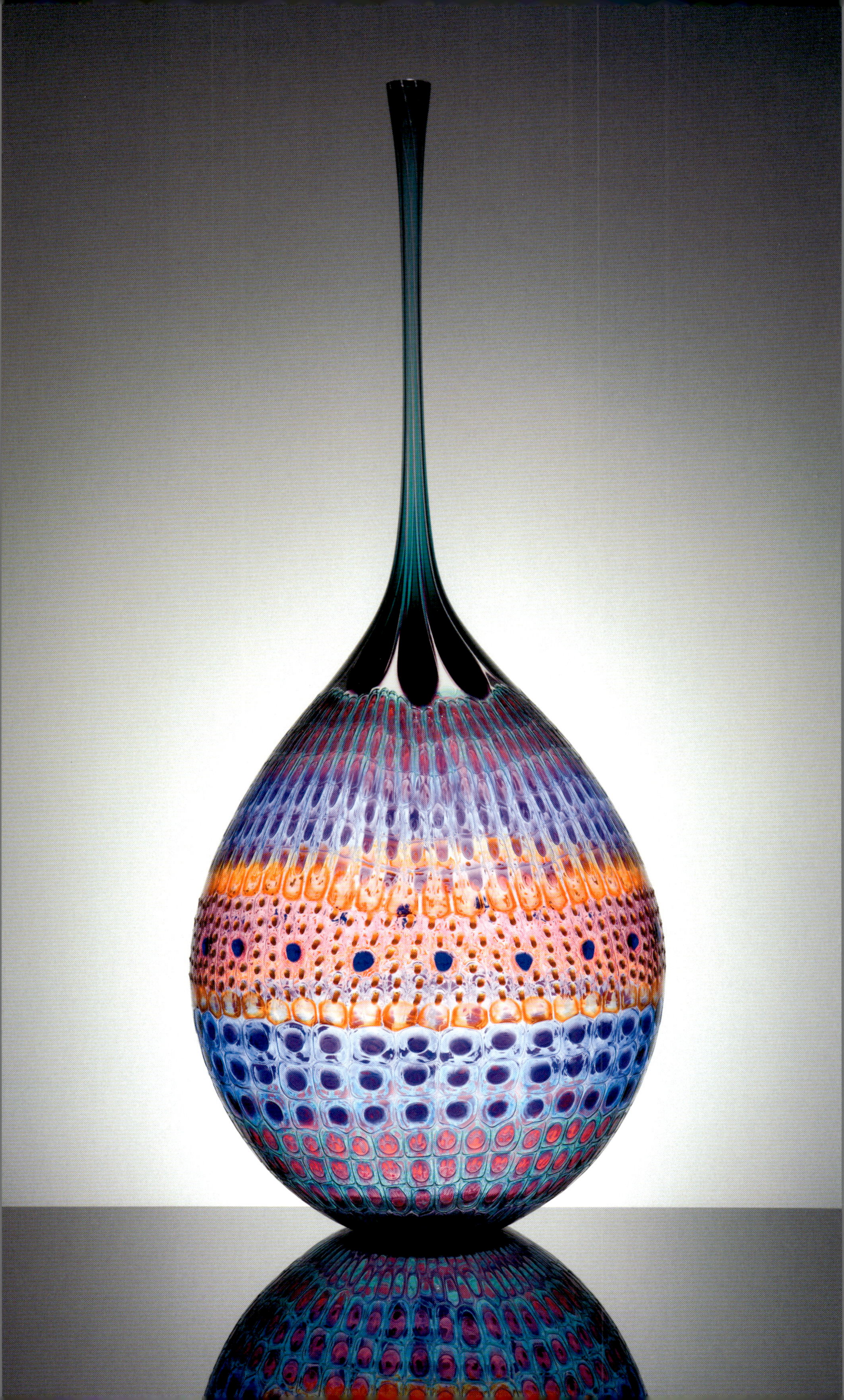

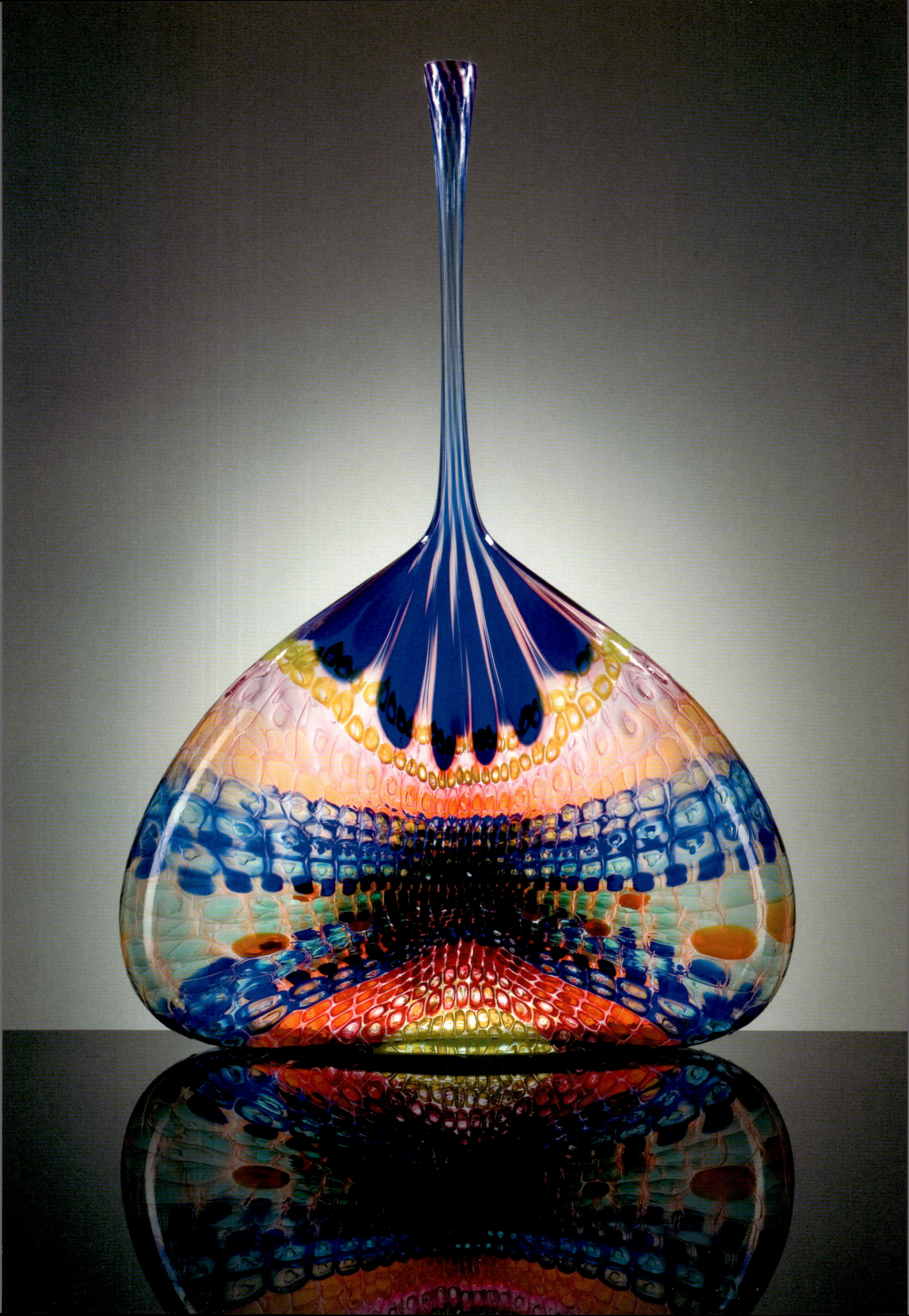

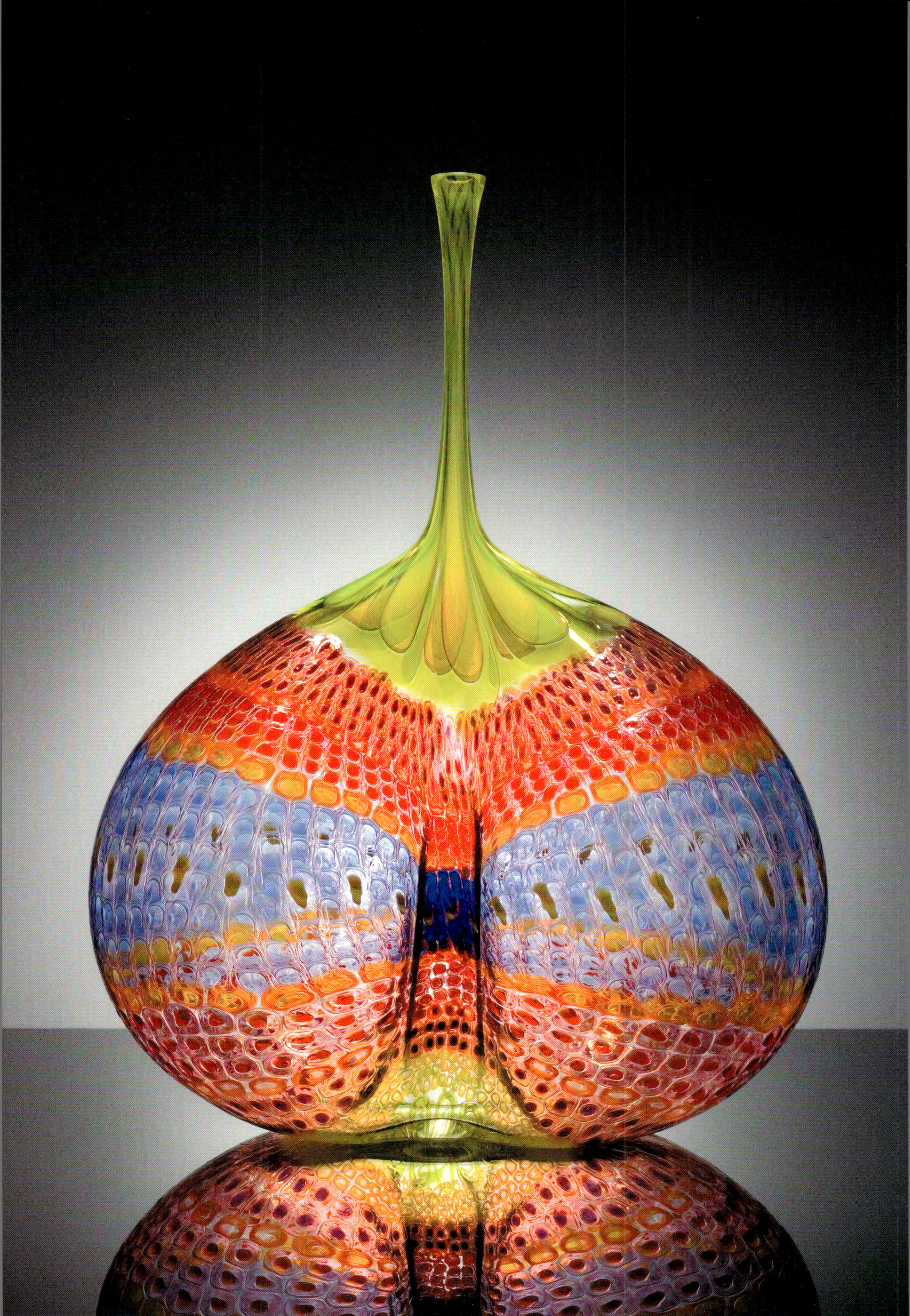

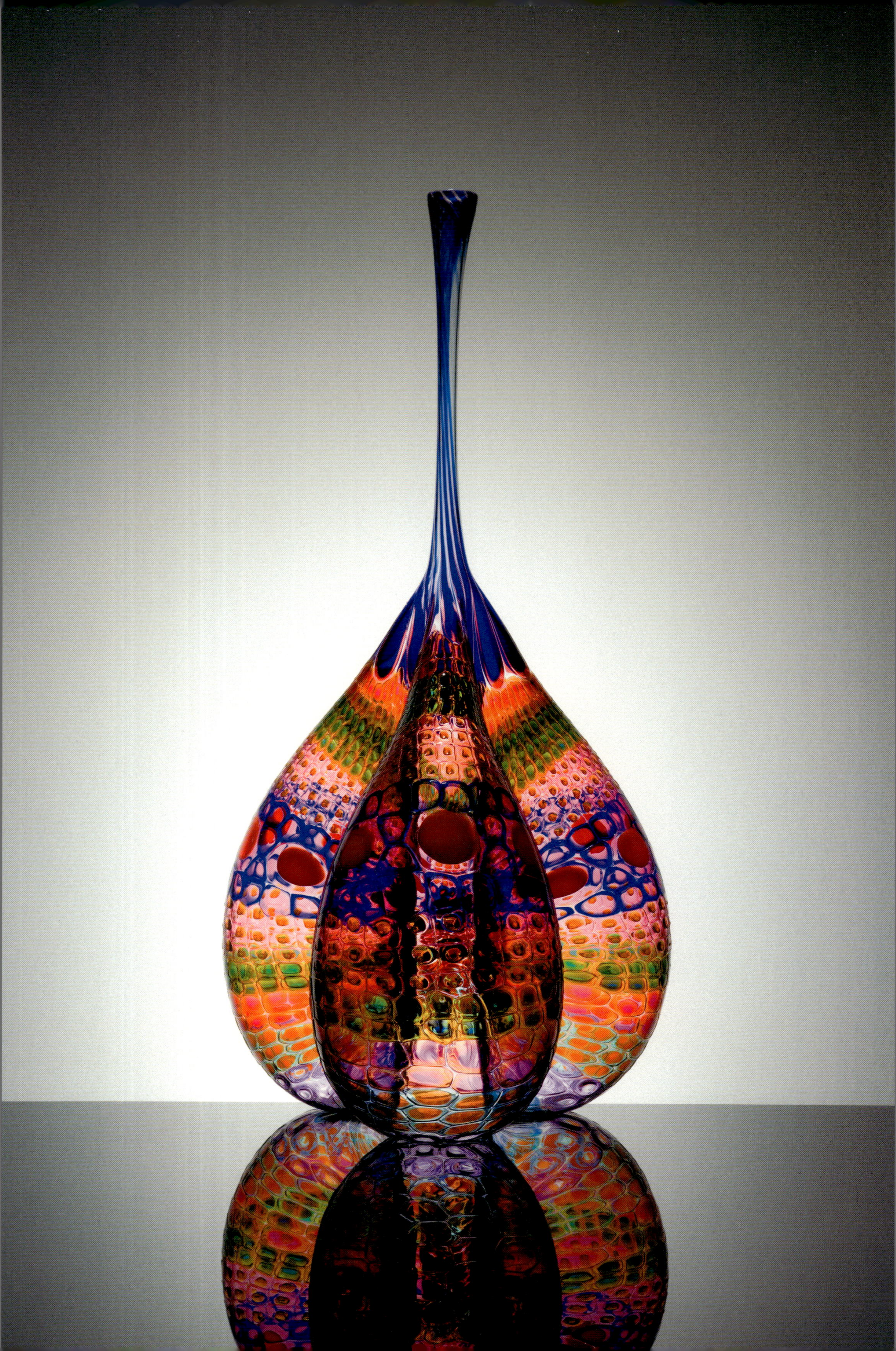

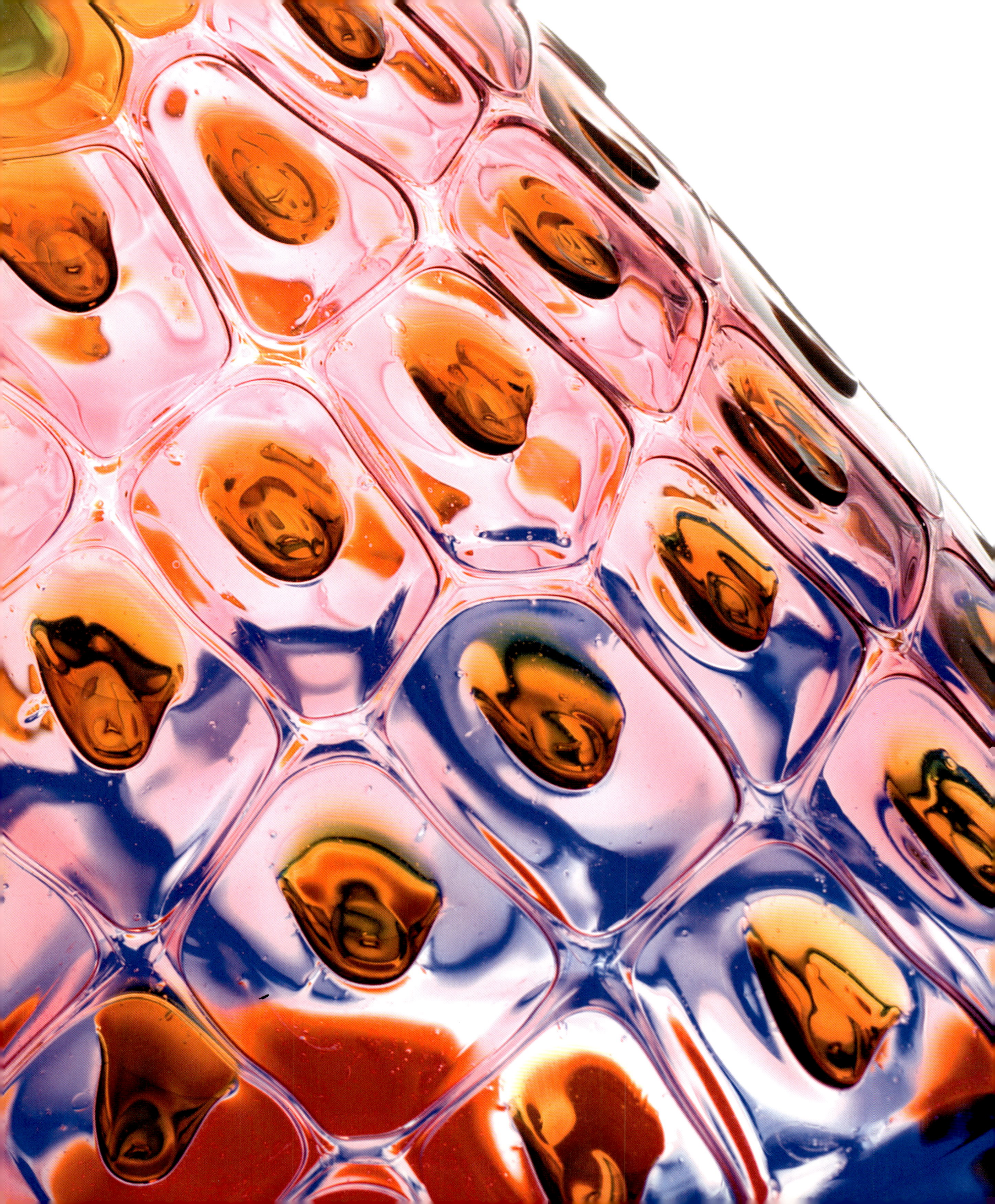

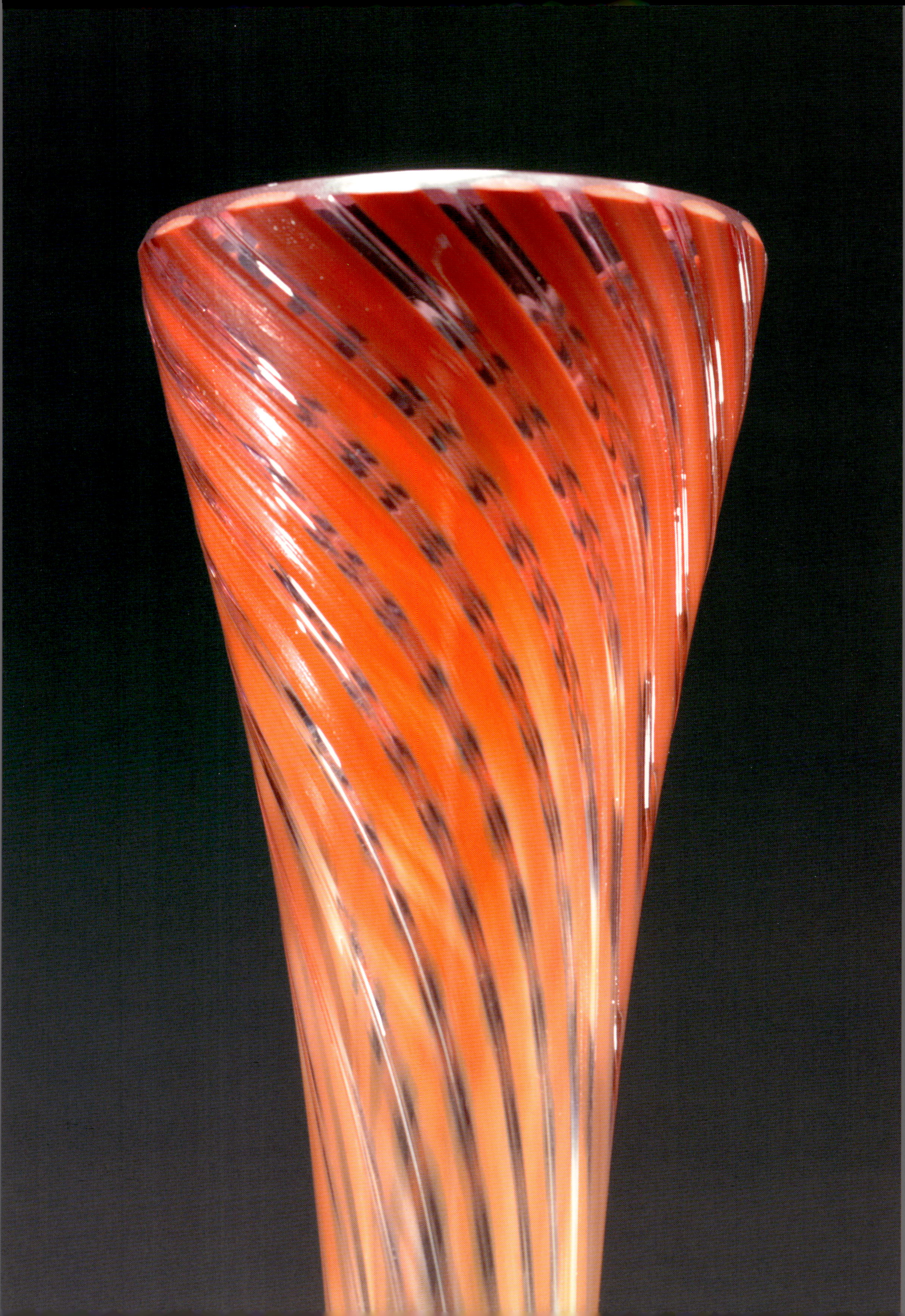

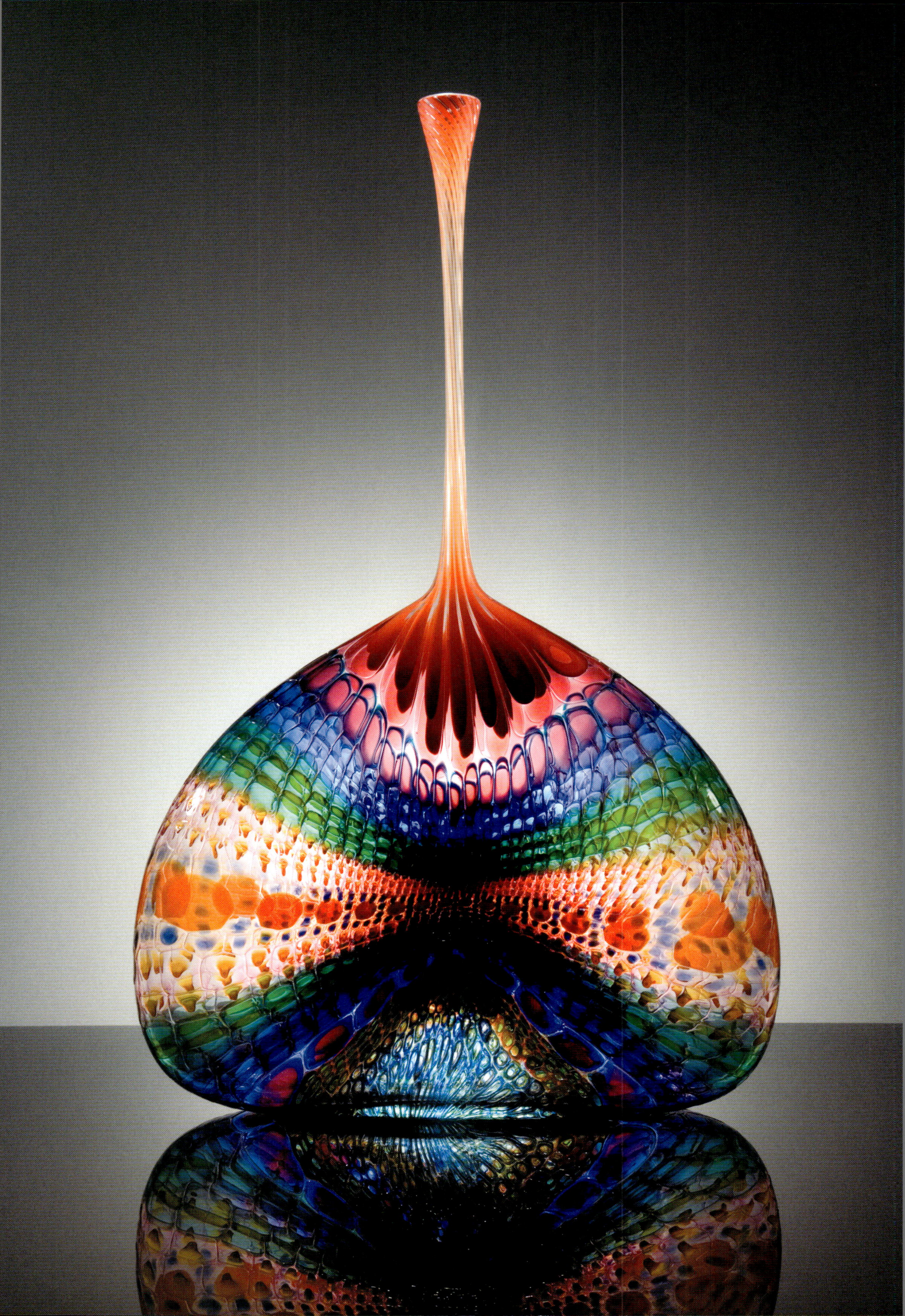

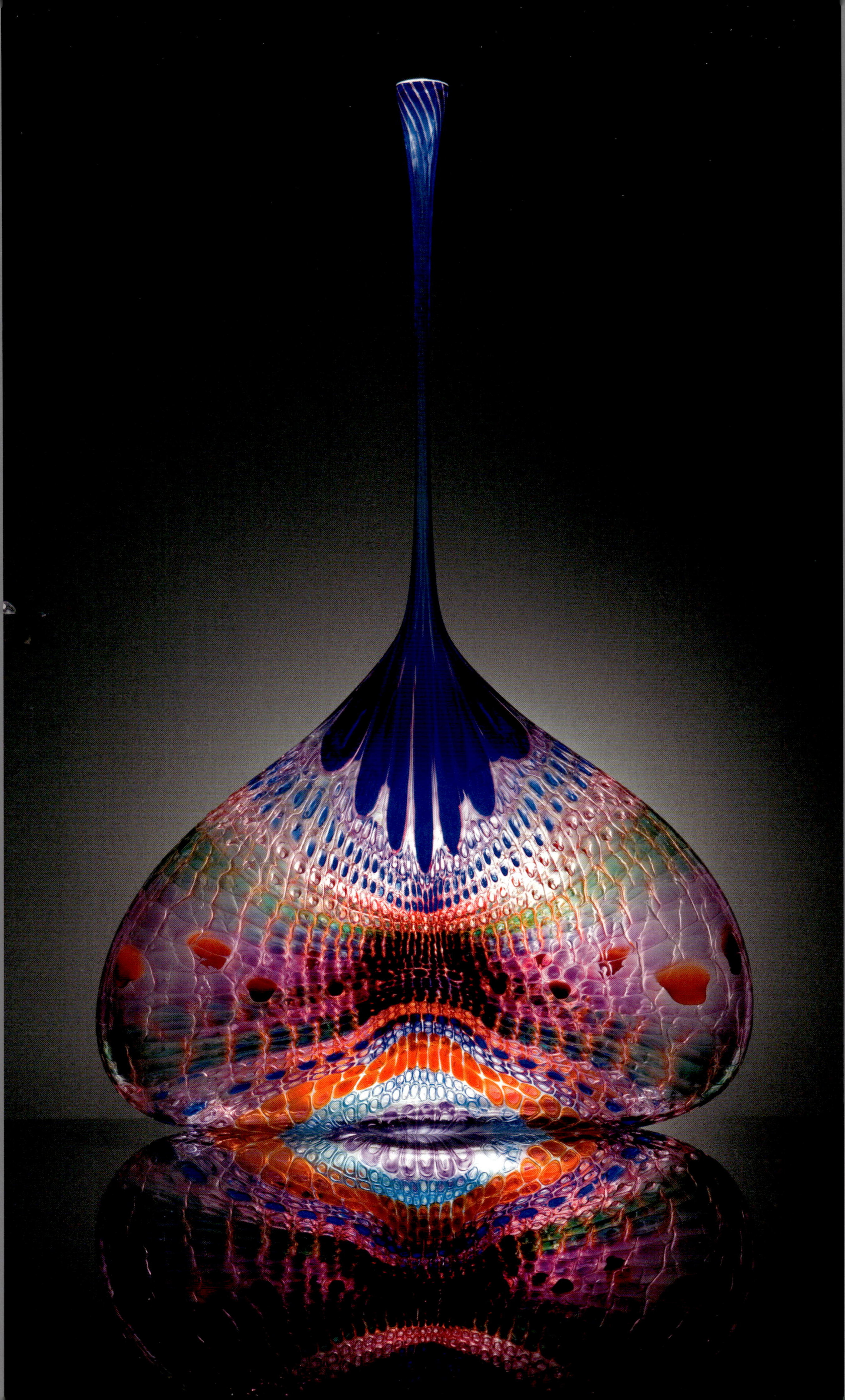

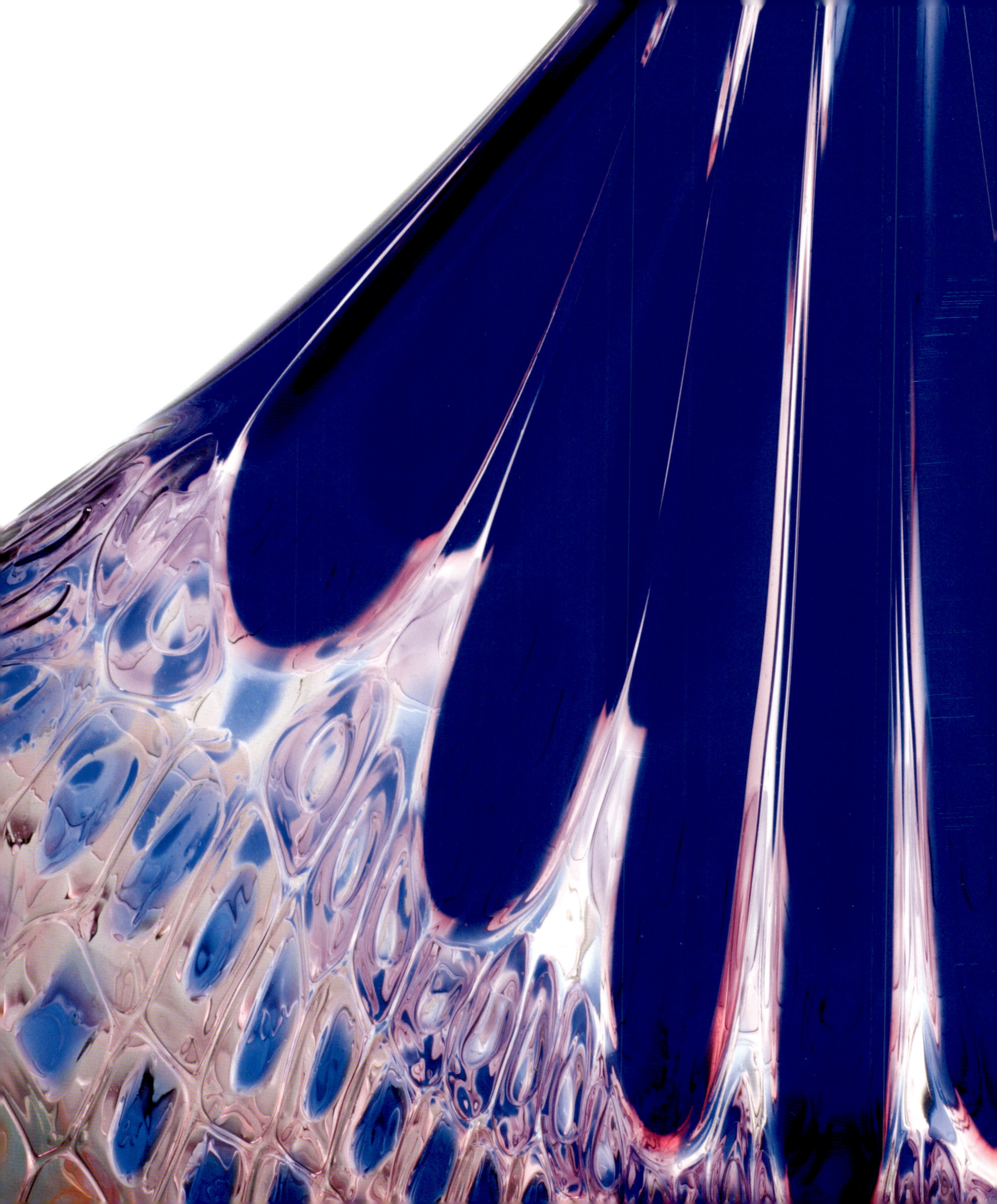

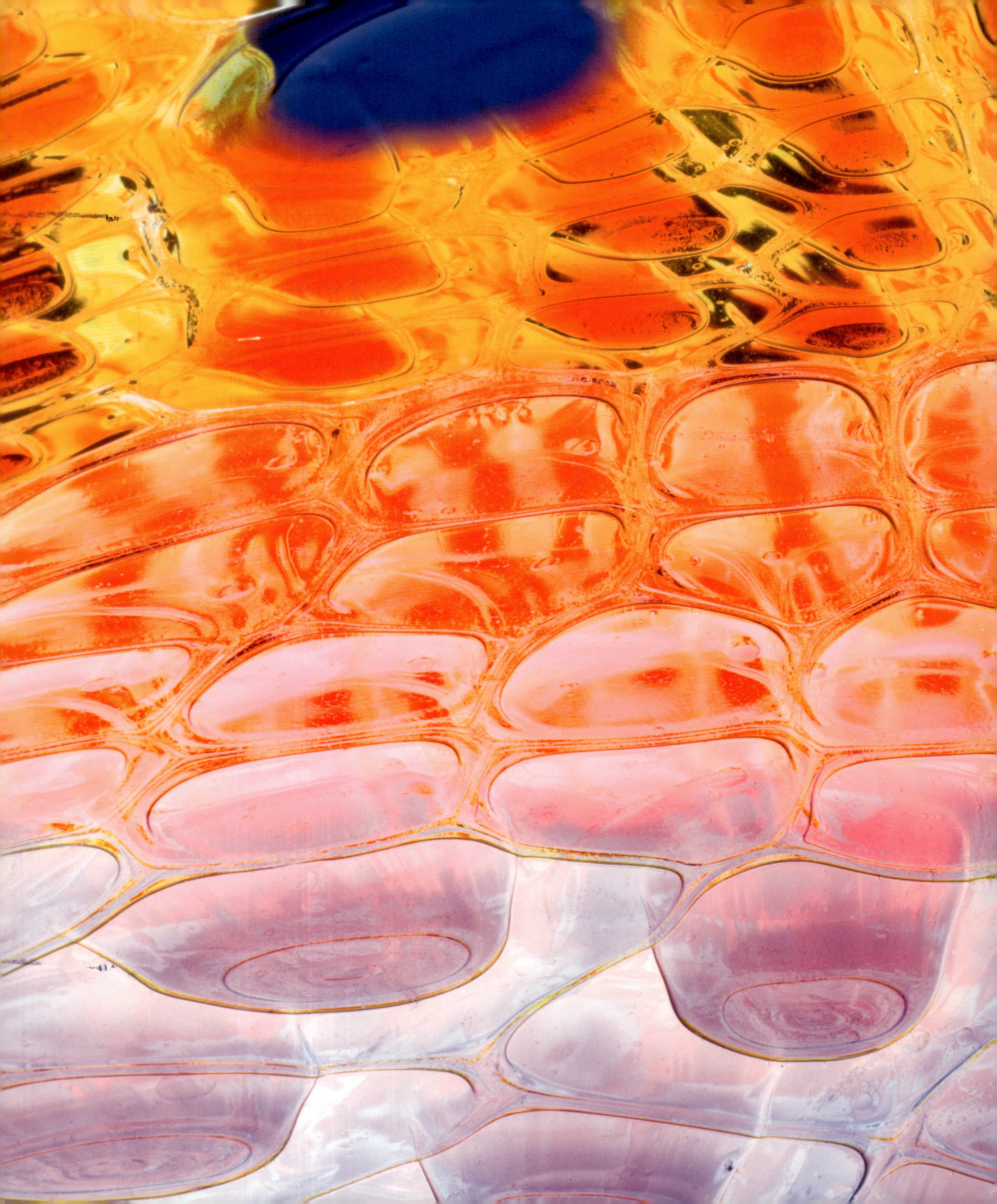

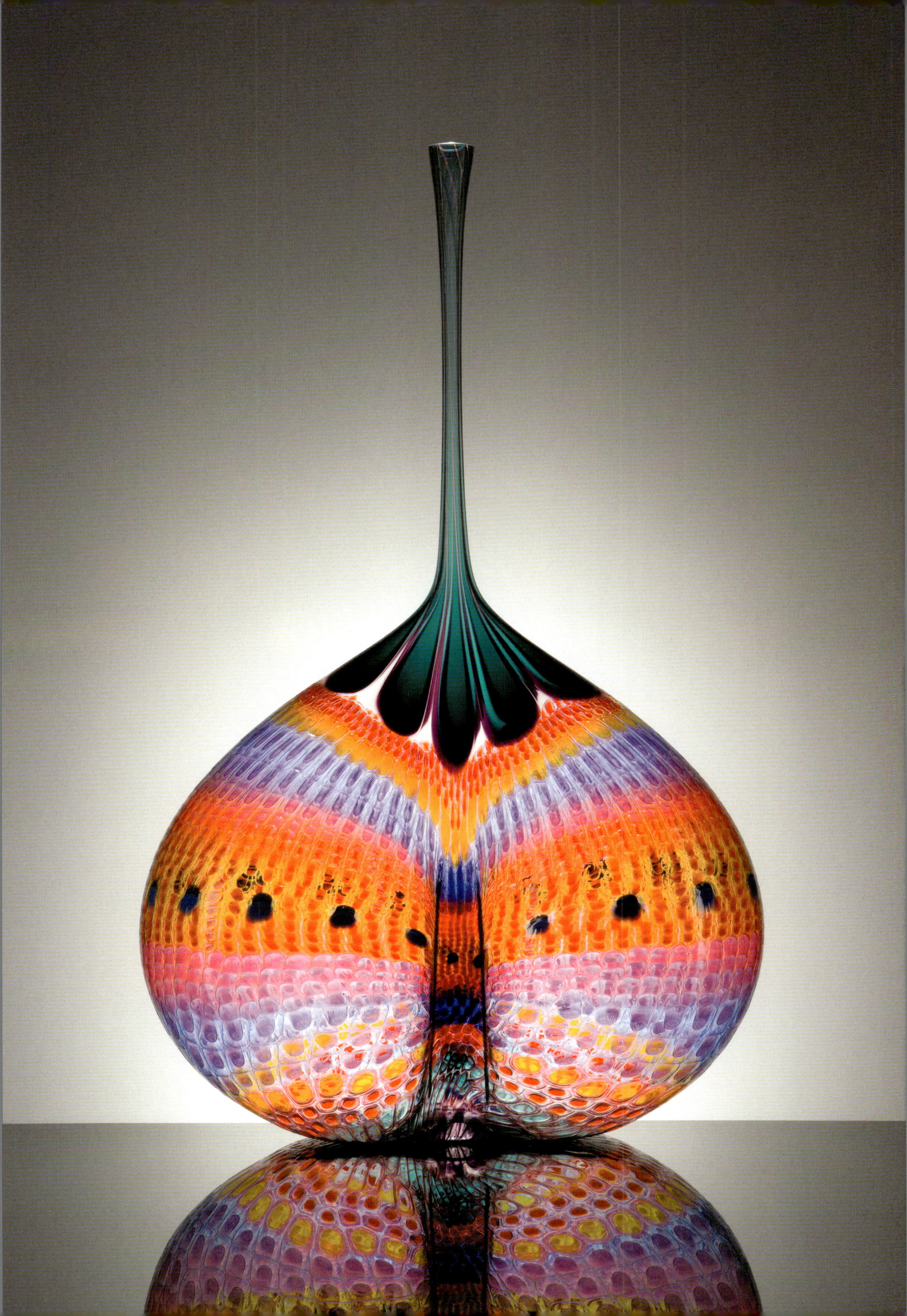

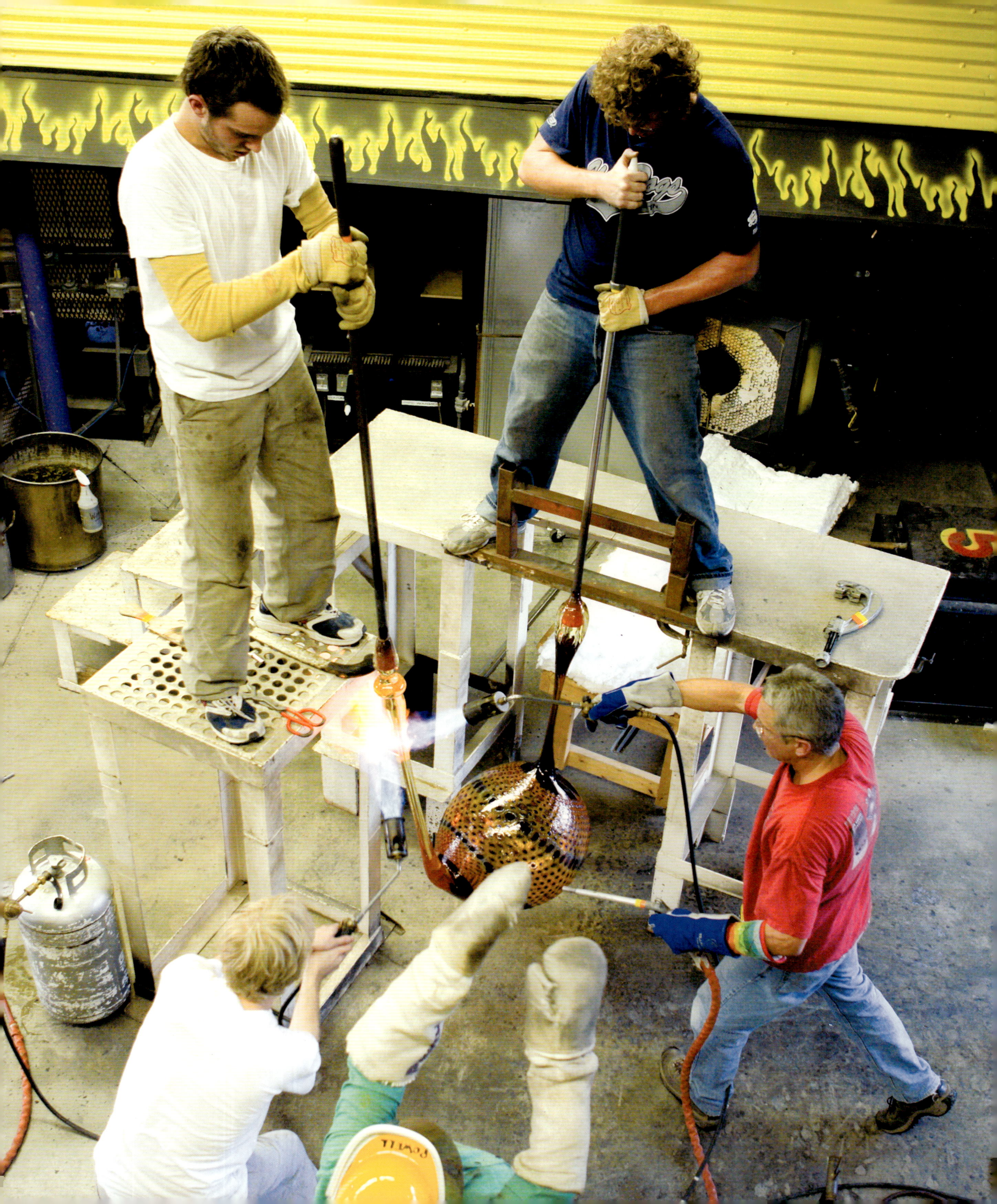

WHACKOS

"The Whackos abandon the security of the vessel and allow me to explore more challenging sculptural concerns. They especially suggest dynamic postures of animals. These shapes, which everyone is so familiar with, allow the viewer ready entry to my use of color. Shapes formed through growth—whether human, plant, or animal—intrigue me. I enjoy shapes that, through the forces of nature, are swollen or puffed into irregular forms. I'm as fascinated by the shapes of okra and tomatoes from my garden as by the contours of people's heads and bodies."

Stephen Rolfe Powell, 2005

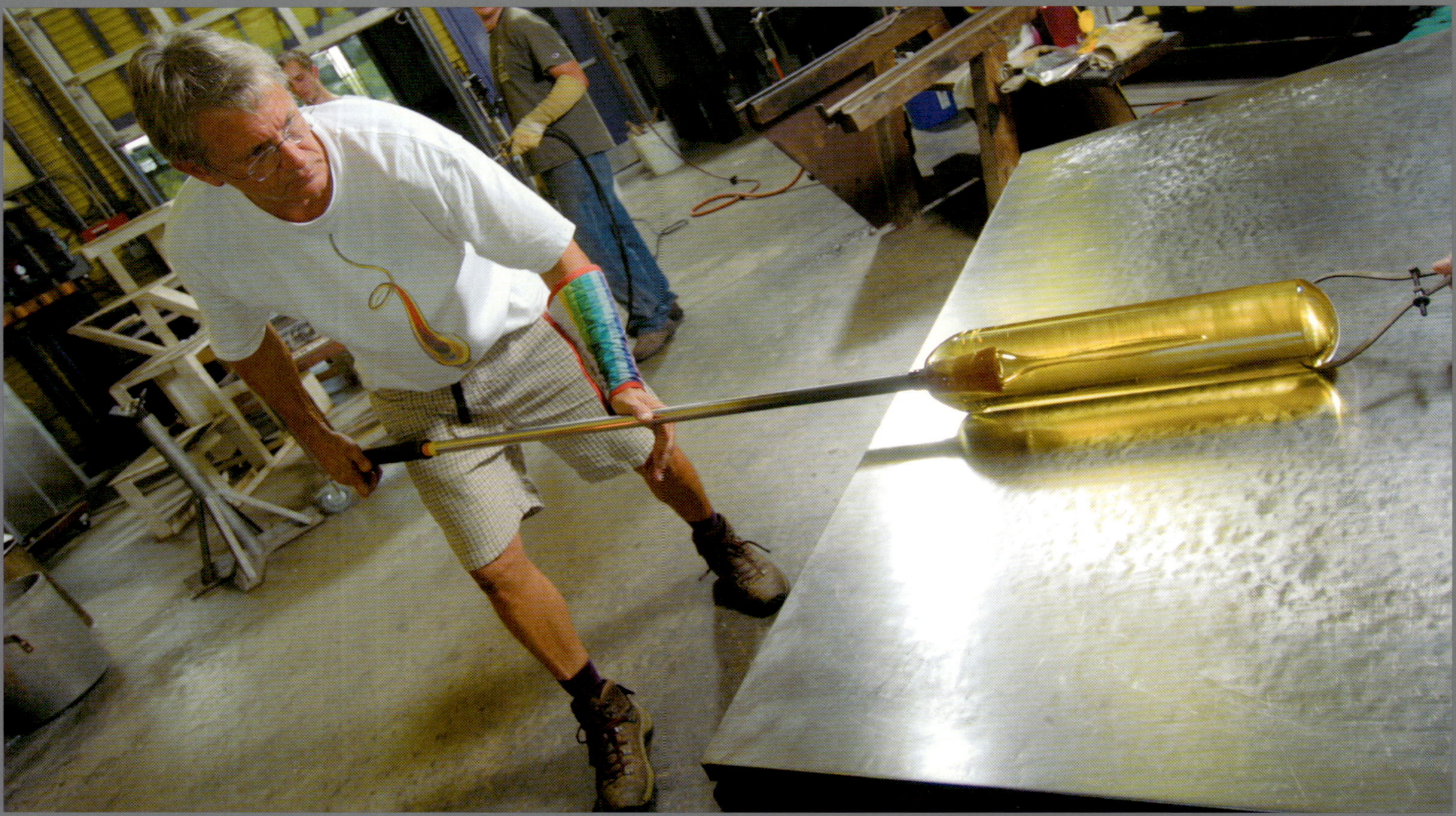

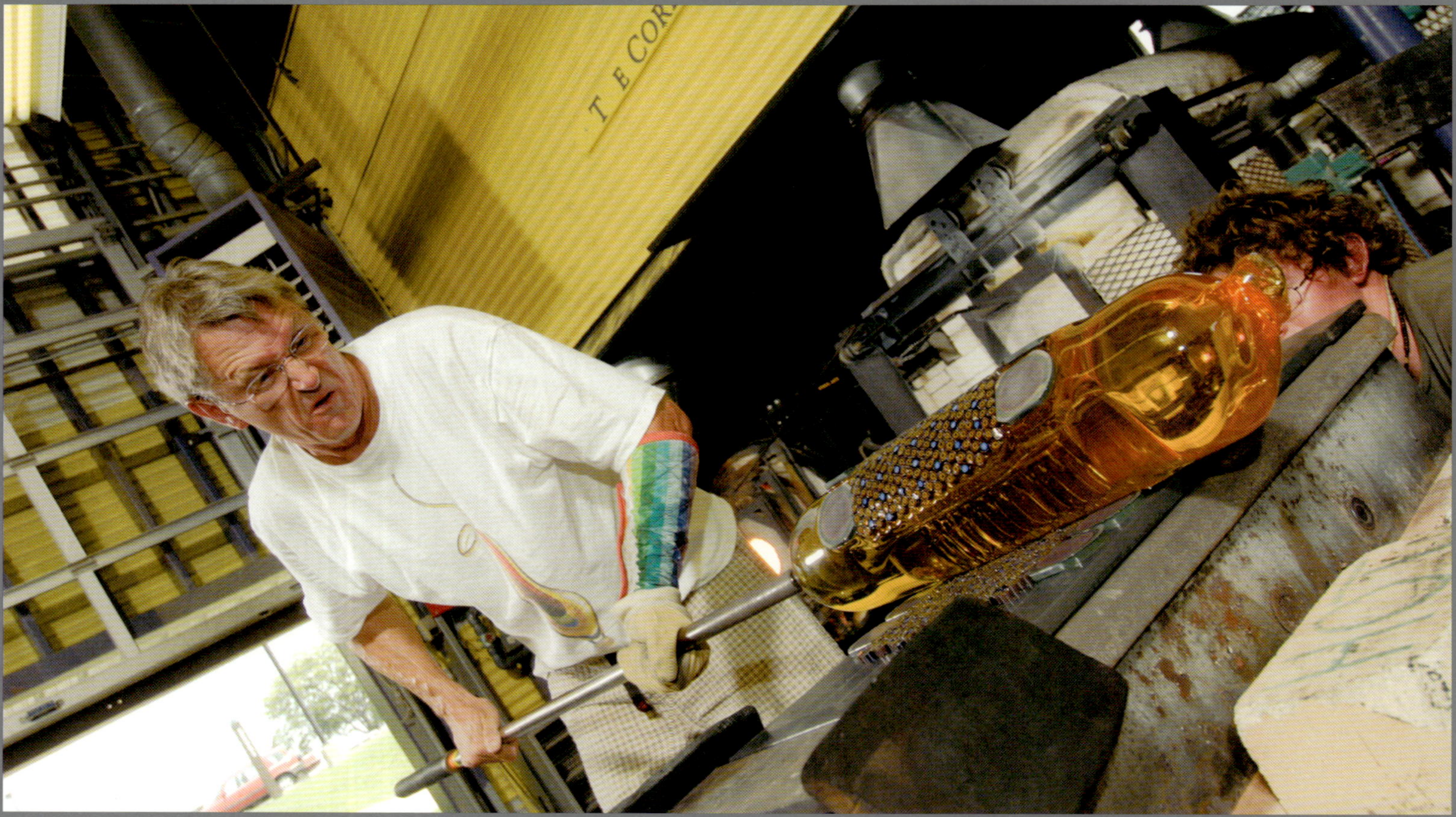

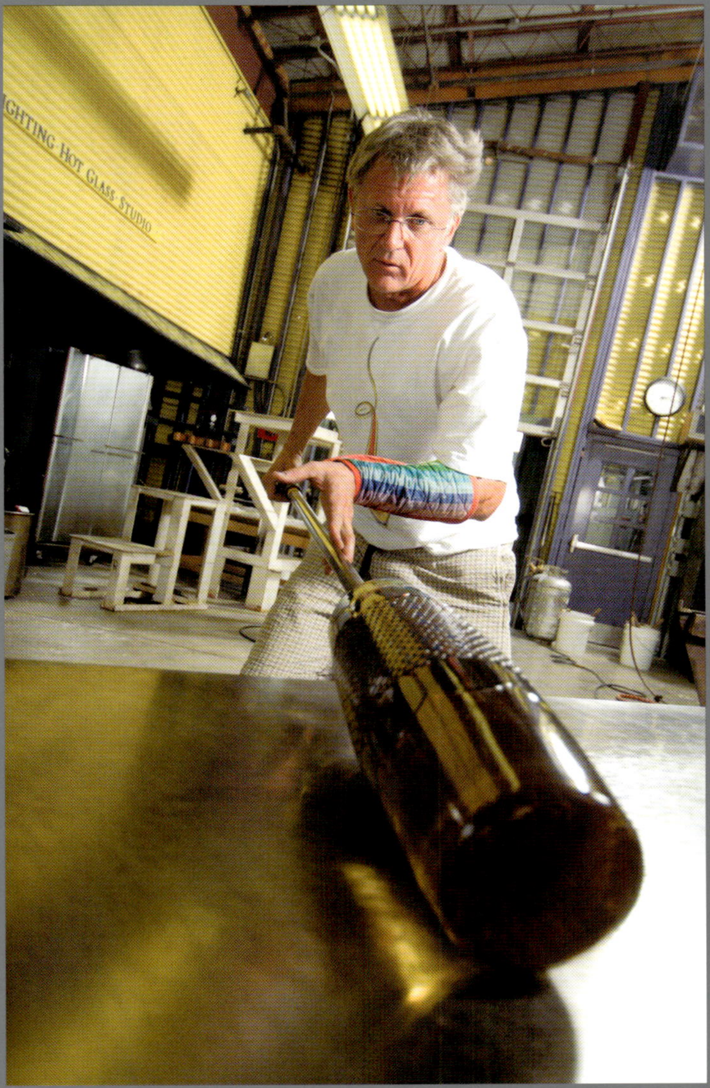
Hot Glass Studio

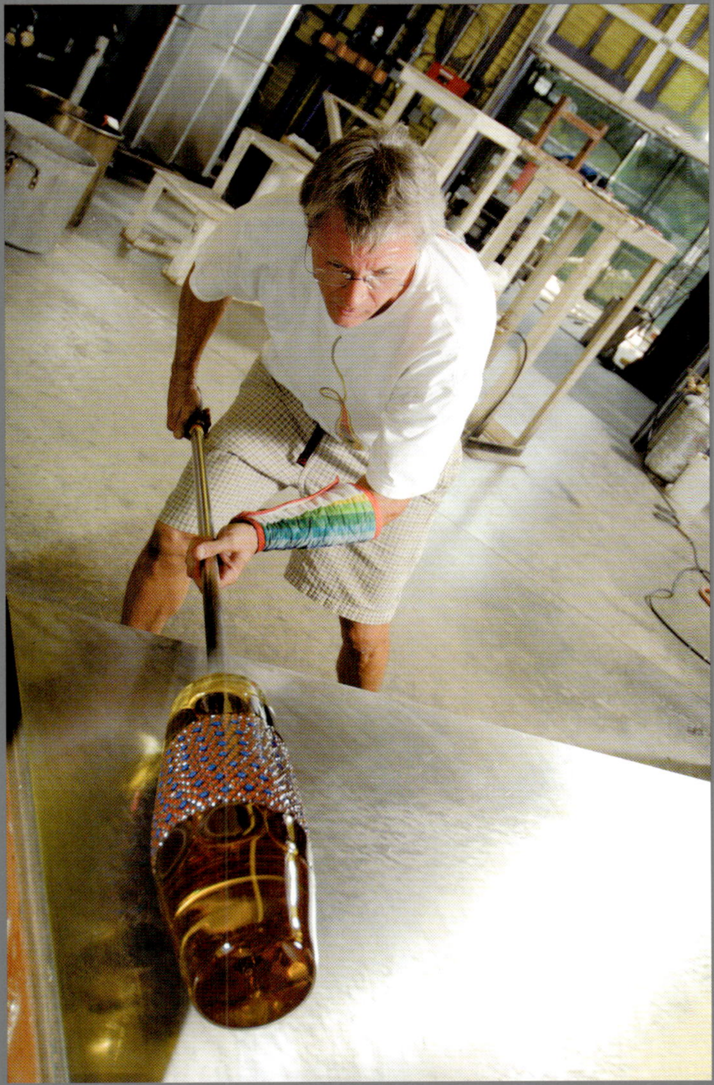

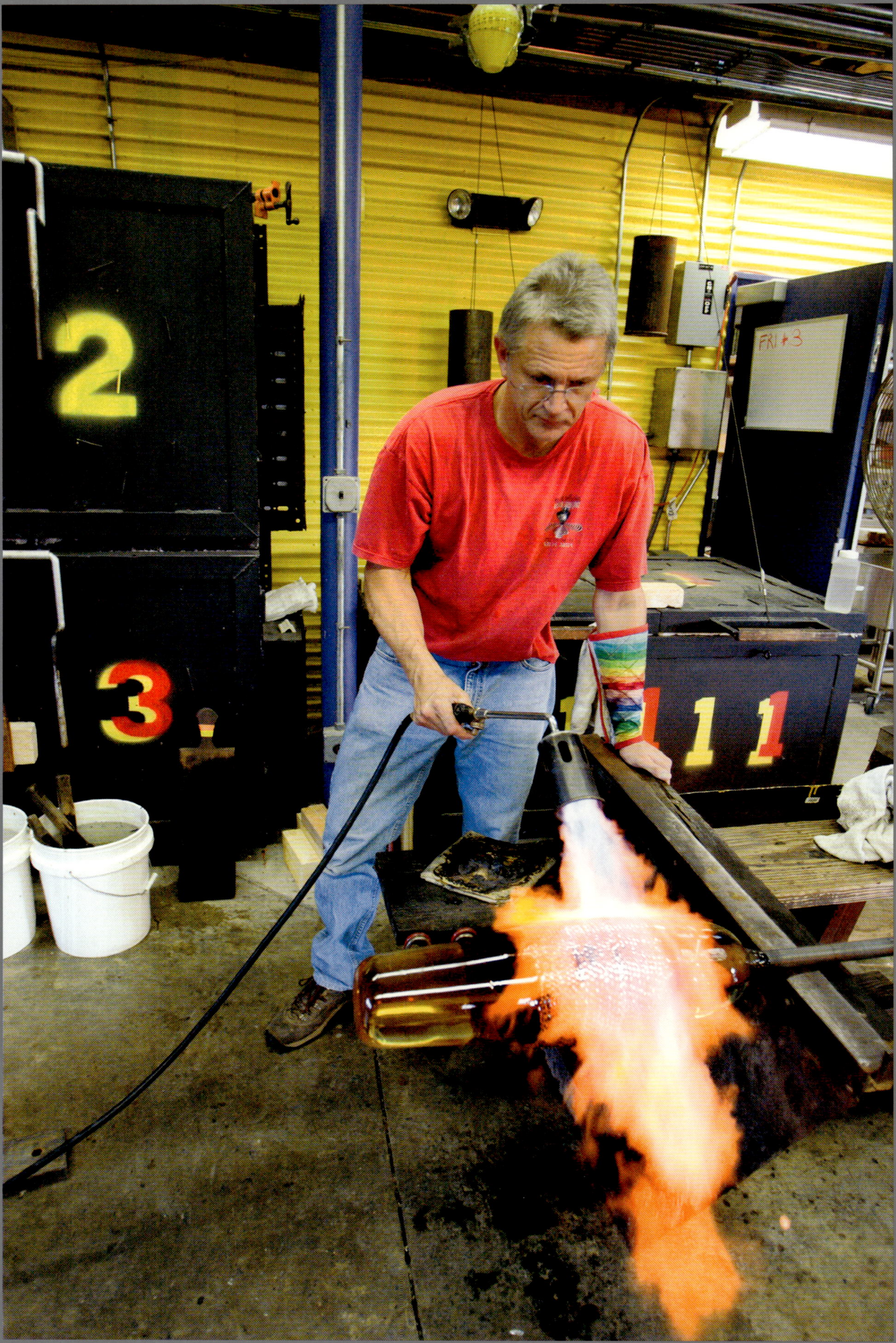
2
3
FRI #3

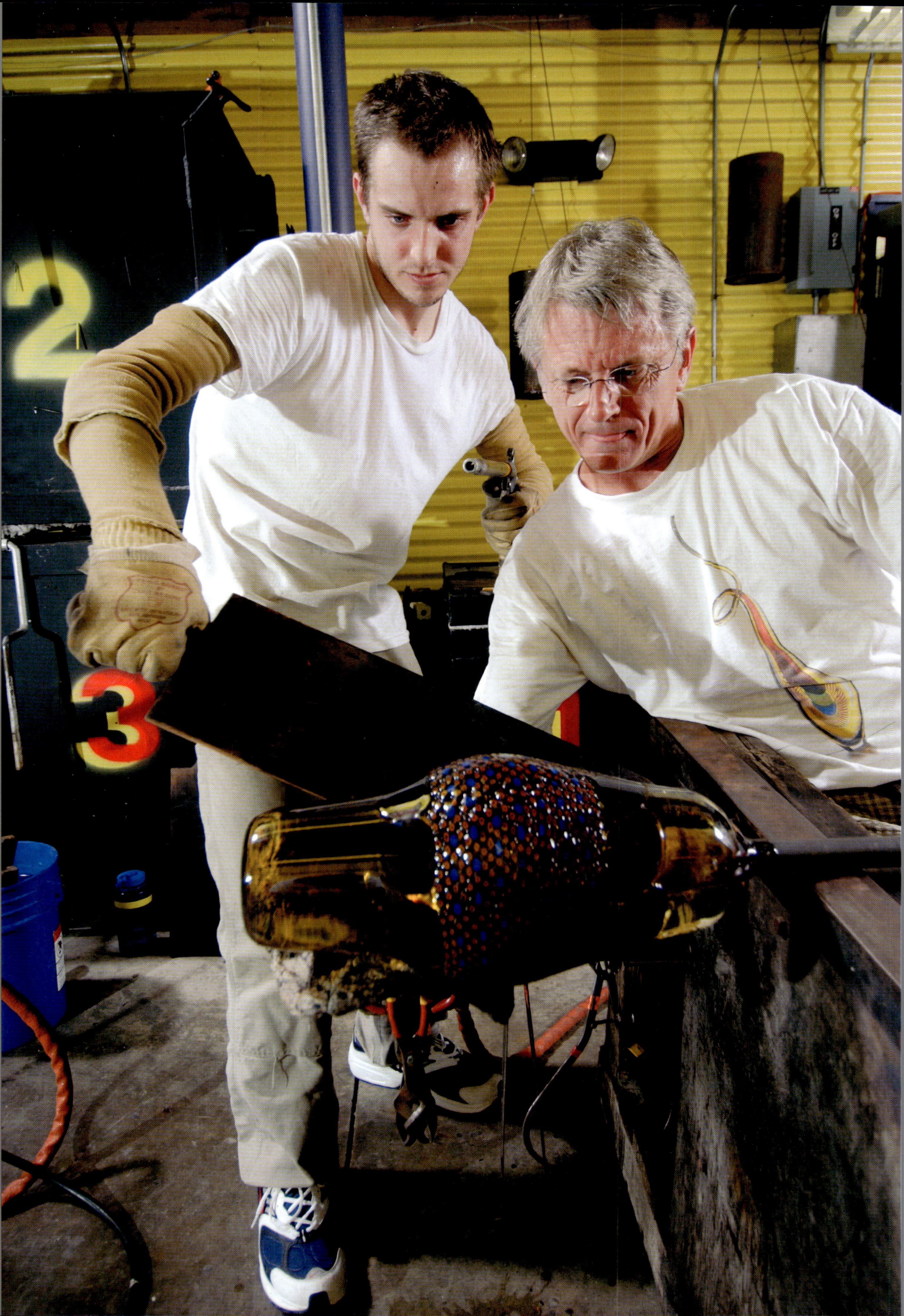

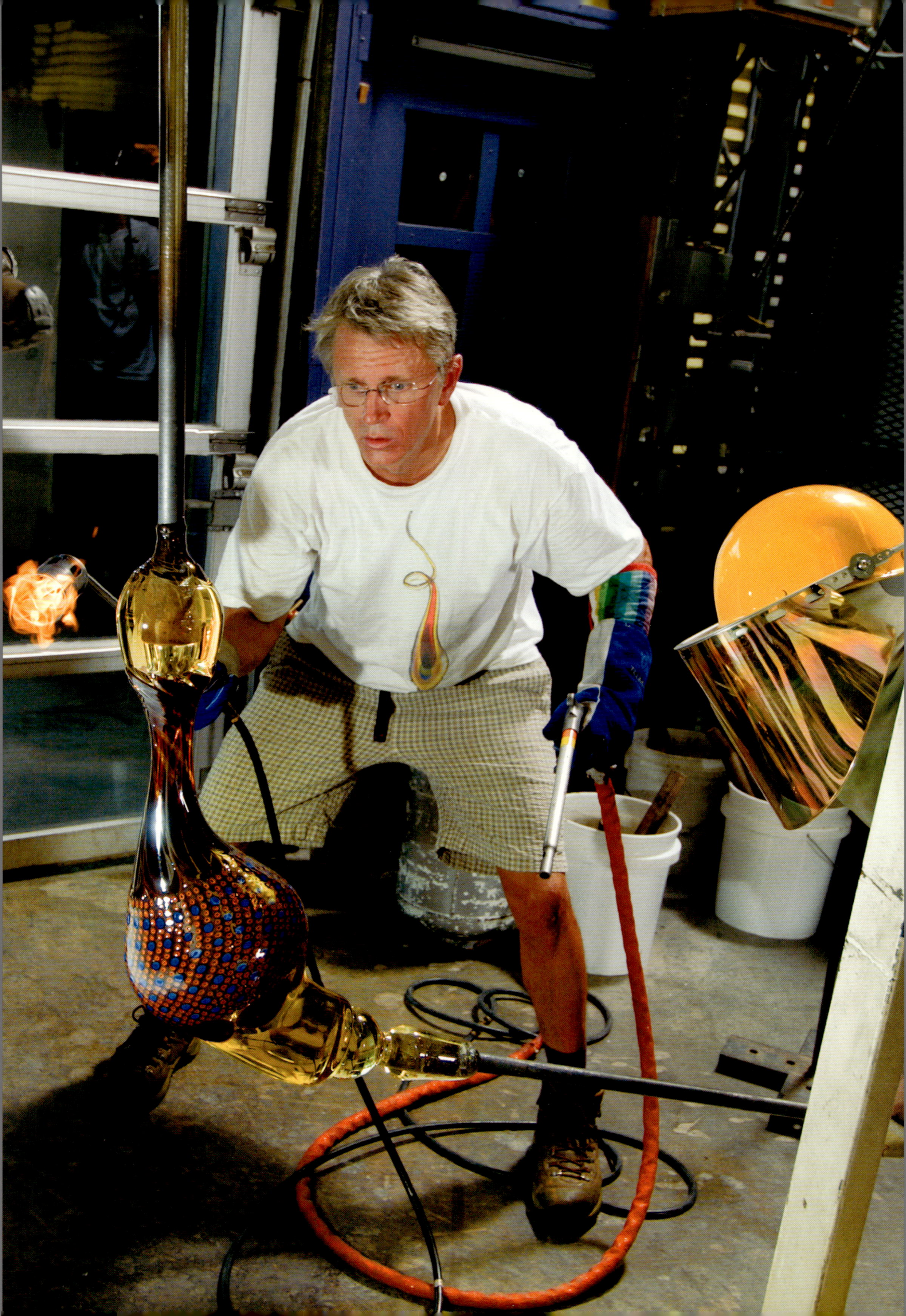

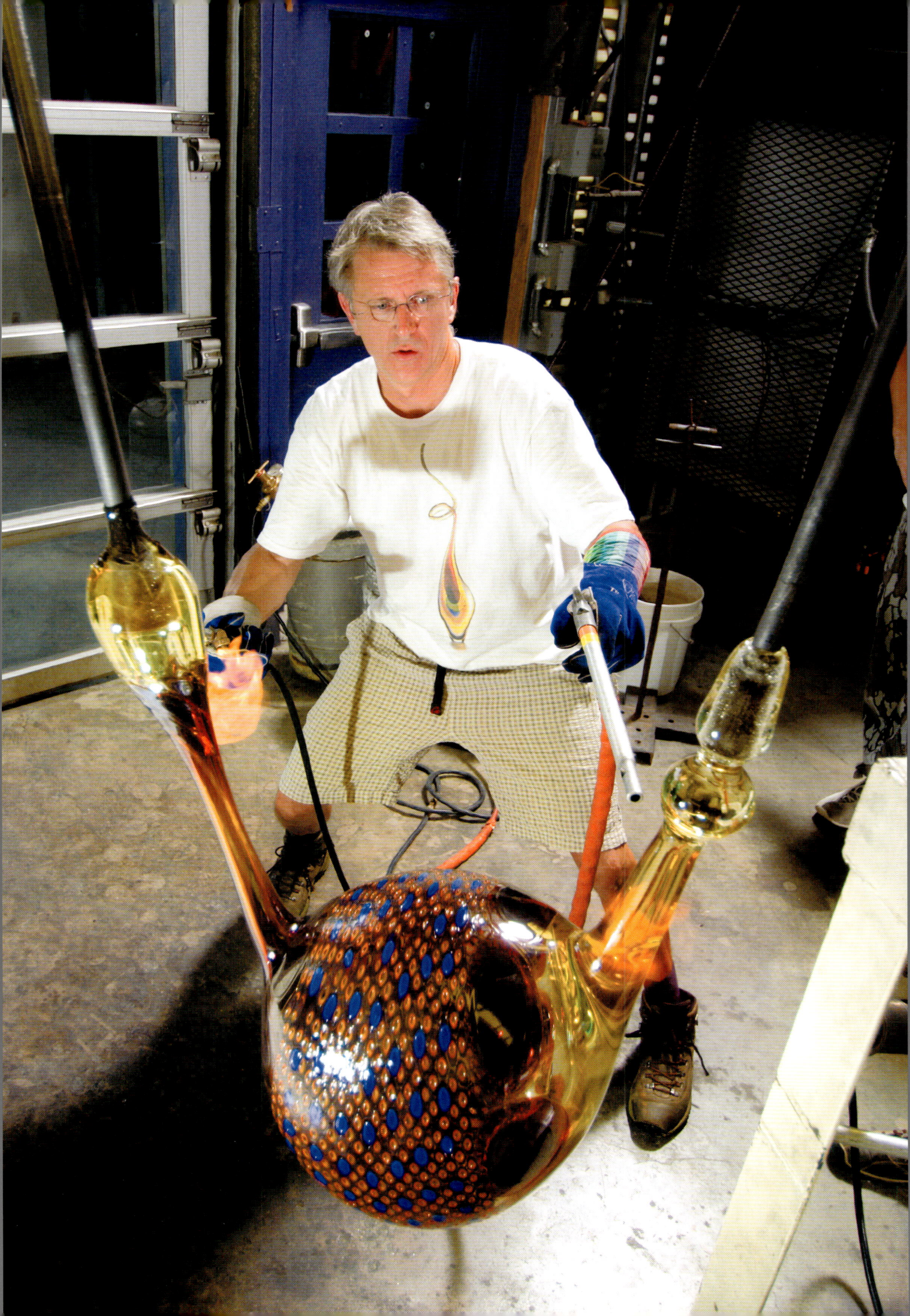

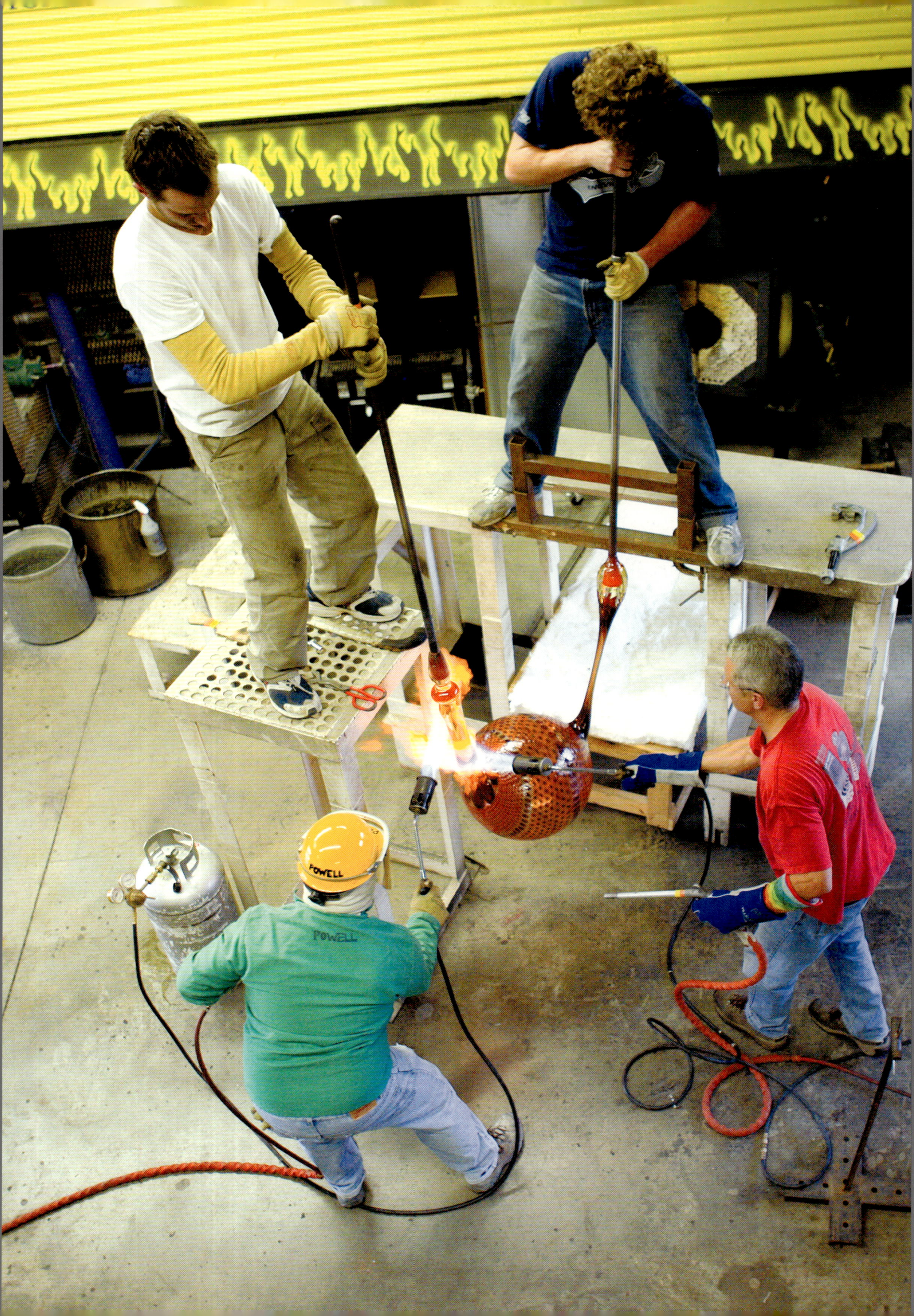
POWELL
POWELL

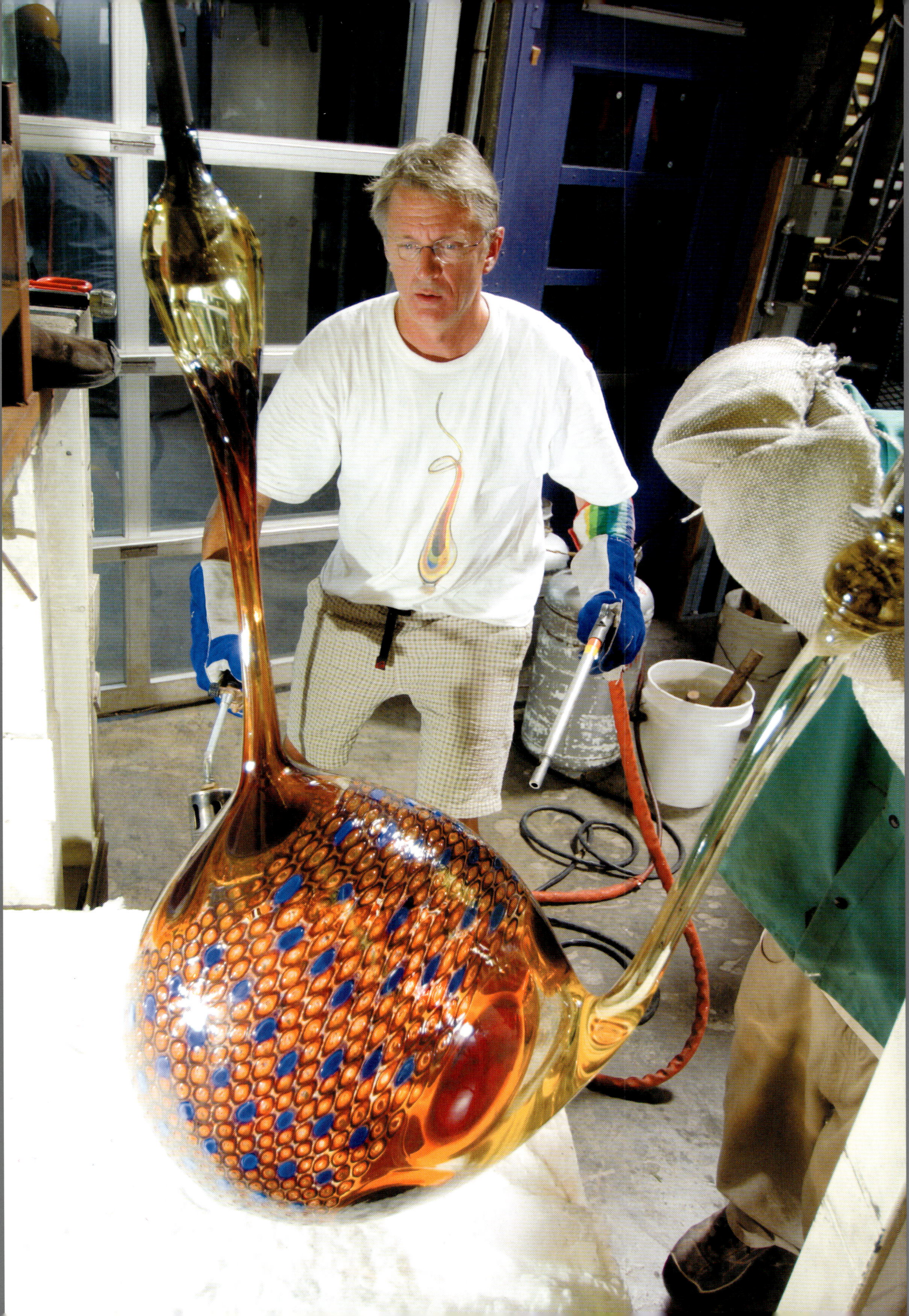

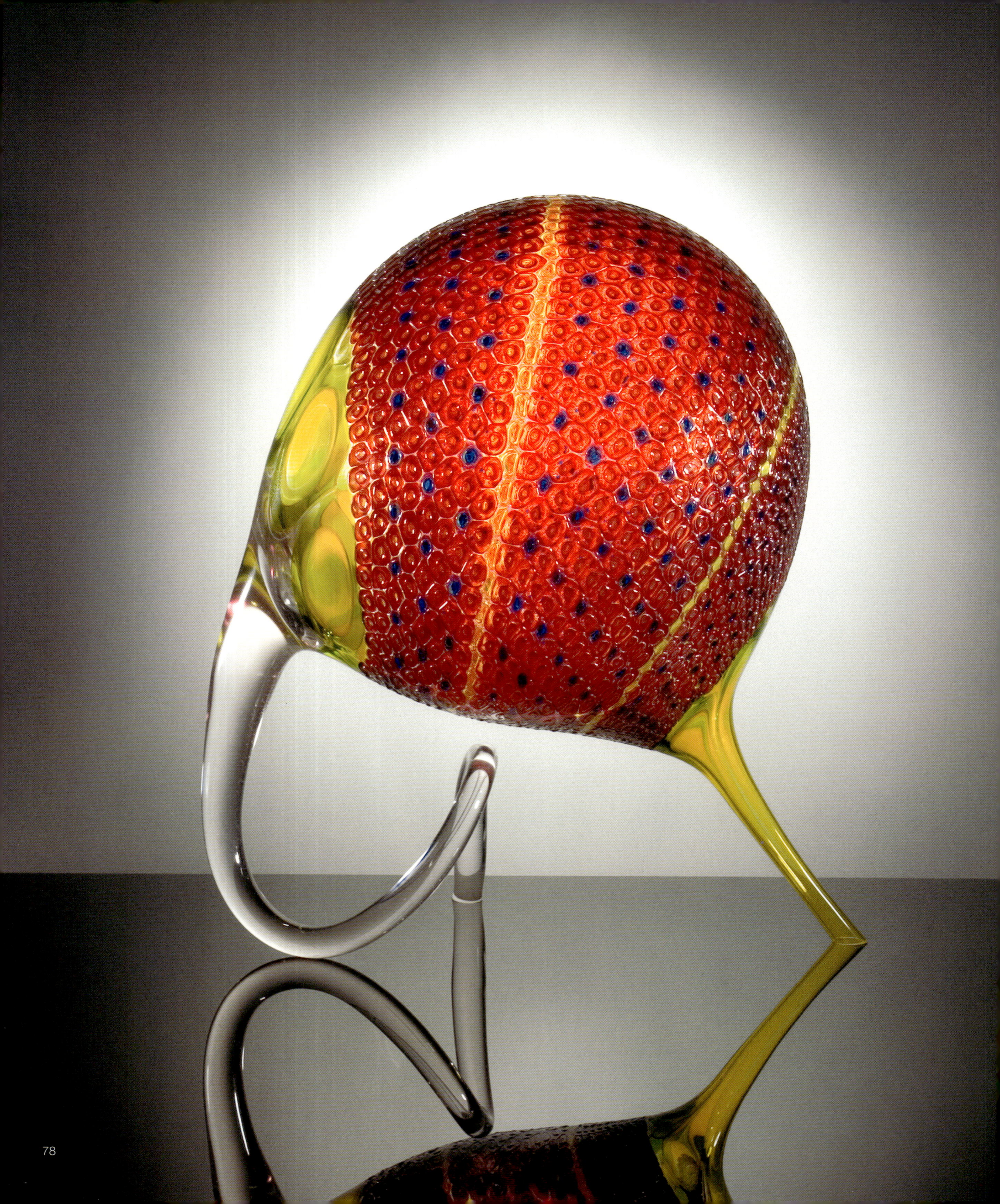

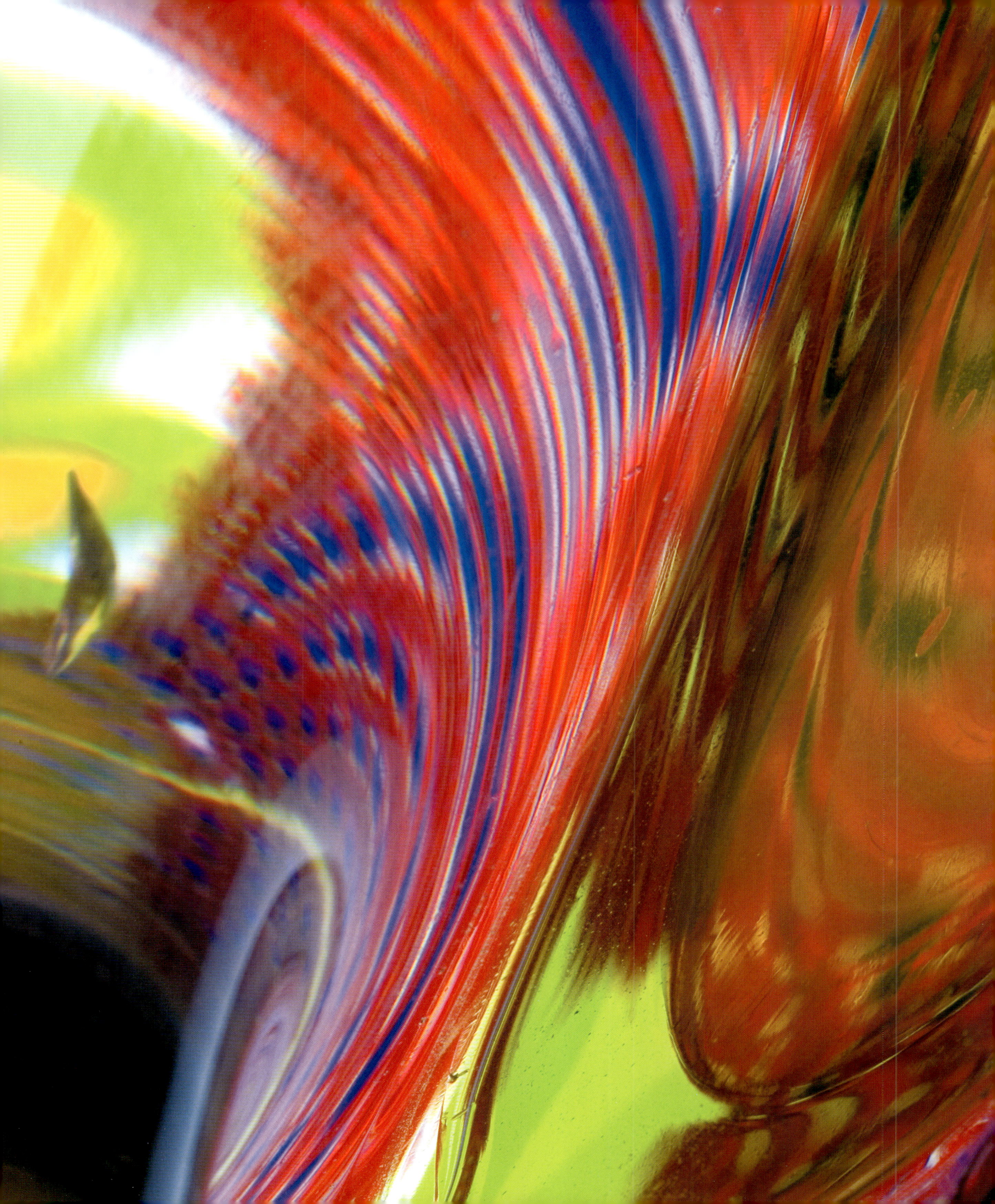

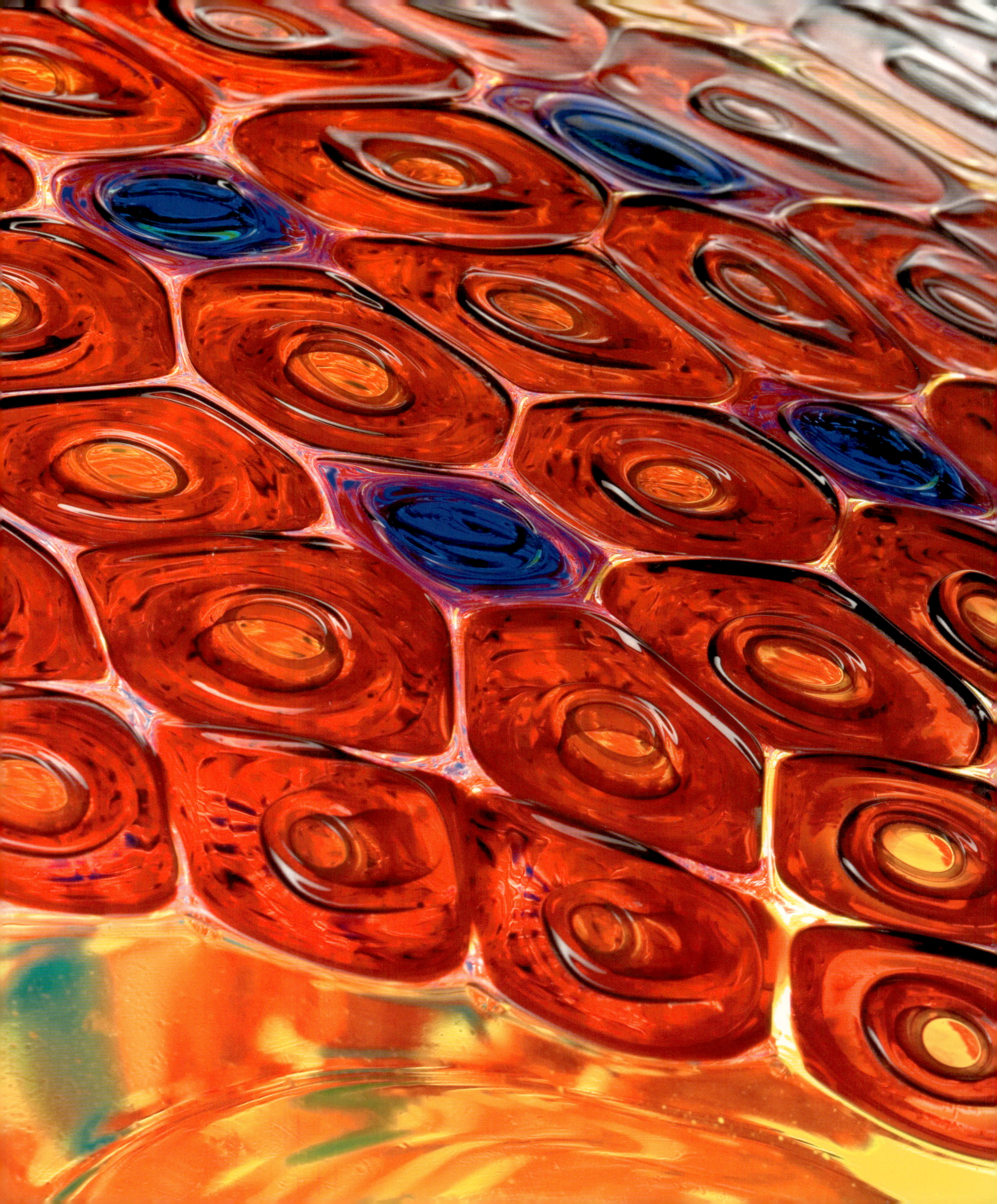

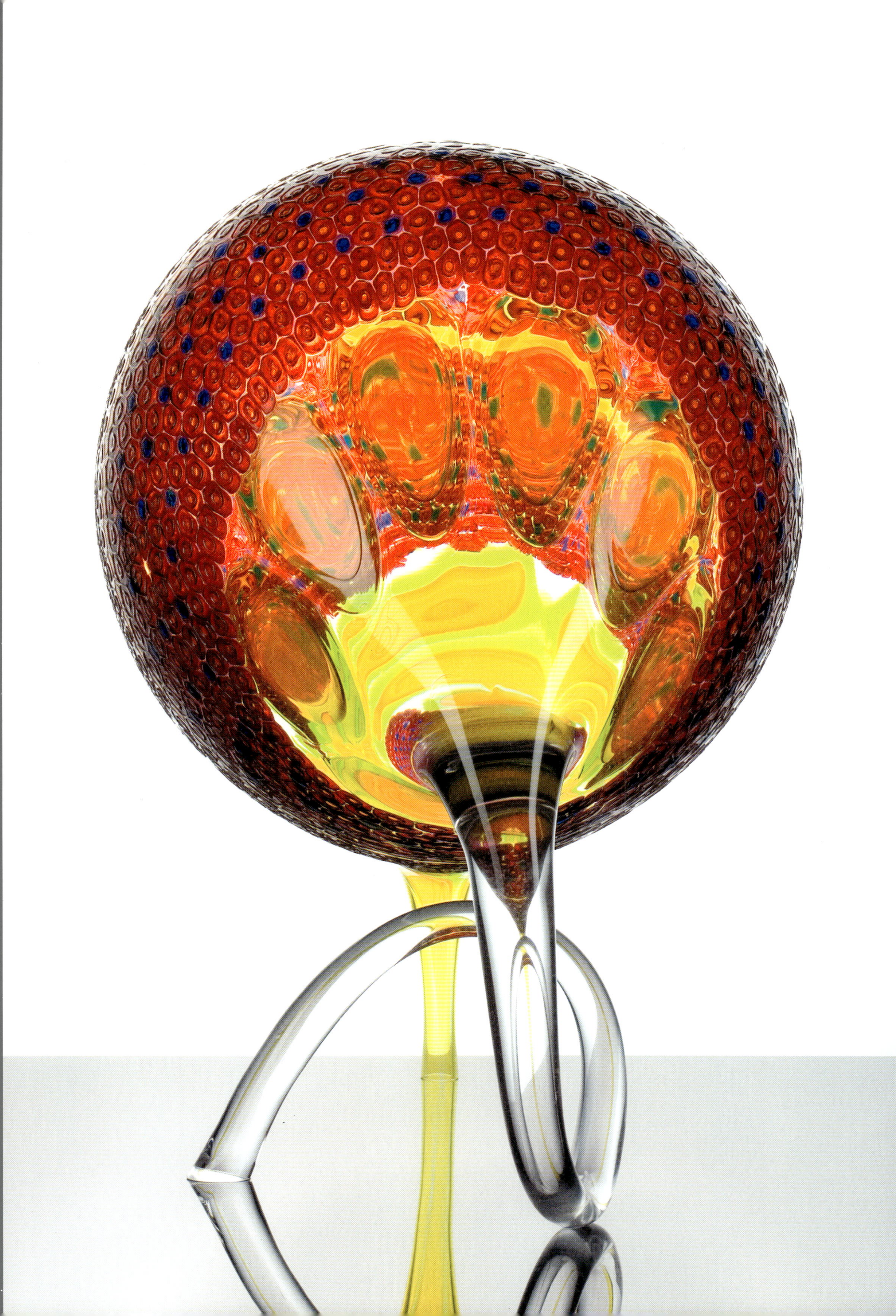

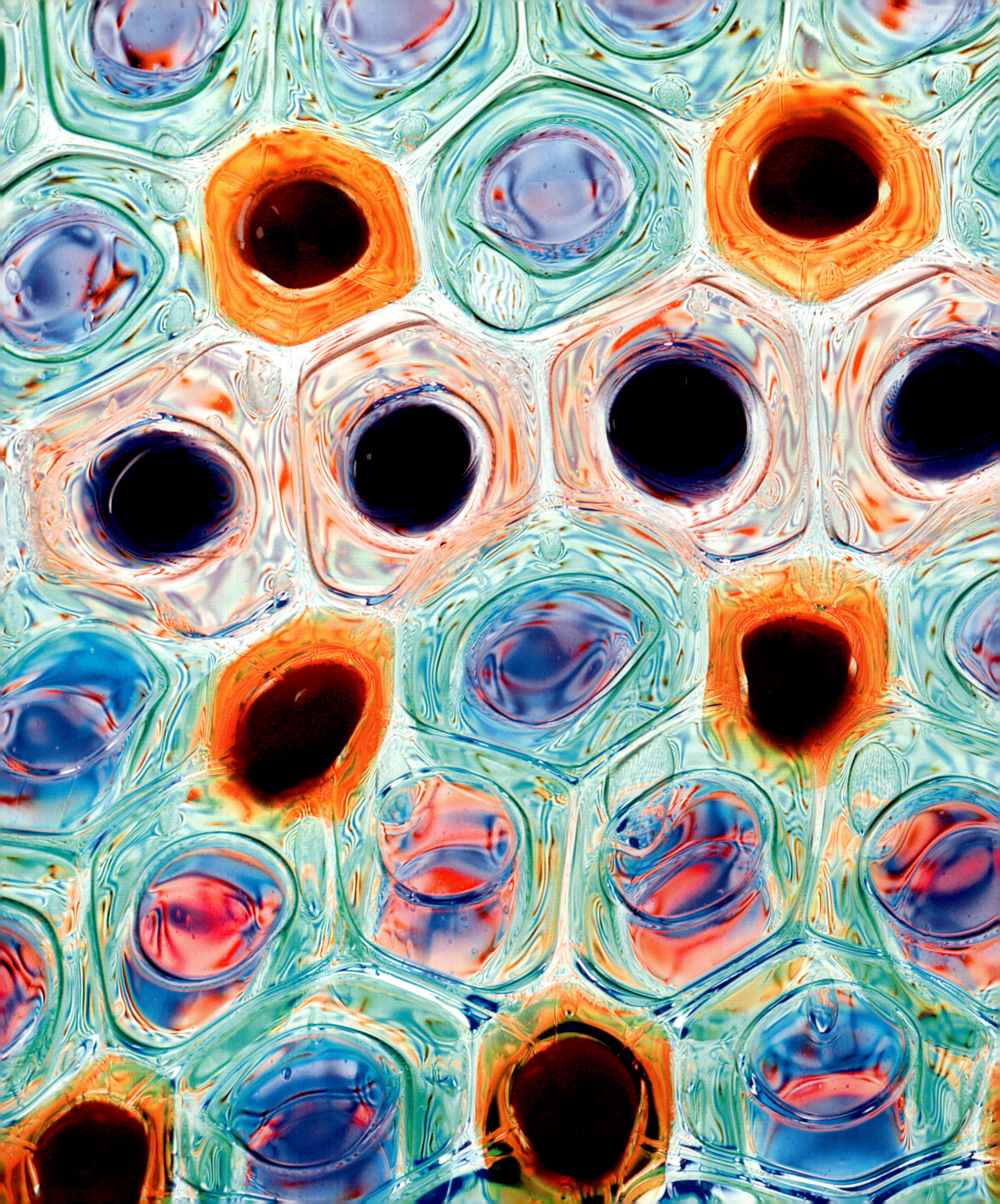

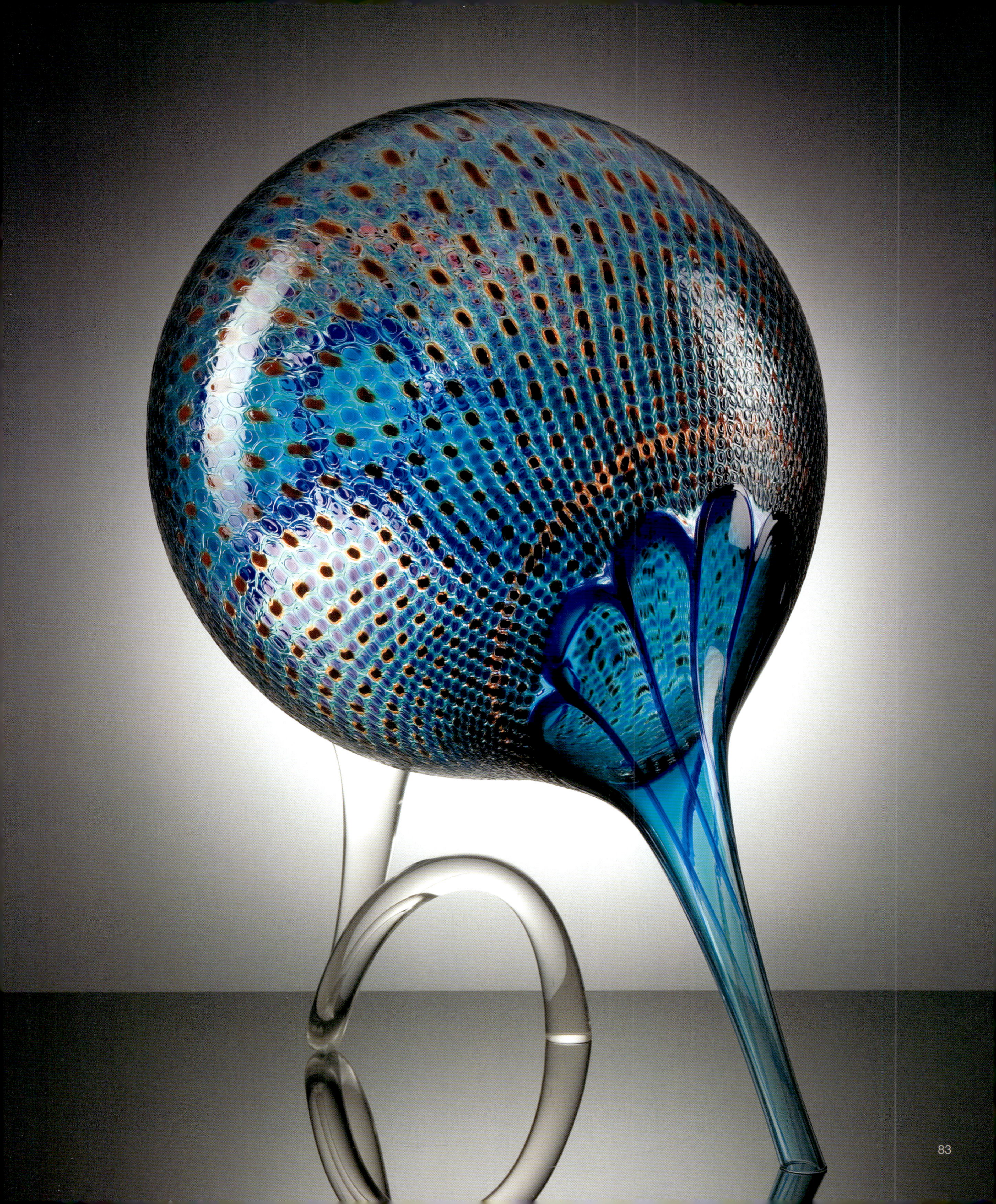

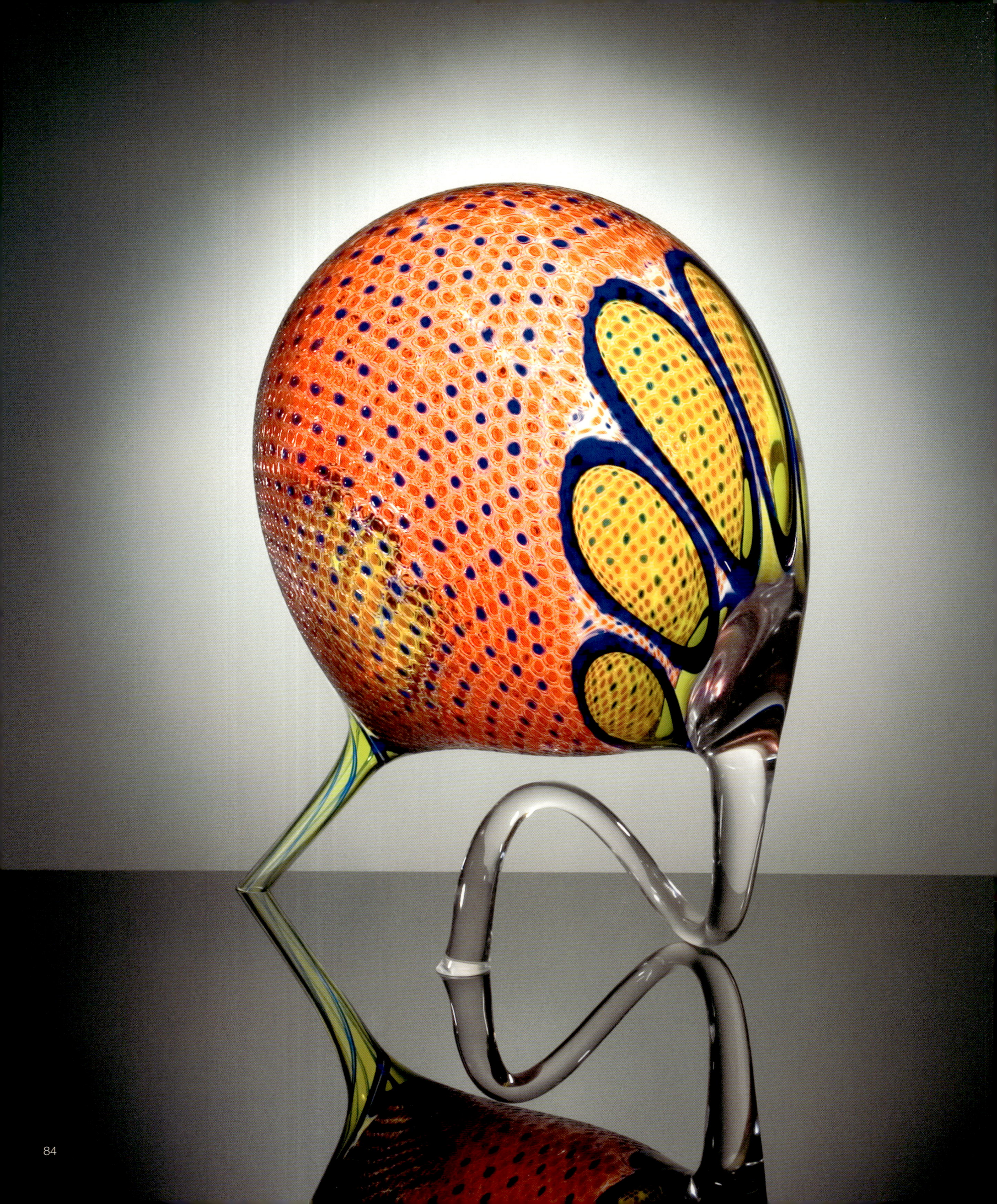

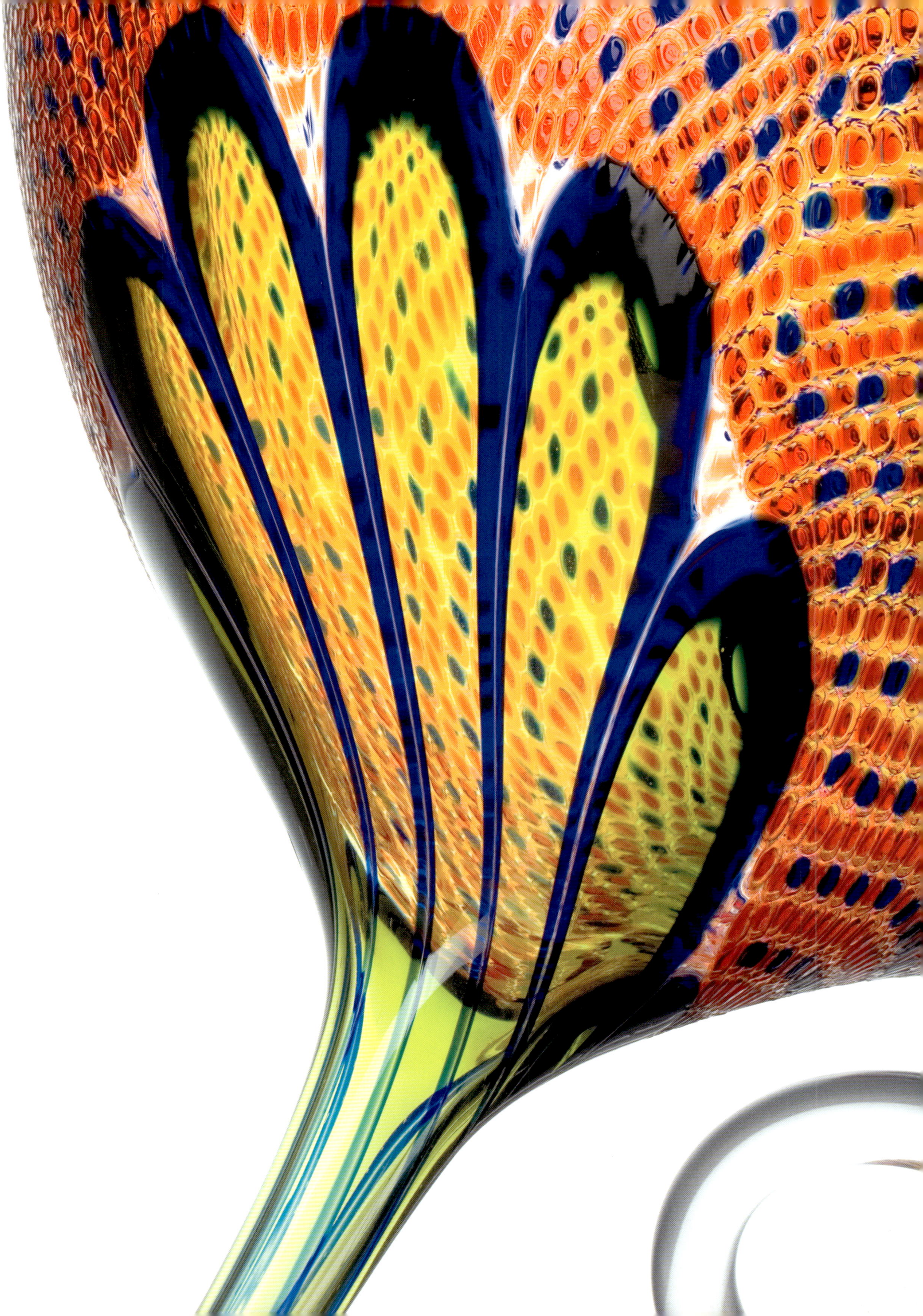

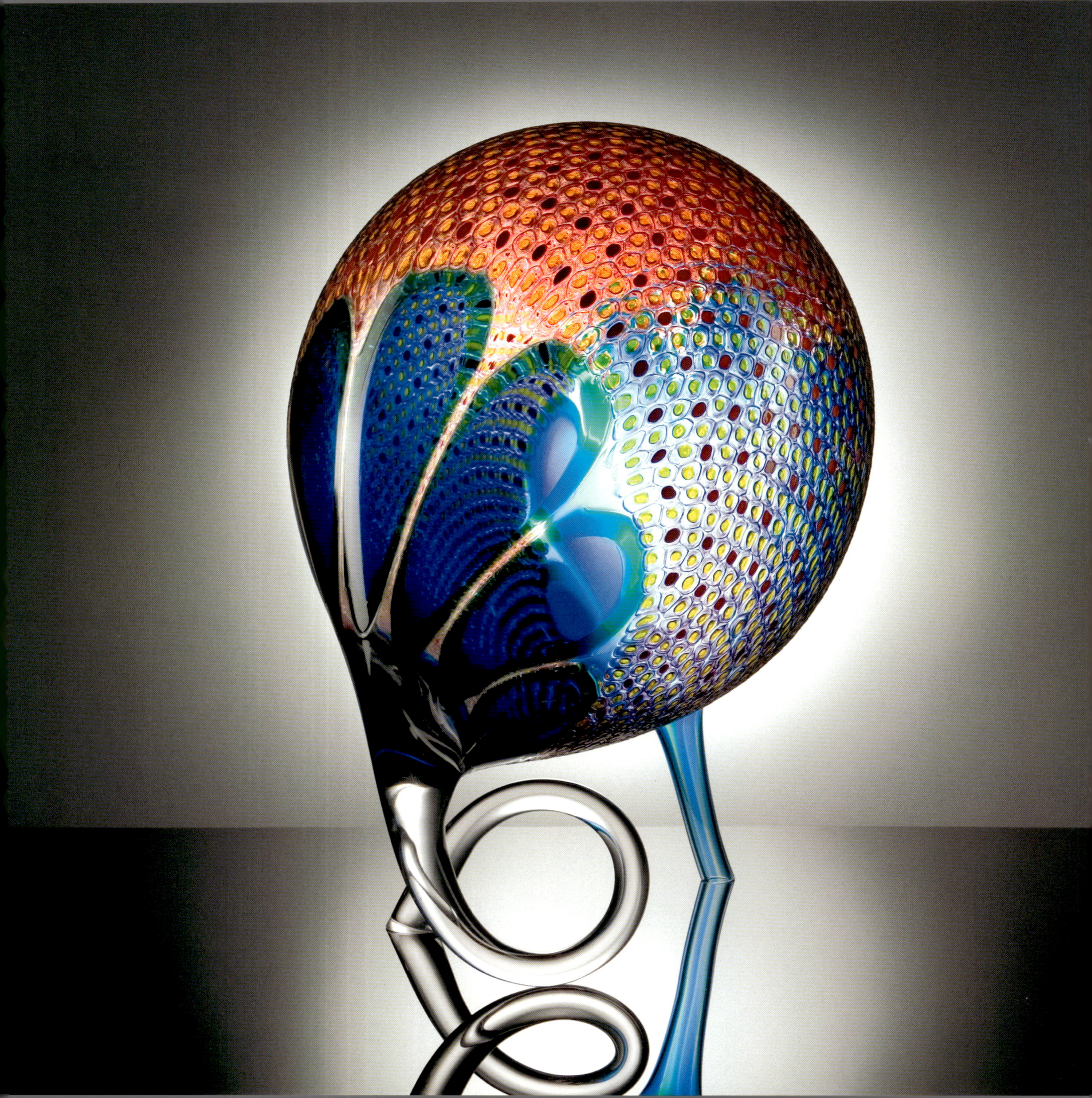

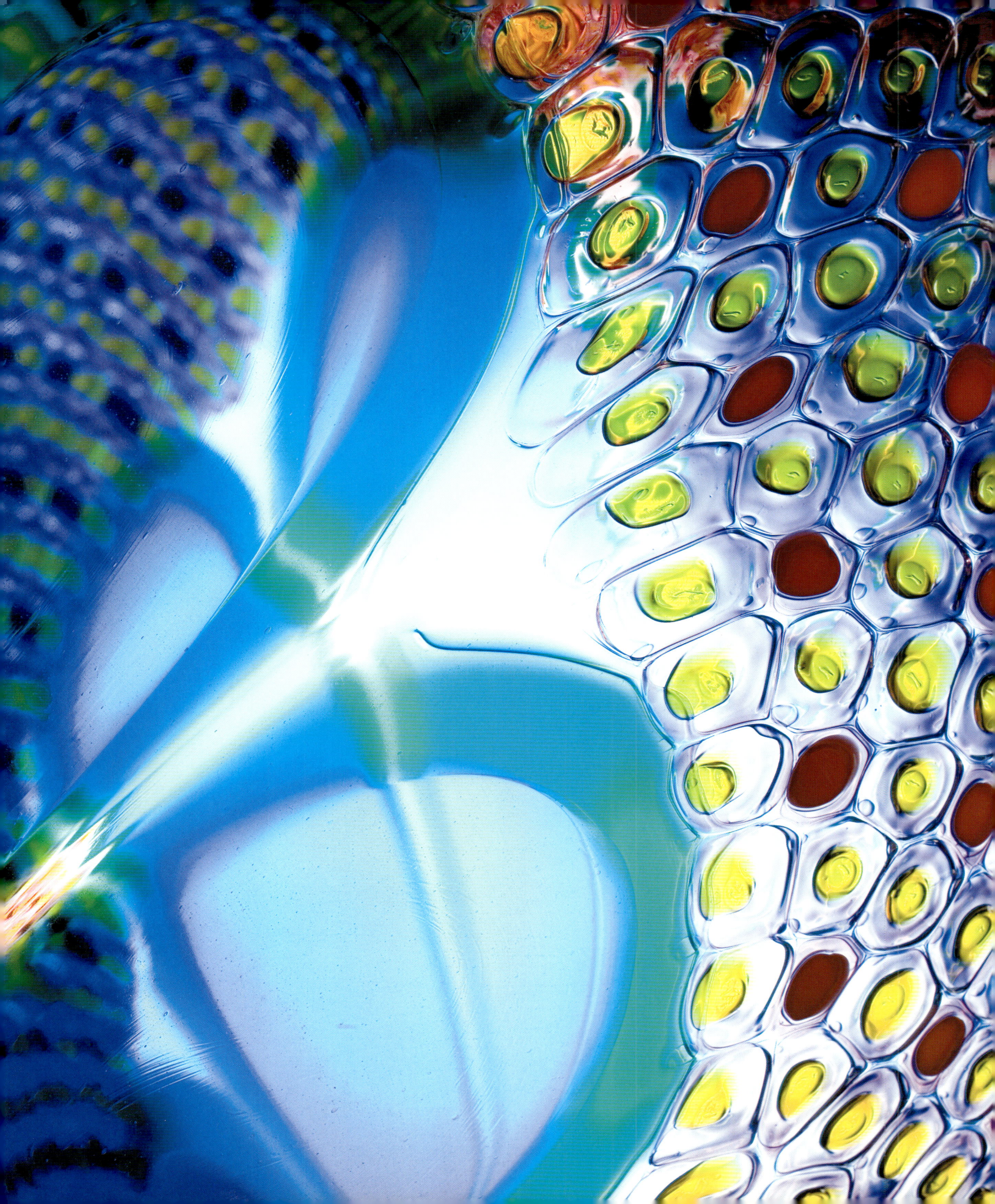

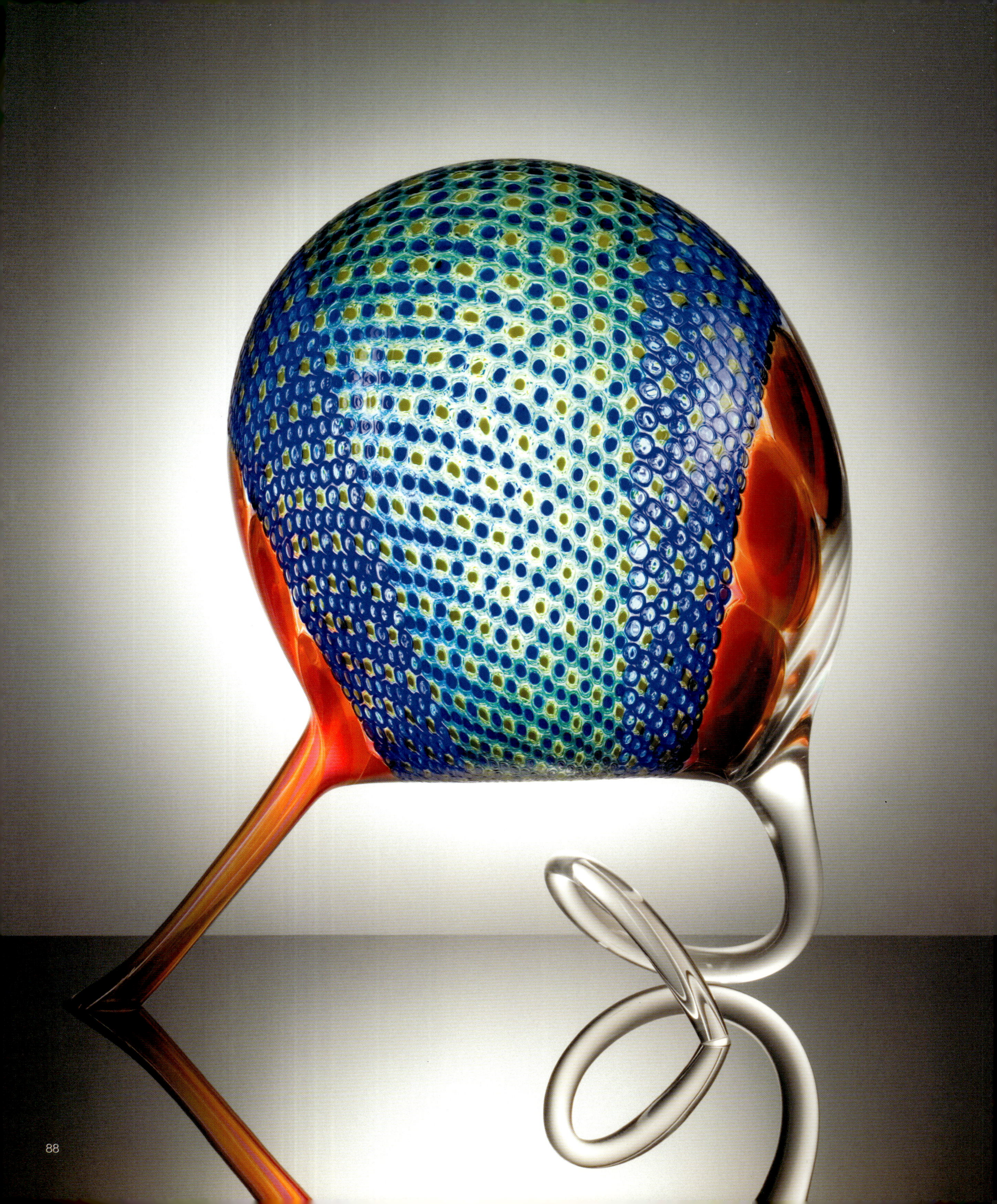

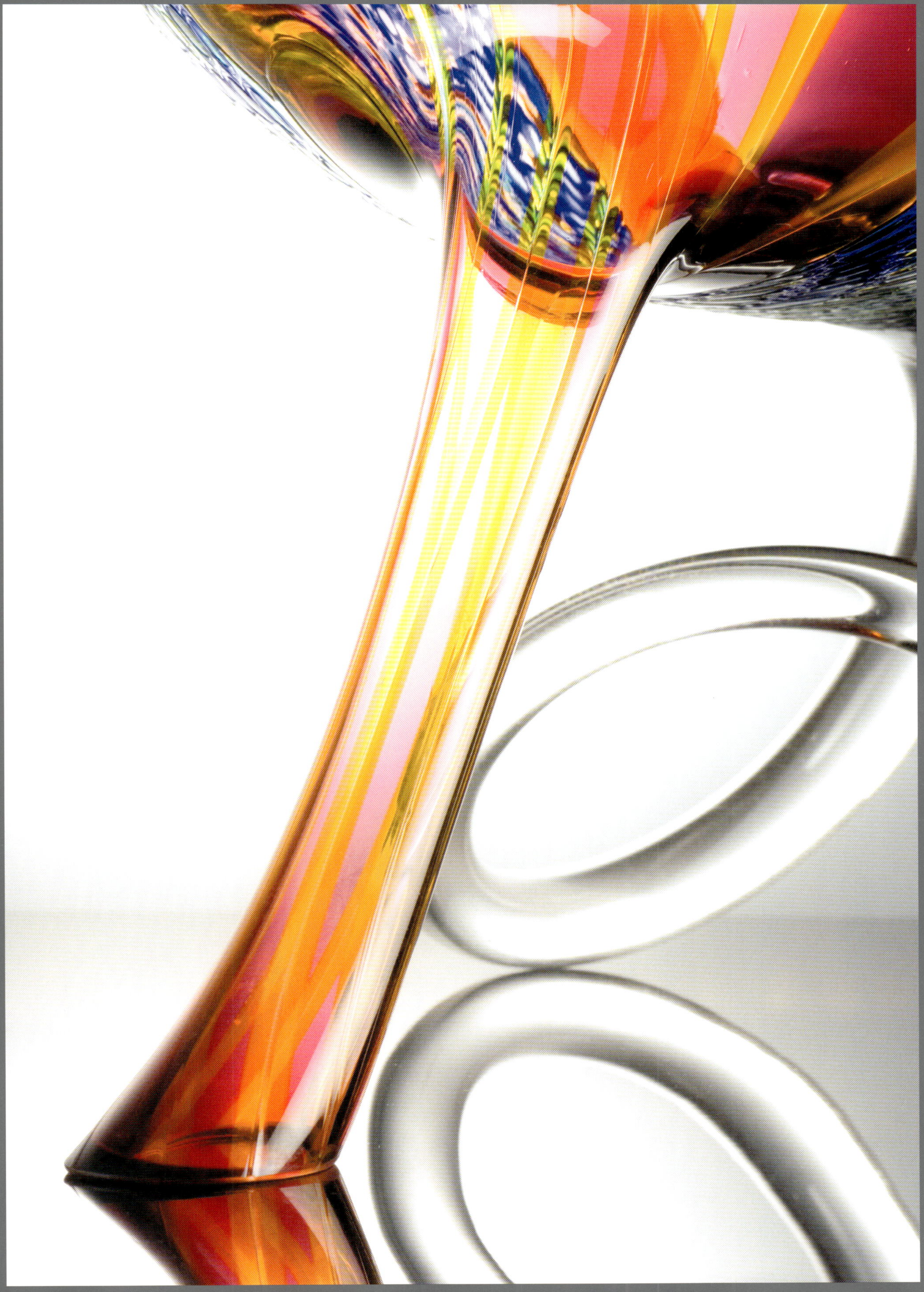

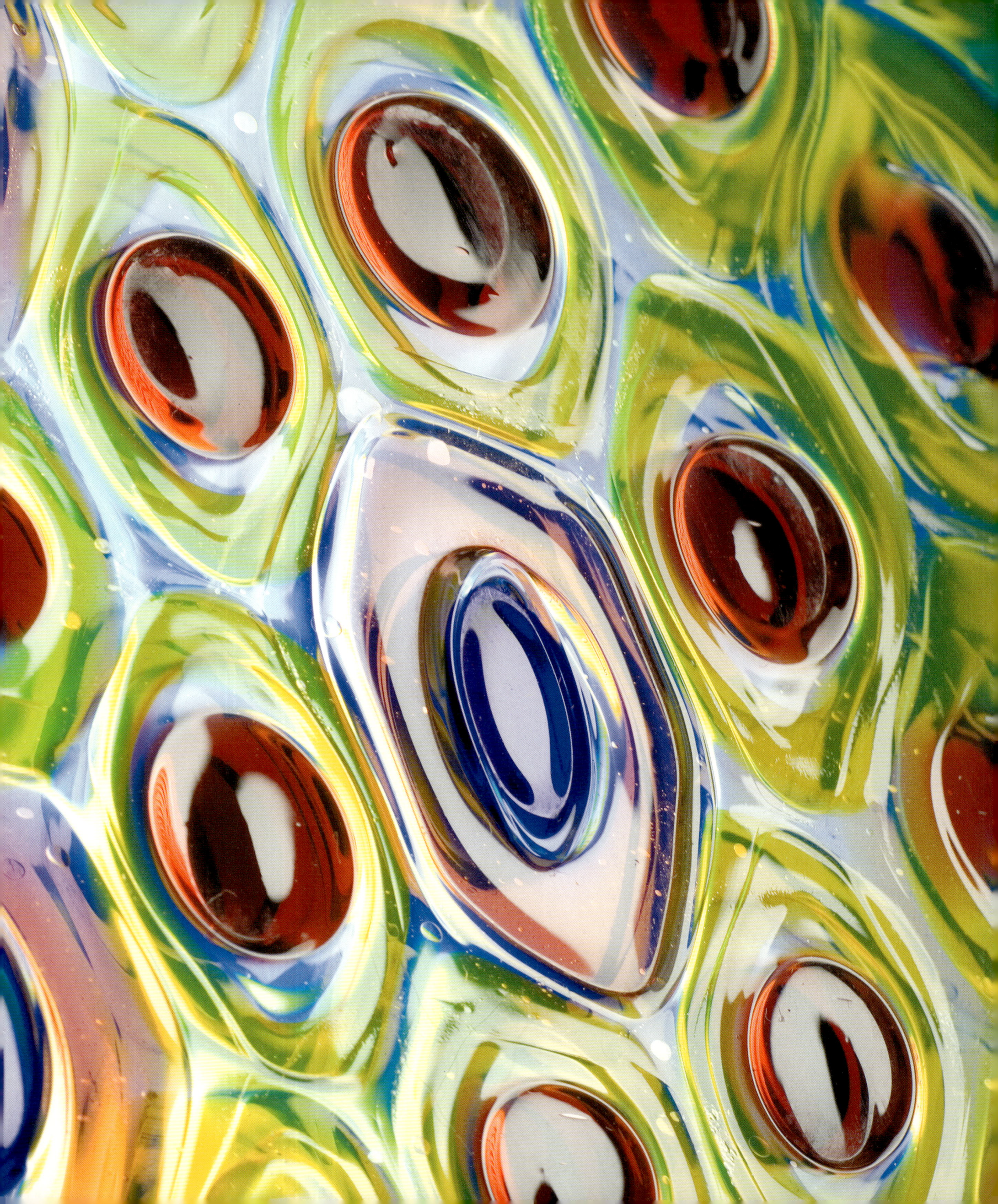

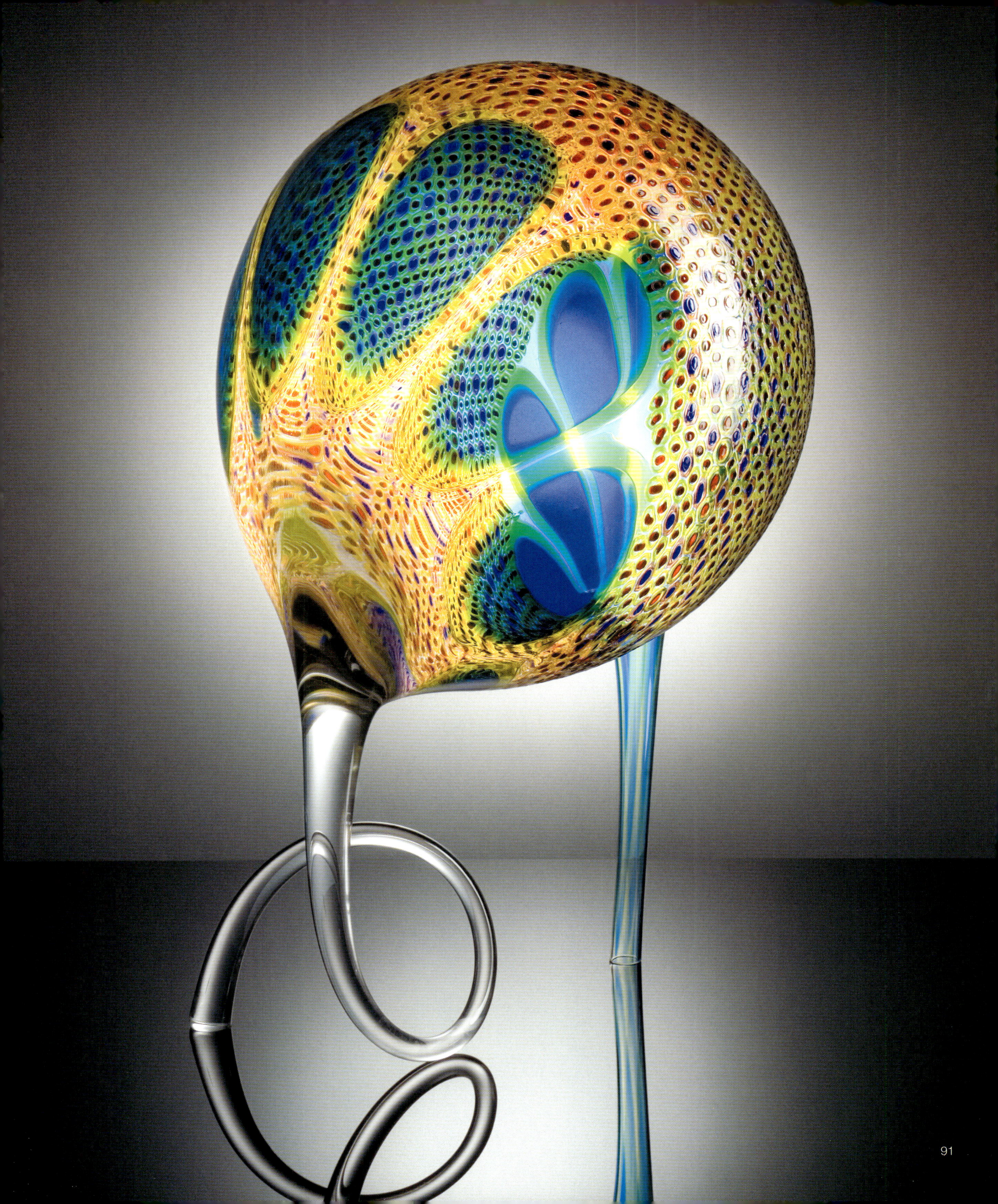

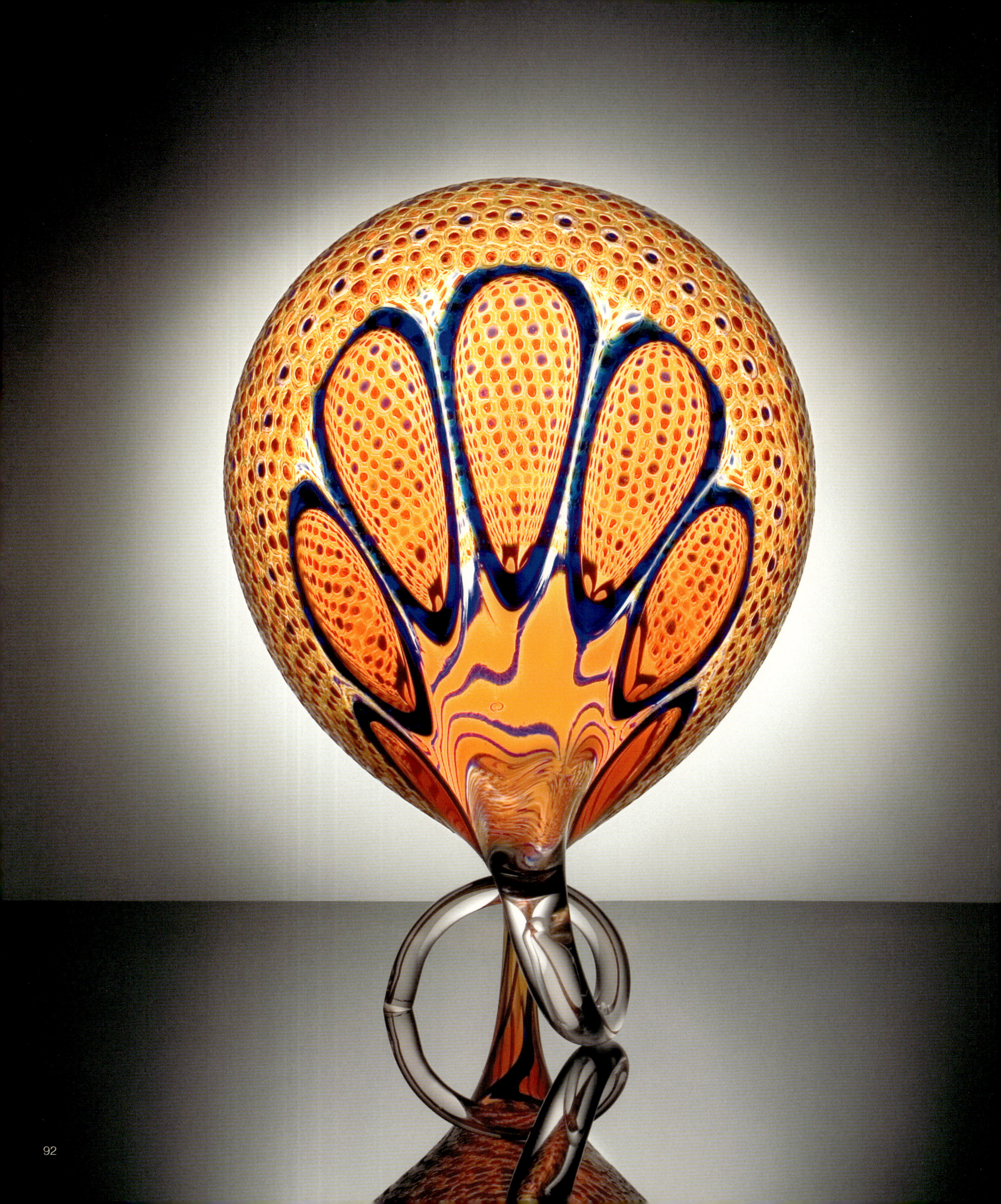

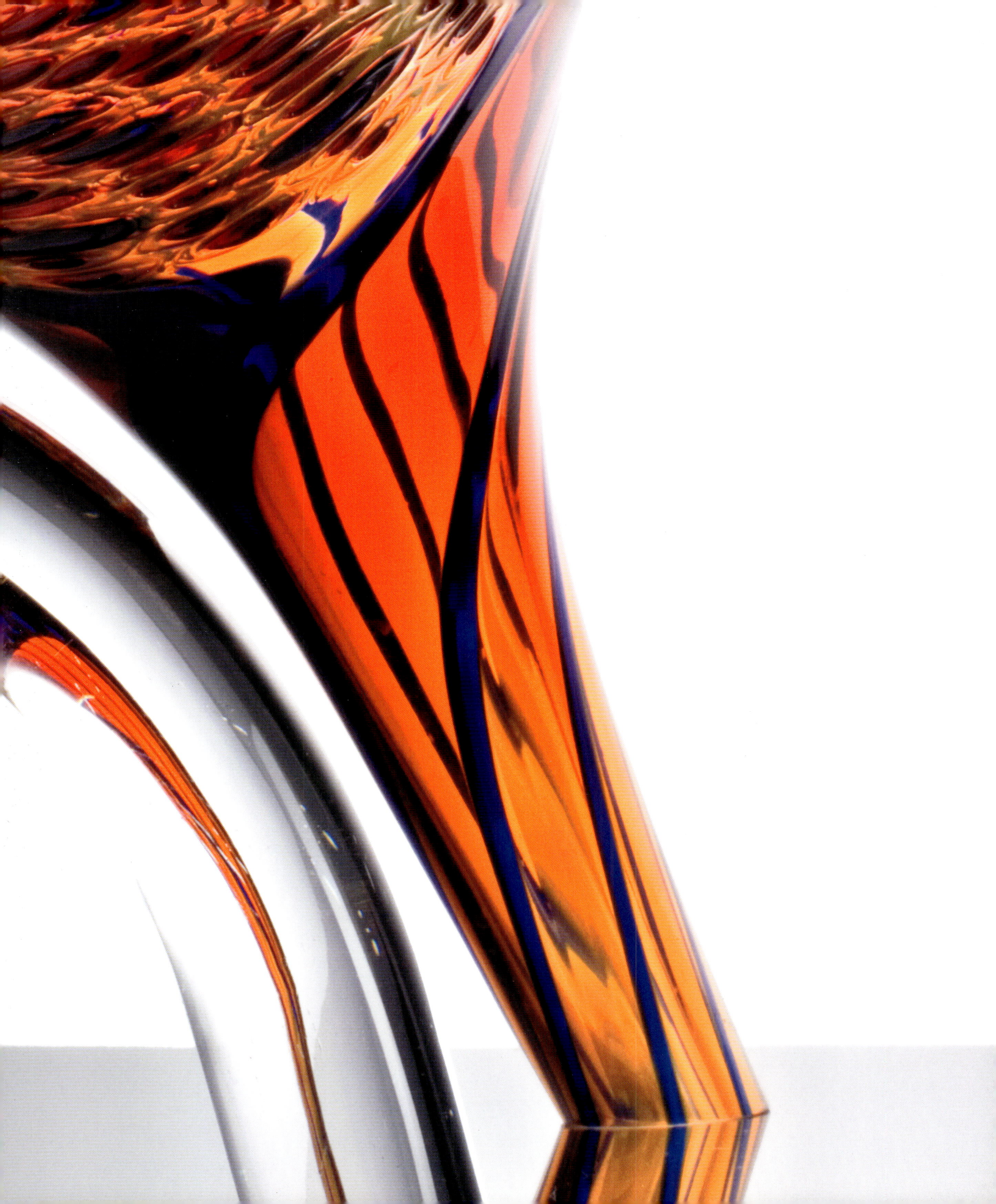

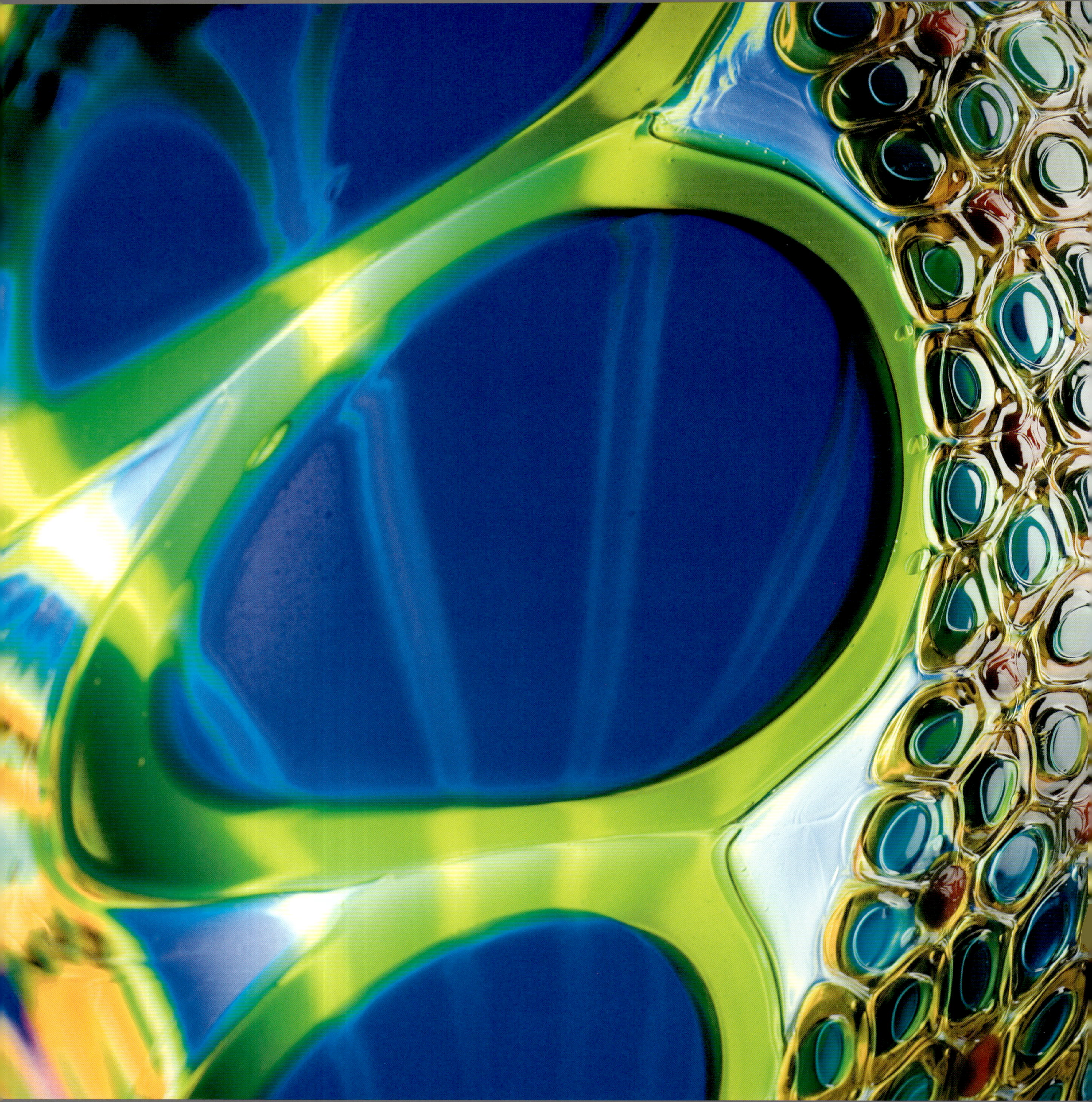

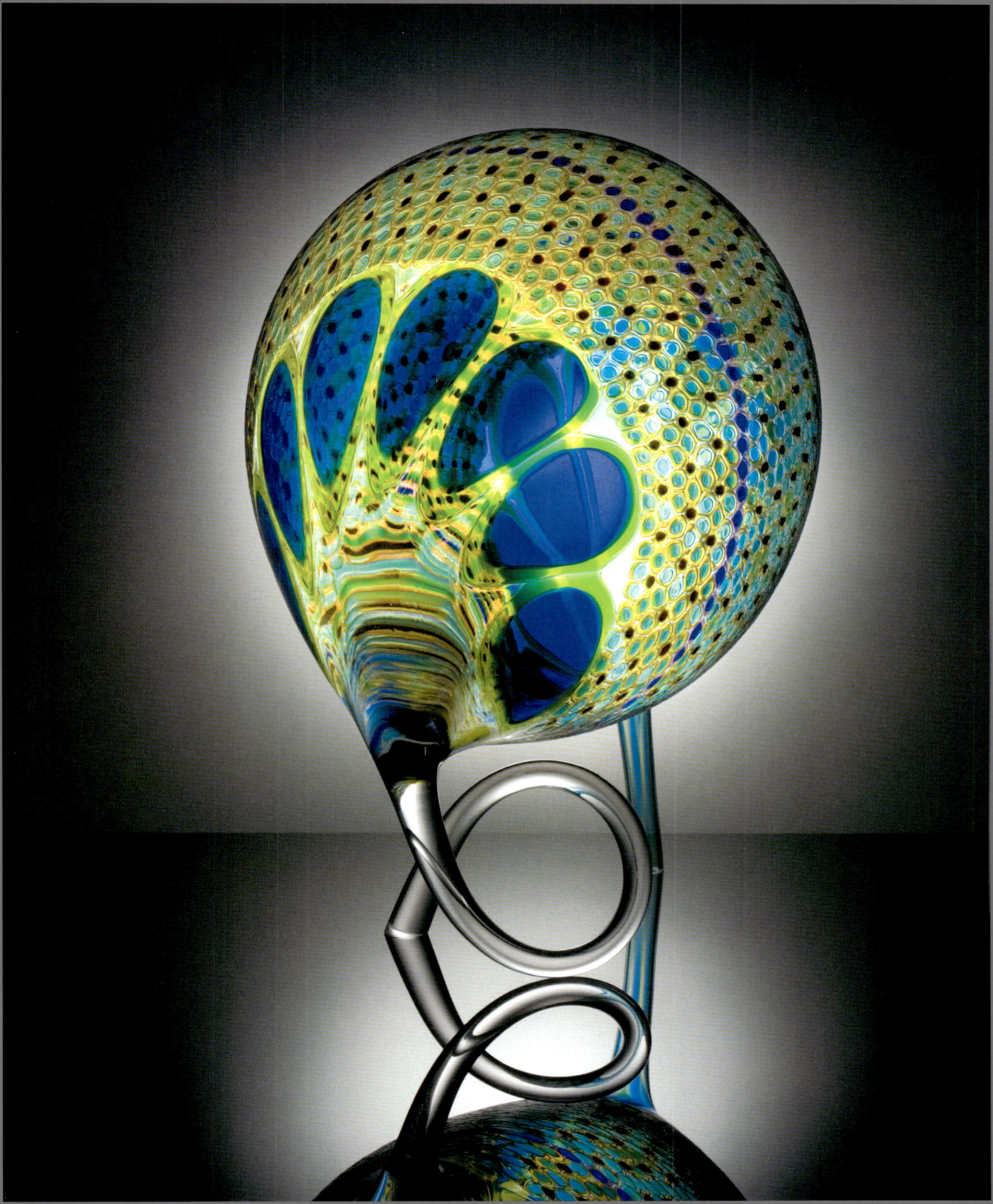

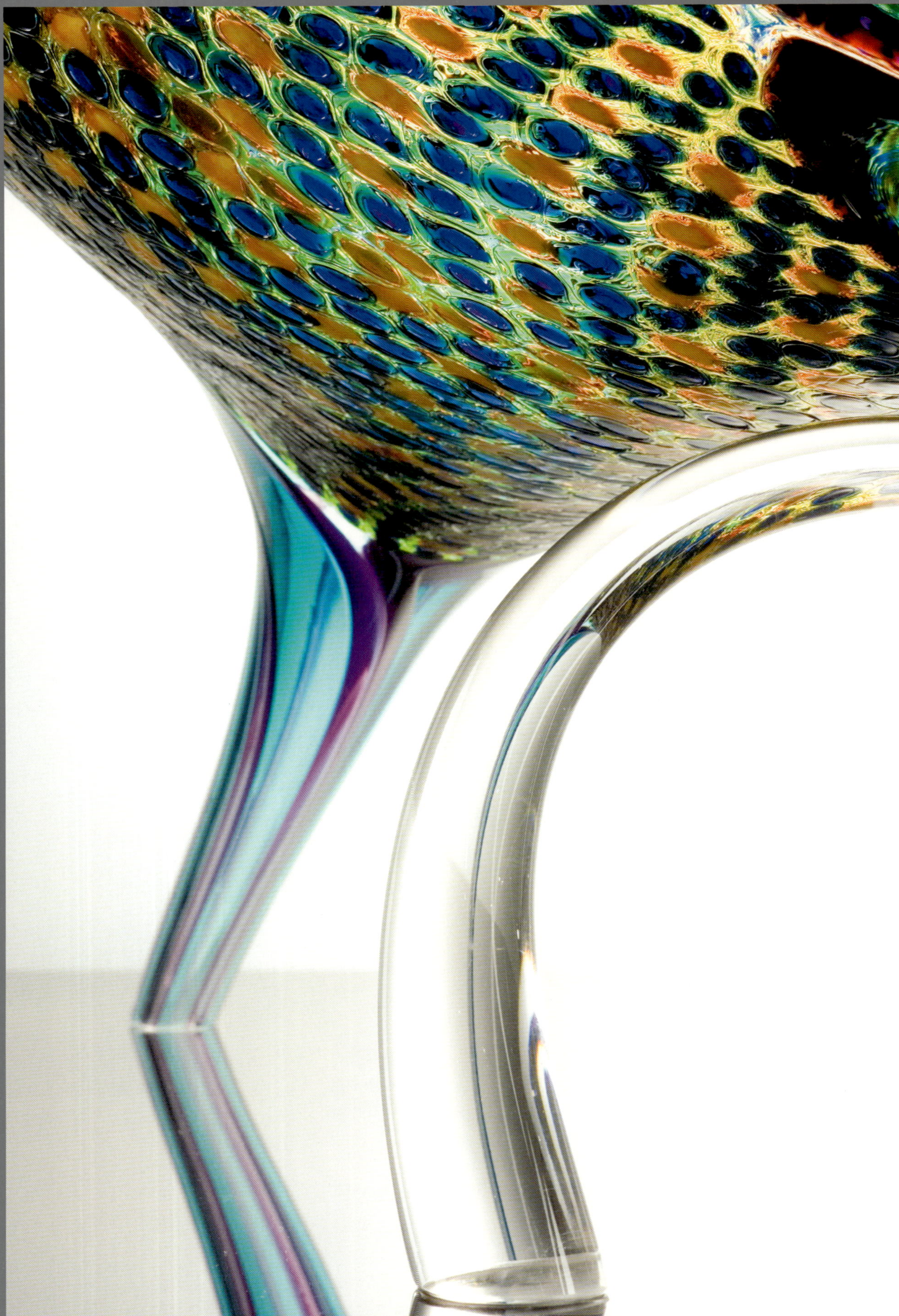

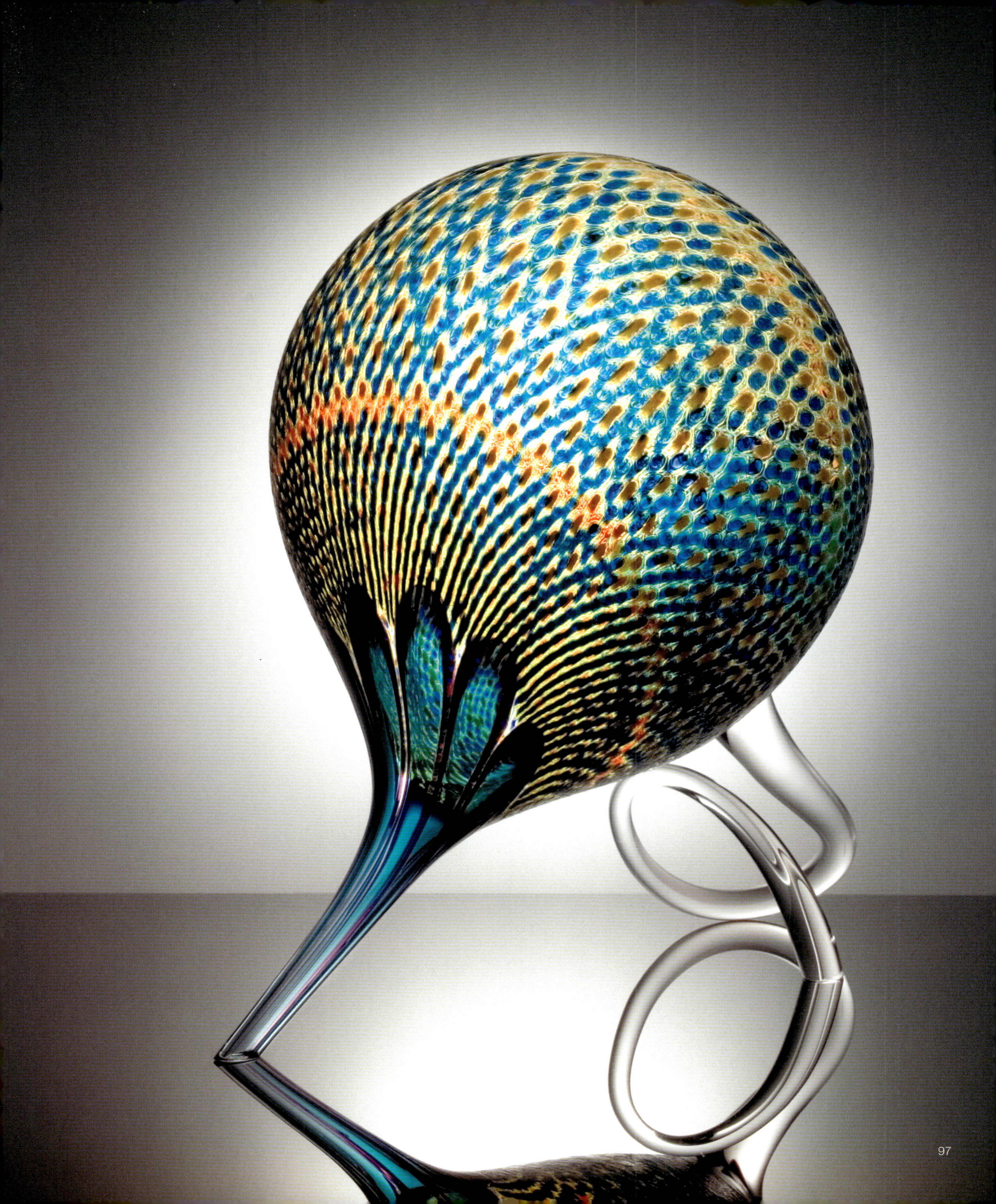

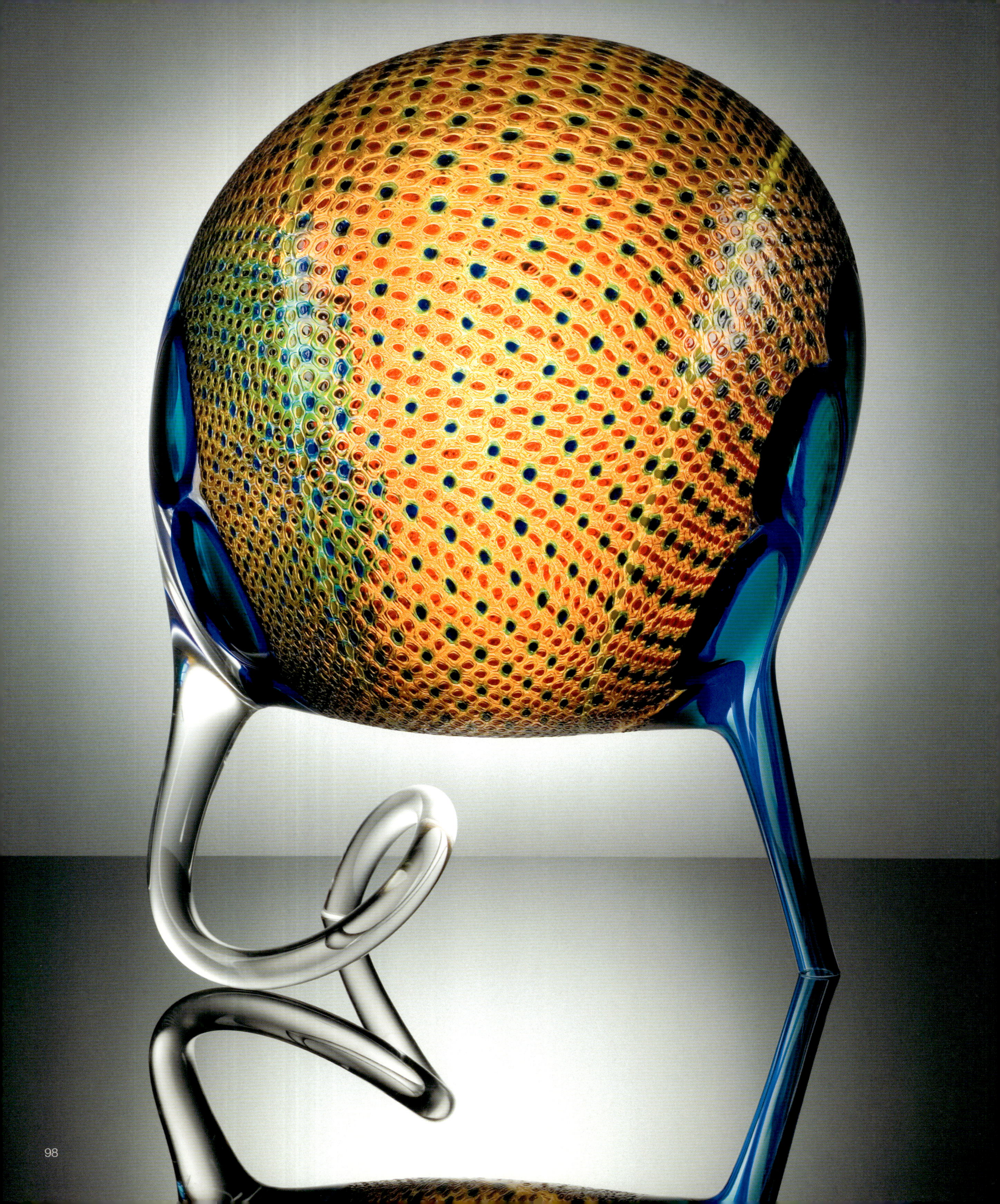

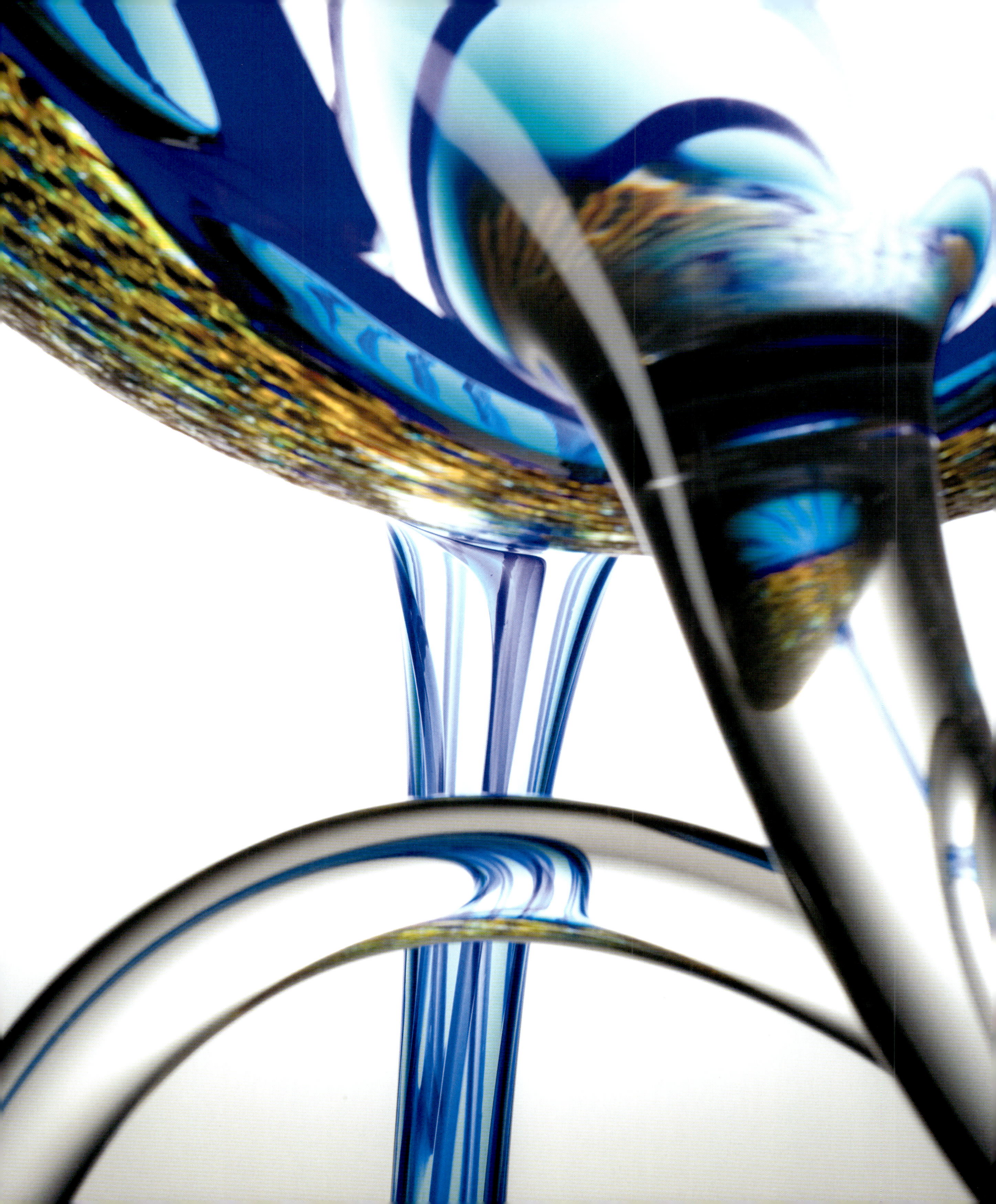

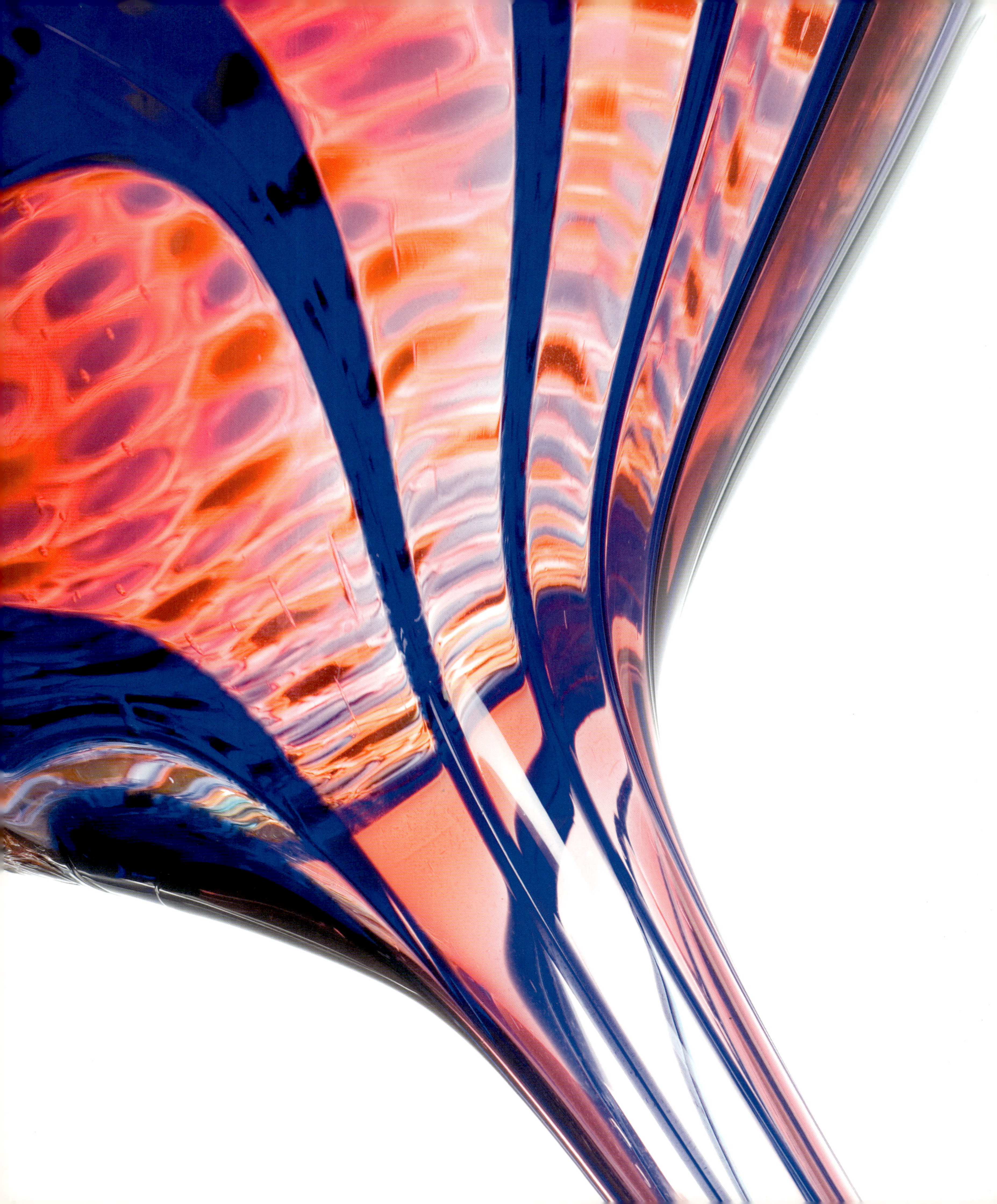

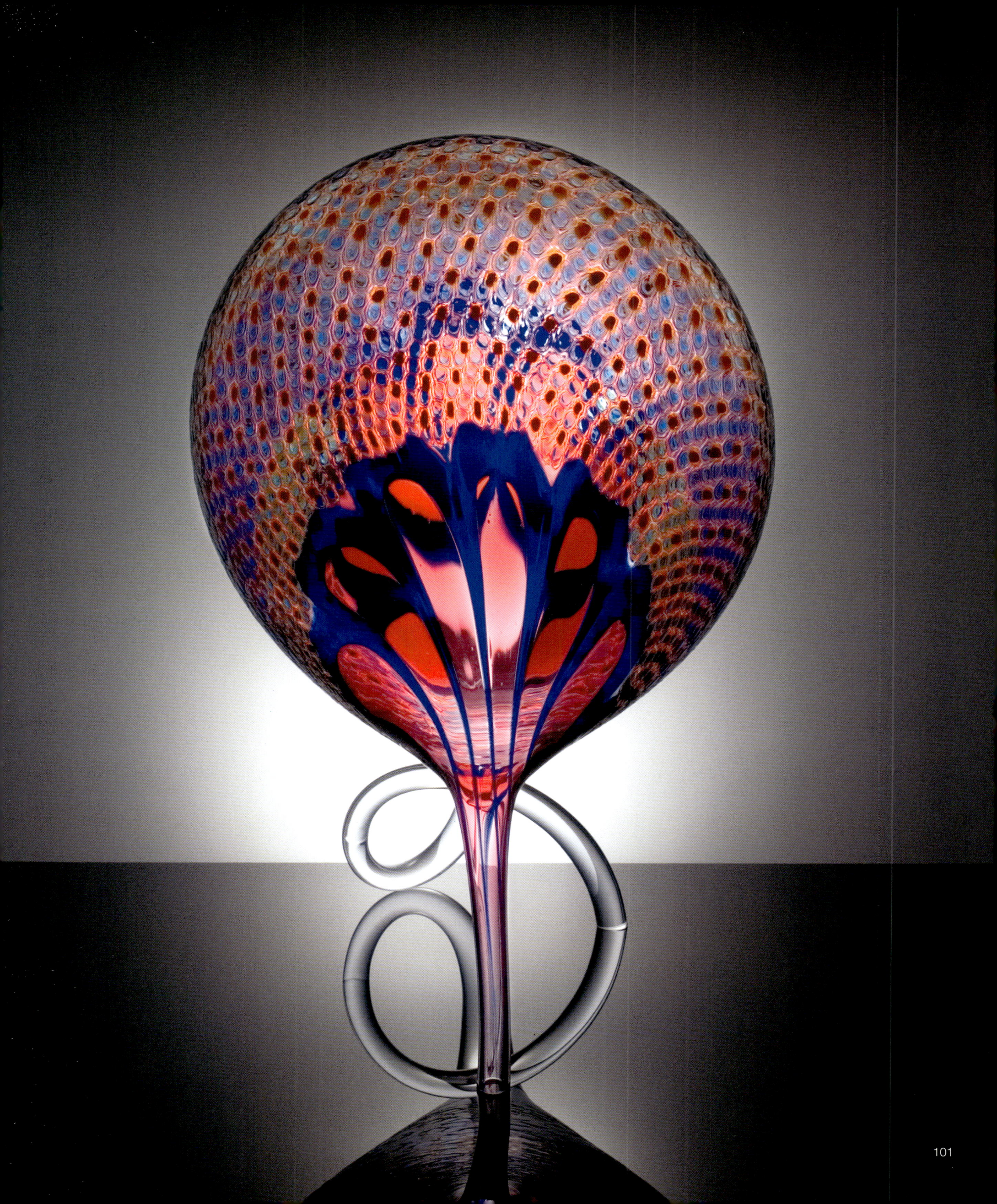

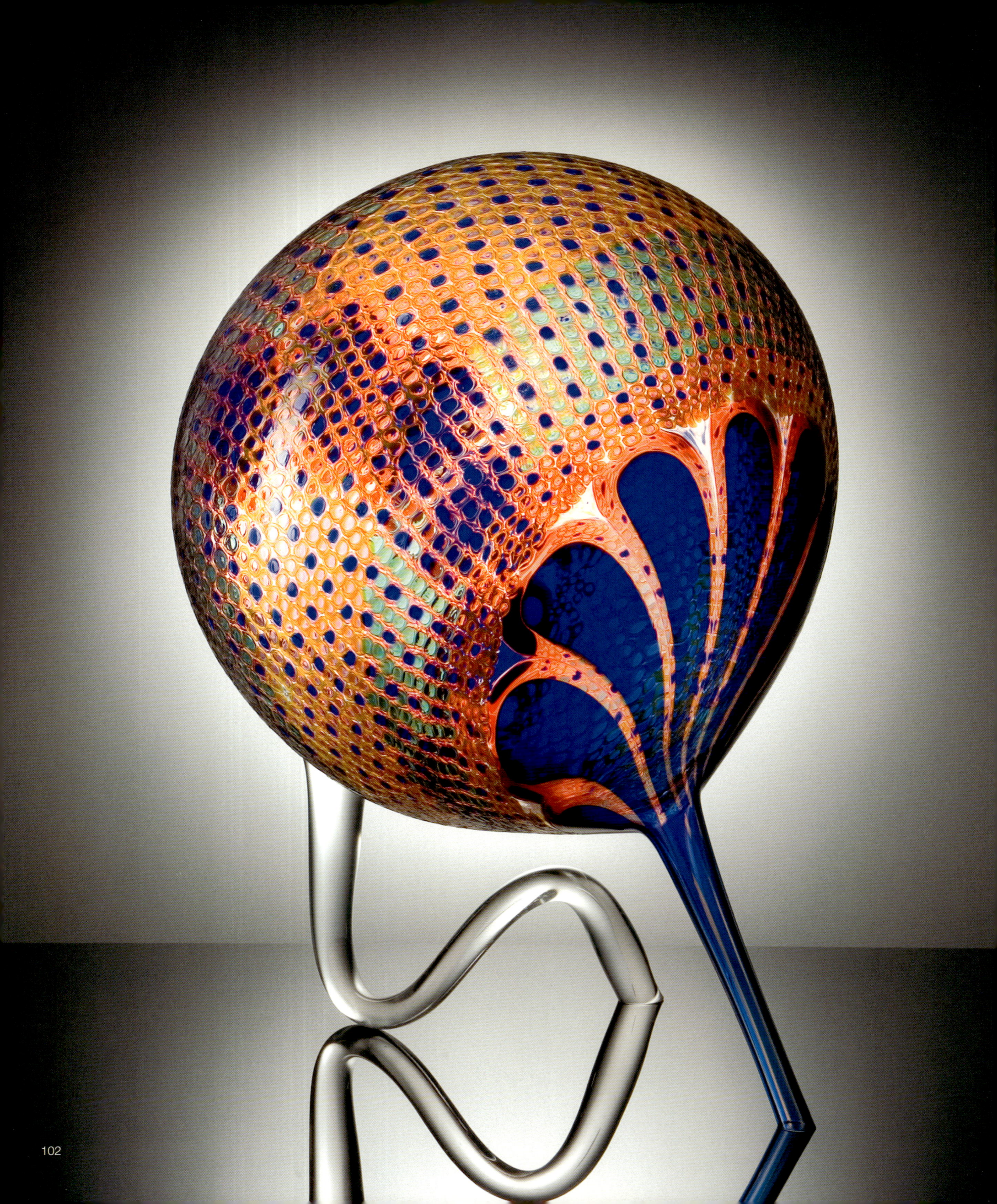

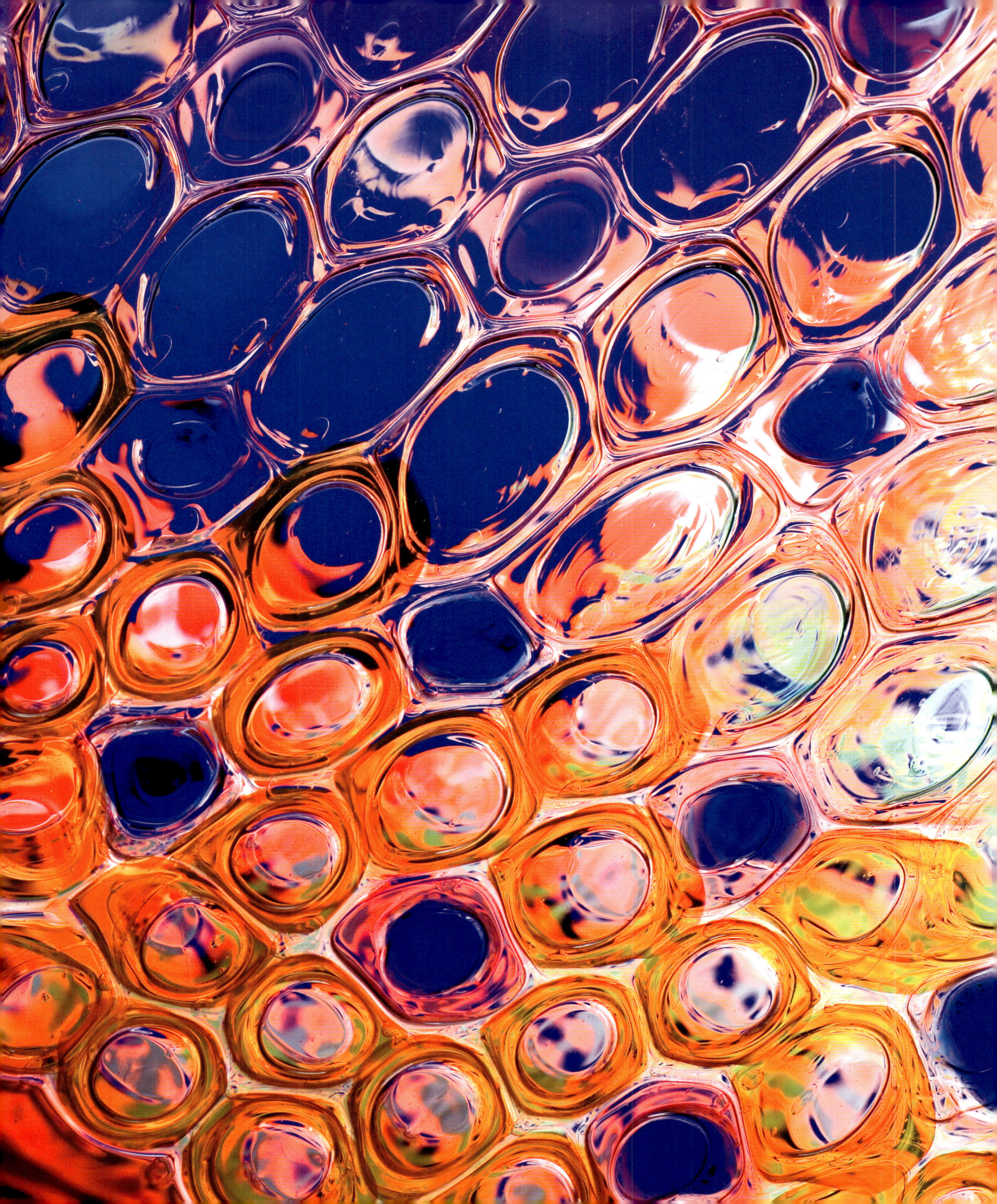

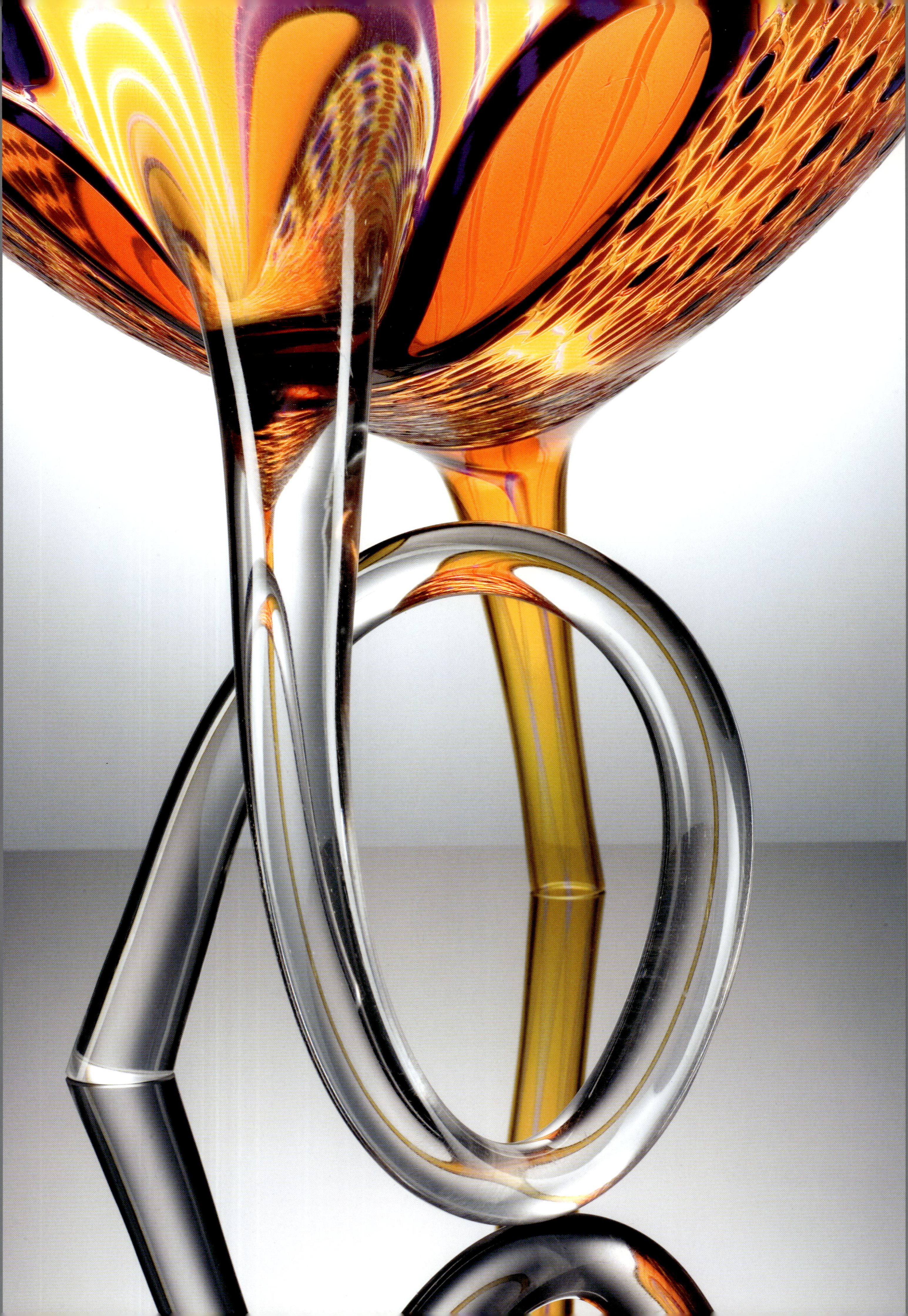

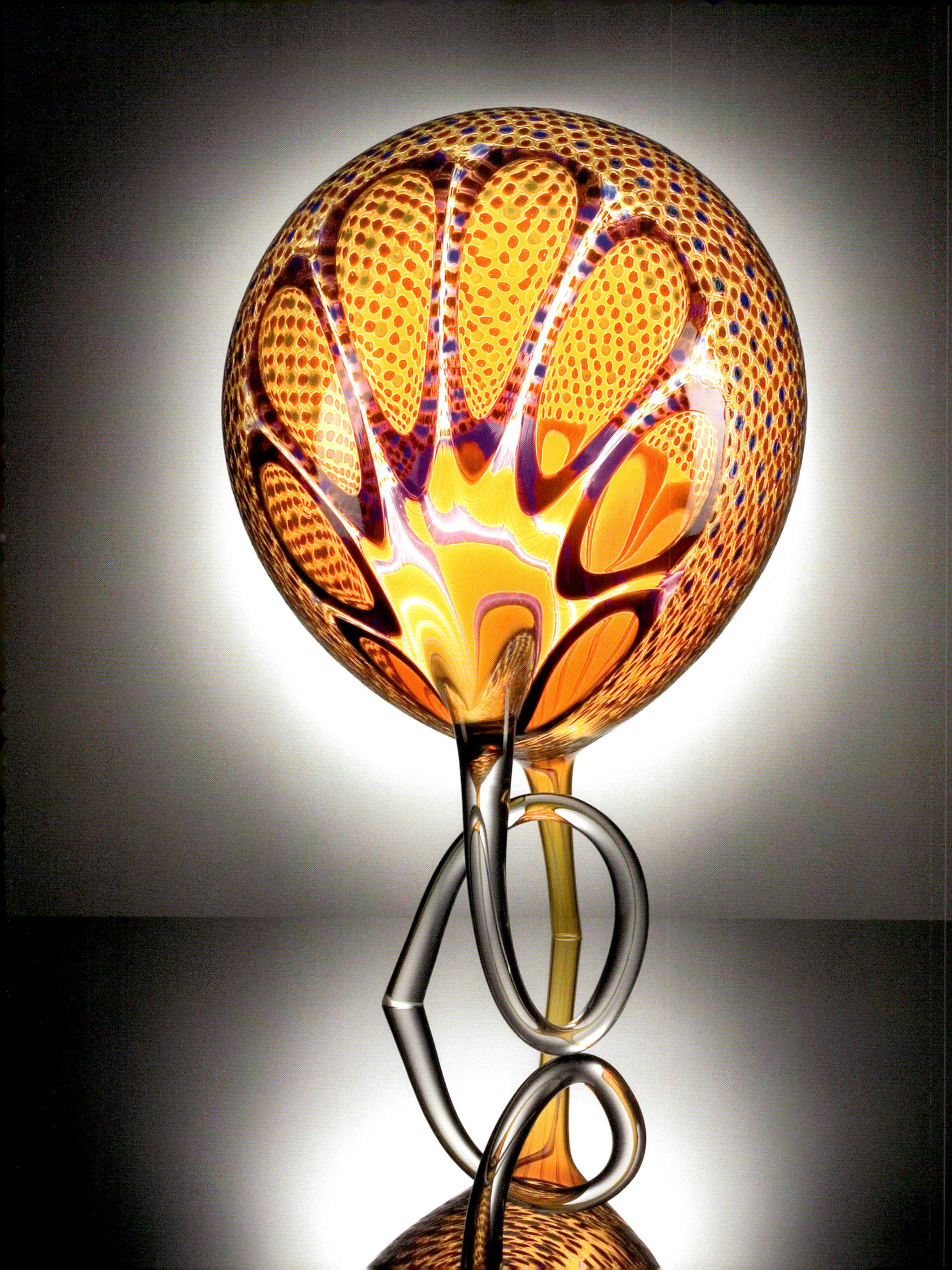

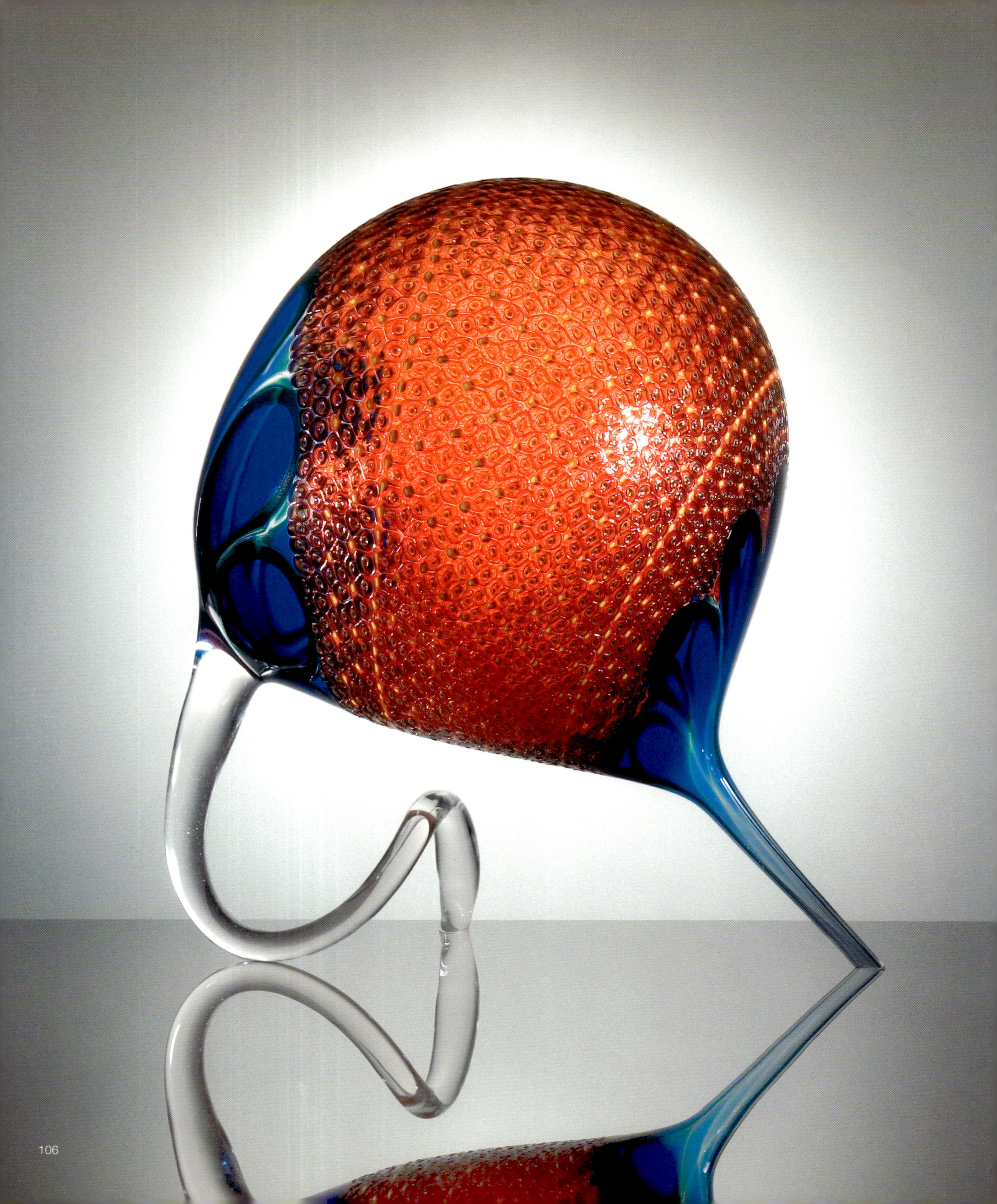

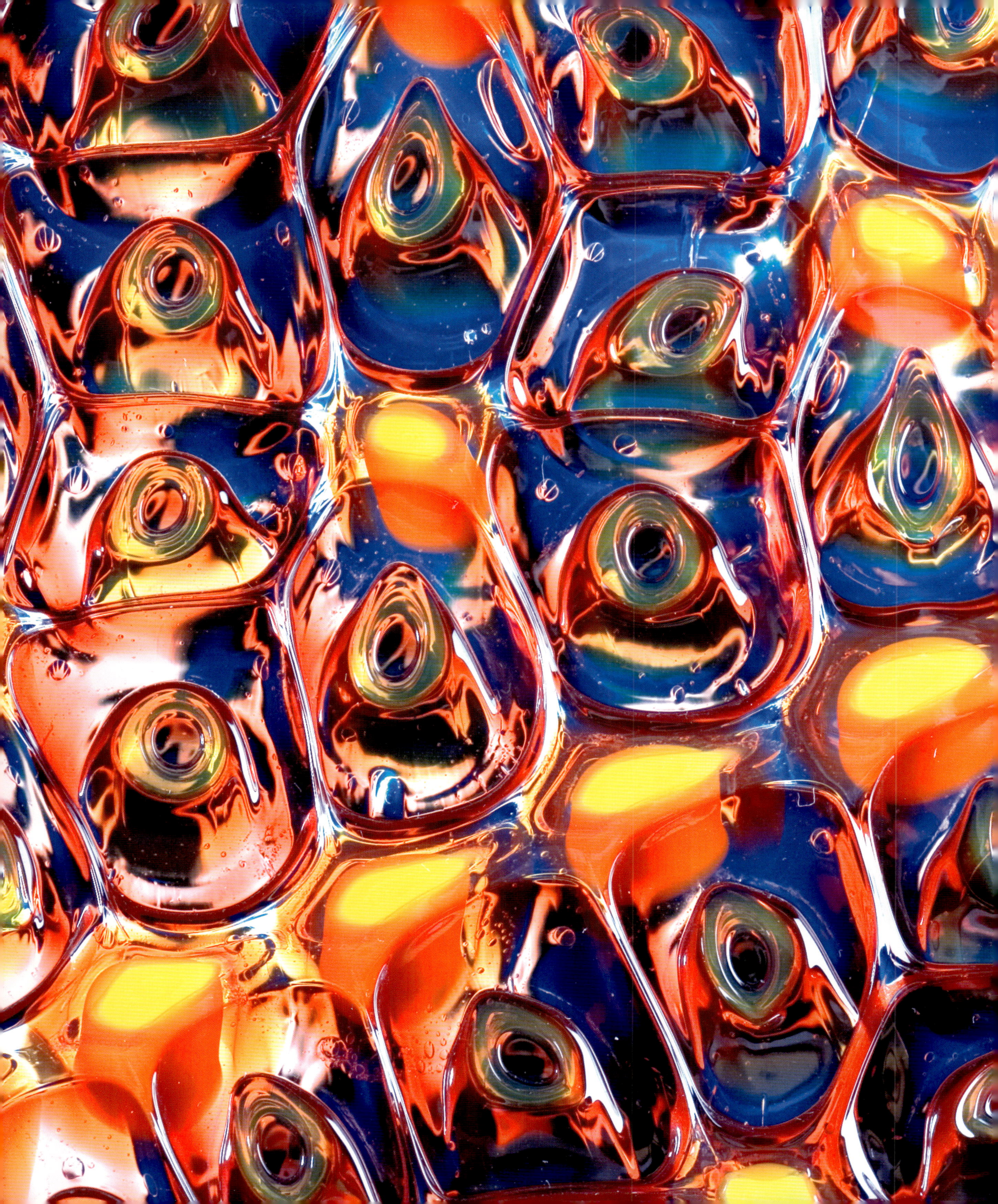

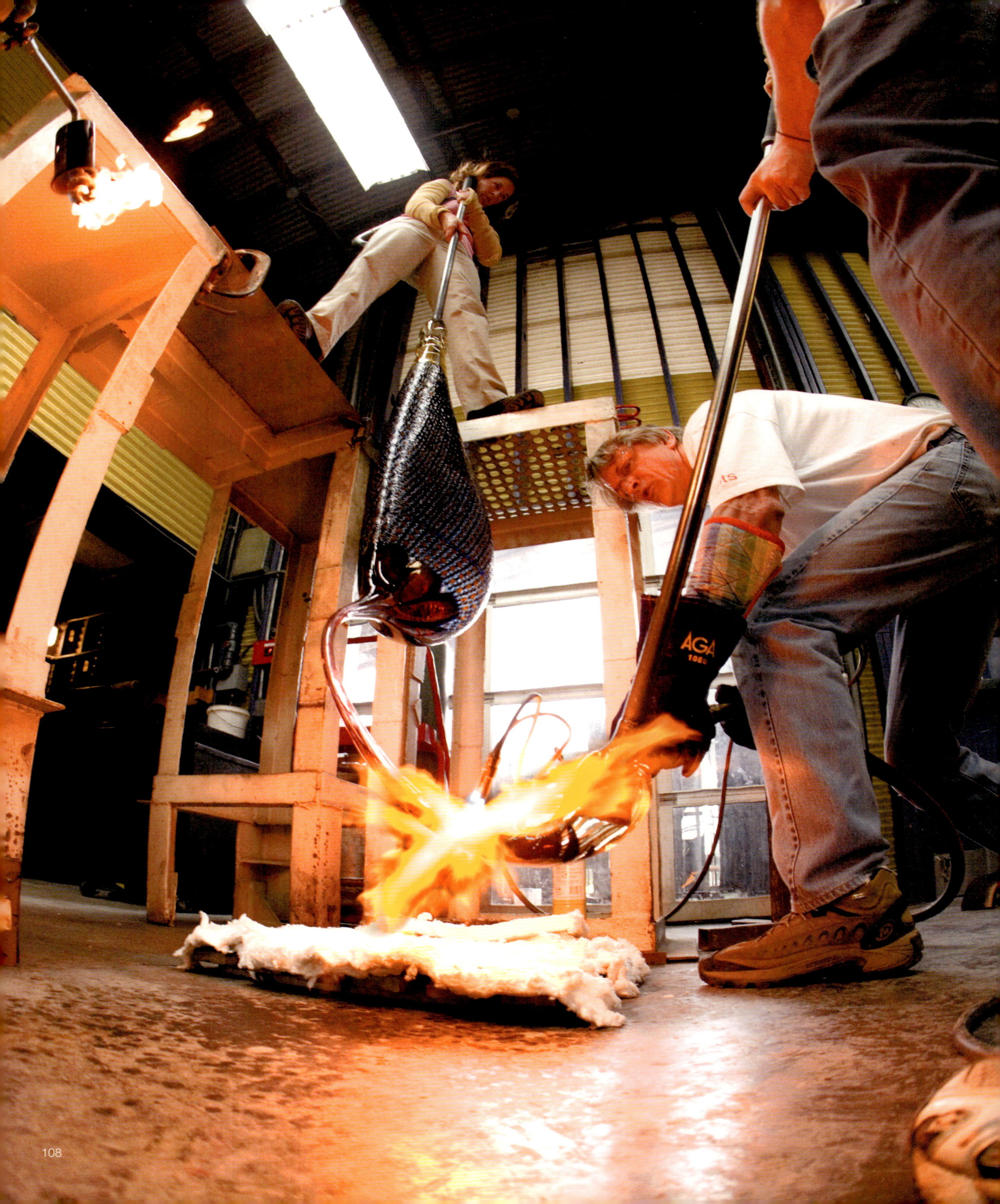
AGA

SCREAMERS

"The Screamers reflect a blend of the asymmetrical sculpture of the Whacko work with the vessel tradition I used for so long. The asymmetry is freeing and allows for more expressive forms—forms that suggest howling, twisting, snorting, contorting. Yet all this craziness is tempered by the order of the pattern and the physical balance of the piece."

Stephen Rolfe Powell, 2006

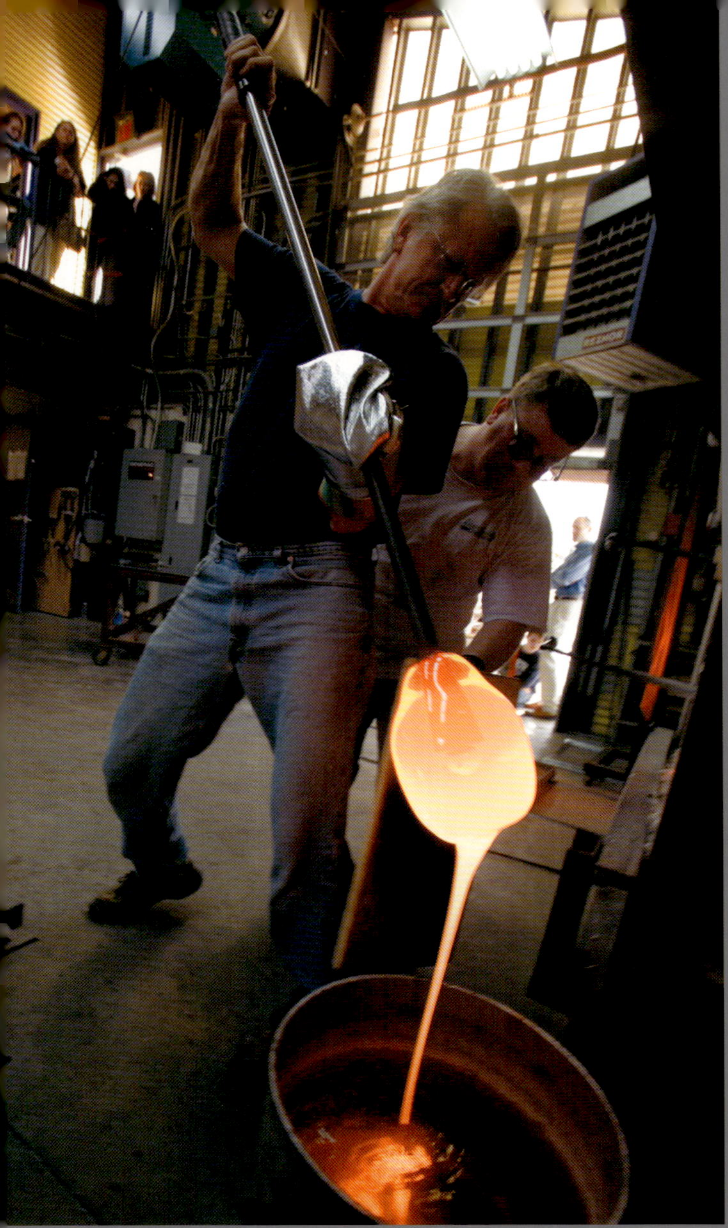
REZNOR

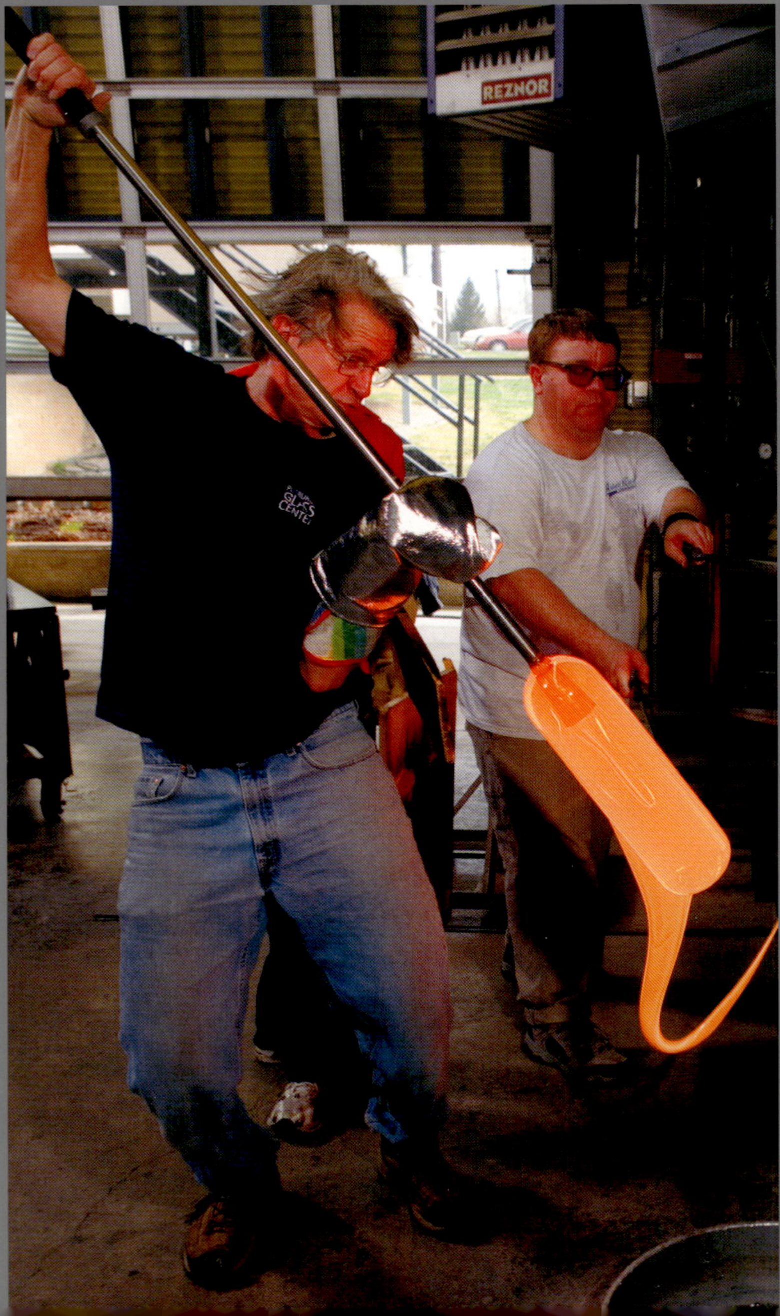
REZNOR

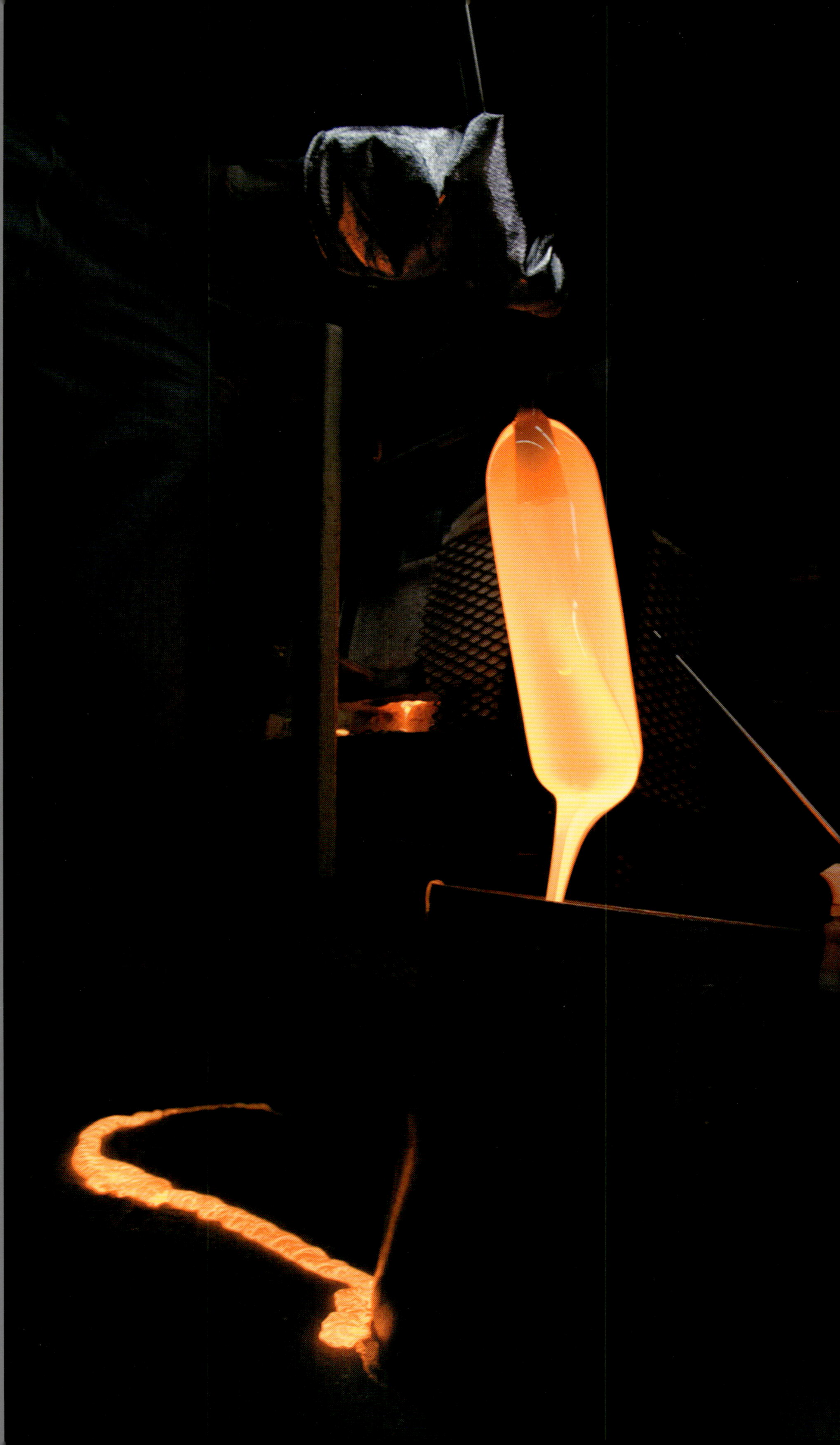

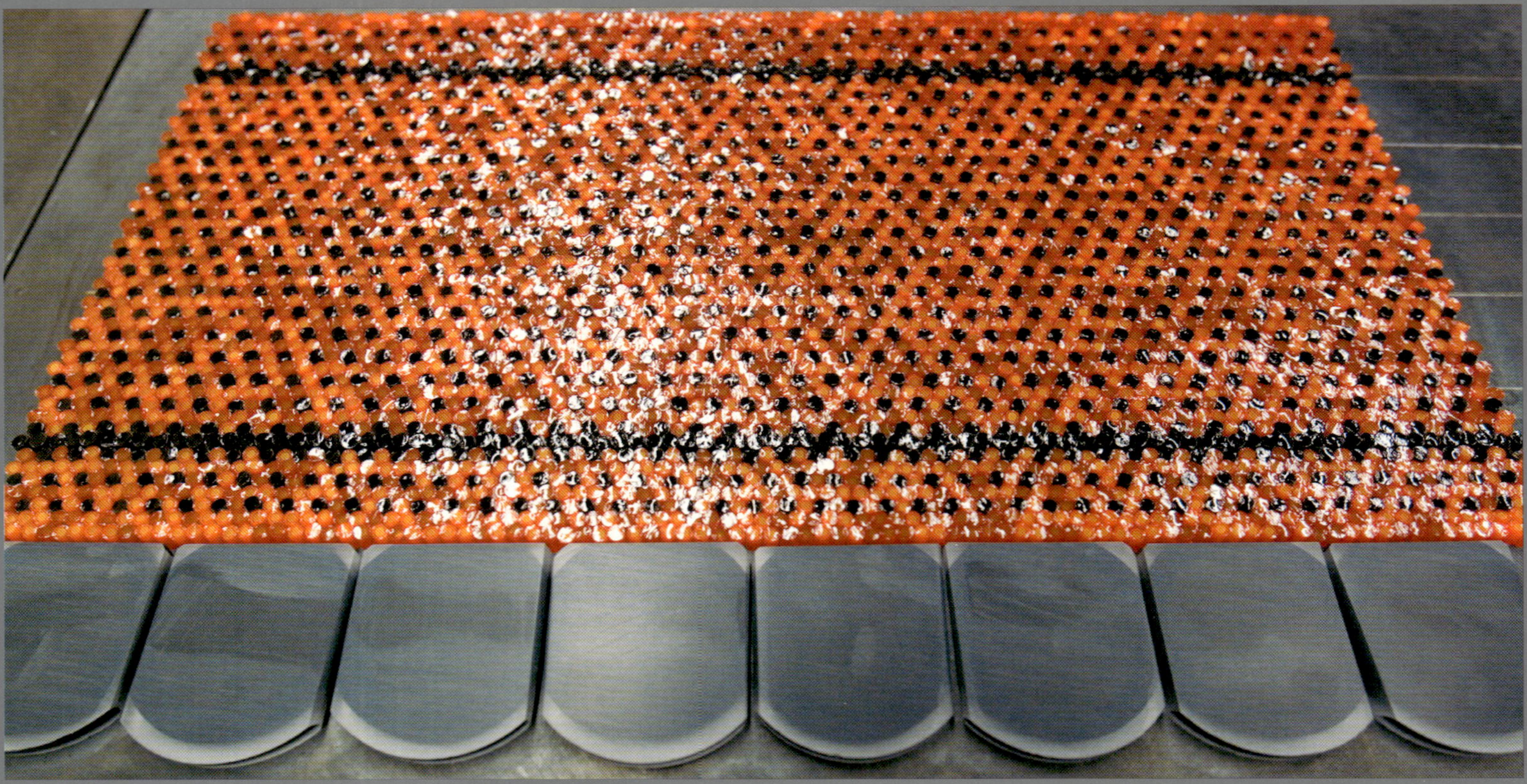

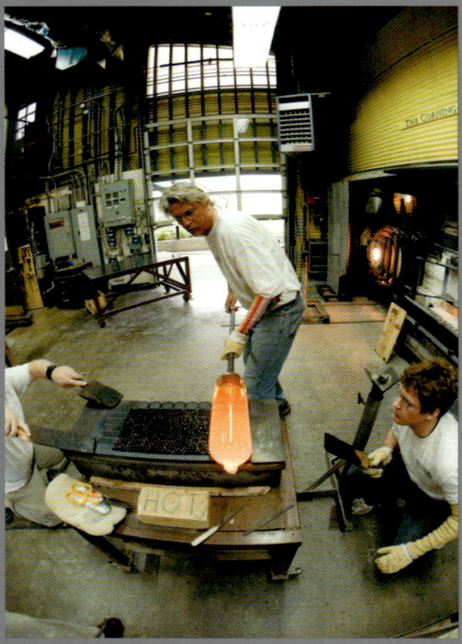
HOT

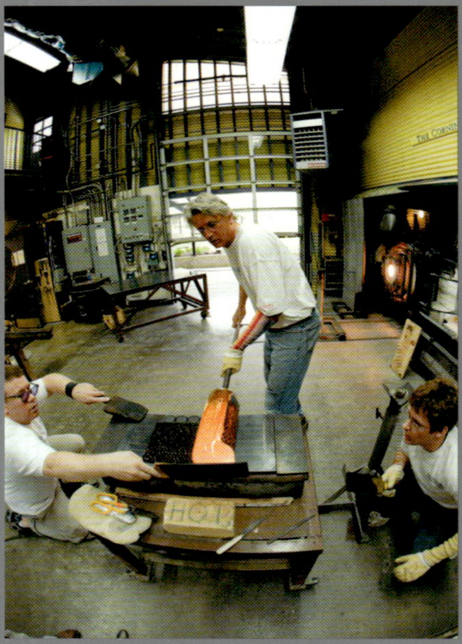
HOT

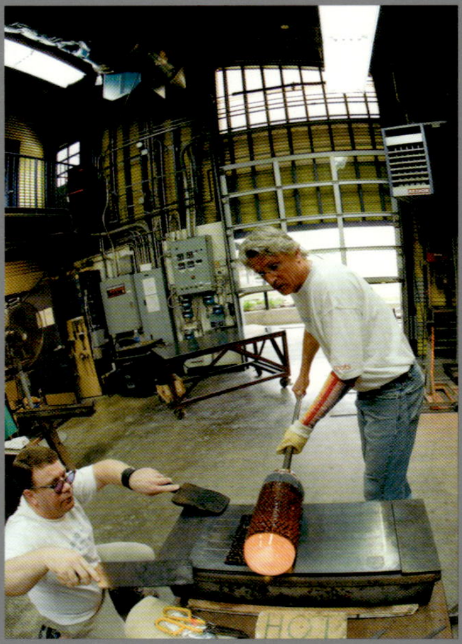
HOT

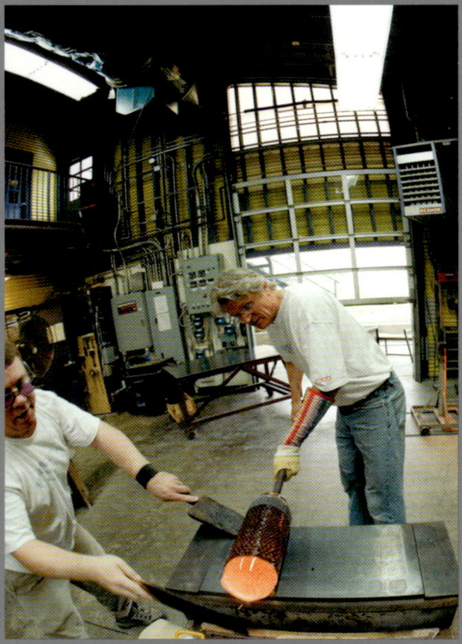

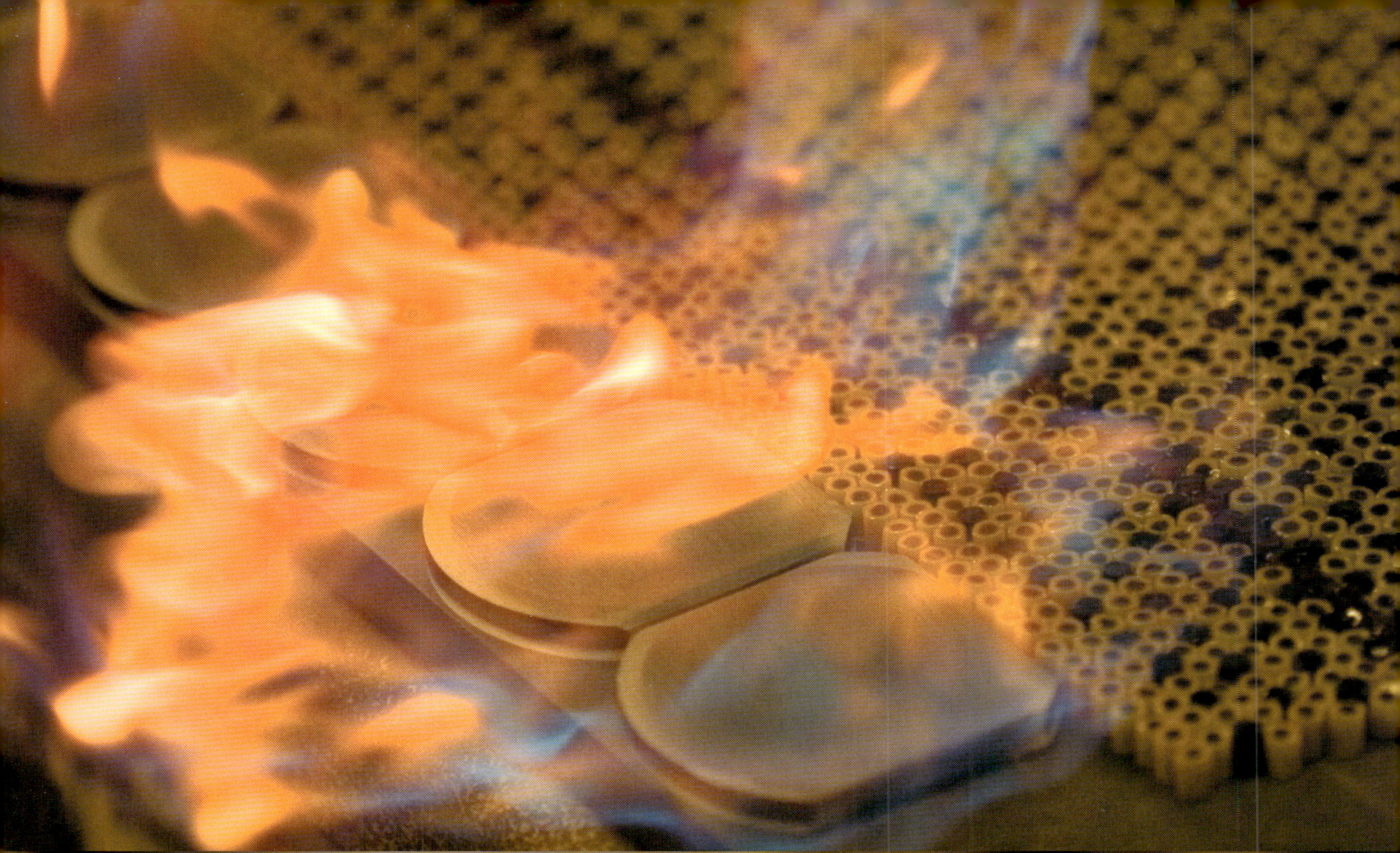

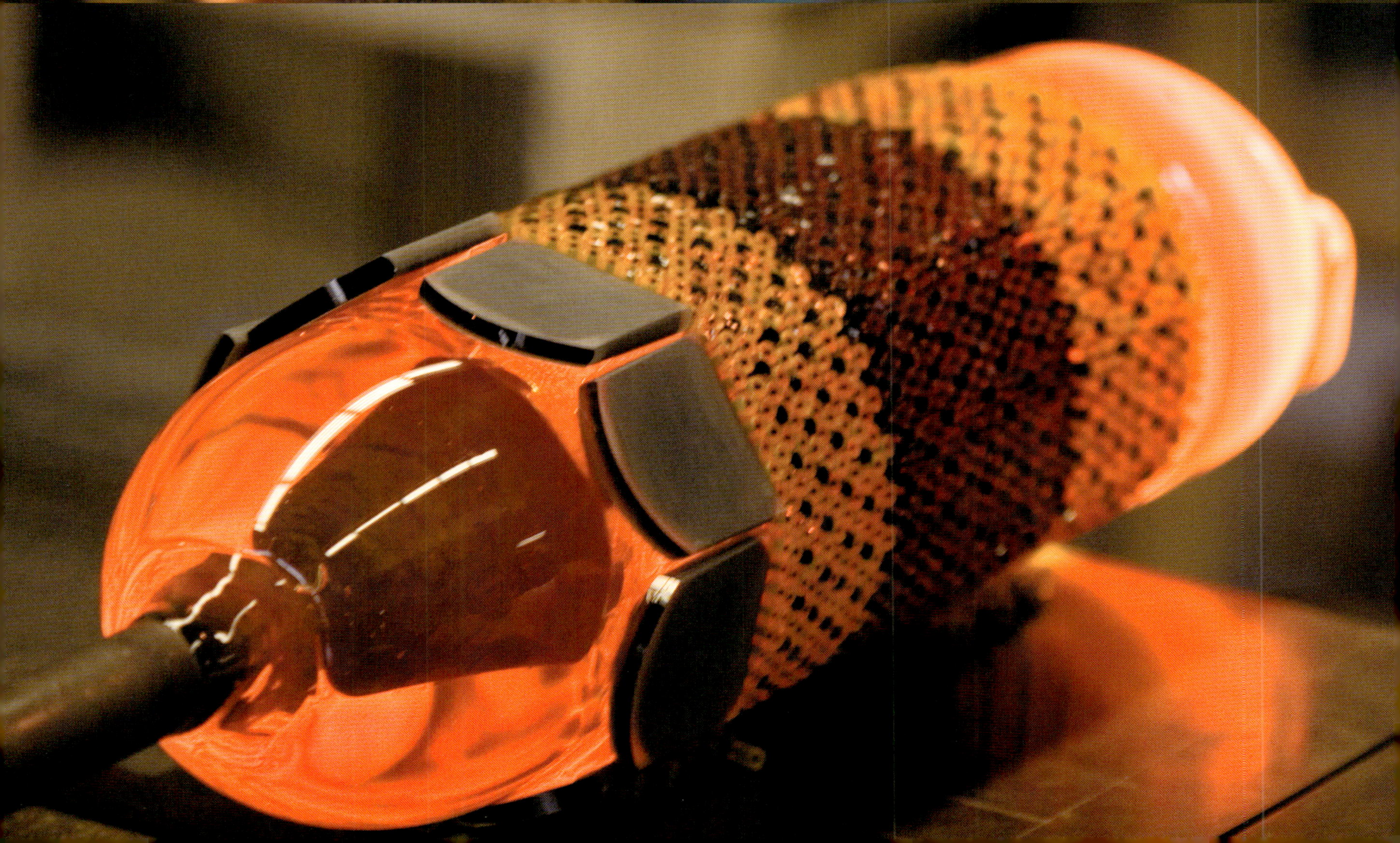

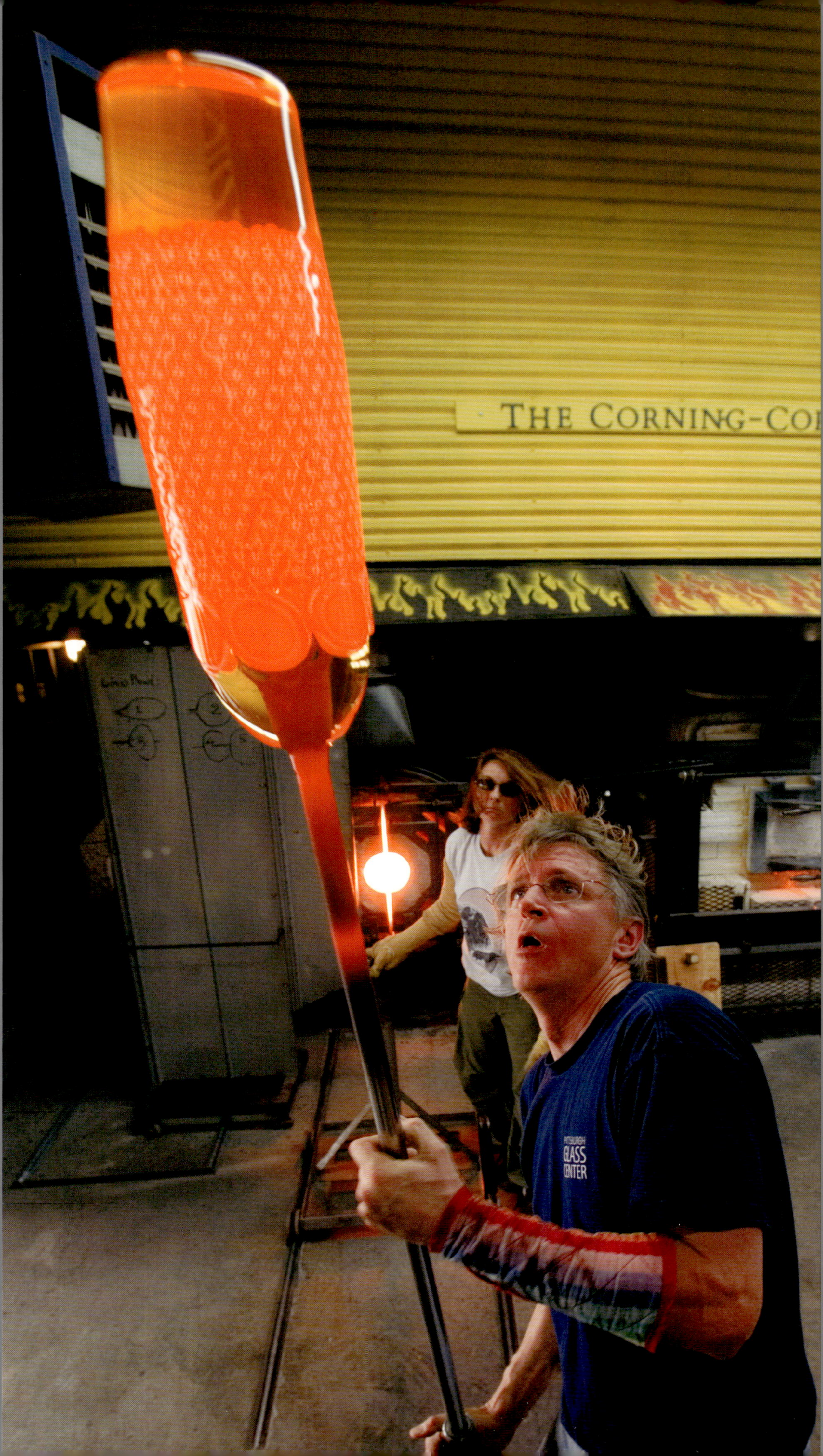
THE CORNING-CO

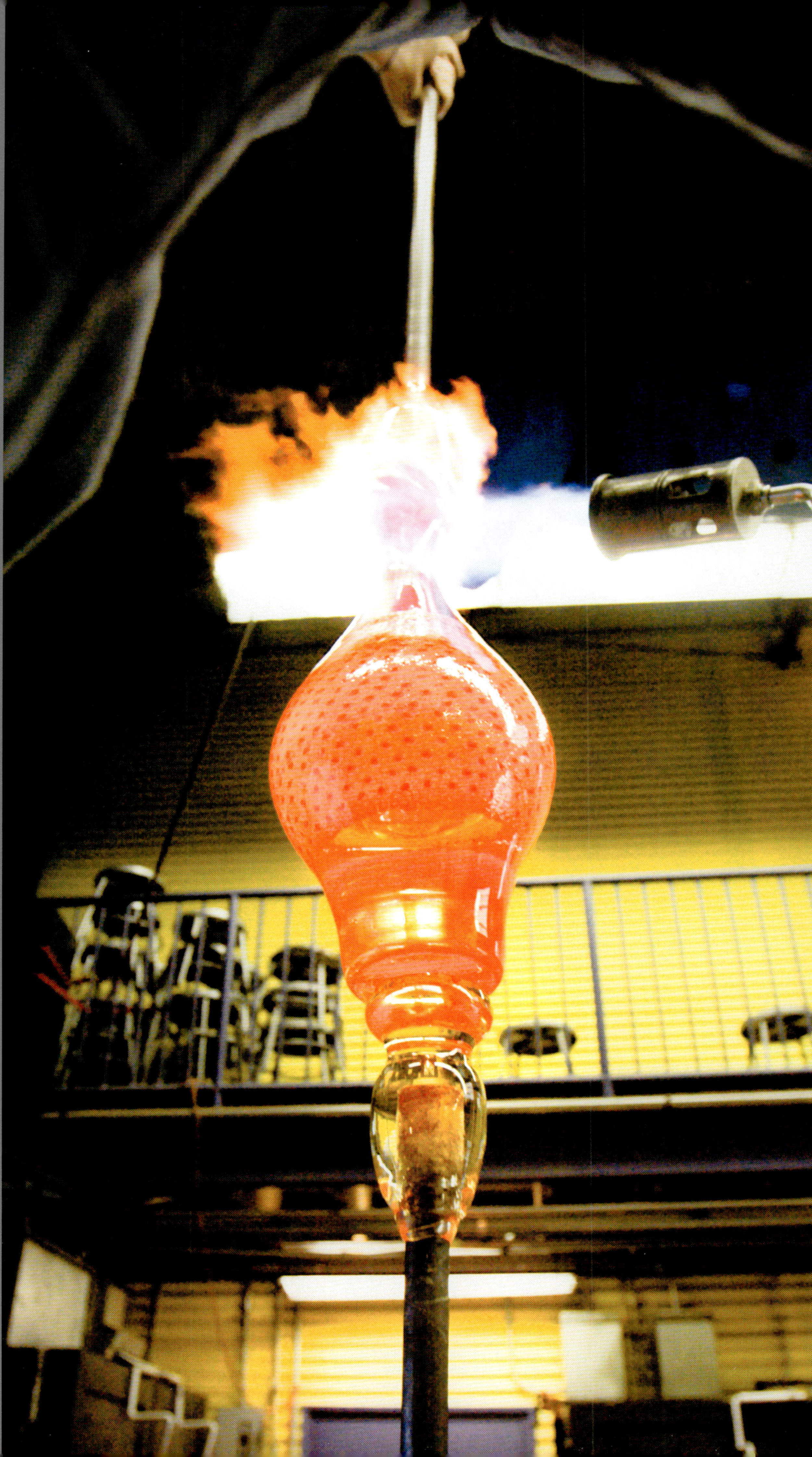

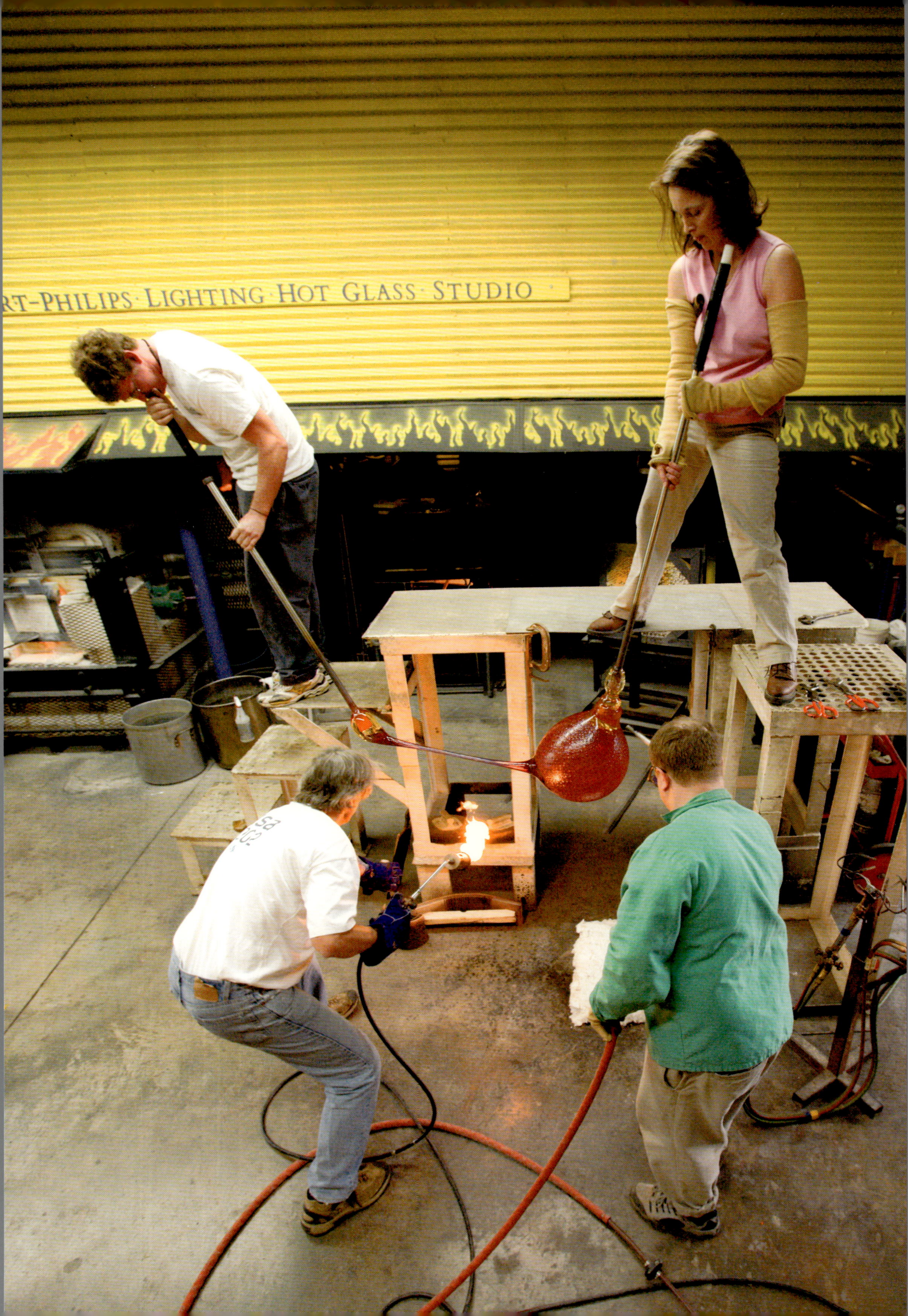
RT-PHILIPS LIGHTING HOT GLASS STUDIO

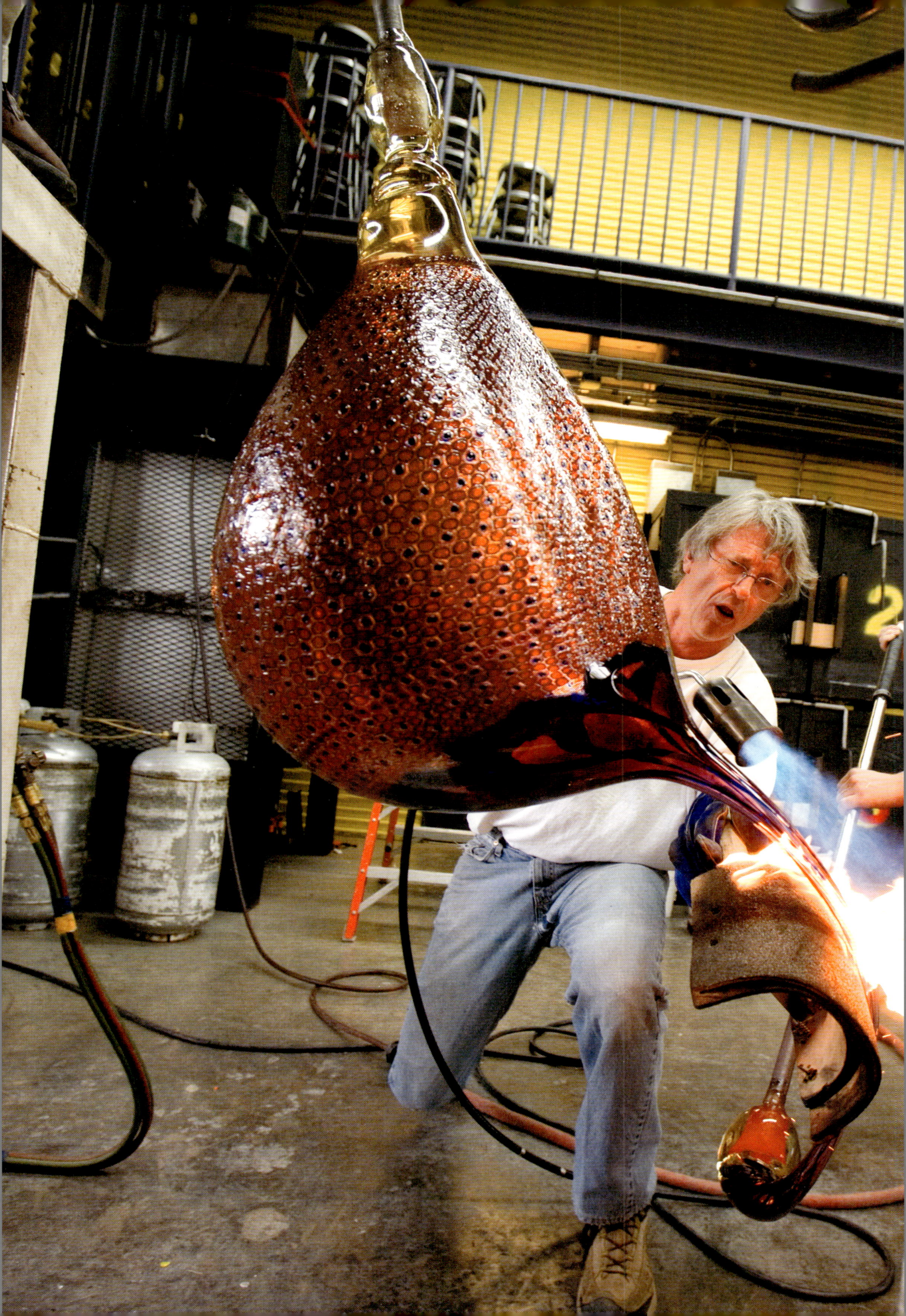

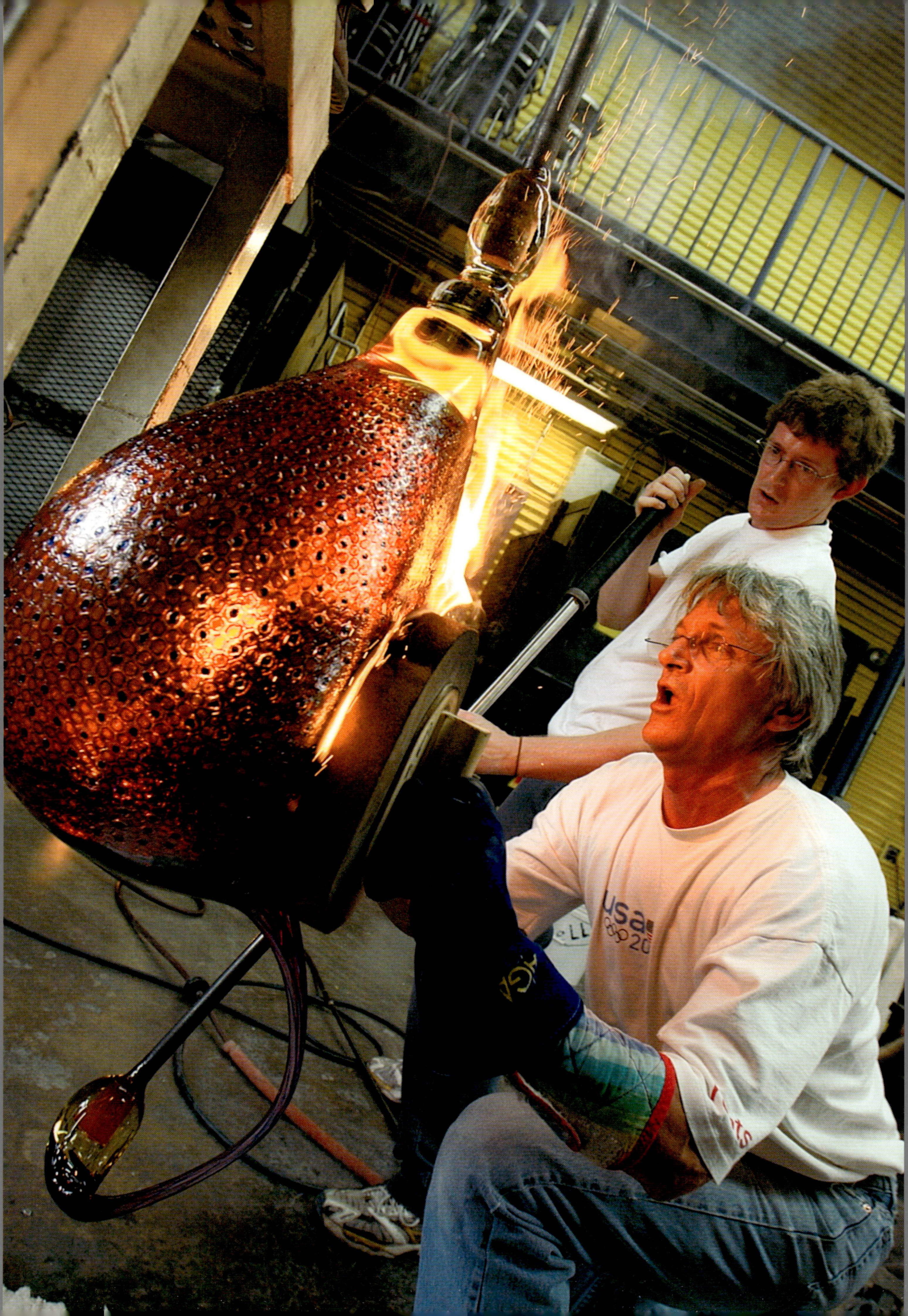
usa

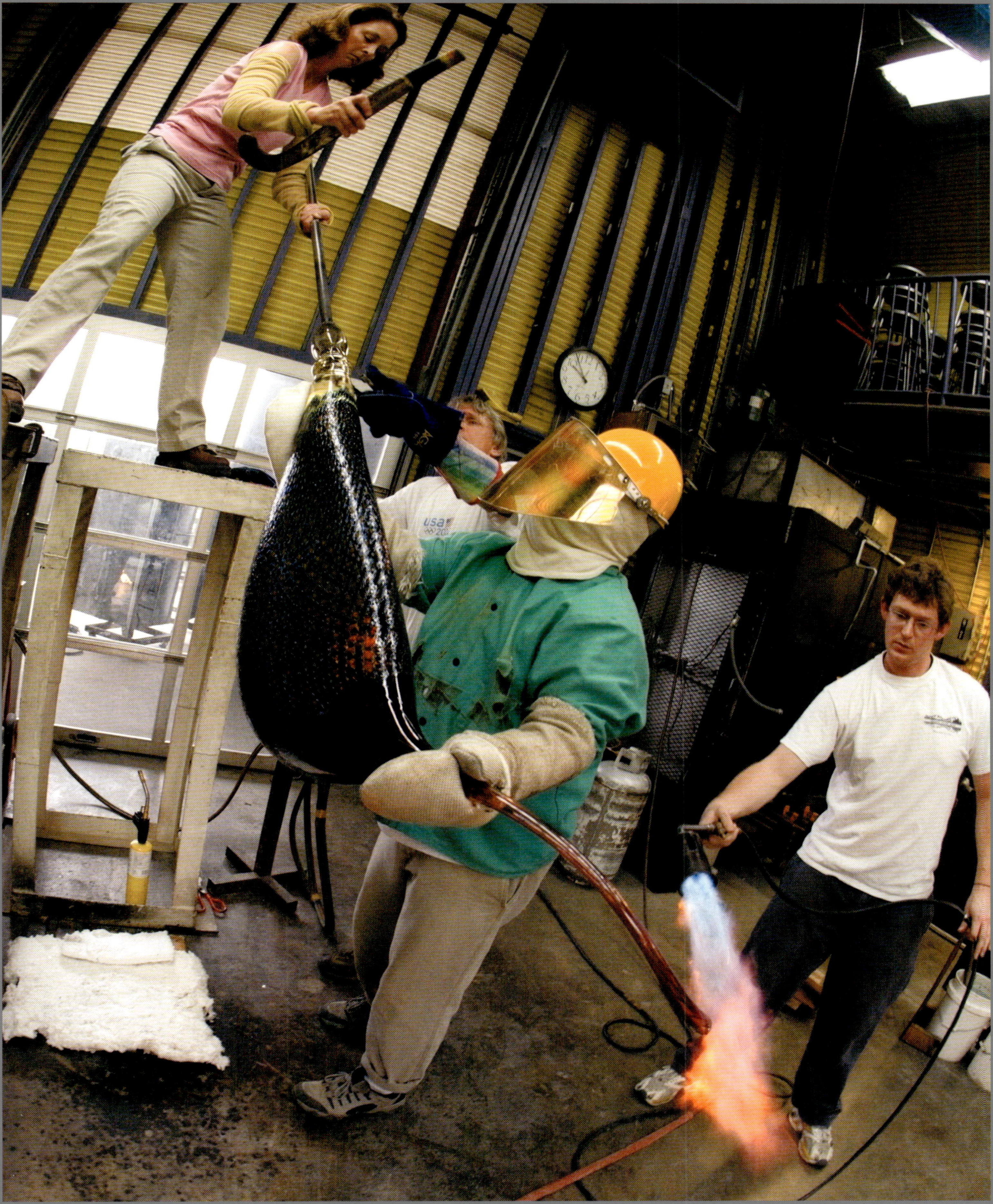

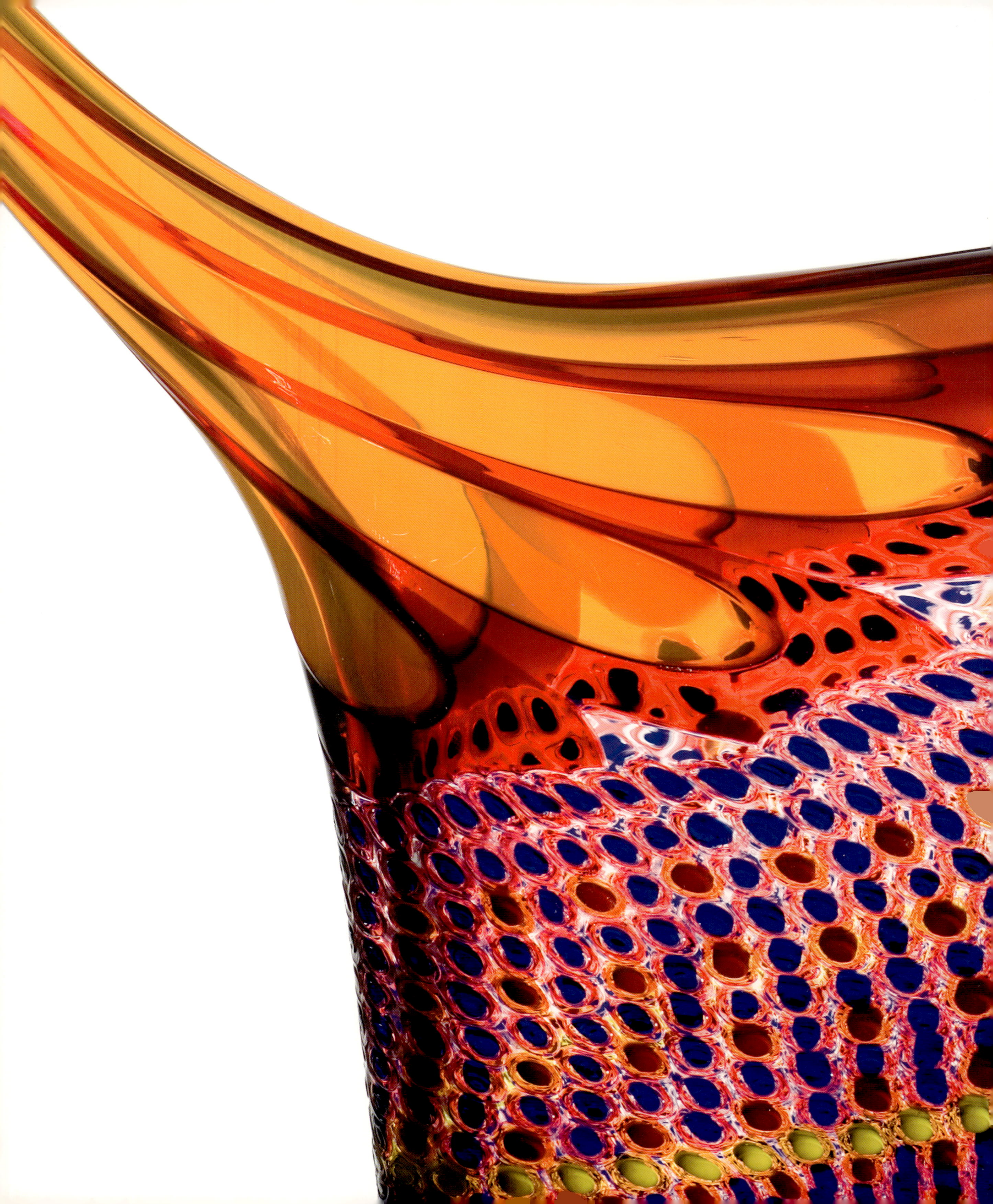

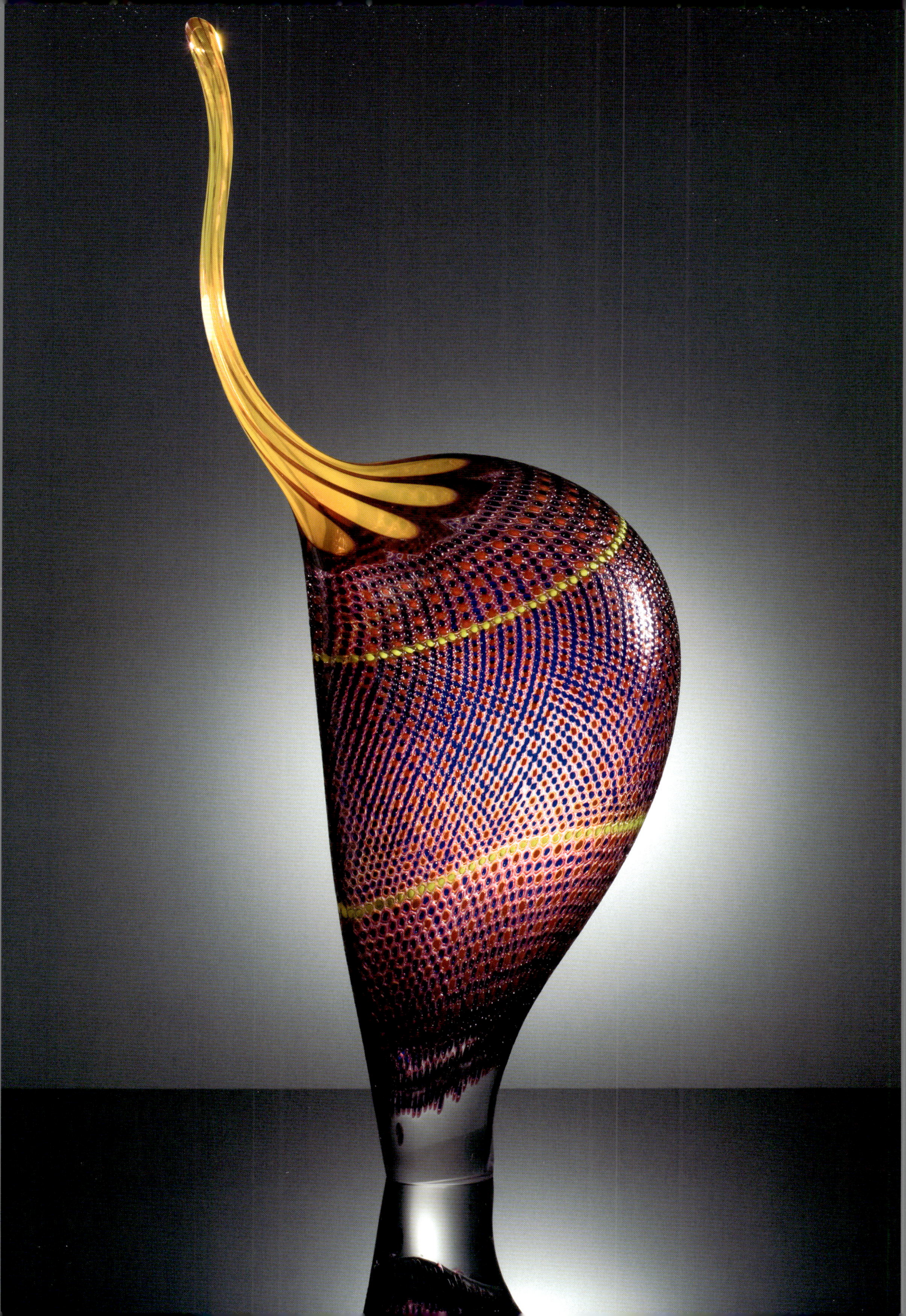

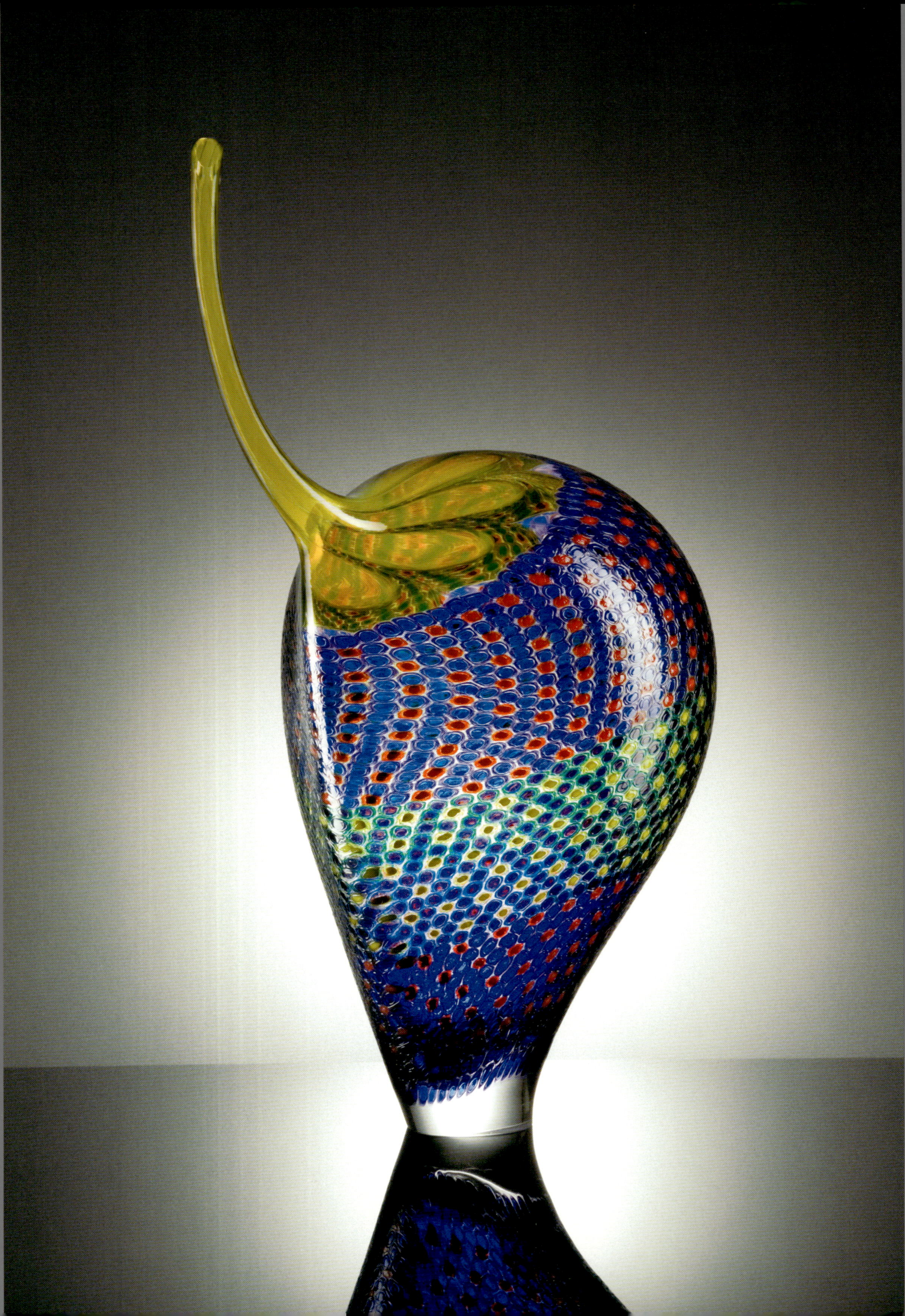

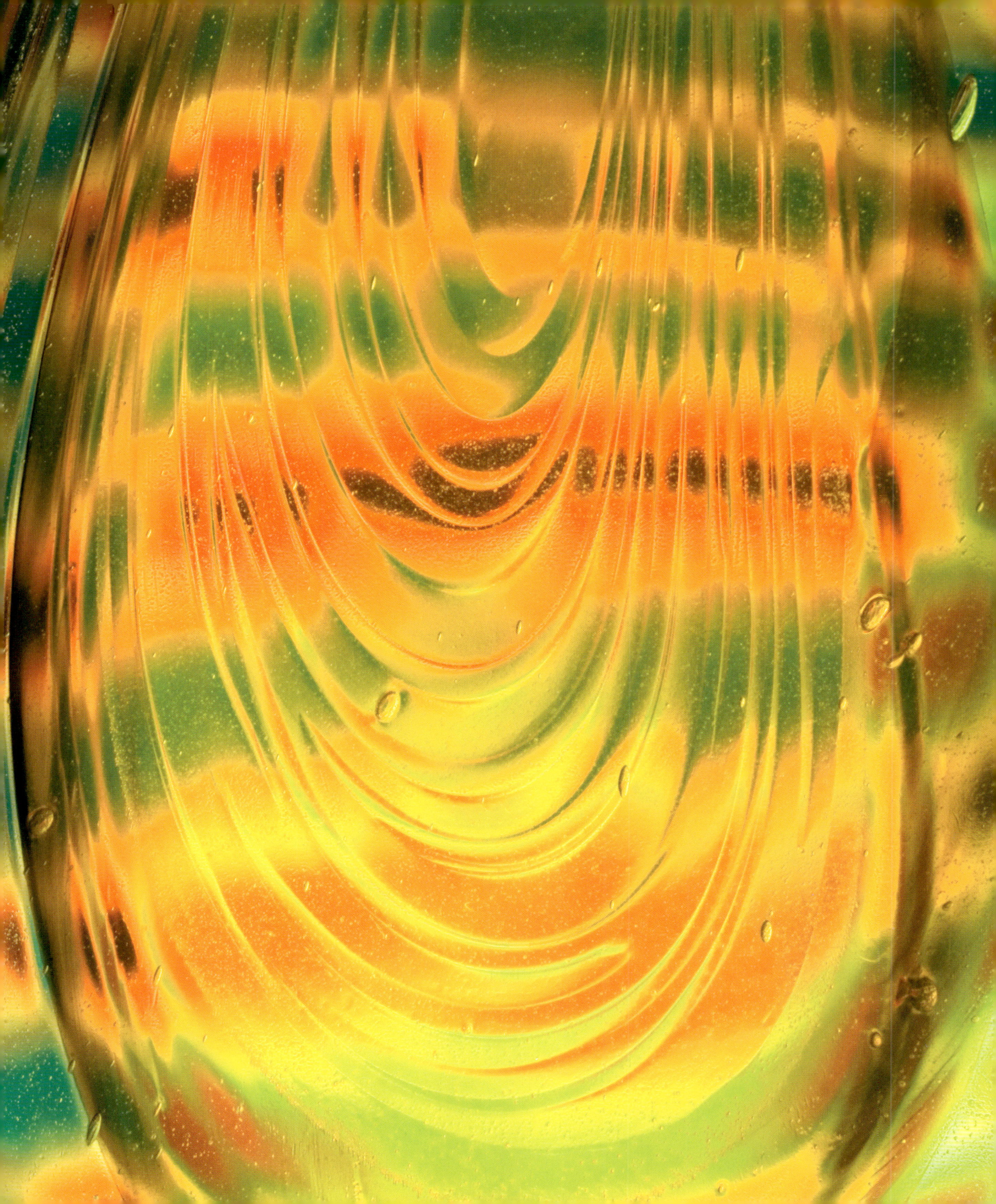

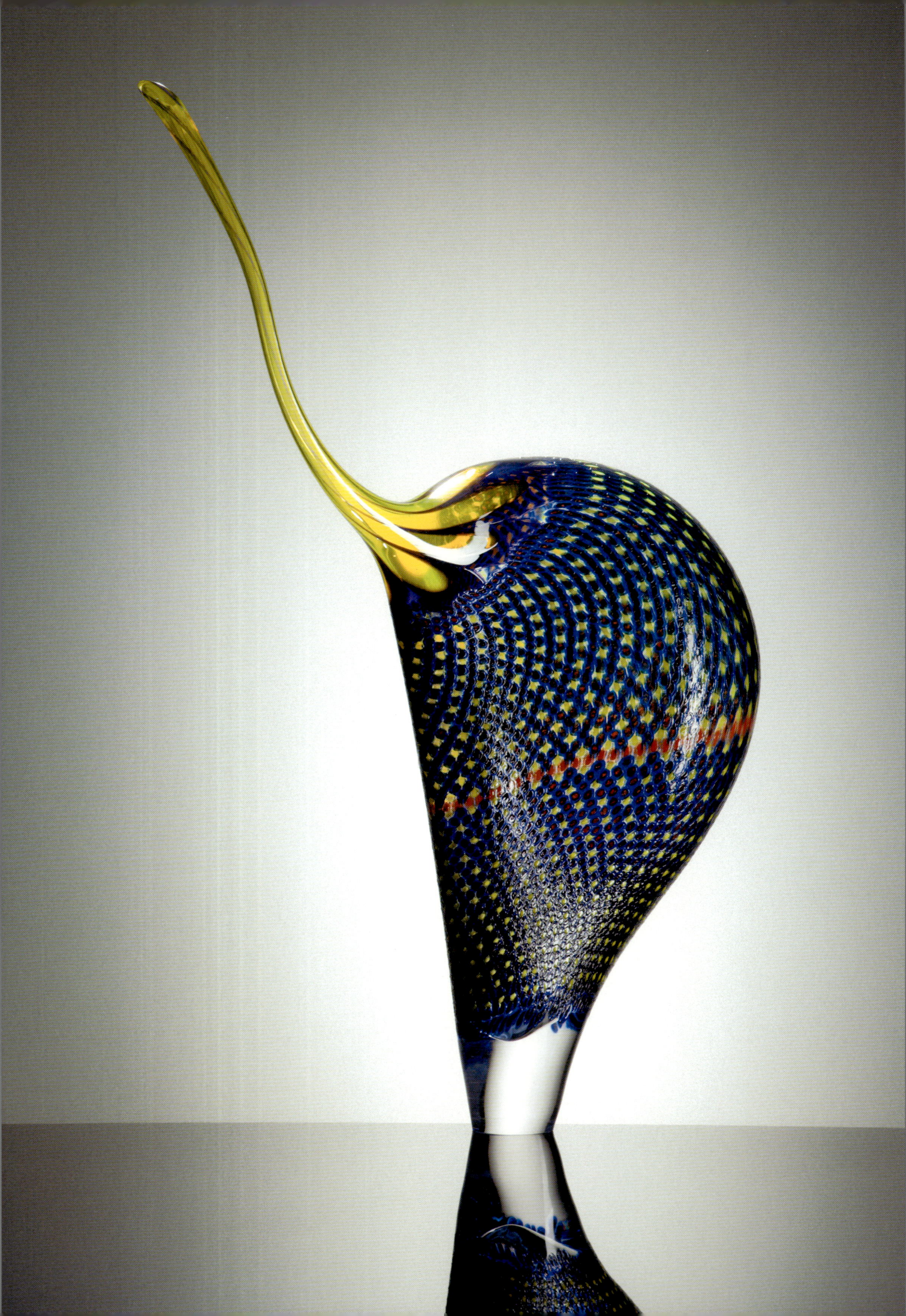

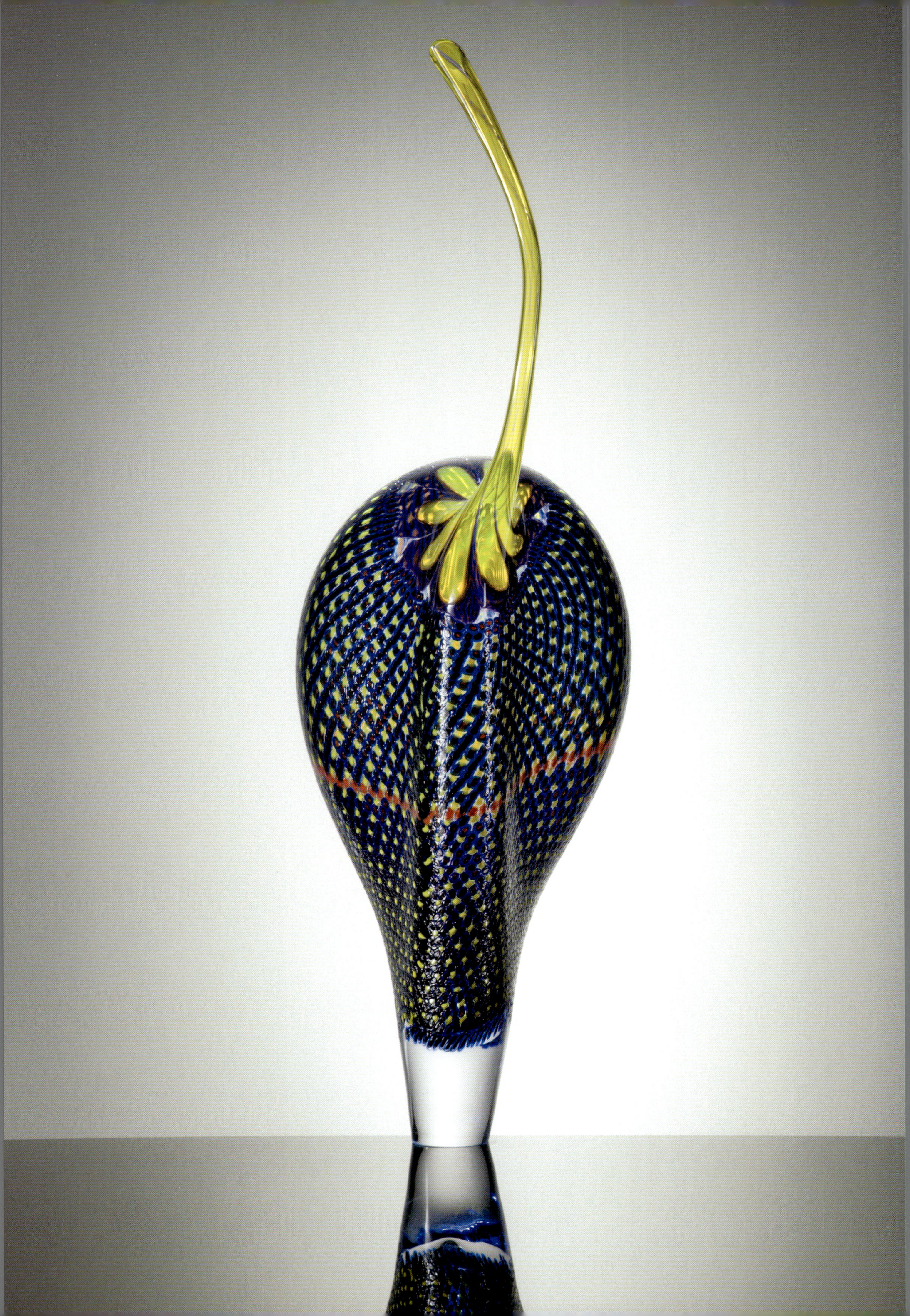

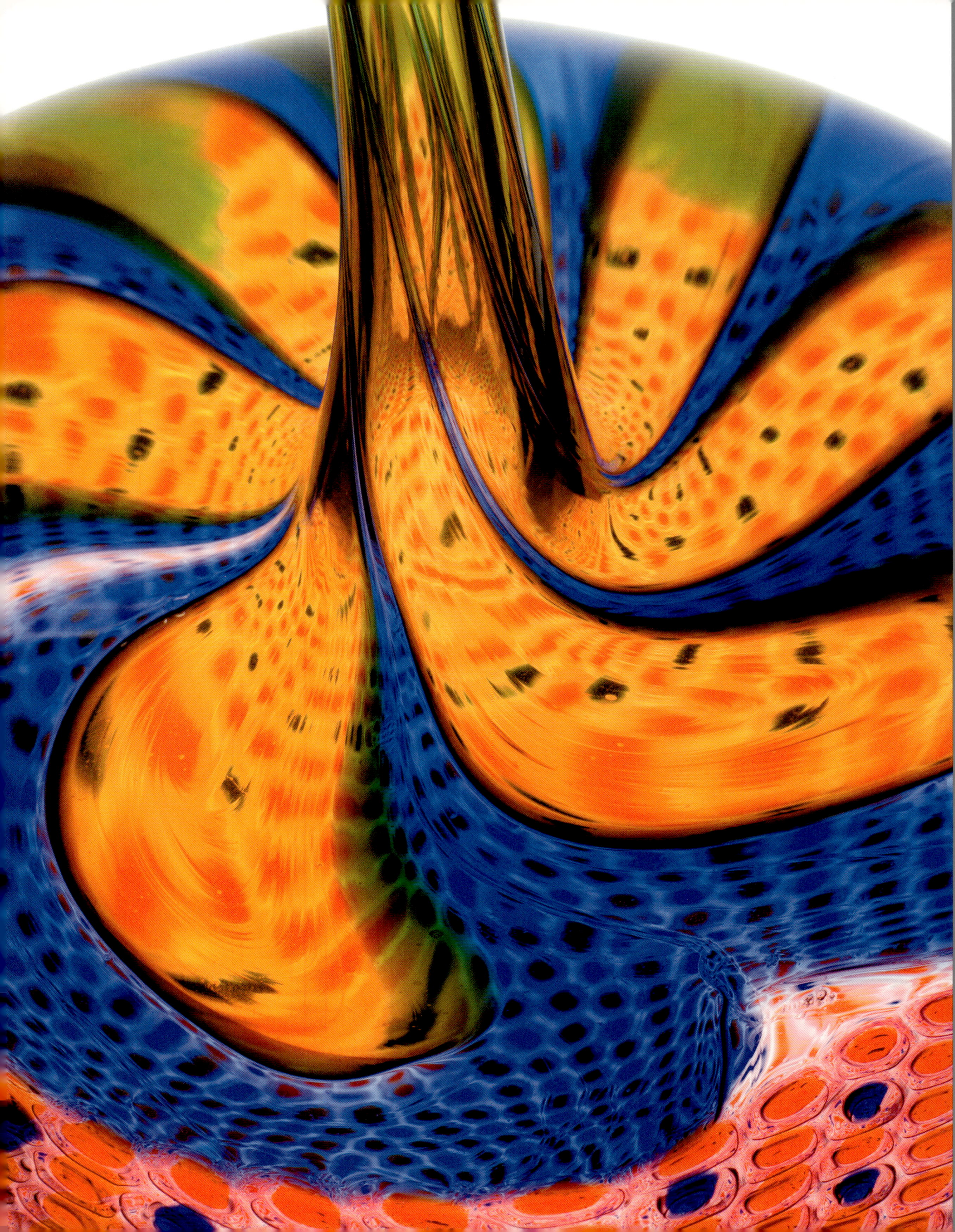

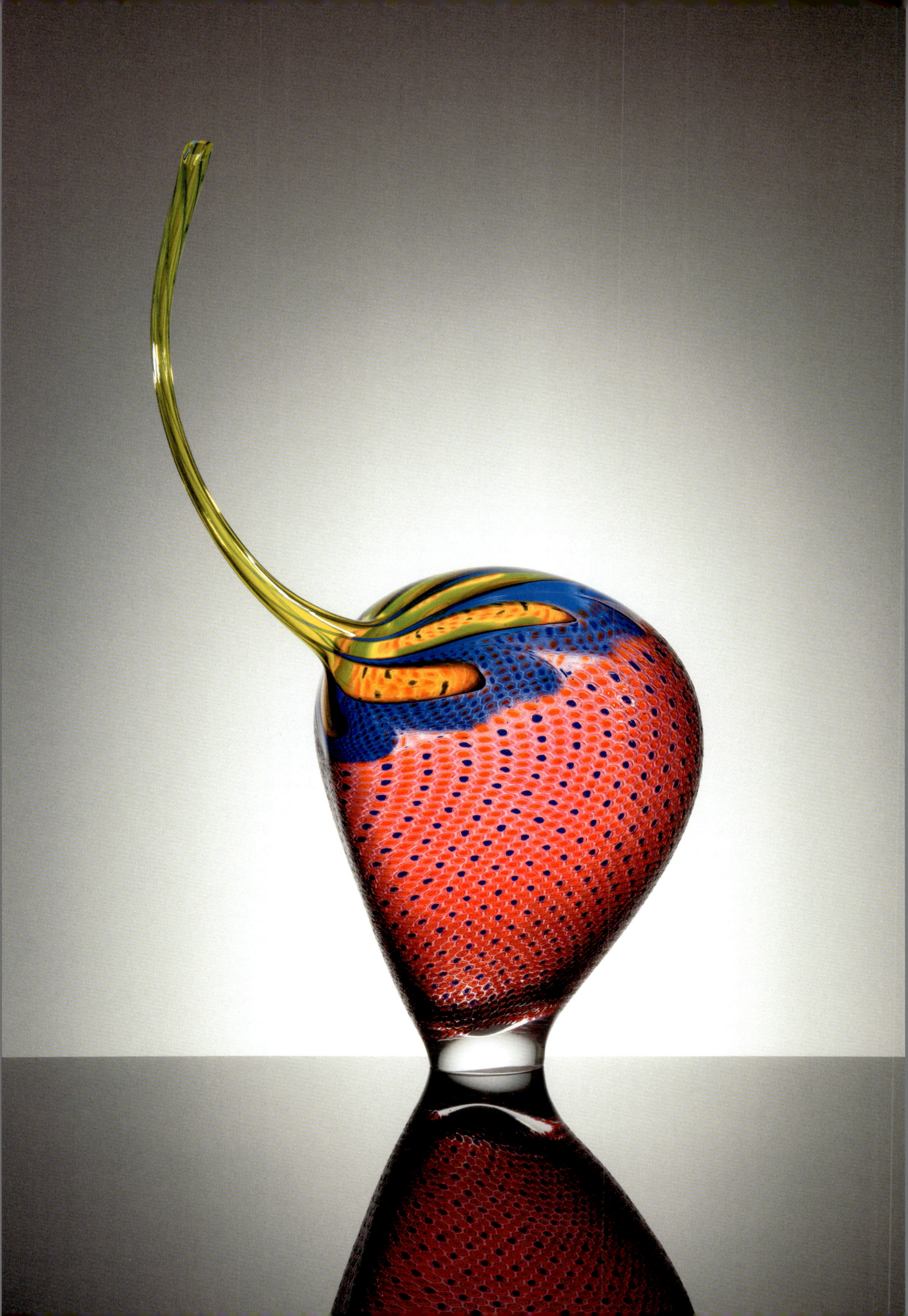

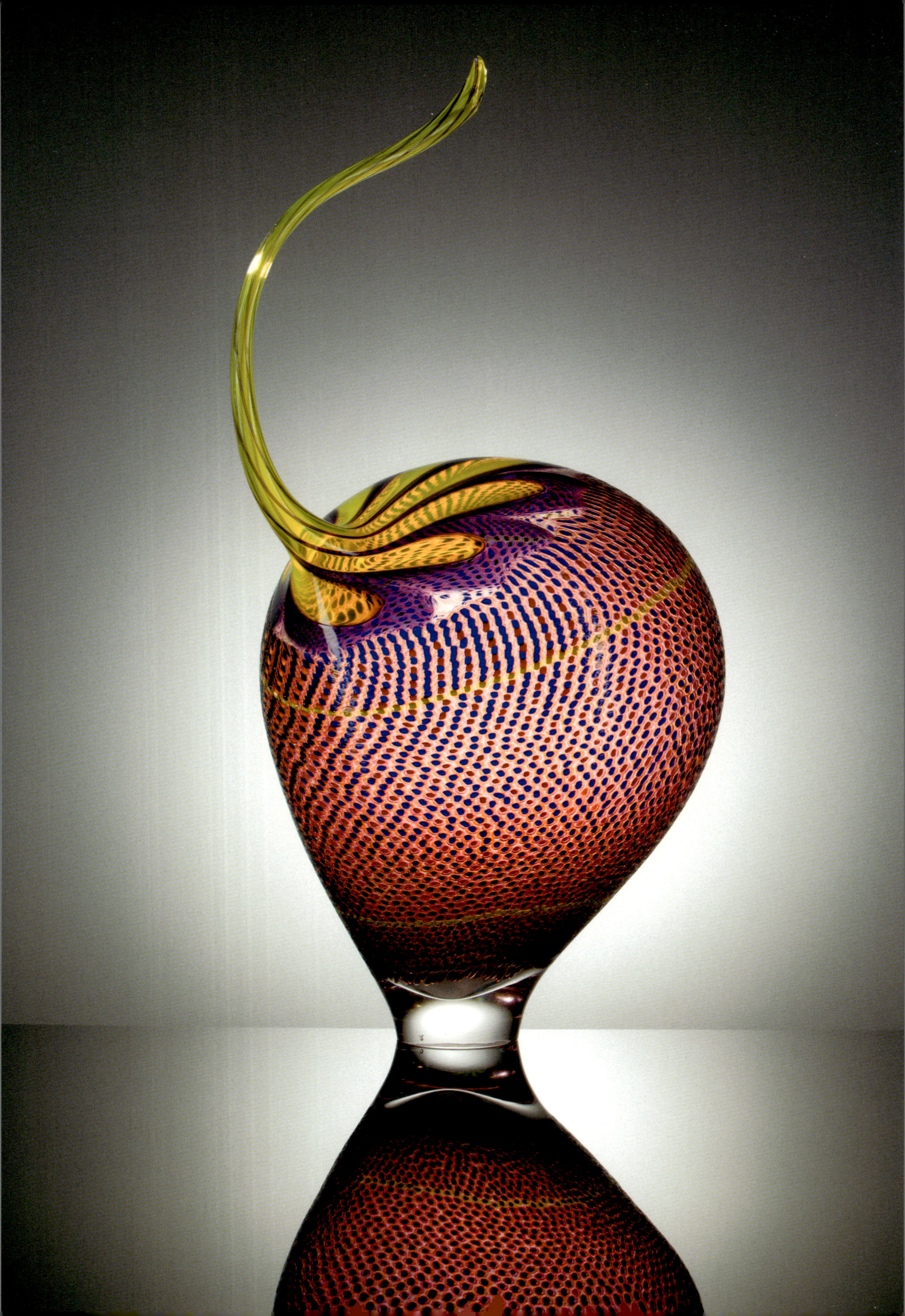

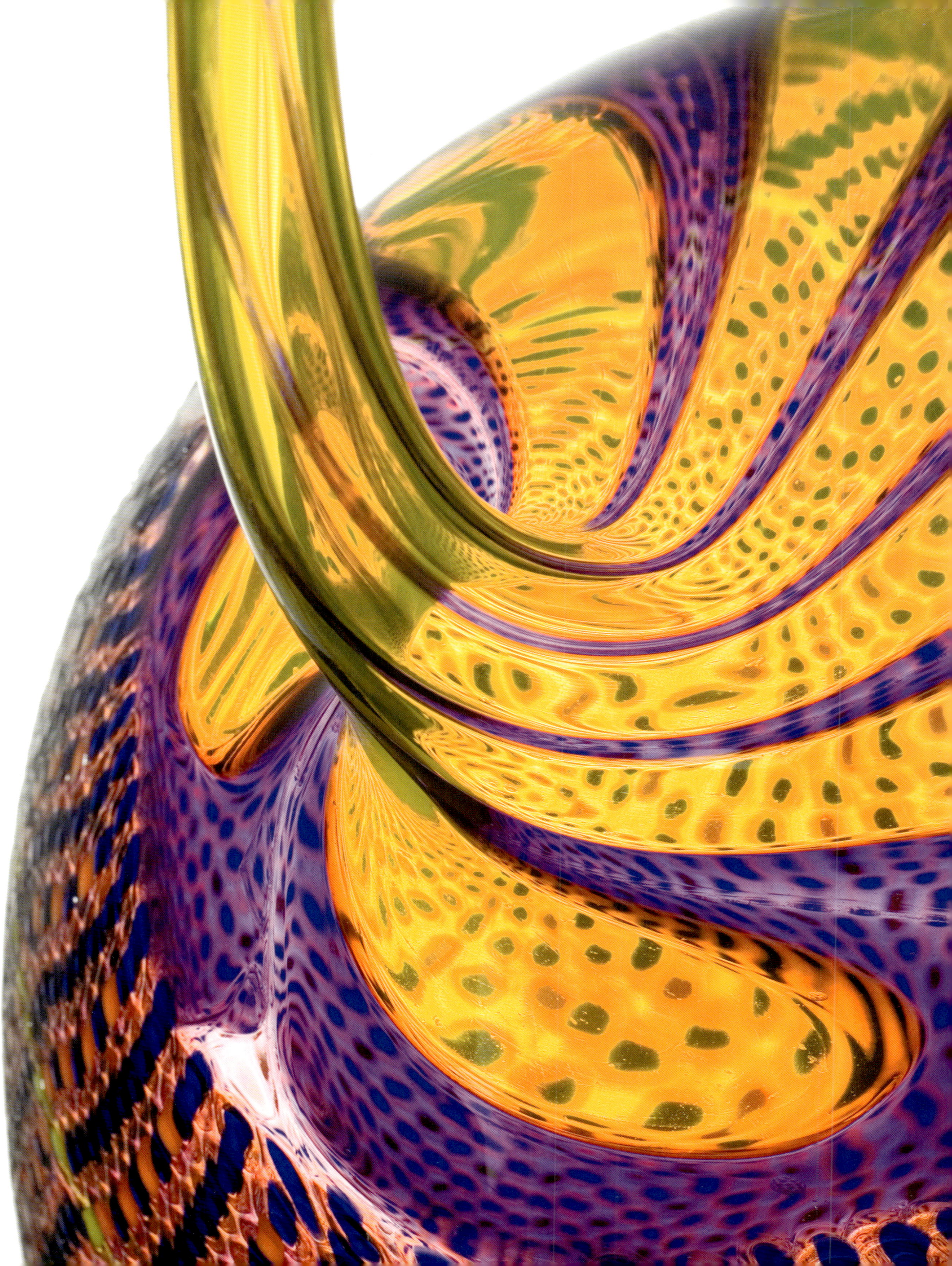

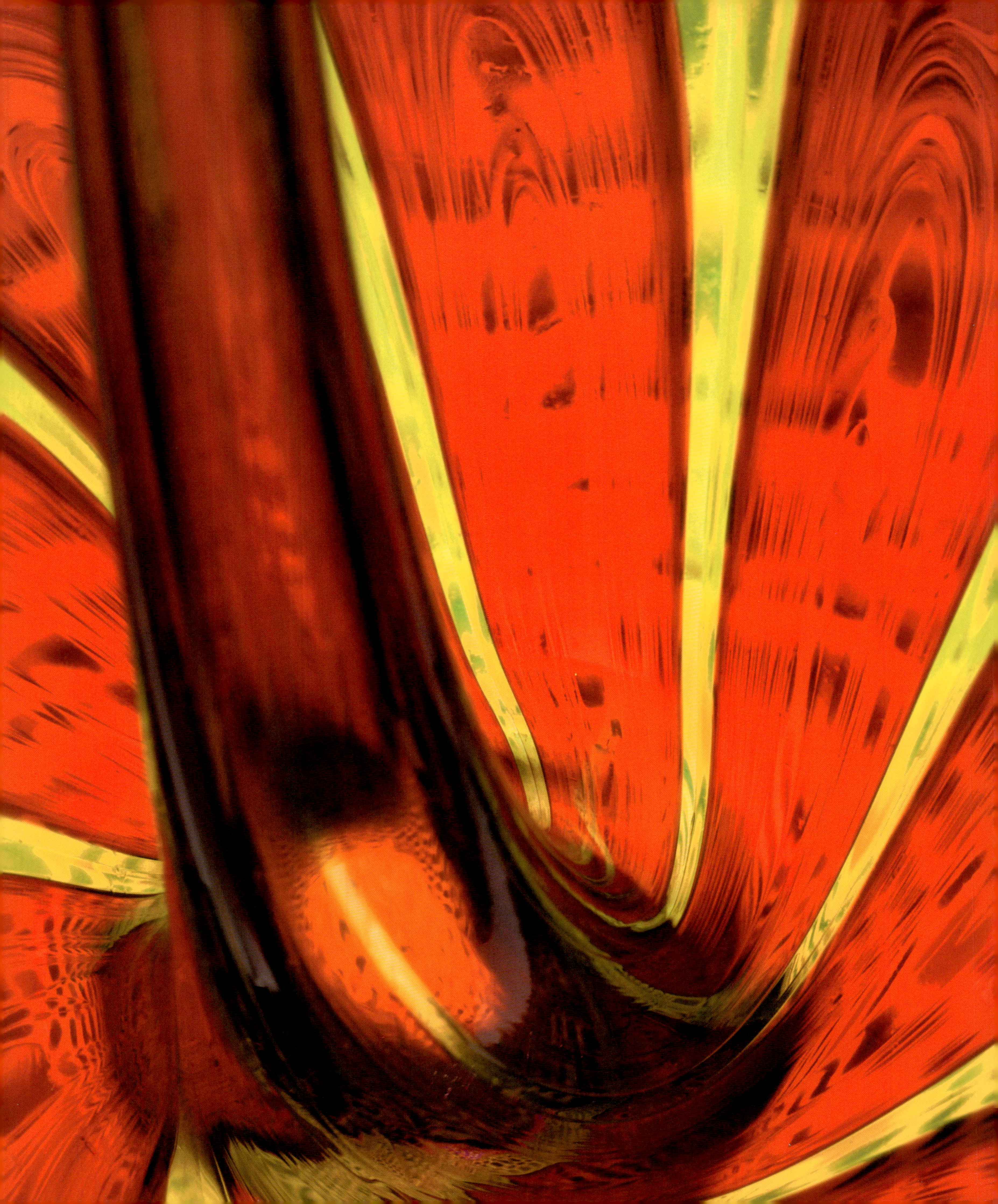

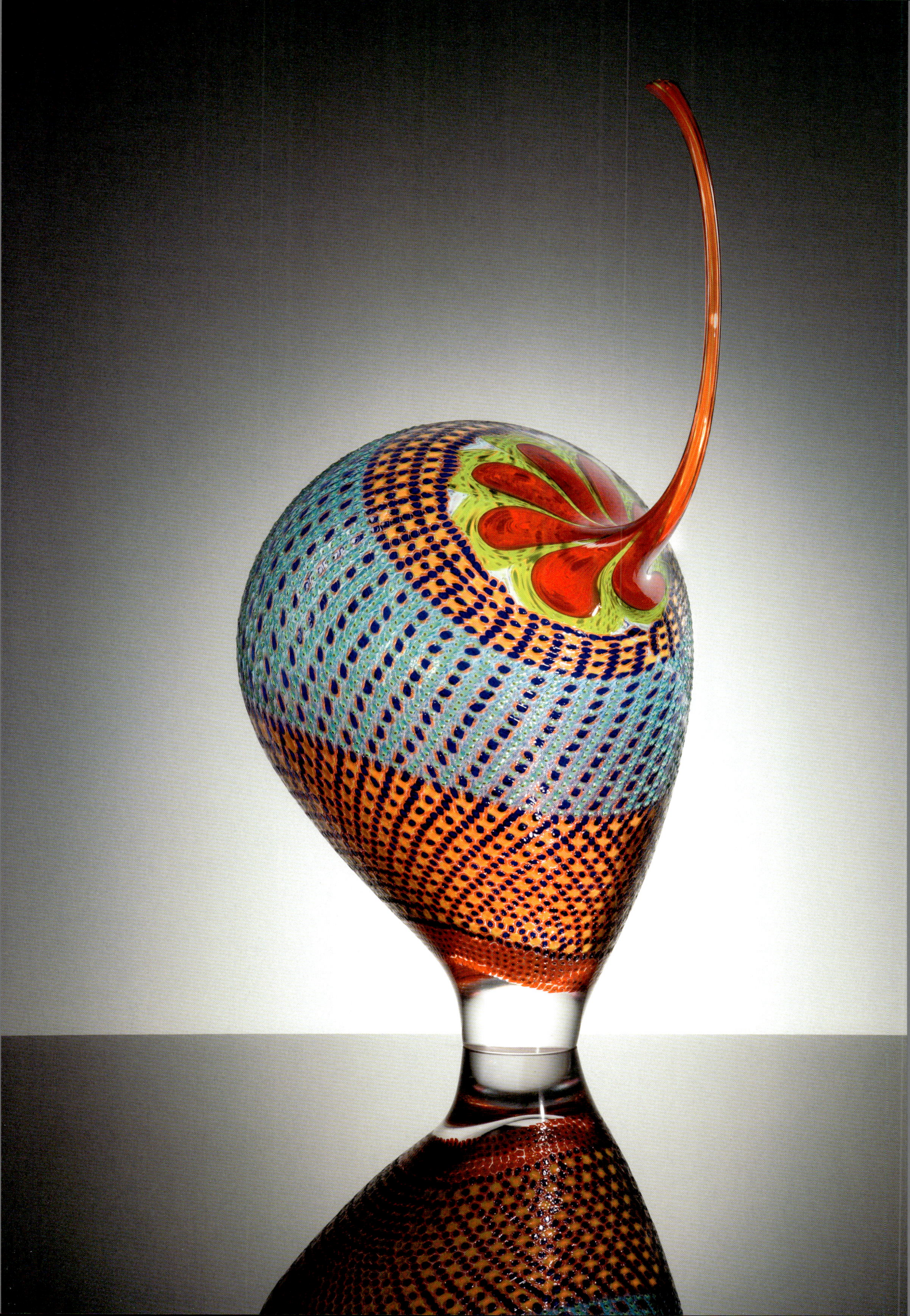

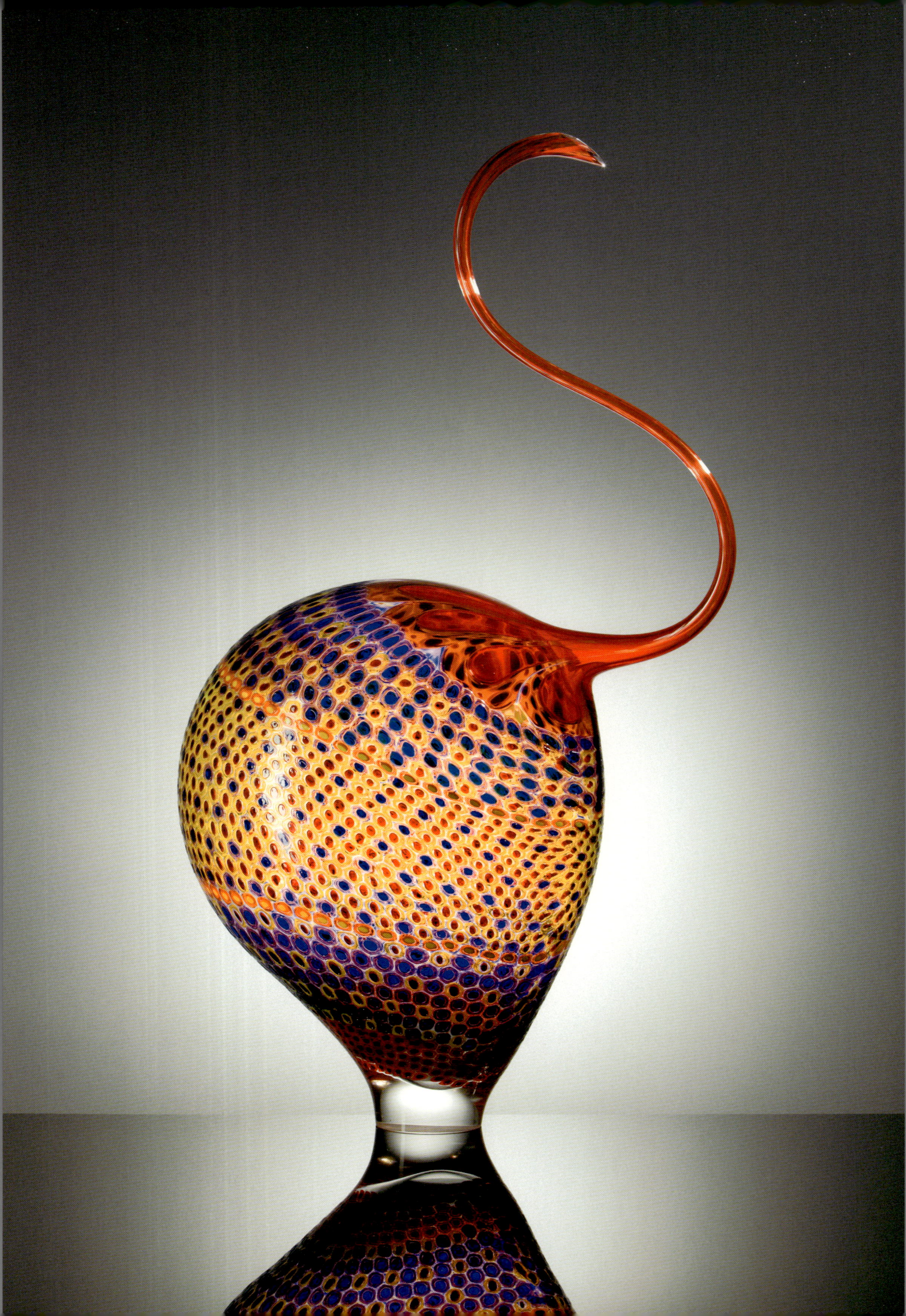

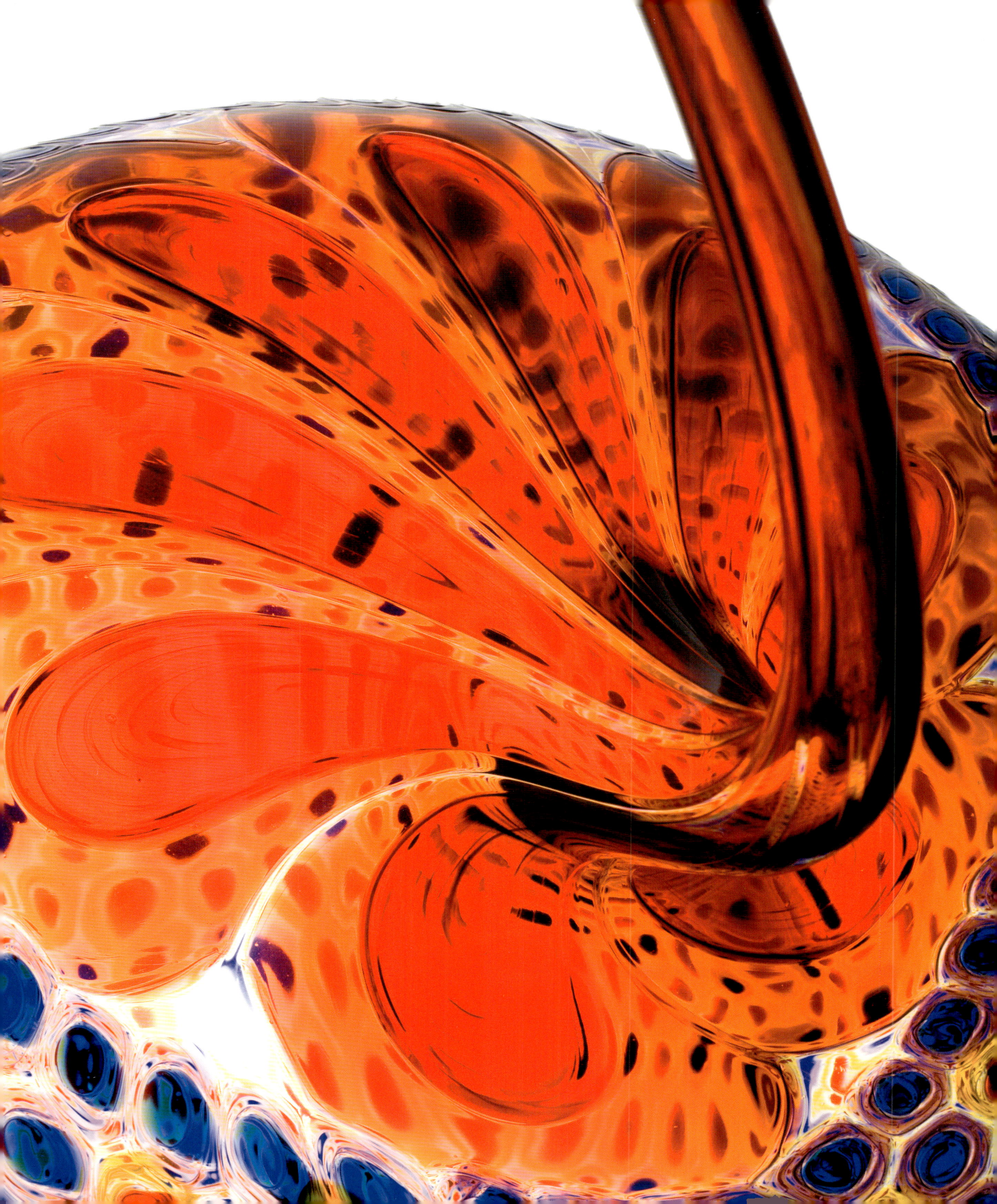

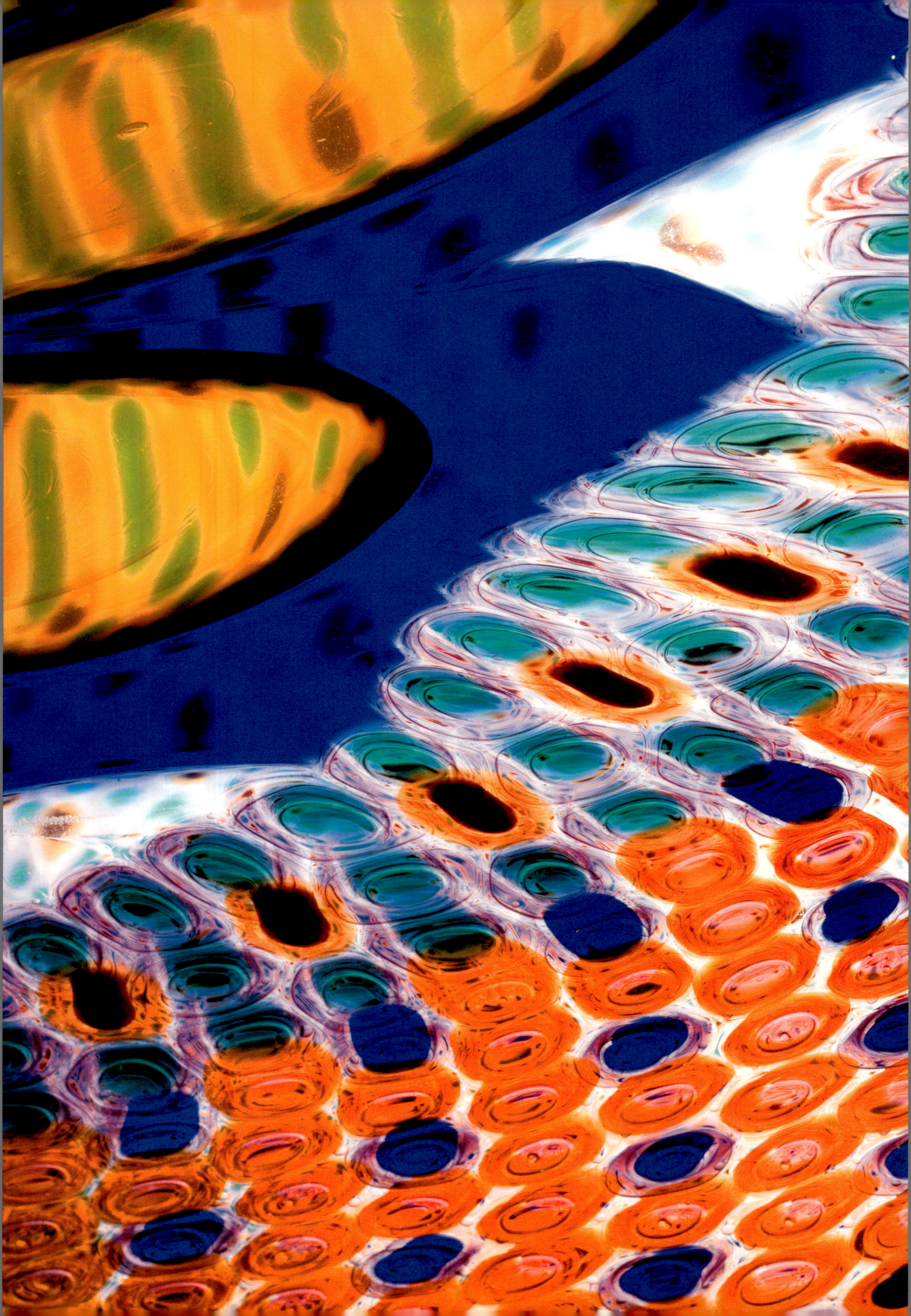

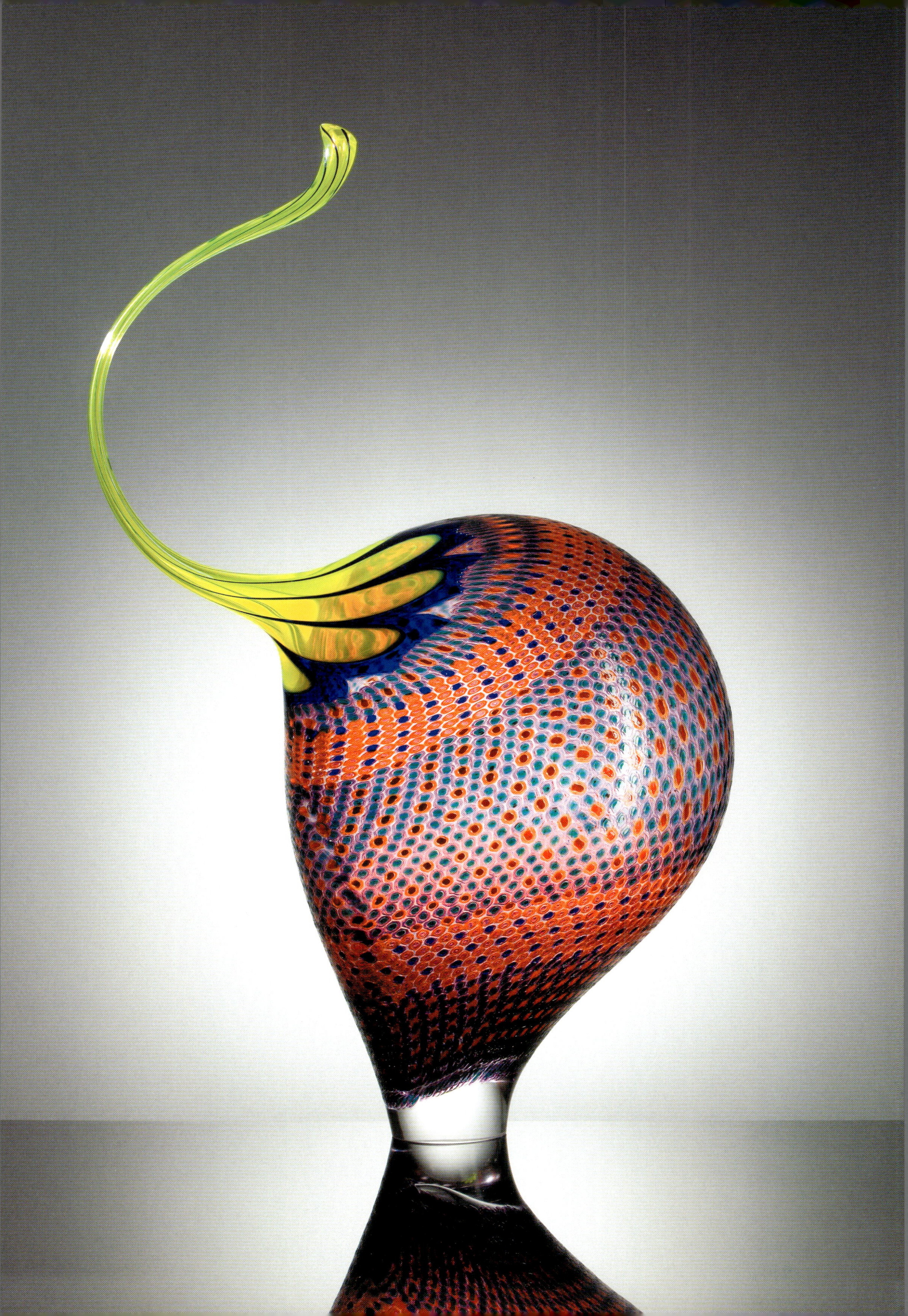

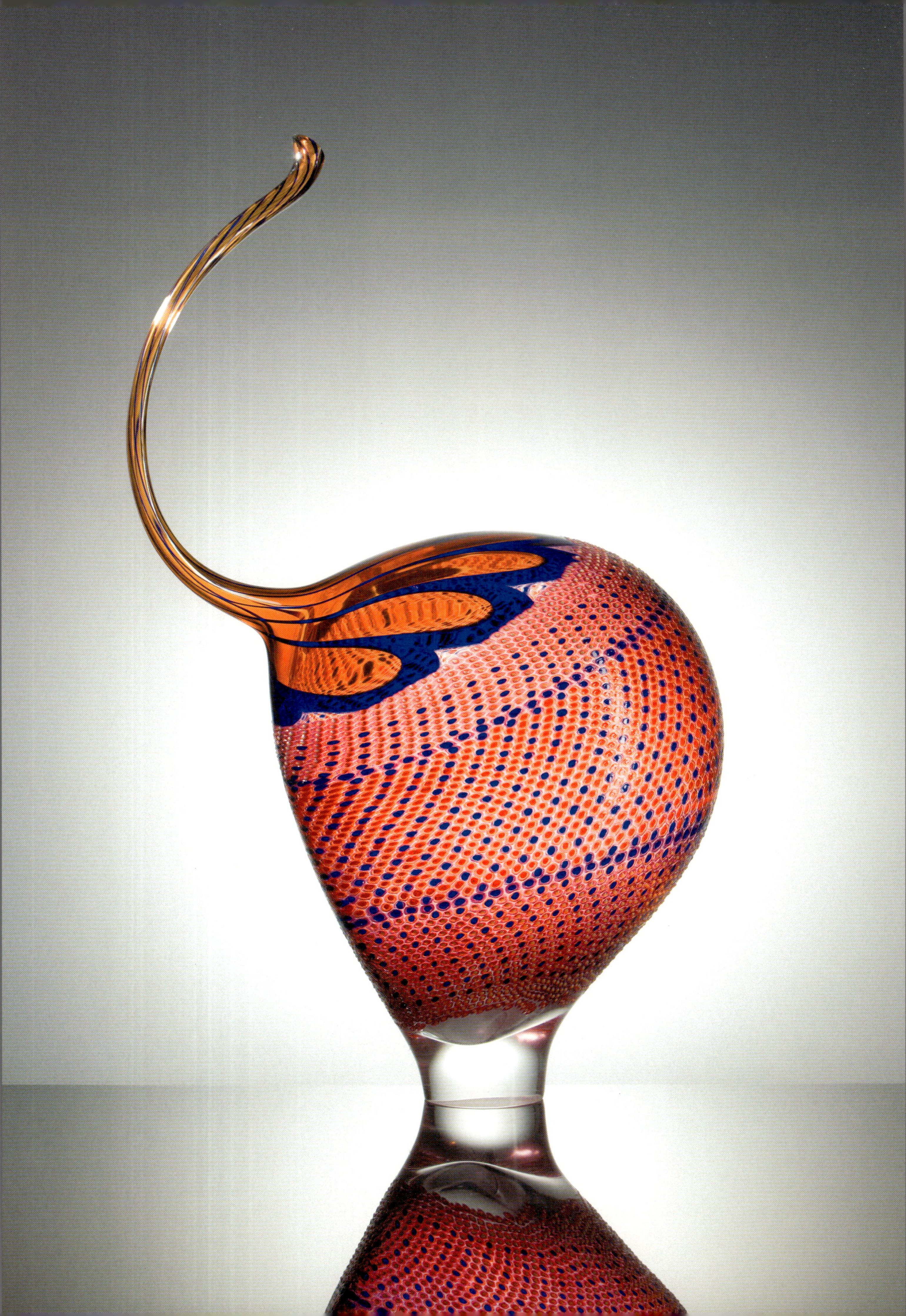

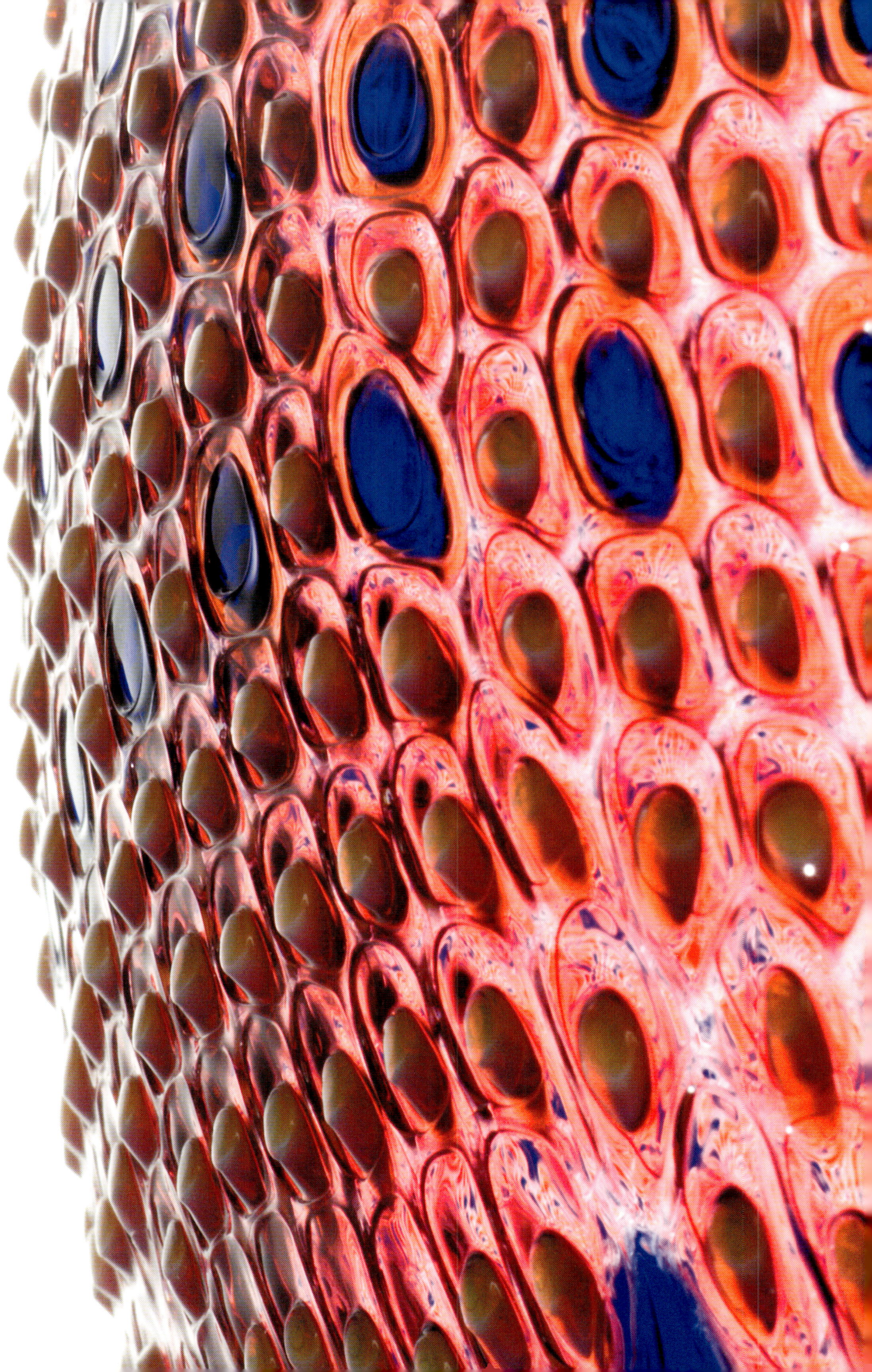

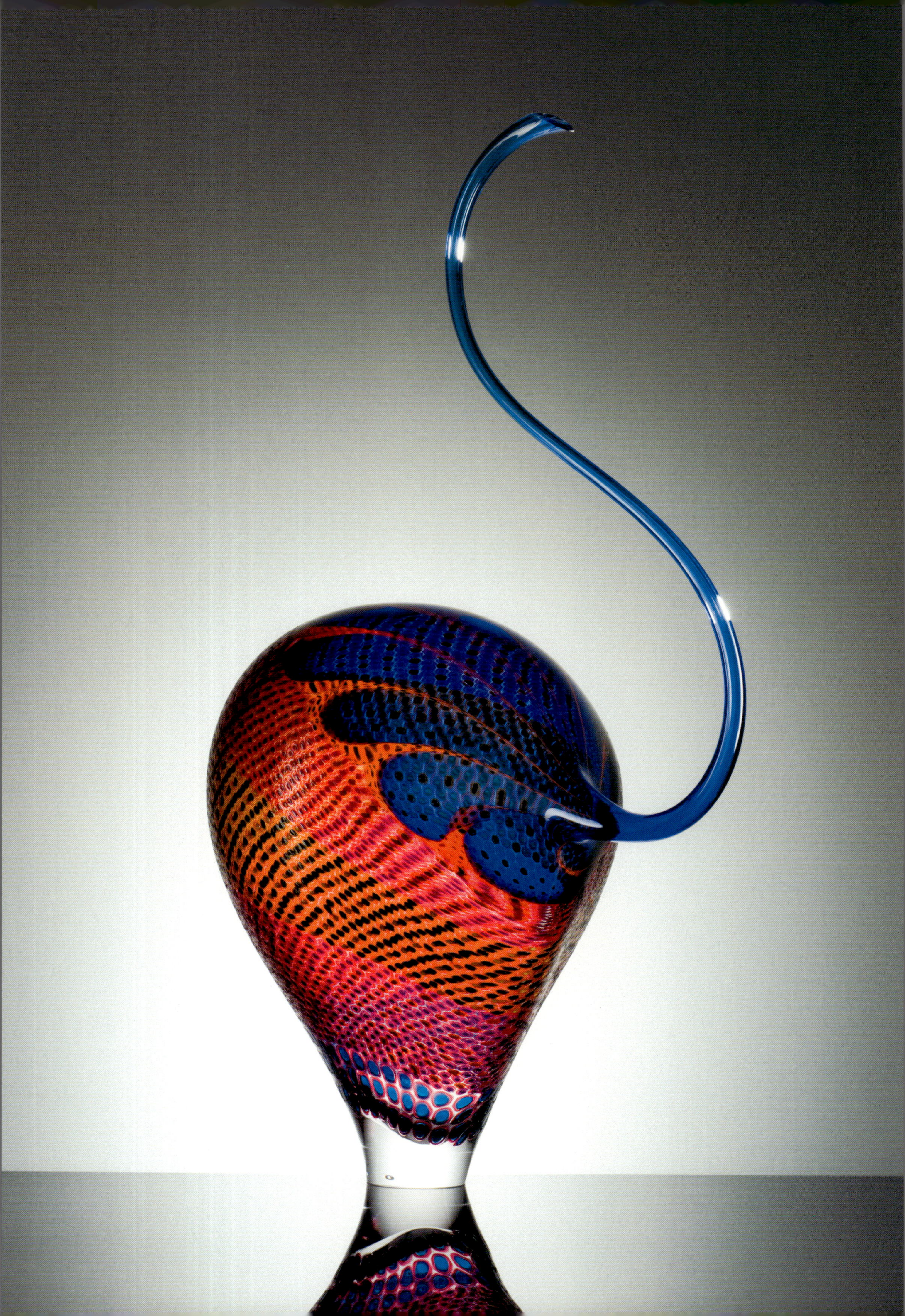

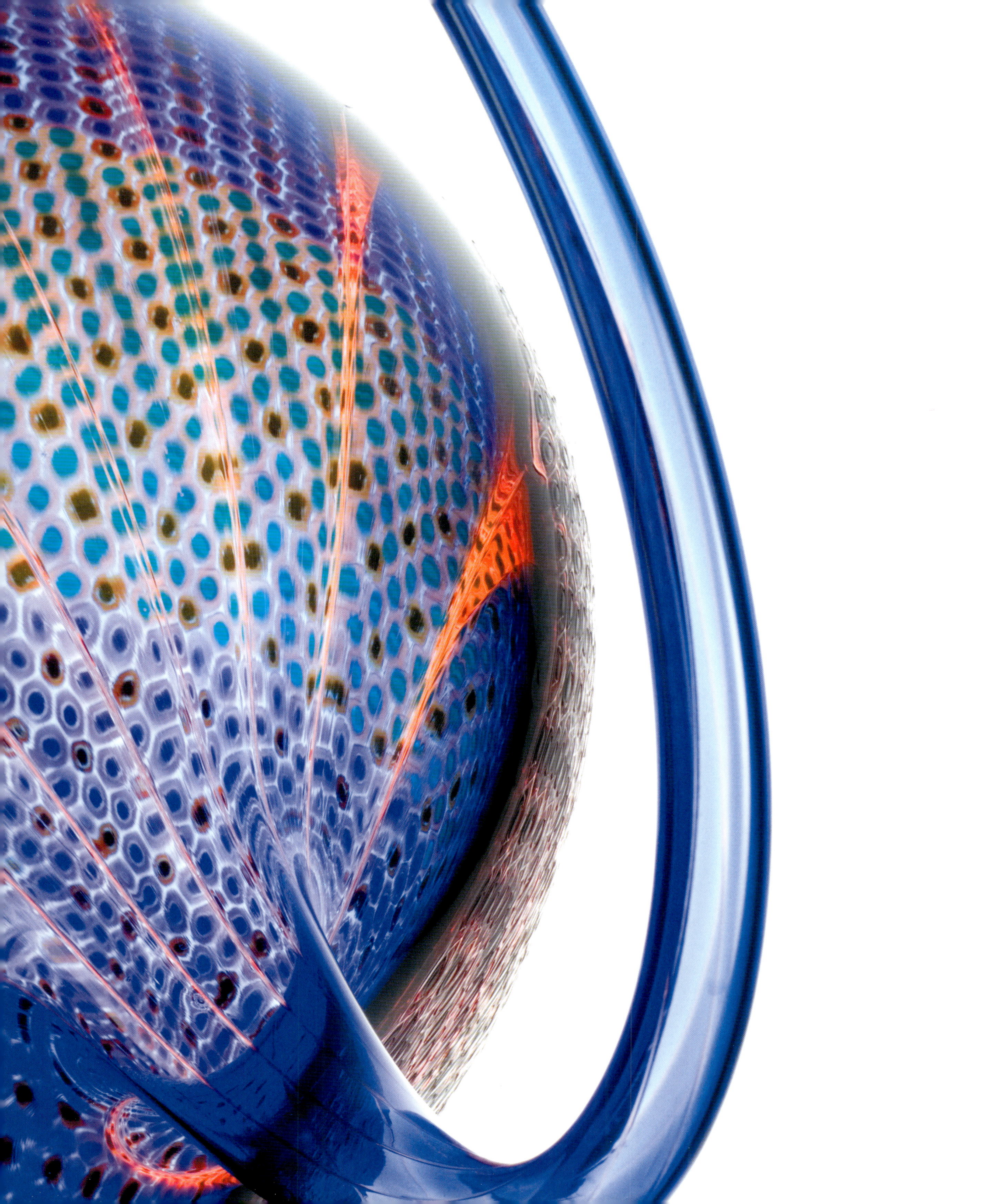

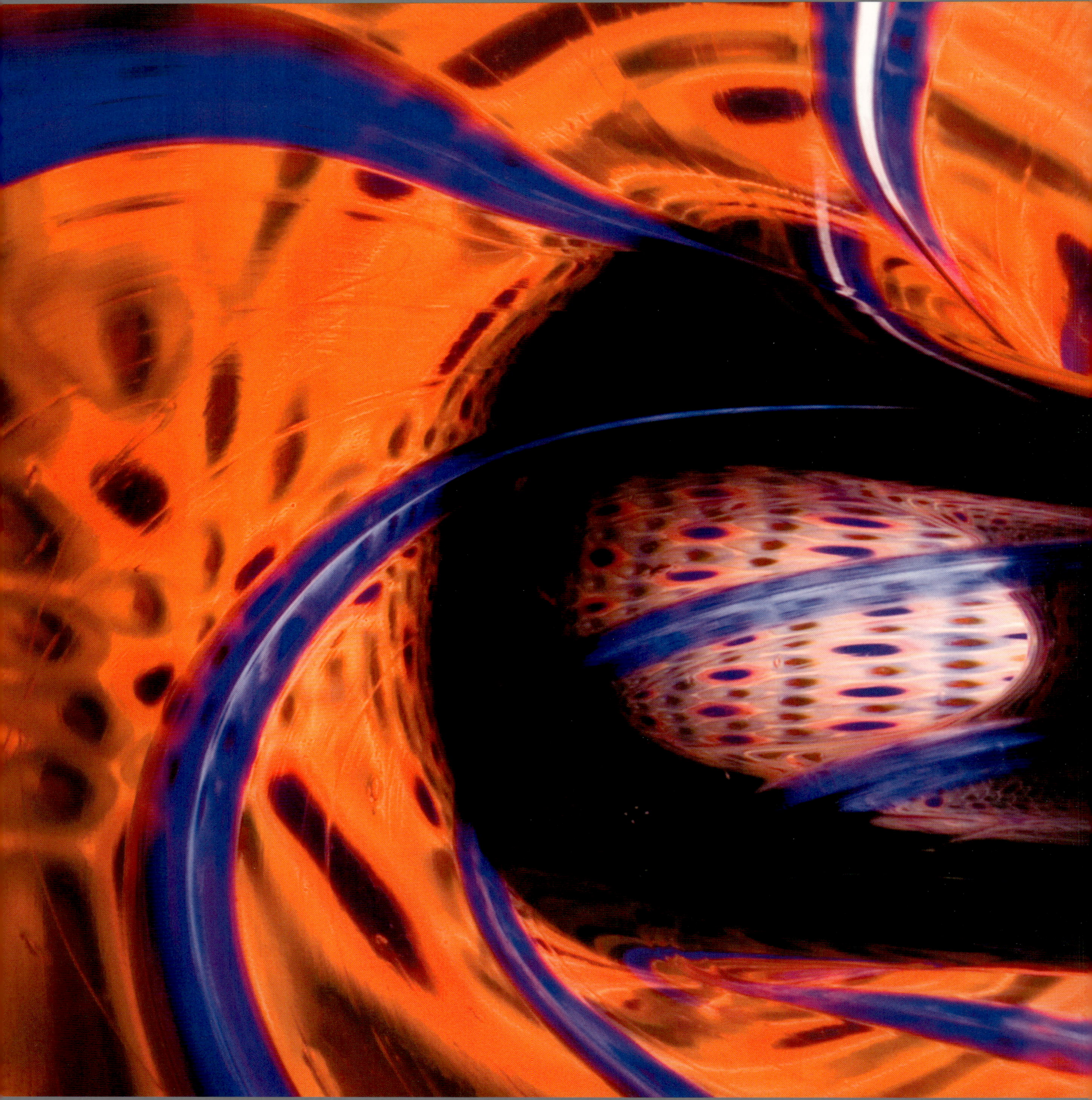

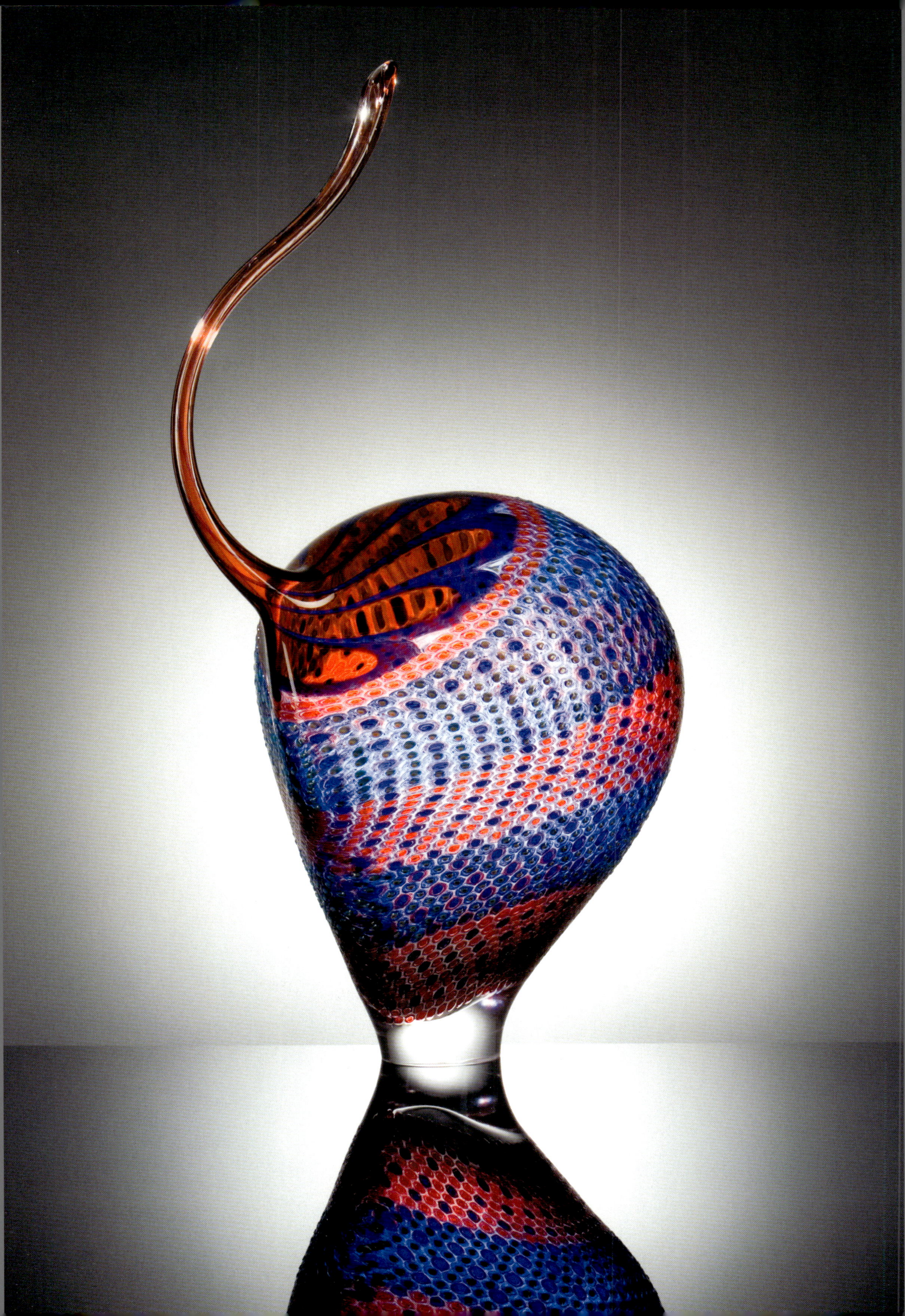

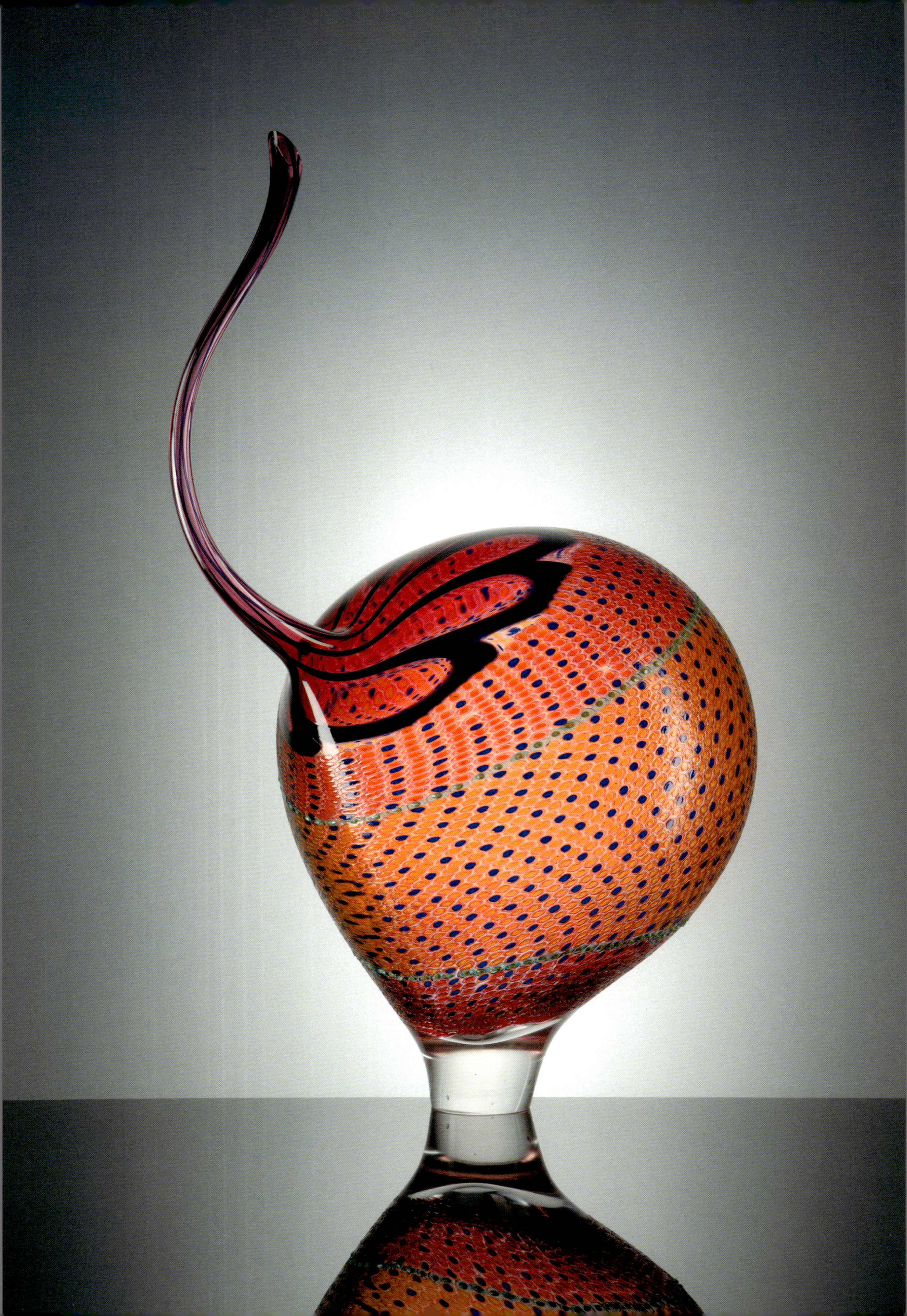

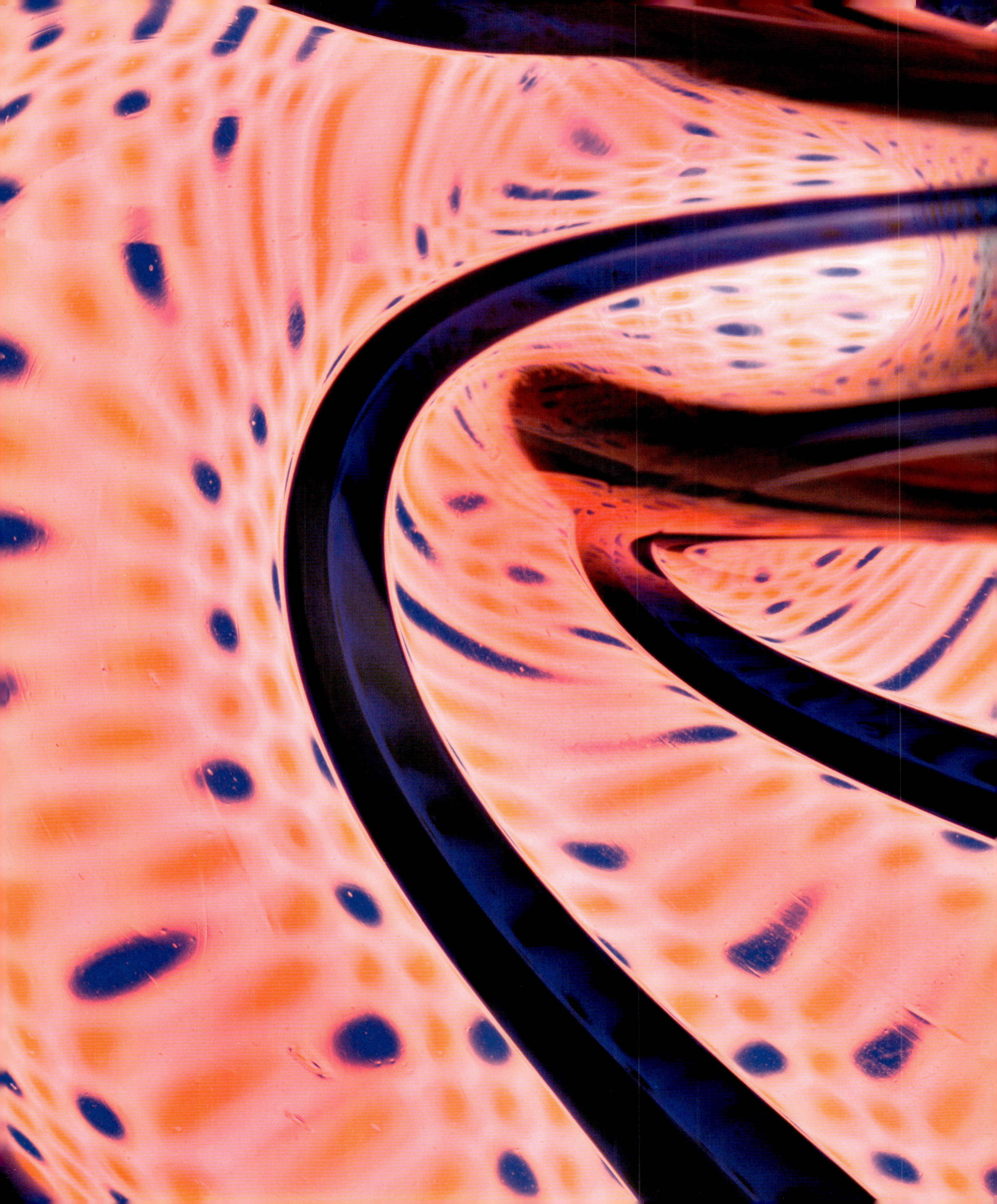

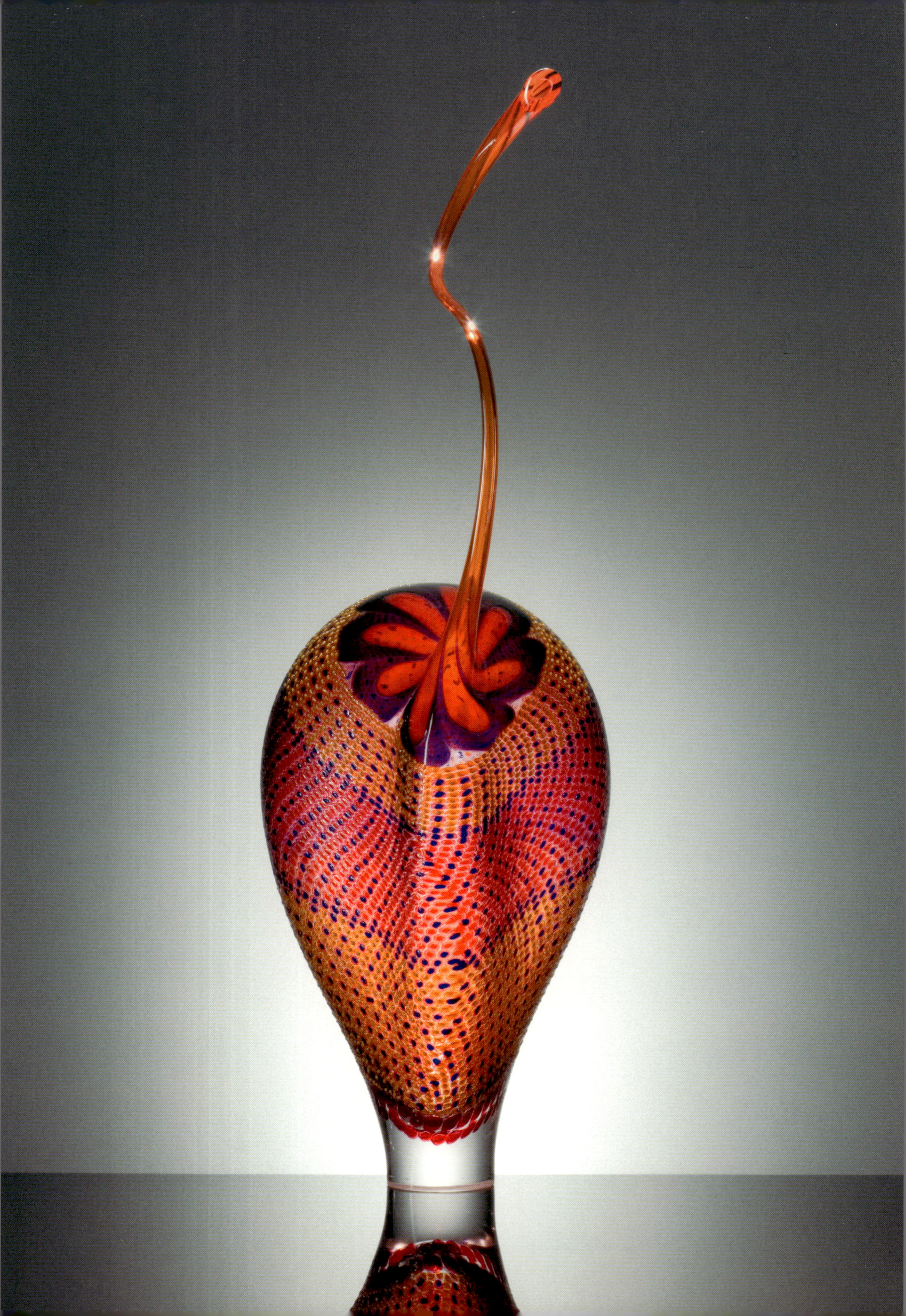

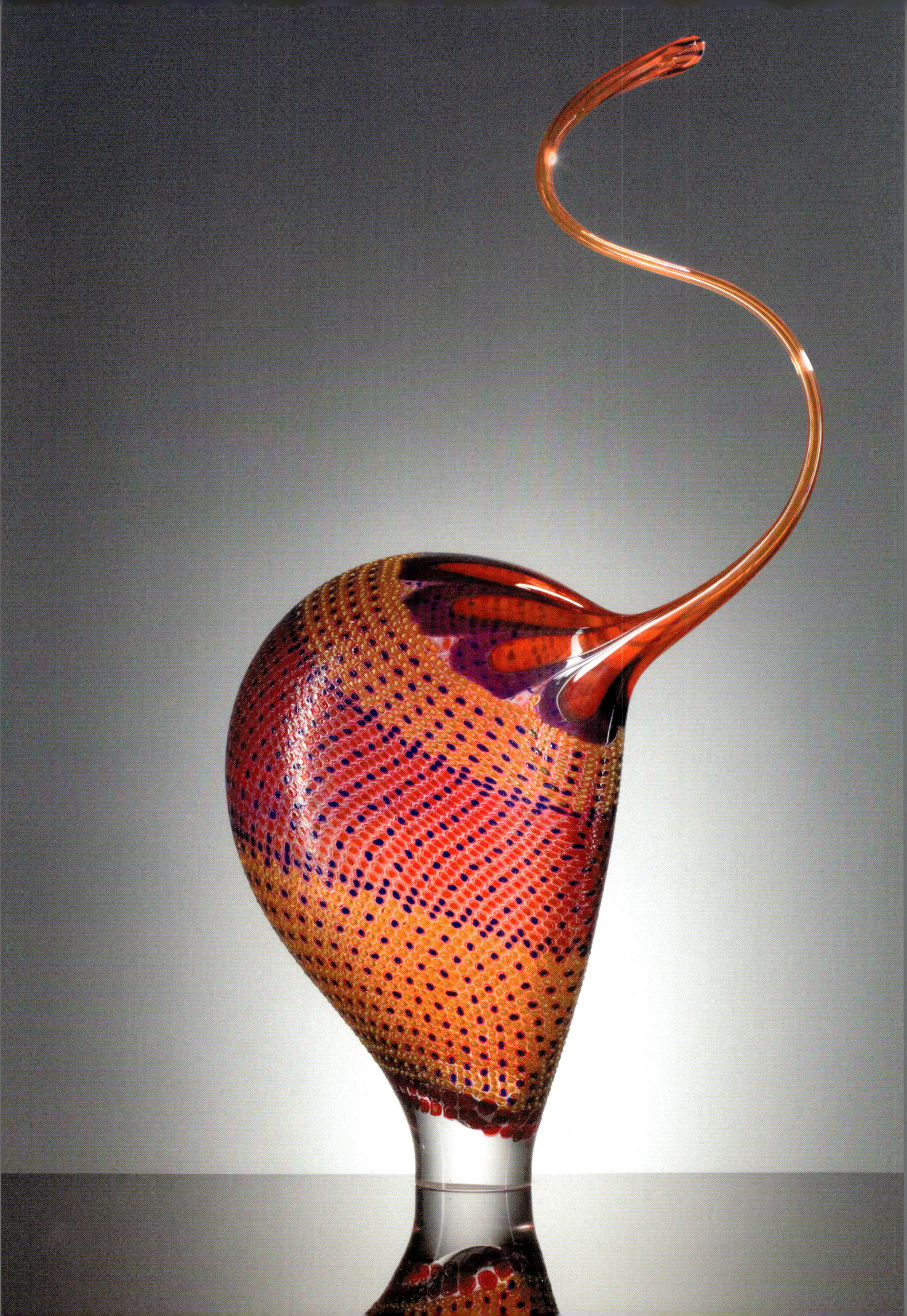

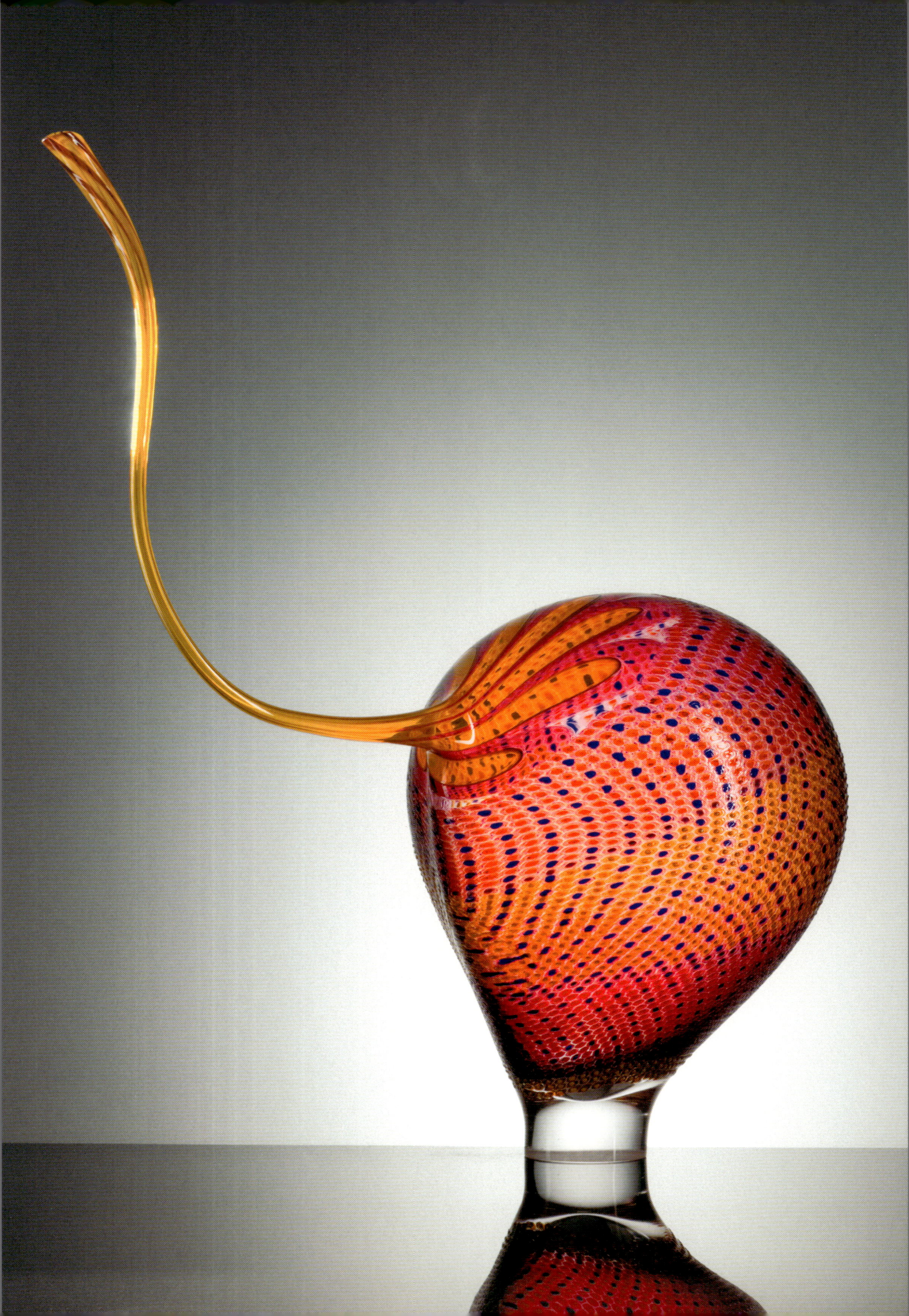

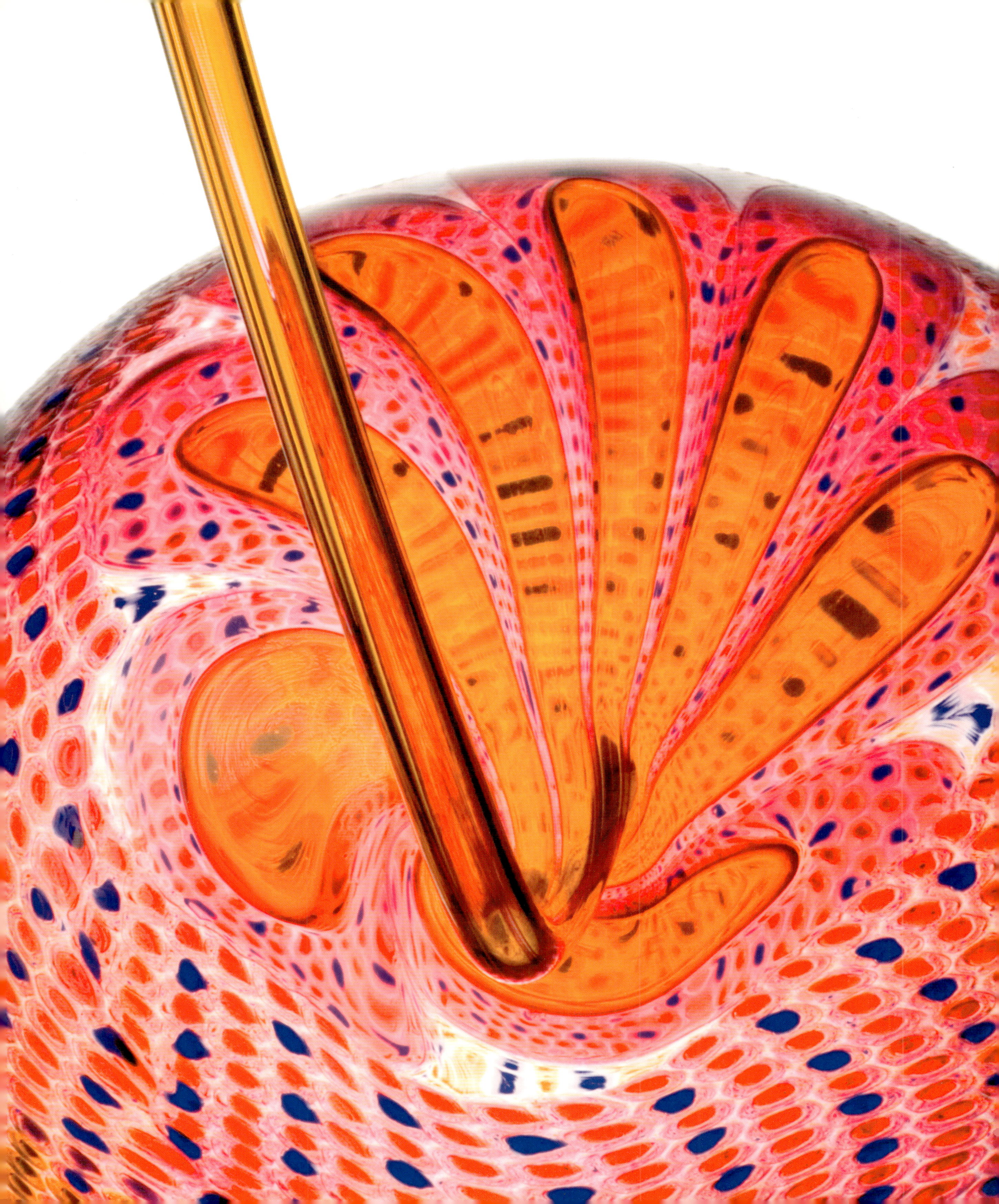

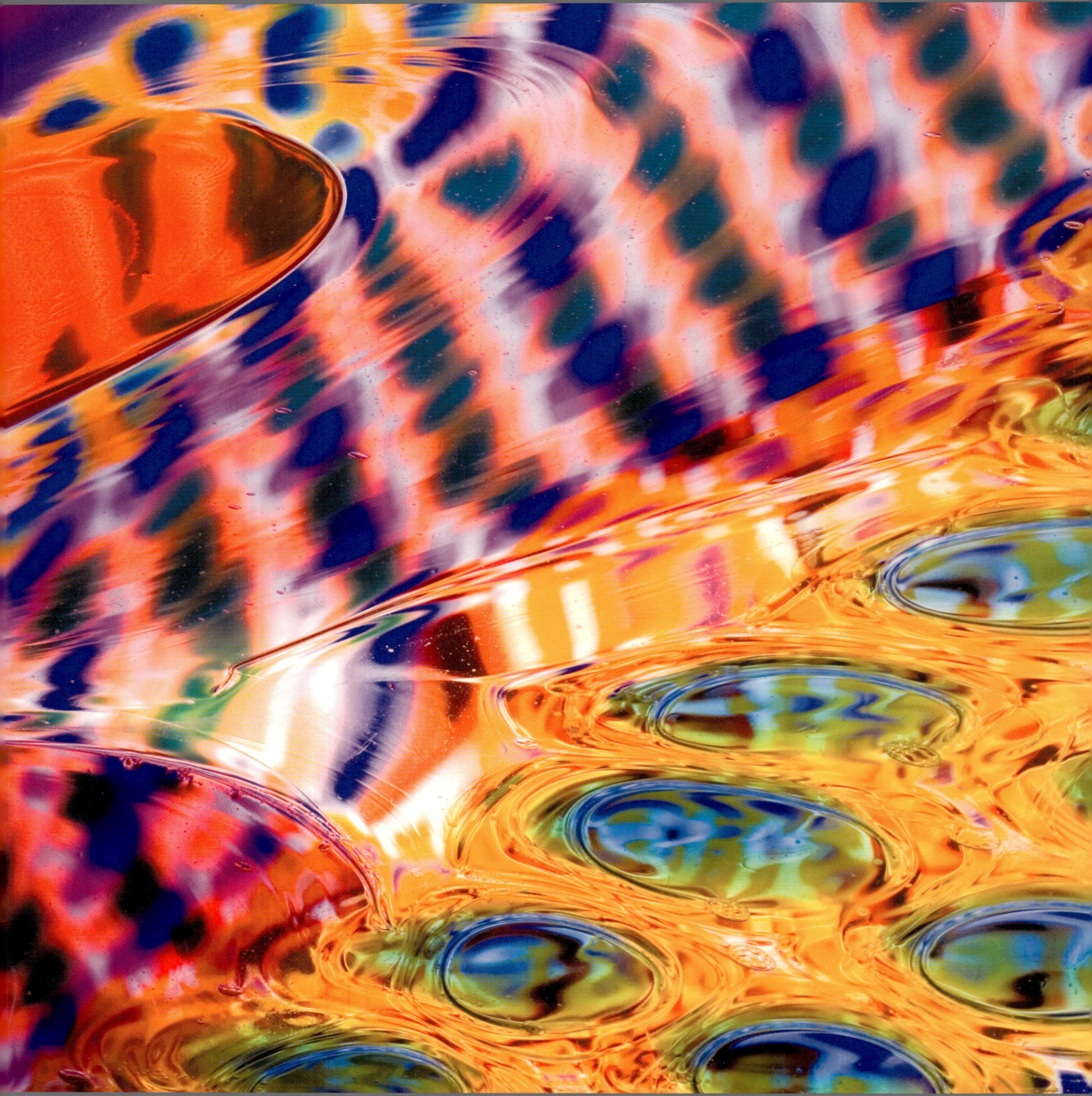

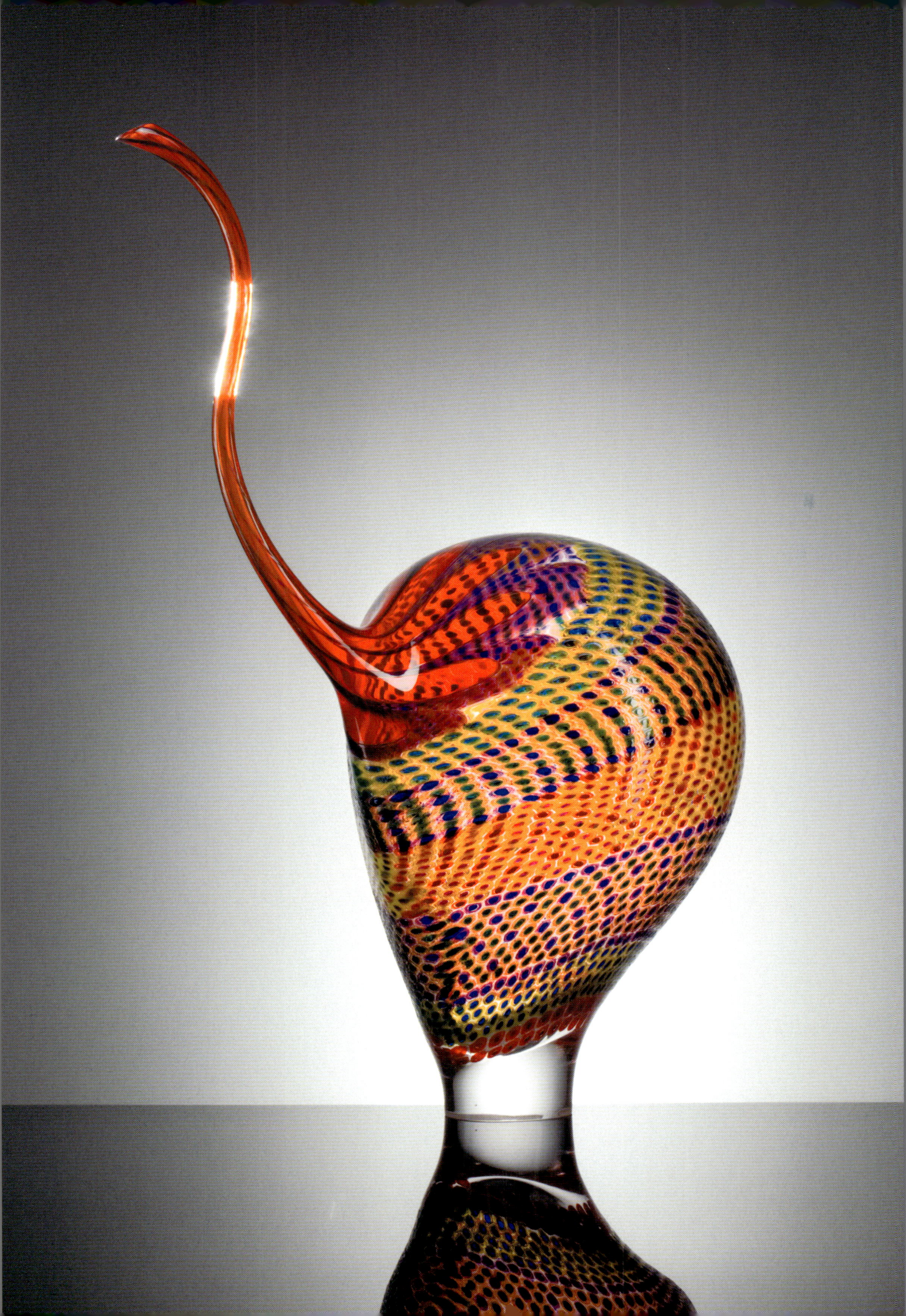

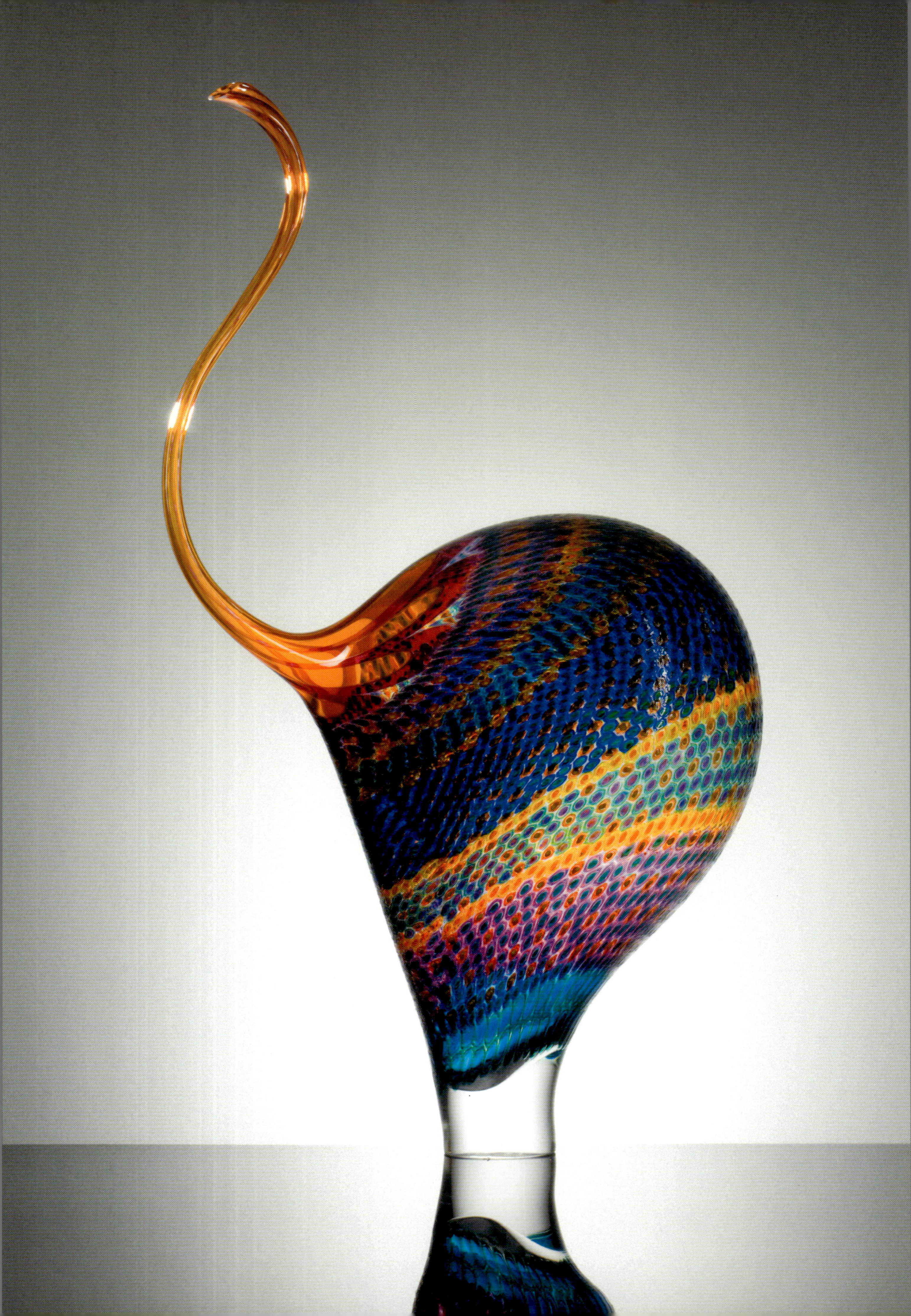

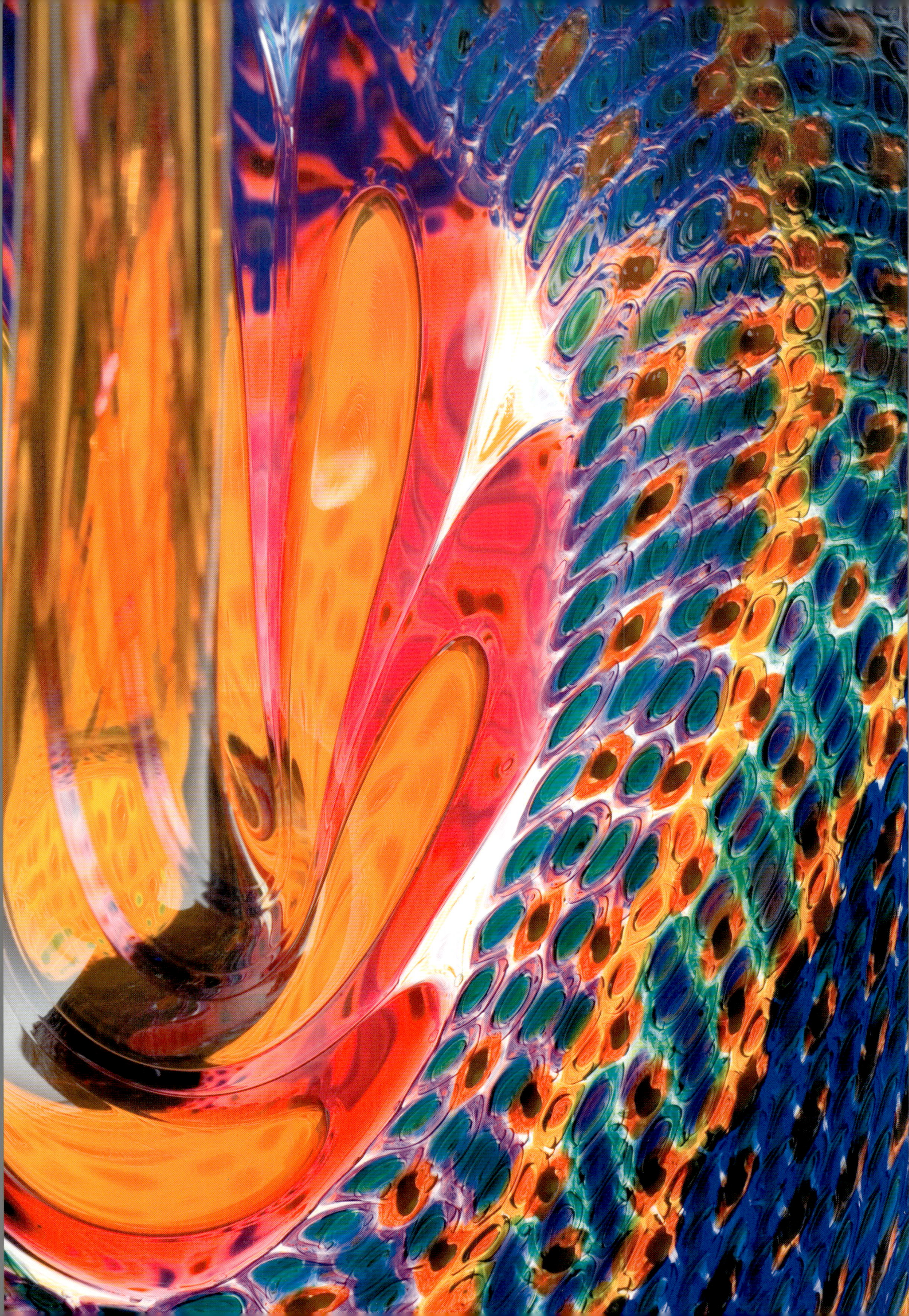

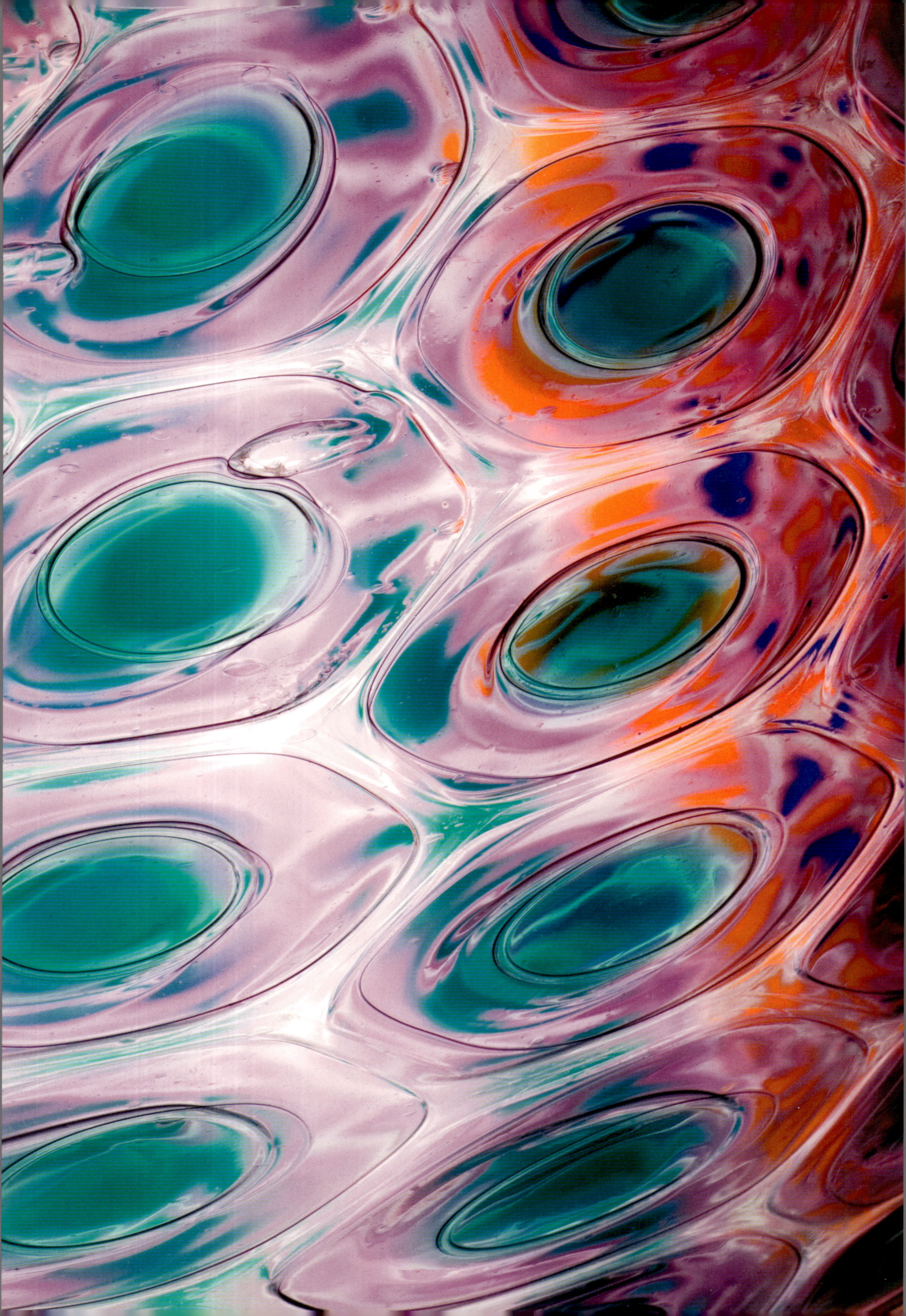

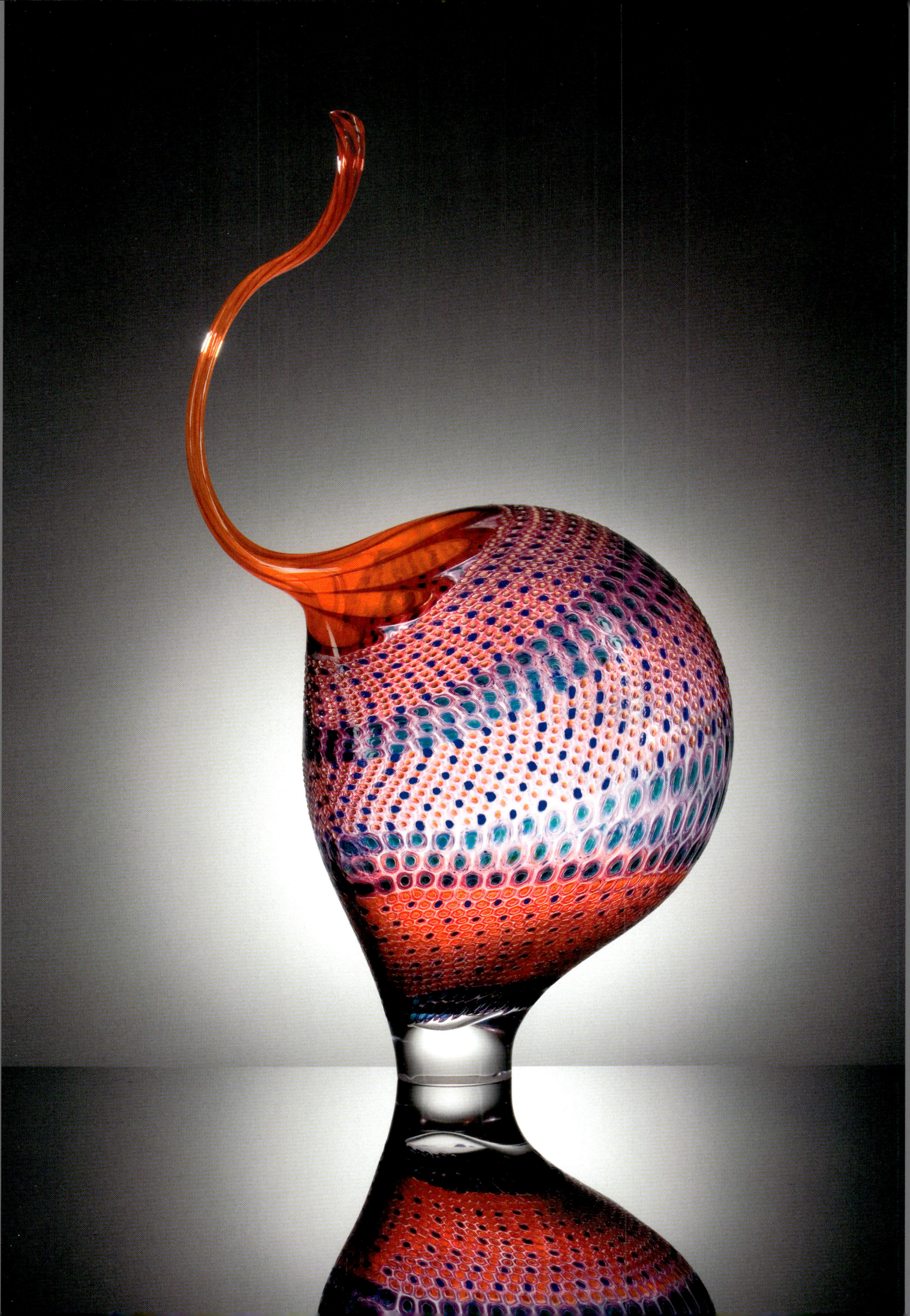

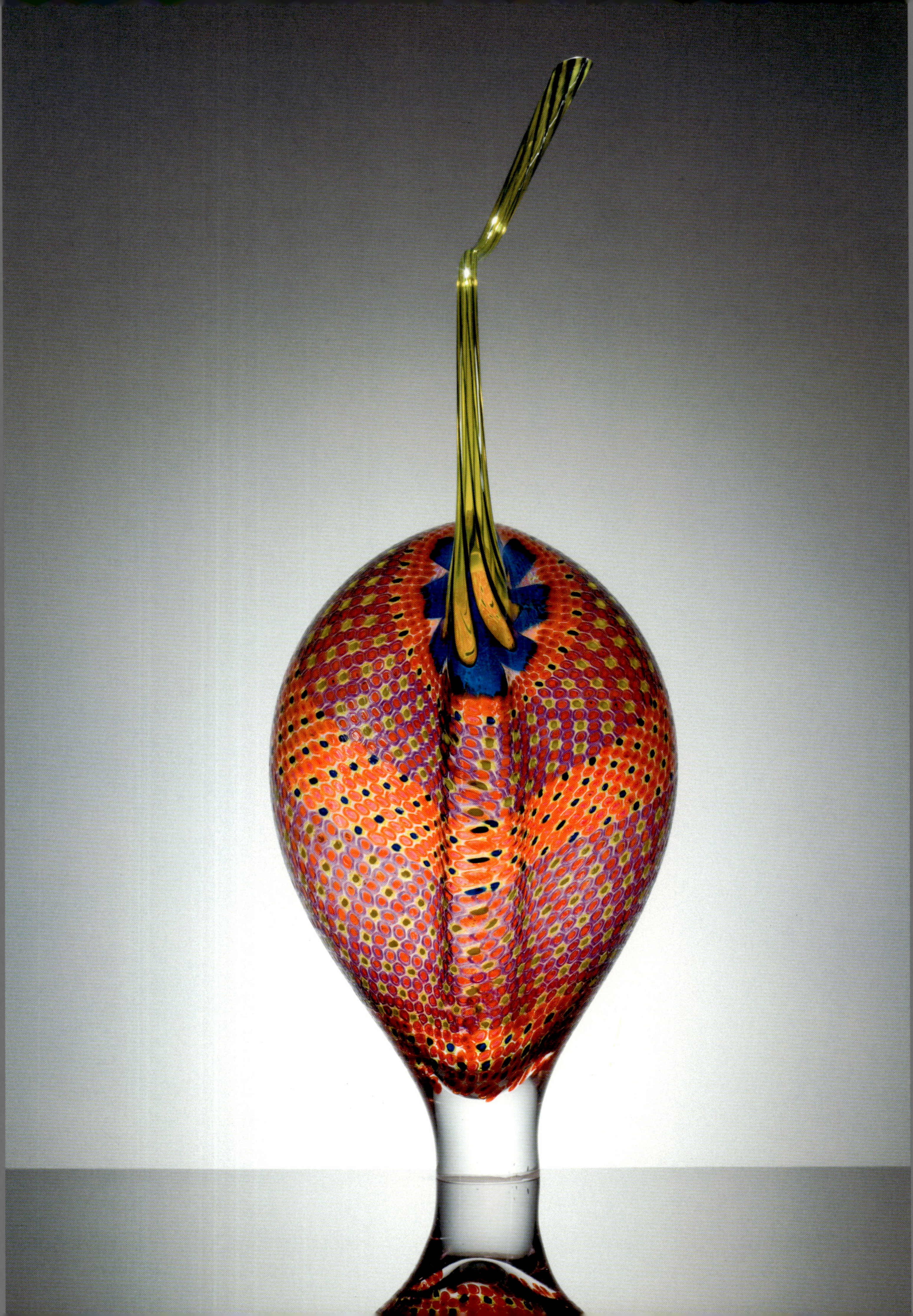

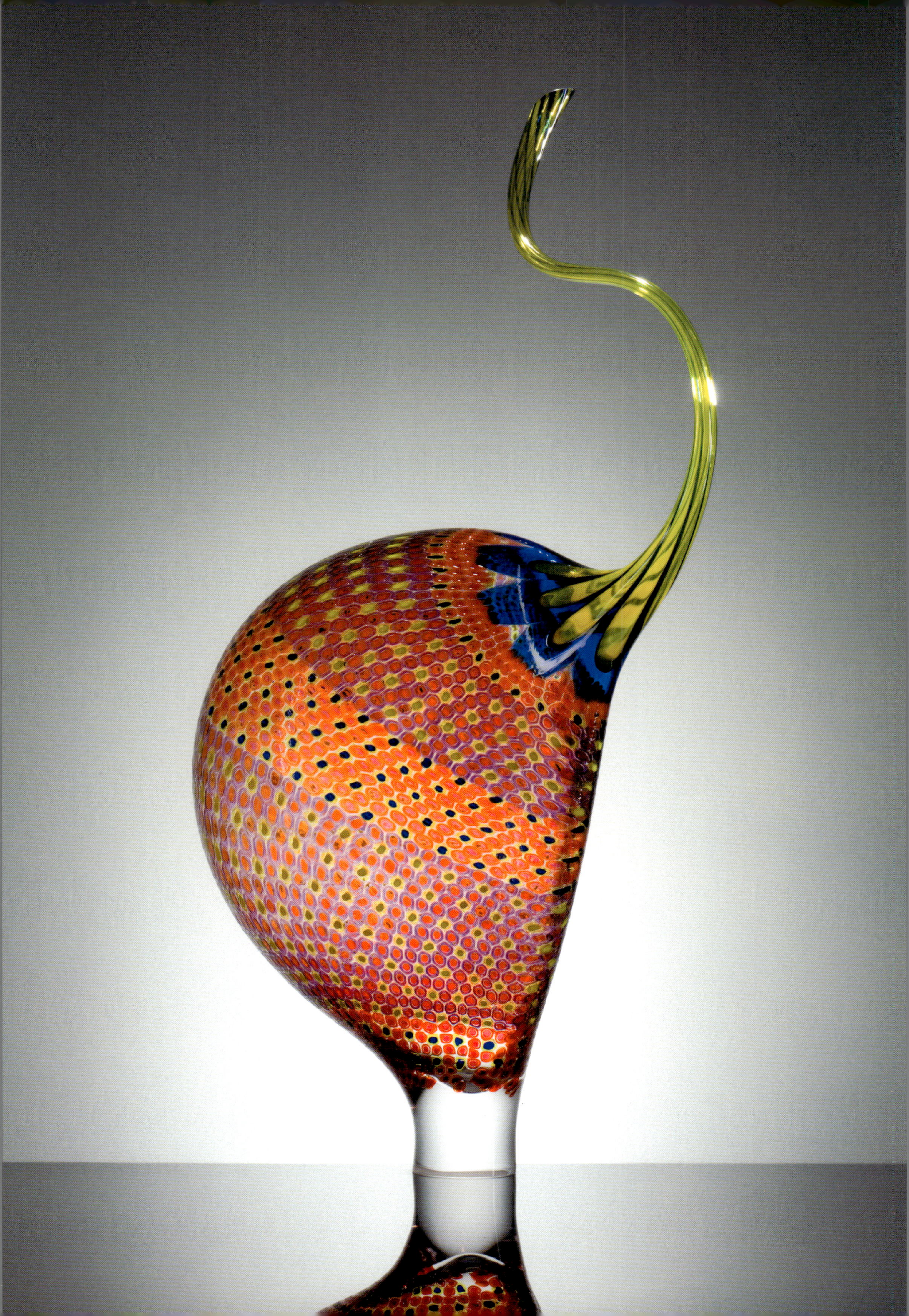

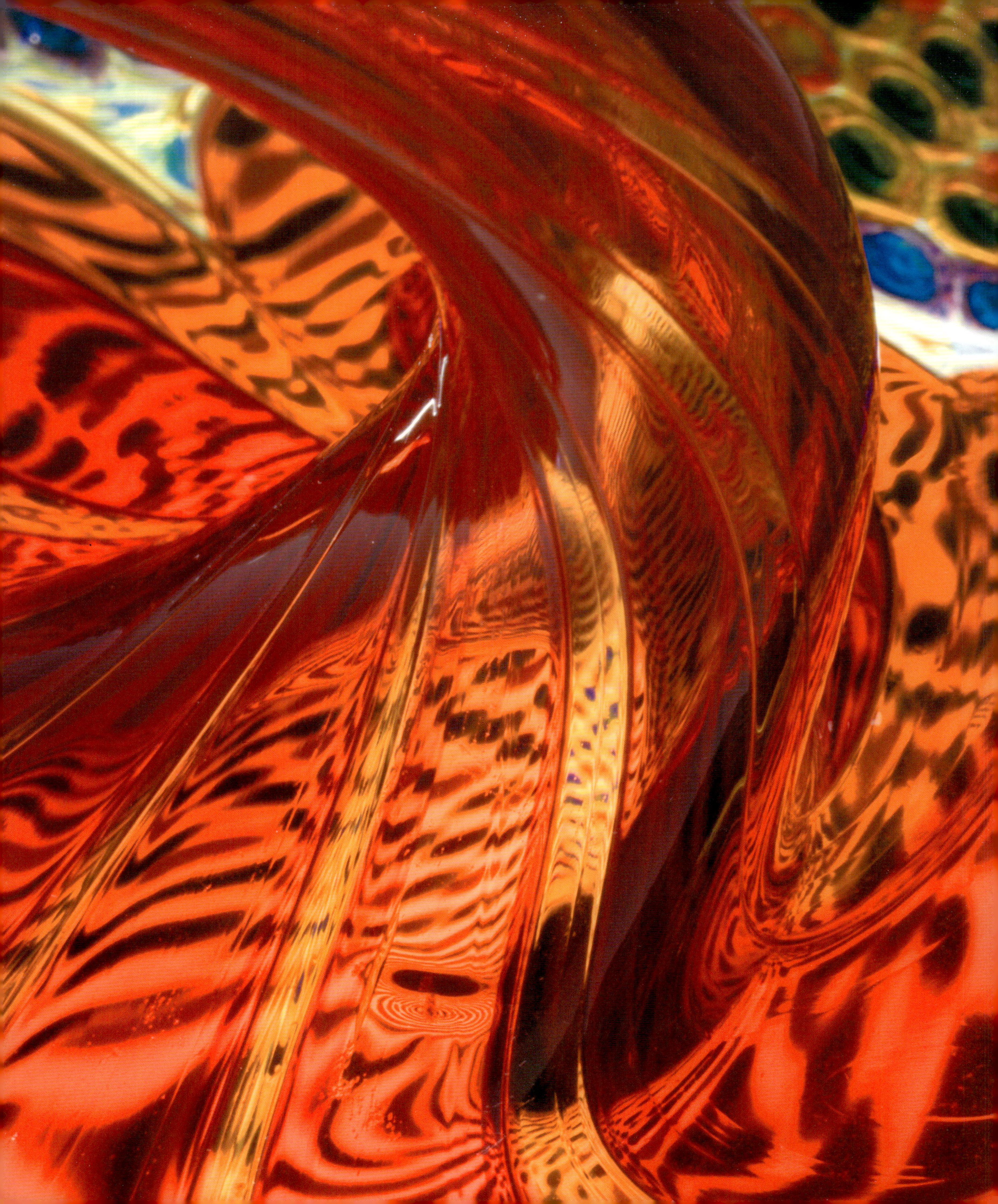

GENESIS AND THE VITREOUS SINGULARITY

The spirit of creation resides in the colossal, multicolored vessels of Stephen Rolfe Powell. Through an evocative Rothko-like use of abstract color fields and a sensual vessel format, his works explore the fragile boundaries of creation: artistic, sexual, divine, cosmic, and mythic. Evoking notions of the heroic and the primal, Powell's vessels plunge both artist and viewer back into the unconscious—back into the cosmological and mythical origins of the universe.

Much of Powell's fascination with the act of creation is driven by a spiritual bond with nature and one of its primary elements, fire. As a direct descendant of the Native American princess Pocahontas, Powell seems to draw his energies and references intuitively from nature and the surrounding landscape of his Kentucky farm. His radiant swelling vessels find easy parallels in the geological stratifications of exposed cliffs and riverbeds, the orbiting planets of the cosmos, the pregnant bellies of the Native American pots and baskets, and the bulging bodies of prehistoric fertility goddesses. Metaphors for creation of all kinds abound in Powell's luminous universes where the glass medium itself becomes a metaphorical expression of creation and, at the same time, the insubstantiality of his artistic quest.

It is not, however, the symbols of creation that preoccupy Powell but the intense singularity of creation itself. His attraction to glass is ultimately linked to a conception of creation that depends upon fire as the catalyst. Each new vessel for him is an attempt to physically reenact the primordial moment of creation through the transformative power of fire. French theorist Gaston Bachelard has explained the universalizing implications of this process in the *Psychoanalysis of Fire:*

"Fire is a privileged phenomenon which can explain anything. If all that changes slowly may be explained by life, all that changes quickly is explained by fire. Fire is the ultra living element. It is intimate and universal. . . . Among all living phenomena, it is really the one to which there can be so definitely attributed the opposing values of good and evil. It shines in Paradise. It burns in Hell. . . . It is well-being and it is respect. It is a tutelary and terrible divinity, both good and bad. It can contradict itself; thus it is one of the principles of universal explanation."[1]

A self-proclaimed pyromaniac, Powell wields fire at the end of his blowpipe with the same intensity and spiritual knowledge as a shaman performing a sacred ritual. His penchant for working at night enhances the ceremonial effects of the roaring furnace and red-hot glass awaiting transformation. To Powell the physicality of this process relates to the action painting of Pollock and de Kooning.

His preoccupation with fire extends beyond the confines of the studio to include a massive anagama kiln on nearby property that has the capacity to fire more than 2,000 pots at one time; it is the largest operating kiln in Kentucky. There are also his annual bonfires and fireworks festivals that can only be described as anthropological throwbacks to practices documented in Sir James George Frazier's *The Golden Bough*. Even Powell's earliest childhood memories focus on such polar experiences with fire as family campfires and Ku Klux Klan cross burnings aimed at liberal-minded professors like his father, who taught drama at Birmingham-Southern College in Alabama.

Just as fire is central to Powell's conception of creation, so is color: Both elements have the expressive ability to evoke, to shock, and to transform. When he began working in the late 1970s, first as painter and ceramist, then exclusively in glass after 1984, Powell tried to incorporate the radical color aesthetics of the New York School of Abstract Expressionism into his art. In the late 1980s he began to adapt the color fields of Mark Rothko and Kenneth Noland to his larger works. It is the raw energy, radiant color and spiritual essence of their paintings that Powell pumps into his giant universes. His aim is not to produce "abstract designs" or "bloodless decorations" but to evoke basic human emotions. And color is a tool to tap into the primordial energies of creation because it conveys meaning in a pre- or extralinguistic way.

Born in 1951 in Birmingham, Alabama, Powell grew up in the shadow of the city's monument to the steel industry, a 56-foot-tall statue of the Roman mythological fire god, Vulcan. He attended Centre College in Danville, Kentucky, where he received his B.A. in painting in 1974. After briefly teaching art at a Birmingham high school and at Draper State Prison in Elmore, Alabama, he entered graduate school at Louisiana State University in Baton Rouge. After receiving his M.F.A. in ceramics in 1983, he worked in the fire-intensive process of raku. Powell had experimented with glassblowing in graduate school and at summer workshops, but his commitment to the medium came only in 1984. While attending an exhibition of his ceramics in Houston, Texas, he visited the Rothko Chapel at St. Thomas University, where he experienced a strong empathy with the aims of the artist and a total frustration with the inadequacy of paint to convey emotion through color. "I realized that Rothko had gone as far as humanly possible," recalls Powell, "so glass suddenly seemed like the logical alternative to painting and ceramics." Powell says he often wonders whether Rothko would have committed suicide if he had considered the expressive potential of colored glass.

Over the next couple of summers, Powell taught at Summervail in Colorado, where he had the opportunity to work closely with such diverse glass artists as William Morris, Marvin Lipofsky, Richard Marquis, and Paul and Dante Marioni. By 1985, he had already acquired sufficient expertise and reputation to assist Dan Dailey and Lino Tagliapietra at the Pilchuck Glass School in Stanwood. The atmosphere of experimentation and innovation at Pilchuck encouraged him to apply the color aesthetics of Abstract Expressionism painting to glass. In the same year, *Corning's New Glass Review* affirmed Powell's chromatic experiments when it featured three of his vessels.

His early pieces are generally small vessels of vividly colored opaque glass with contrastingly bright horizontal stripes or "wrappings" of molten glass. The vessel format became a crucial component in his work at this time, and he adheres to it now even in spite of its current negative associations with "craft." The vessel shape appeals to Powell because of its ability to serve both utilitarian and ceremonial purposes and because it is the oldest significant glass form, dating back to early Phoenicians.

Around 1988 he began to experiment with classic Italian techniques using murrini as a way to increase the number and visual impact of the colors in each piece. He subsequently developed a process that involved fusing thousands of hand-cut glass beads to a cylinder of hot glass, which he then blew out into complex accordion and multiple lobe shapes. Introducing the murrini allowed him to explore the relationships and effects of multicolored bands as well as the possible visual tensions between mixed areas of opaque, translucent, and transparent glass on a single surface. The swollen glass beads have organic, amoeba-like shapes that engulf the entire glass surface in highly calculated patterns of color akin to the Neo-Impressionistic dots of Georges Seurat. The earlier, thread-thin "wrappings" have expanded into thick registers of vividly colored beads that hug the vessel's fluid folds. These zones of color create a lively organic character that variously suggests geological strata built up through the millennia and cosmic implosions born of the "Big Bang." Such diverse associations are encouraged by the geological, planetary, and incendiary terms he includes in many of his complex titles. Powell's adaptation of classical murrini techniques has allowed him greater "calculation" in the choice of colors and, as a consequence, greater control in the relationship between the body of the vessel and the viewer.

Powell further clarified his personal vision of glass art in 1990 when he accepted an invitation from the former Soviet Union to teach and study at the Mukhina Glass Institute in Leningrad and at the Lvov Glass Factory and Art Institute in Ukraine. The lack of information about Soviet glass in the West had long intrigued Powell, and he was literally the first American ever allowed to enter many of the sacrosanct glass factories of the former U.S.S.R. What he discovered there was a dramatically different method of working: Soviet glass production typically divided the act of creation between an "artist" who generated designs and a "technician" who executed the piece. His brief encounter with this division of labor helped him to recognize in his own work the necessity of a direct "hands-on" approach that imparts traces of his physical presence as well as embodying the mental acts by which a work is conceived.

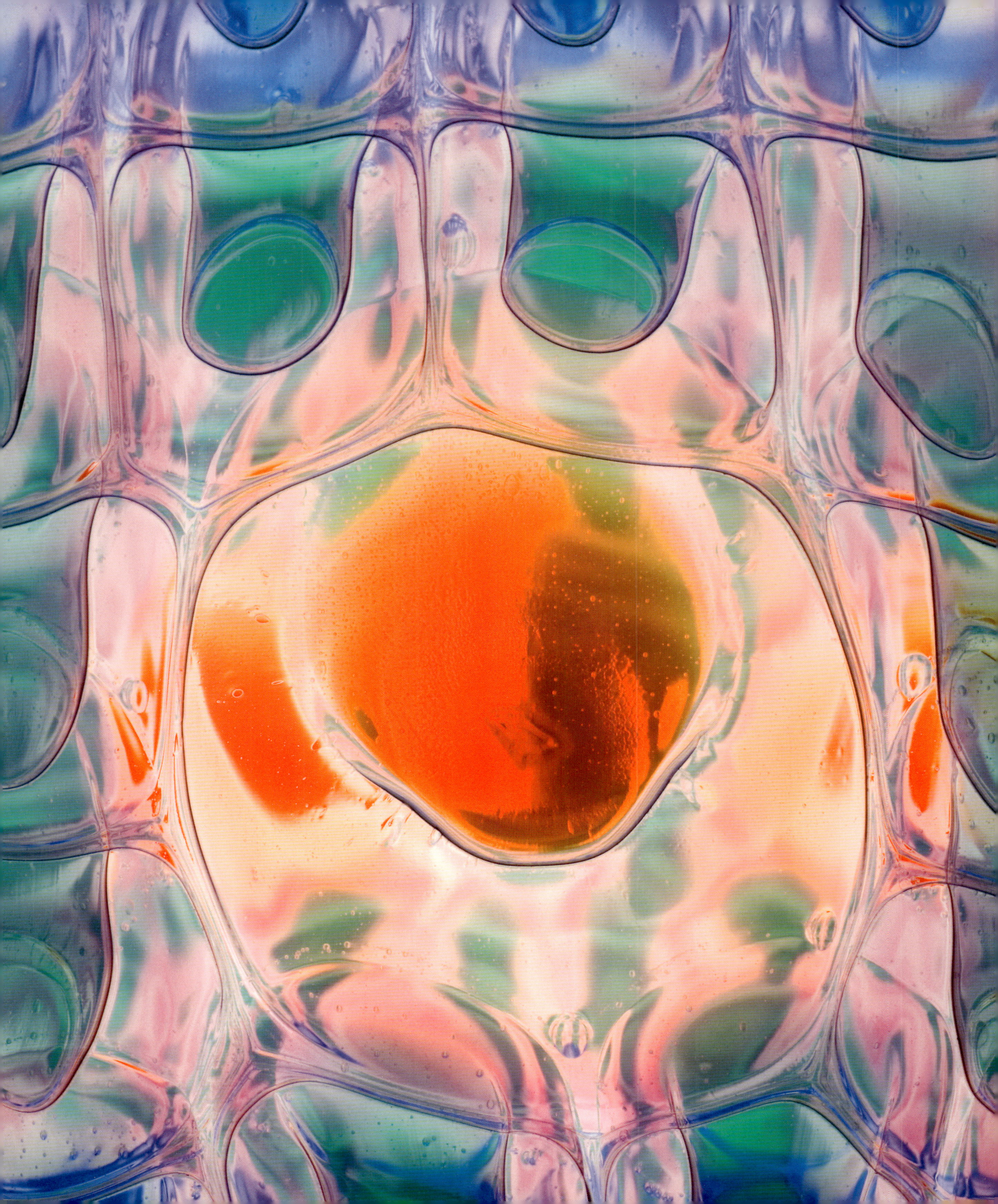

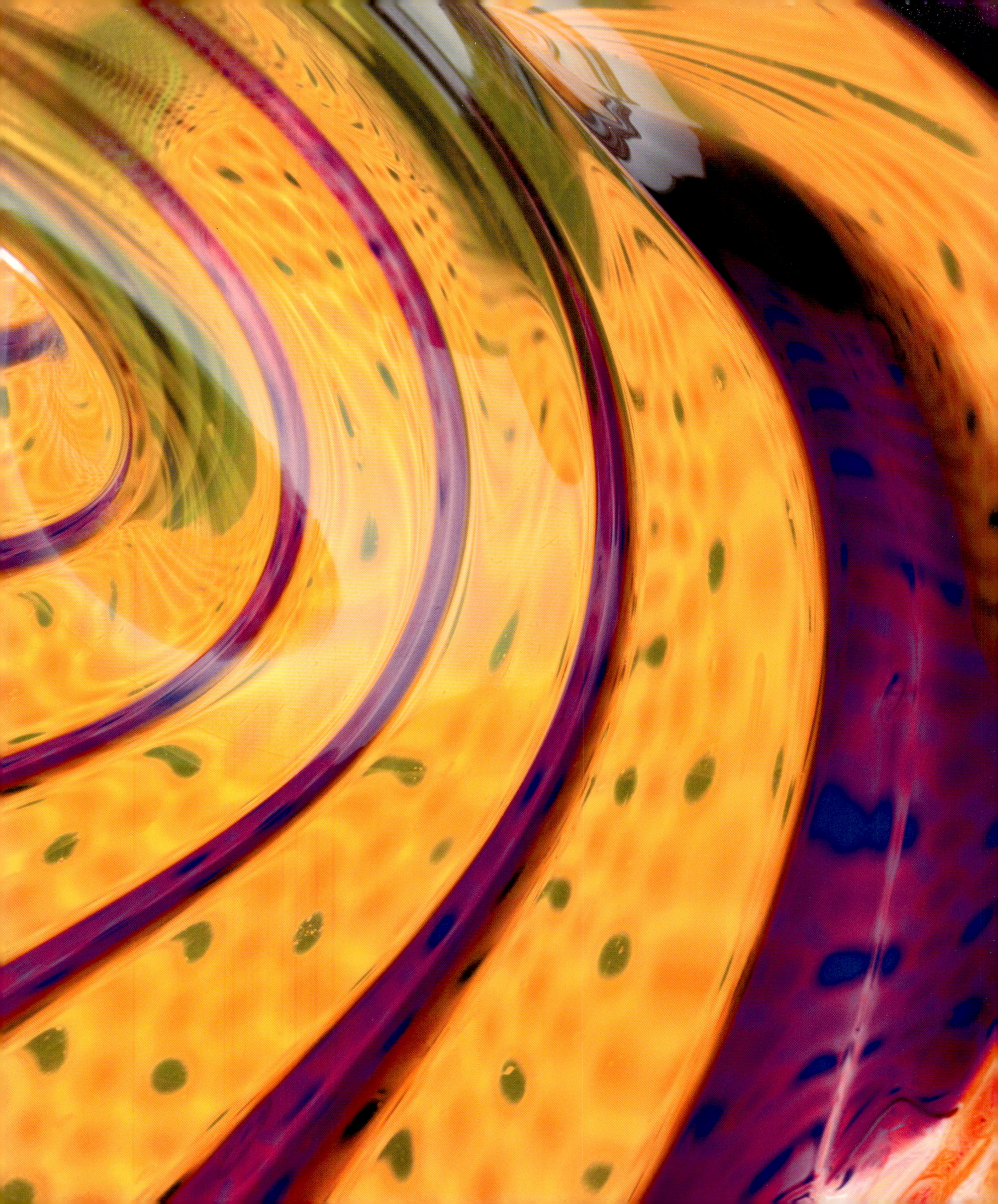

Powell's vessels reflect the insights of his Soviet experience in their unabashed emphasis on sheer physicality and a robustness of size that measures the very limits of his physical capabilities. They easily doubled in size, becoming more sculptural and sensual with long tapering necks that aspire to heights above a meter. The earlier complex shapes gave way to the bulging double lobe, full, and flat orb shapes that allowed him to strengthen the optical intensity of the abstract color fields. The light-filled registers now pulsate with radiant colors from the approximately 3,000 murrini that make up the color fields of each vessel. No two pieces are ever alike, and their color harmonies vary widely; some are based on natural elements—earth, air, water—while others are ethereal and otherworldly. The suggestive sequences of bands and slight modulations of bead size compel the viewer to examine surfaces and to question the relation between the outer tactile surface and the inner space of reflected light. The previously neglected interior of the vessel is here permeated with a vaporous cathedral light that creates a pregnant void—if not The Void. With these subtle shifts and almost painterly manipulations of light and color, Powell successfully merges the power and luminosity of glass with the color aesthetic of the Abstract Expressionists. While crossovers between glass and sculpture have become commonplace, Powell is one of only a few artists working today whose art may genuinely be described as bridging the gap between the traditional color aesthetics of painting and the traditional sensibilities of glass.

The sensual shapes of his vessels are also intended as vehicles into the unconscious experience of primordial creation. The rounded bellies of the orb shapes and the sagging buttocks of the double lobes, replete with vaginal slit, all speak to the sexual, life-giving aspect of creation. Their archetypal forms offer modern analogies to Paleolithic fertility goddesses such as Venus of Willendorf or Venus of Lespuque. To borrow a phrase from Lucy Lippard, Powell's works function like "symbols of lost symbols";[2] they hover between past and present, permanence and transformation, ritualistic symbol and decorative artifact. Their dichotomous nature even appears in their unusual titles. Powell often gives the vessel a last name of Smith, Jones, or Johnson as a way of paradoxically emphasizing the universality of their forms and the banality of art itself in the late 20th century. He also incorporates sexually loaded words into many of his titles, such as cleavage, cheeks, buns, sigh, and gasp, that mock the modern viewer's preoccupation with the epiphenomena of sex and simultaneously invite a more focused second look that might glimpse the common visual language of the collective unconscious.

Powell's most recent works have added the element of chromatic movement. An accident in the summer of 2003 left Powell with a fractured wrist that made it physically impossible for him to hold the heavy glass-laden blowpipe above the emerging vessel. The accident fortuitously freed him from his traditional method of working and became a catalyst for invention. Over the next year, he gradually shifted the format of his vessels from a vertical to a horizontal orientation, pulling out and twisting the long tapering necks and the previously flat bottoms to create supports for the luminous glass bellies. Powell simultaneously strengthened the optical intensity of his vessels by limiting his palette to fewer and more brilliant colors like lemon yellows, tangerines, and vibrant greens that appear to radiate with movement when combined. The use of large murrini around the neck and the bottom of every vessel explodes into broad, colored panes of glass that open up the interior world of the vessels and activate their inner life with light.

The once statuesque icons of sexuality now writhe and pulsate with movement like yoga zealots stretching and pulling to find their spiritual center. The anthropomorphic effect of the glass bodies is further asserted by titles that now include active, life-defining words like puffing, throbbing, lurching, nodding, and listening. Powell playfully and self-deprecatingly refers to these horizontal vessels as his "Whackos" series, suggesting that they are detours to a correct and rational progression of work. In truth, they should be seen as part of Powell's larger and continuing struggle to find and understand the power of color. In 2005 Powell returned to a predominantly vertical orientation for his vessels, but the life-asserting elements of his work remain a constant theme of exploration.

However important the symbolic and the formal elements are to the work of Stephen Powell, the physical, momentary act of creation remains his primary focus. Every wielding of the blowpipe for him is an attempt to connect with the primordial essences of creation through the transformative power of fire. Every new vessel with its varied shape and color is a constant reworking, a constant search for the "one coming answer" that will satisfy the creative impulse. If Powell's giant universes seem to have little in common with the parodic juxtaposition and politicized specificity of our postmodern era, it is because their references are drawn intuitively from the unknowable realms of the mythical and the metaphysical. His vessels are intensely private quests to understand and convey the invisible links that bind the fragile boundaries of creation.

Laurie Winters

Curator, Milwaukee Art Museum

Permission to reprint Laurie Winters' "Genesis and the Vitreous Singularity" kindly granted by *Craft Arts International*, in which the essay was originally published in Issue 39.

1. Gaston Bachelard, *The Psychoanalysis of Fire*, trans. Alan C. M. Ross (Beacon Press, Boston, 1964) p. 7.
2. Lucy R. Lippard, Overlay: *Contemporary Art and the Art of Prehistory* (Pantheon Books, New York, 1983) p. 8.

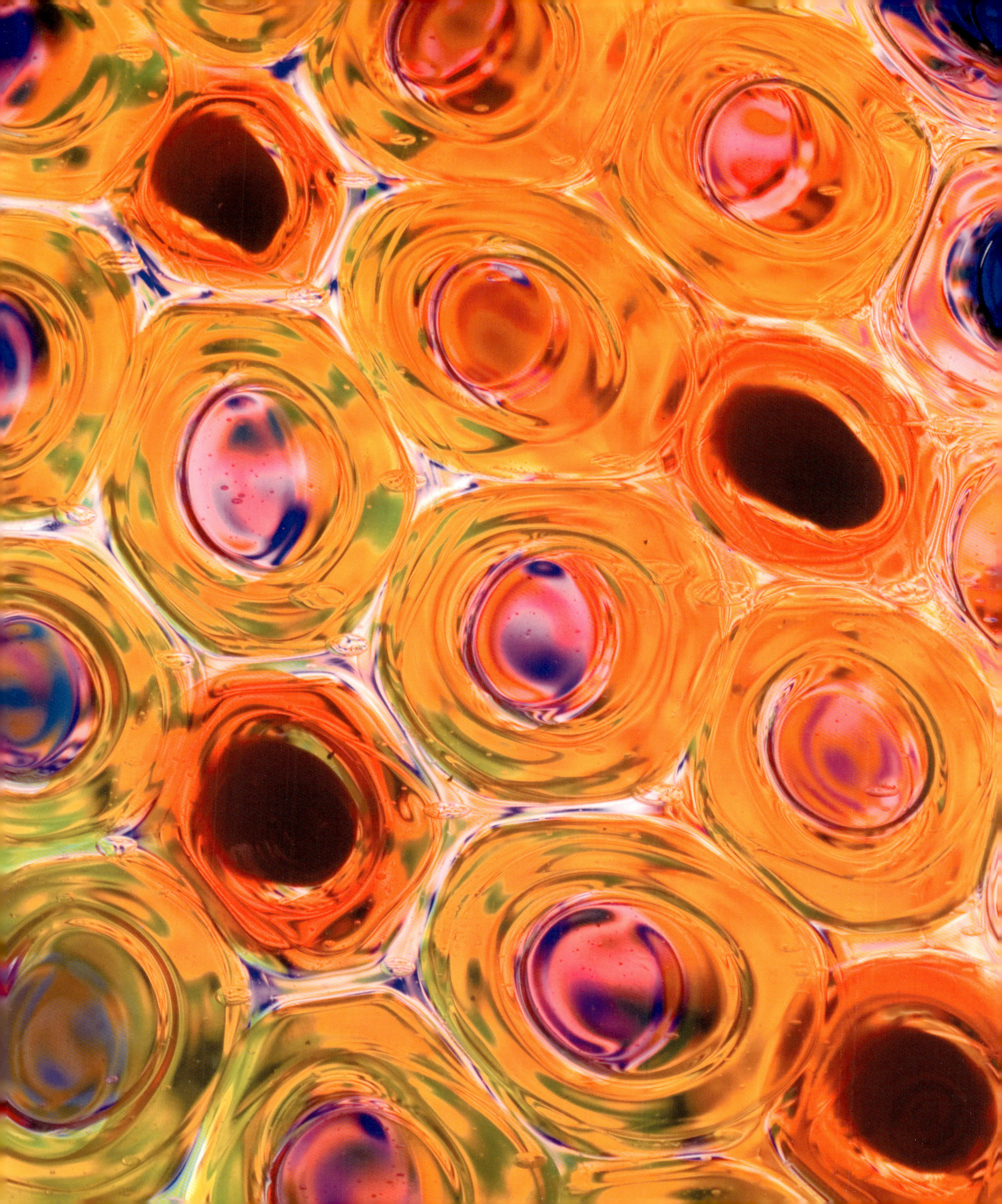

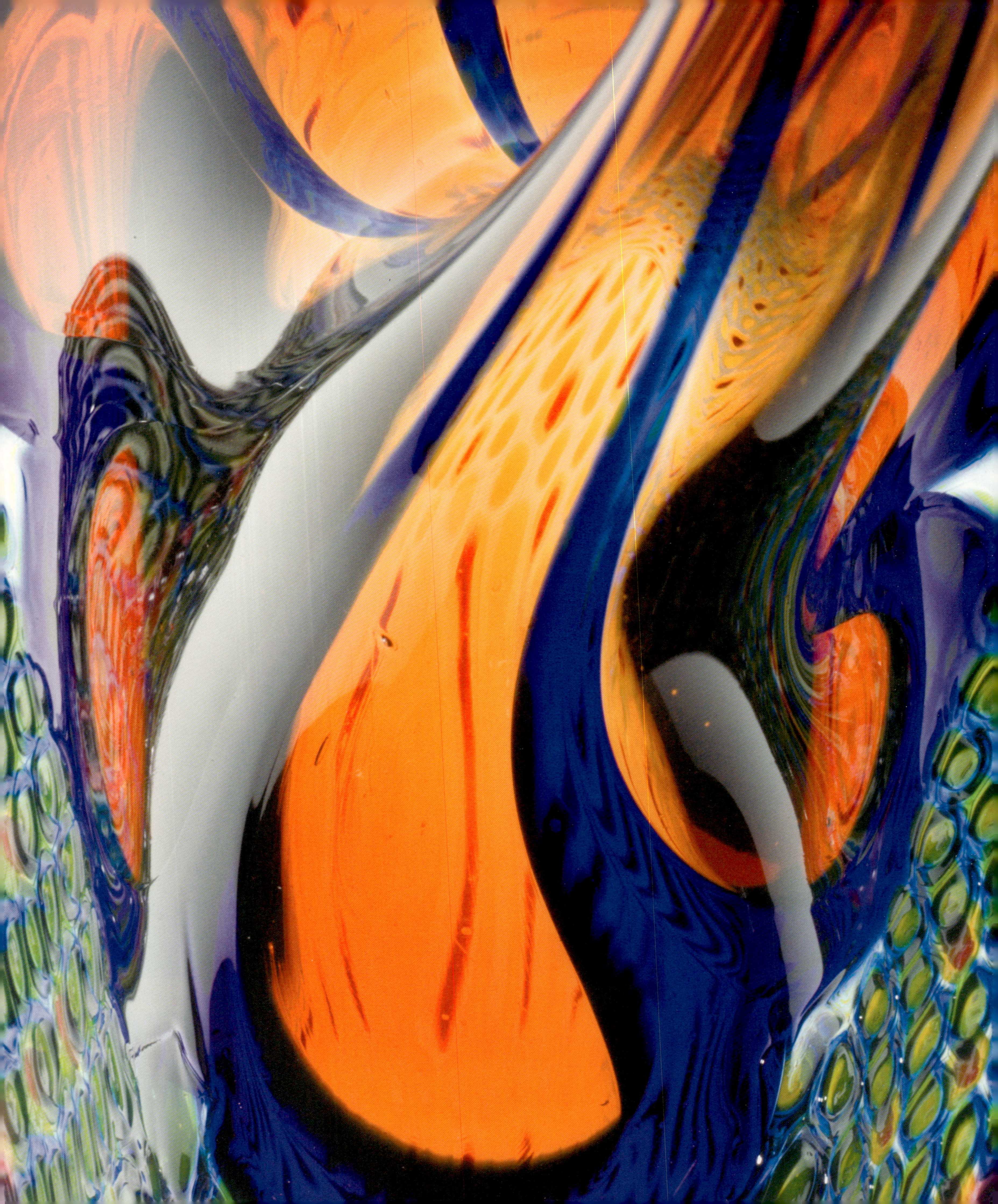

ROAD TRIP TO NEW ORLEANS

In the summer of 2004, I made a trip to New Orleans by way of New York City and Danville, Kentucky. It started out at the SOFA show in New York. My old buddy Stephen Powell was there at SOFA as well, and he had graciously invited me to come down to his spread in Kentucky right after the show to cool out for a few days, then ride with him down to the Glass Art Society conference. I was to present my dad with the Lifetime Achievement Award there at the conference in New Orleans.

We got off to an appropriate start by watching the big horse race on TV at Mickey Mantle's bar on 57th Street in New York. Then it was off to Kentucky. Arriving at Stephen and Shelly's place, we settled into doing nothing—at least I did. The Powells busied themselves with the two boys, but we all did spend time at their pool. There seems to be a steady stream of visitors around there, and I was really impressed with Shelly's patience.

I can be good at lying around doing nothing, but Stephen has a big old place there and a fancy "ride 'em mower." I had to have a go. I mowed the whole place, which took most of the day, all the while working on my tan. Steve didn't seem to mind. I had not mowed grass since I was a kid, and I found it to be a satisfying, calming experience, but not one that made me want a lawn that big.

Preparation for the ride to GAS began the evening before we left and almost turned into an all-nighter. We were taking the school van. Every inch was packed with gear and suitcases and Steve's helpers. Steve was going to be doing a demo at GAS, and he makes sure he has everything he needs, including his whole crew (mostly Centre students). There were seven of us in all, and it was going to be a 14-hour drive. Stephen wanted to take us through Birmingham, his hometown, and I was psyched to check it out. We left at around 4 a.m. Steve's buddy Mark Lucas rode in the front, and the youngsters gave me the whole backseat to myself. It did not take long for me to doze off. I woke up around the time that we were stopping to eat breakfast. I really enjoyed watching Stephen interacting with the young guys that make up his team. A lotta laughs. He has a great way of relating to the students. There is a lot of teenager still in Steve, and the kids all love him.

Lunchtime found us in Birmingham, and we had to eat at John's, a restaurant downtown that features Southern cuisine. When I travel I love to sample local fare and was not disappointed by this place. Stephen and Mark did a great job of enlightening me on the merits of sweet tea and other stuff that you just ain't gonna find on the West Coast. I really loved it. We then went up to the "Vulcan," the big figure that guards the city, I think, and went up in the top to take in the view. Steve then drove us through his childhood neighborhood. I personally really like to see where people come from, and it was great to see a friend I'd known so long reflecting on the good old days of his youth.

Back on the road and rolling towards N.O., trying to make time, we finally pull up to the hotel where we are all staying, and naturally it is full of conference-going glass people. It took forever to get checked in as we had to chat with every other person we saw. And it was so hot too. Being a West Coast guy, I just am not used to the heat and humidity. We went out for supper, which Stephen was pretty enthusiastic about (he seems to be that way when it comes to food, I've learned), and went to some famed local place. It was so hot there I could not get much of an appetite together, so the whole deep-fried, spicy gumbo thing just was not working for me. Stephen, though, ate like it was his last meal, relishing the fried okra and other creole specialities. The guy really likes his Southern food.

I had decided that I was going to hang out with this crew while I was there for the conference as they were all such great guys and I could blend into the crowd rather than having to socialize the entire time and be "on." It was nice to feel like I was on the team when really I was along for the ride, and I wanted to contribute, if I could, when the big demonstration happened, which was the next day. The guys were all really nice to me and let me participate. I had not ever seen Stephen make one of his pieces before in the 21 years that I'd known him, so the whole process was new to me. Where I come from, the glassblowing frame of reference is all about Murano. That is to say, in Seattle we all work in a Venetian style of glassmaking that Lino Tagliapietra has passed on to us. Stephen and the boys have developed their own style over the years making his work there at Centre College.

I don't think that I was much help, really, but they let me on the pad anyway. I loved it, and I have to say, as jaded as I am, having seen just about everything in glassmaking, or so I thought, it was a heart-stopping demo. A lot of careful preparation and methodical procedure and then two minutes of full-on chaos, people up on platforms, everyone holding a torch, shouting with face masks on, running around, then it's in the annealer and over, just like that. It was very exciting. Amazing even. I did say that I kind of felt like I had seen it all having grown up in glass studios and at the Pilchuck School, but this was something else, and they made a really good one too. It was a great show. Good job, guys.

The rest of the trip was spent doing some tourist stuff together and, of course, eating at places Stephen knew about and taking in the craziness all around while I waited for my dad's big moment later in the conference. Seeing the way that Stephen and his team work made an impression on me. As I've said, there is a lot of specific structure to the way that glassblowers make things in the Northwest, and it has become a global hot spot for studio art glass. Artists come from every corner of the planet to teach, to exhibit, and to just look around at what is going on out here. Stephen's approach and the things that he makes are, in my opinion, so very American. He has figured out how to do this work from the center (or Centre) of Kentucky where there is not much of a glass peer group or opportunity for dialogue, and he has refined it to what it has become today. As much as I have always admired his work, I like it even more now that I have experienced it being made and have seen, up close, where it is from and the people who help him do it. It was a great trip.

Dante Marioni
Glass Artist
Seattle, Washington

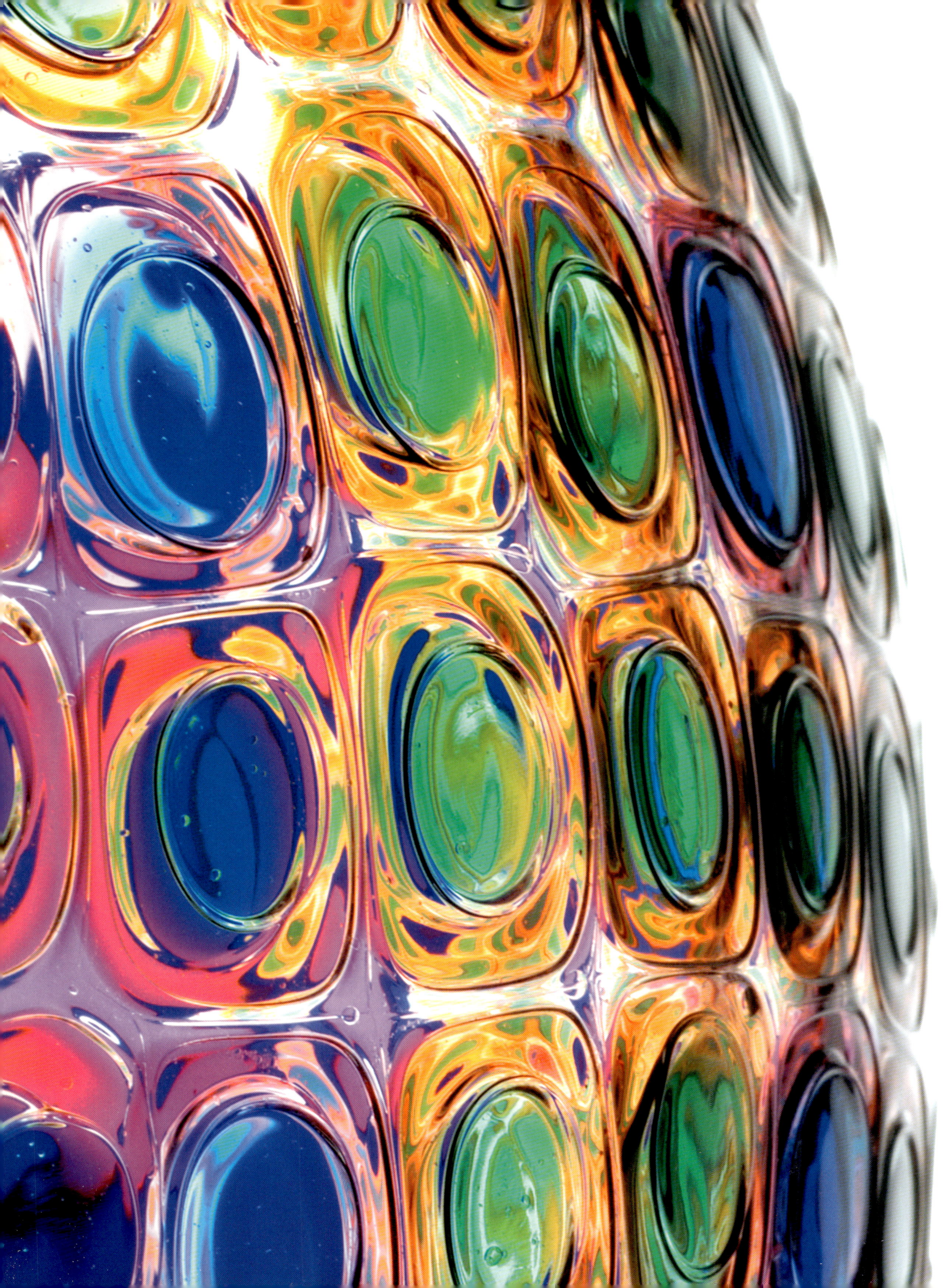

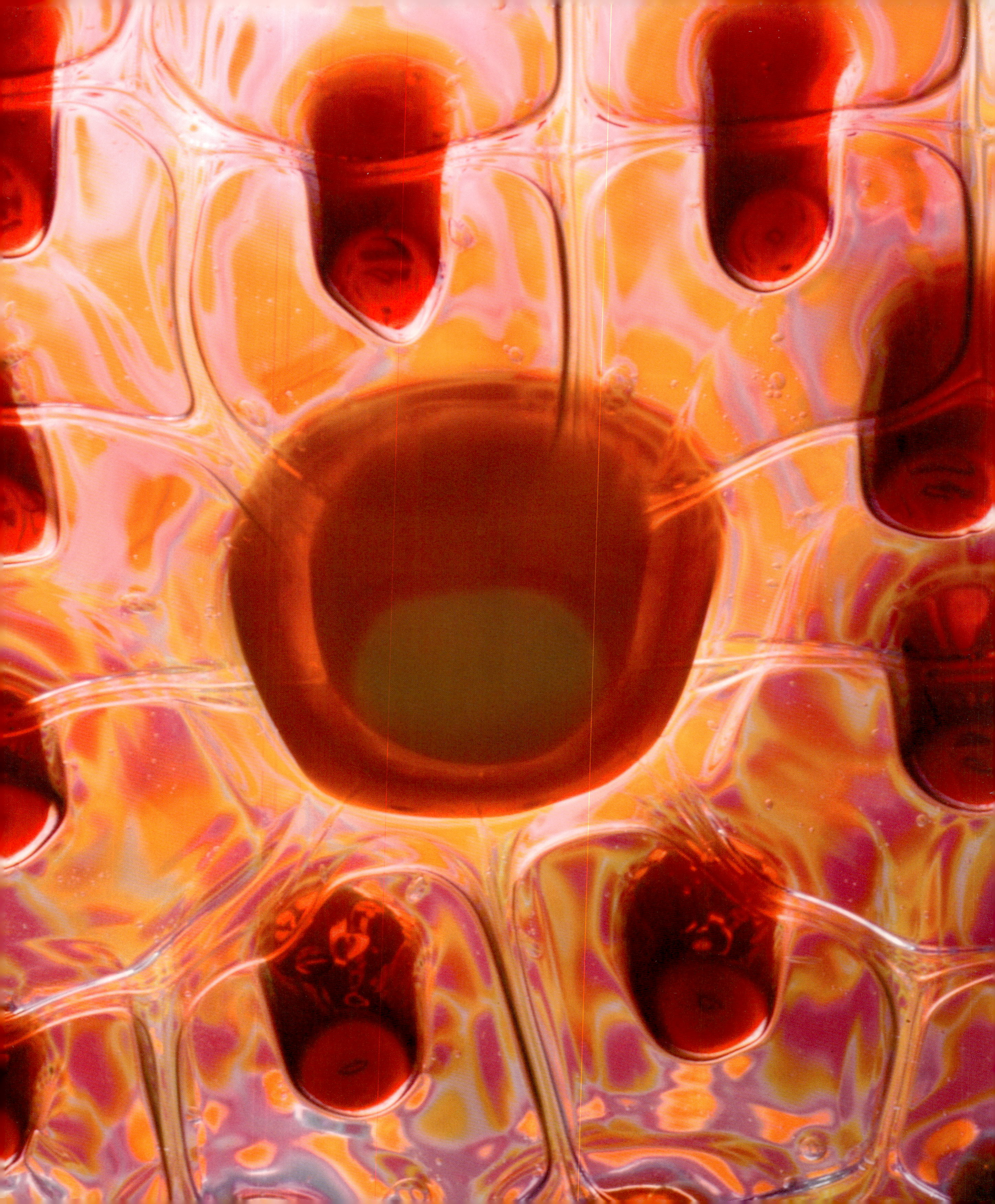

IN LOVE WITH GLASS

The first time I observed the work of Stephen Powell, I was attracted to his use of particularly colored murrini, and I was drawn into the objects themselves. At the time, I was unaware that the artist was American, and my first thought was "To which Venetian maestro can I attribute such artistry?" The multitude of colors captured my sight, and I had the strong desire to touch those objects, to perceive their asperity, or simply to feel their form. When I finally met Stephen for the first time, I was immediately taken by his kind friendliness. This first impression was soon fulfilled by many other positive qualities, first of which is his utmost generosity—and all of this makes me proud and honored of his friendship. Stephen is an excellent artist and teacher; he is open, and he is helpful to others. He has a great character, and, above all, he is in love with glass. I believe that such qualities are fundamental for transmitting a true love and passion—that goes beyond mere notions—for working with glass. Stephen, for me, is most importantly a great example of humanity. With friendship and esteem,

Lino Tagliapietra
Glass Artist
Venice, Italy

AN EXTRAORDINARY MAVERICK

One moonlit and starlit night, I stood atop the roof of a building on the campus of Centre College in Danville, Kentucky. There I witnessed the single most remarkable performance of all my years with the studio glass art movement. I was standing enveloped by the roar of glass-melting furnaces, the flare of gas torches, and the sound of incessant, throbbing rock music. At the center of this whirlwind of sight and sound was Stephen Rolfe Powell, hard at work. Powell, with the assistance of his team, was giving birth to a stupendous, sinuous, multicolored, four-foot-high, swollen glass vessel. As it shimmered against the soft sheen of that night sky, I realized I was witnessing something very special.

I was not alone in realizing that this primal act of creation was a unique moment. Powell was surrounded by more than a dozen groupies (myself now included). This was his standard entourage of locals, collectors, and dealers who regularly witness these stupendous Stephen Powell "blows."

Perhaps I should have realized that I was in for some inimitable experiences when I saw Stephen's work for the first time. This initial experience was at the 1990 Glass Art Society conference in Seattle. There I heard Libensky and Brychtova speak for the first time about their new freedom in Czechoslovakia. Dale Chihuly unveiled his new Boathouse showcasing Lino Tagliapietra himself demonstrating his own incomparable techniques. But no exhibit in Seattle was more dramatic that the one in a local painting gallery that featured several large contemporary Impressionistic-style canvases. Juxtaposed alongside the paintings were colorful, monumental glass vessels sporting sensual elongated necks on exaggerated bulbous bodies. This was the work of Stephen Rolfe Powell.

This rich new body of work must be created by a maverick, I could not fail to realize. Who is Stephen Powell? Where did he come from? He had somehow bypassed the established academic glass programs and was not connected with Pilchuck, Corning, or Penland. How did he land this opportunity to exhibit during a GAS conference at a fine art gallery? Other dealers were asking the same questions.

From that moment on, the seduction of my eyes by the luminous drops of transparent color joined together like a psychedelic dream has kept me pursuing one of the most pleasant journeys of my life. Suddenly, many dealers were dreaming of these magnificent vessels in their gallery too.

I worked at my job as a dealer while Stephen worked at his as an artist. At the first Powell opening at Marx Gallery in Chicago in 1991, Stephen strolled in, tall, lean, and with long flowing hair—smiling and graciously greeting the staff and guests. His warm Southern, gentlemanly manner, enriched by his thoughtful, academic style, left everyone with fond first impressions.

In my case, first impressions have only been deepened and broadened over the years by strong feelings of professional respect and personal friendship. Stephen is a natural giver and taker. He mentors well and enjoys being mentored. His favorite teacher and closest friend in the glass world is Lino Tagliapietra. The love and respect they share encompasses a rich language about their shared passion for life, glass, family, friendship, and learning.

The stunning forms and colors of a Powell sculpture initially fascinated me in Seattle just as their very creation blew me away on the roof atop Centre College on that night of sound and light in Kentucky. But learning about the complex techniques Powell has created to realize his work keeps me guessing as to what he will do next. Stephen is always experimenting and challenging the material to realize a new idea. This constant exploration of possibilities keeps artists, collectors, and gallerists all eagerly awaiting the next release of work by this extraordinary maverick.

Bonnie Marx

Marx-Saunders Gallery

Chicago, Illinois

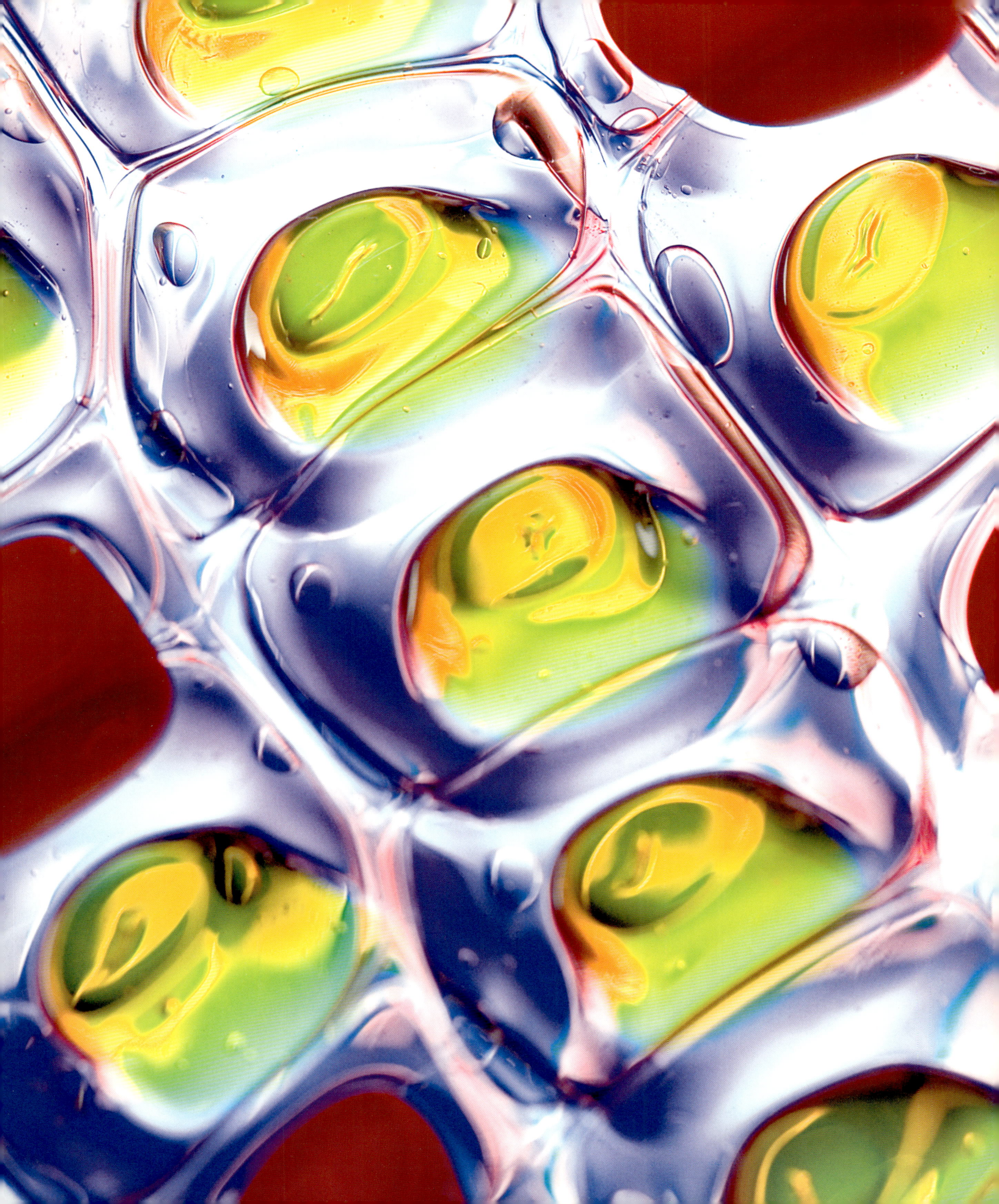

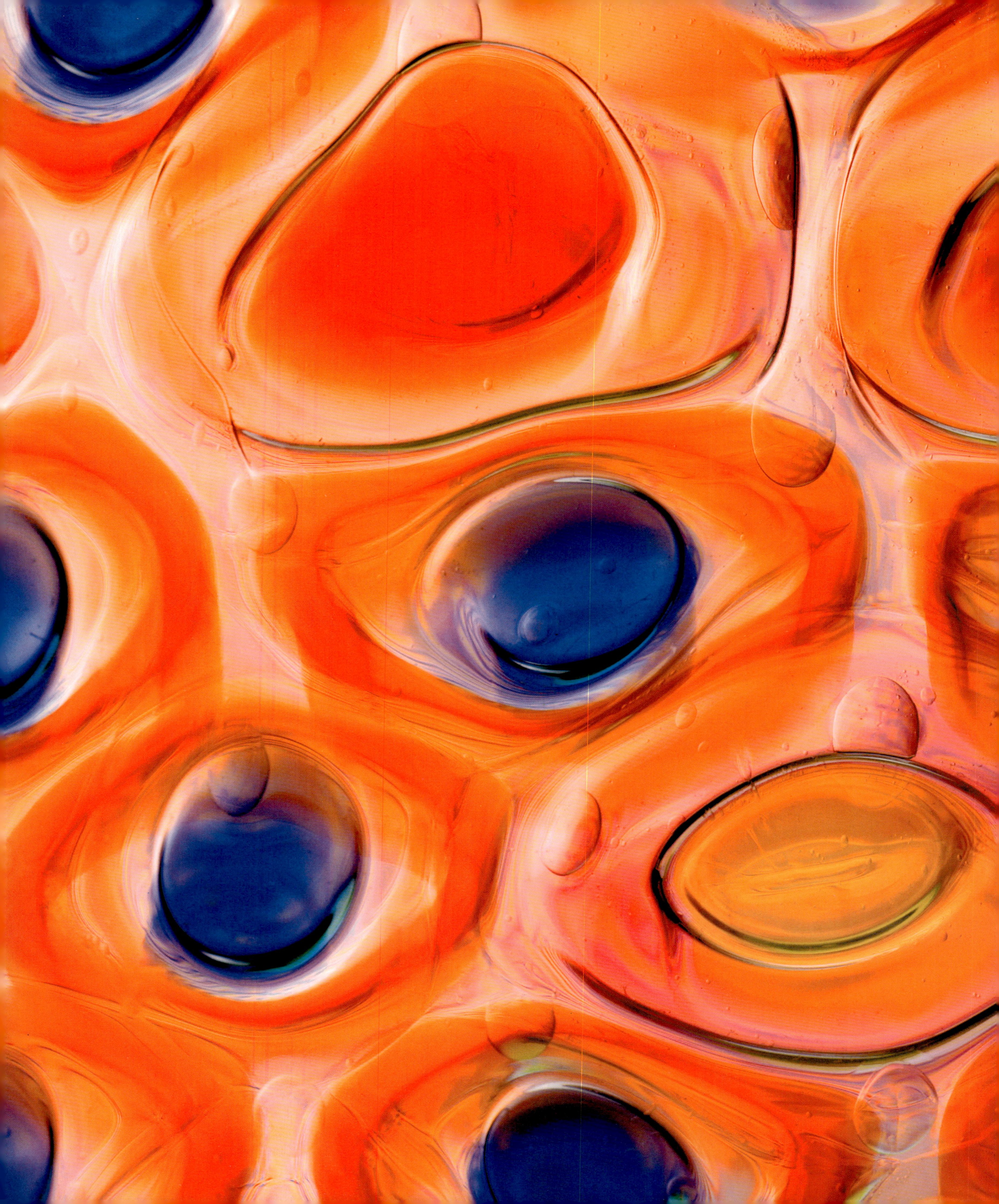

A COMMENCEMENT WEEKEND

I have known and represented Steve now for over 10 years. During that period there have been many opportunities to get to know him personally. Several times he has spent a few days with us at the gallery in Stockbridge. These times have always been during special collector events, and Steve has been very generous in sharing his knowledge and skills both in glassblowing demonstrations and slide lectures. He is articulate, is rather humble, and has a great sense of humor. He has a certain charm, which I would almost characterize as "Old World." He has that special knack of making people around him feel comfortable and welcomed. I believe that is because he is comfortable within himself.

My favorite example of these qualities was the weekend Jim Schantz (art director of Holsten Galleries) and I spent with Steve and his family in Danville in May 2004. The occasion was the commencement ceremony at Centre College, where Steve is a professor of art. What made this particular commencement so special was the fact that Lino Tagliapietra was receiving an honorary doctorate. Lino and Steve are very good friends, and Lino has visited Centre College several times as a guest of the college and is much loved by Stephen's glass students. Lino had brought his whole family over from Murano for this special weekend.

From the moment Jim and I arrived at the Powells' beautiful country home, we were made to feel very welcome by Steve, his wife, Shelly, and a number of Steve's current and former students who were there to help out with the activities of the weekend. The presence of these students was evidence of the great love they all have for Steve. Our first evening was spent mostly in Steve and Shelly's new swimming pool! It was already summer weather, and the pool was the perfect place to congregate. There was plenty of beer (despite its being a "dry" area) and a great barbecue. Throughout the weekend Steve and Shelly could not have been more hospitable. A game of pool basketball and later an Italian card game with Lino and his family are moments that particularly stand out in my memory.

The next morning we attended a demonstration that Lino gave at the college. Although Steve and his assistants were an important part of the team that morning, never did Steve try to occupy the spotlight. Rather, he stayed in the background, keeping a careful eye on the demo and welcoming the guests, including the president of the college and his wife. It was very clear that this was Lino's special weekend and that Steve's only concern was that it be as special as possible and that all the guests have a great time.

The weekend culminated with the commencement ceremony Sunday morning. Lino was one of three dignitaries to receive an honorary doctorate (one of the others was none other than Sandra Day O'Connor). Professor Powell introduced the maestro. Somehow seeing Stephen in his cap and gown made me see him in a whole new light. He became not only the friendly, funny, talented glassblower that I had known for years but a full professor of art at a respectable college.

The party following the commencement was held at Steve and Shelly's home. There was a huge tent and at least 100 people. Throughout the evening Steve circulated from table to table: "Did you get enough to eat?" "Can I get you some more wine?" "Wasn't that a great ceremony?"

Jim and I were a bit sad to leave this wonderful environment. Throughout the weekend Steve and Shelly were the perfect host and hostess of this unforgettable event. I left feeling an even greater respect and admiration for Stephen Powell, not just as a great glass artist, but as a human being.

Kenn Holsten

Holsten Galleries

Stockbridge, Massachusetts

A FEW DAYS IN KENTUCKY

Stephen Powell and I first met in 1984, when I was a visiting artist at Summervail, Colorado Mountain College. Since then I've valued our friendship and professional relationship over the years. Among the things that impress me about Stephen are his technical skills, his dedication to his own work, and his willingness to give time and attention to others in the pursuit of their art.

In 2000, Stephen invited me to Centre College as a visiting artist to demonstrate with the idea of producing a series of work. As usual when I'm in a new situation, I had some apprehension about the working environment. I wondered how well I could work with his assembled team and what I could draw upon for the inspiration for my sculptures.

Before we began our work, Stephen introduced me to the Kentucky culture by taking me to the Keeneland Race Track. Watching the pre-race ceremonies and observing the jockeys' multicolored racing silks, I realized that the jockeys' silks could reflect "my day at the races." Stephen offered his excess mosaic glass murrini that he no longer needed for his own work. I was excited to try a new technique of introducing color in my work. Such willingness to share his personal resources set the tone for my time working at the college.

As I began working with the team, it was clear that Stephen had prepared them well. His team was, in fact, so well disciplined that it took them a while to loosen up to my more fluid way of working with glass. But the rigorous attention to detail serves him well. It was an absolute pleasure to work in the creative environment that Stephen had established. The team was focused, supportive, and ready to work.

After we had worked all day and made a number of pieces, I thought we would stop, but Stephen would say, "We can do one more," so we'd complete another piece. Though it was clear everyone was tired, the team continued to work. The enthusiasm was contagious and persistent; in fact, I wanted to keep going as well. After a couple of days of work, the glass forms we made were especially successful. The pieces were shipped to my studio in Berkeley, California, where I cut, sandblasted, and acid-etched the glass forms into final sculptures.

Stephen's attitude enables people to work at their best and helps them to create quality work. The "Kentucky Series" I created with the aid of Stephen's team was of exceptional quality. Although I've worked in a number of countries and factories with various glassblowers, the "Kentucky Series" proved to be one of the more successful and popular series among the glass collectors. My time at Centre College with Stephen and his assembled team was a rewarding and satisfying experience, one for which I am grateful.

Marvin Lipofsky
Glass Artist
Berkeley, California

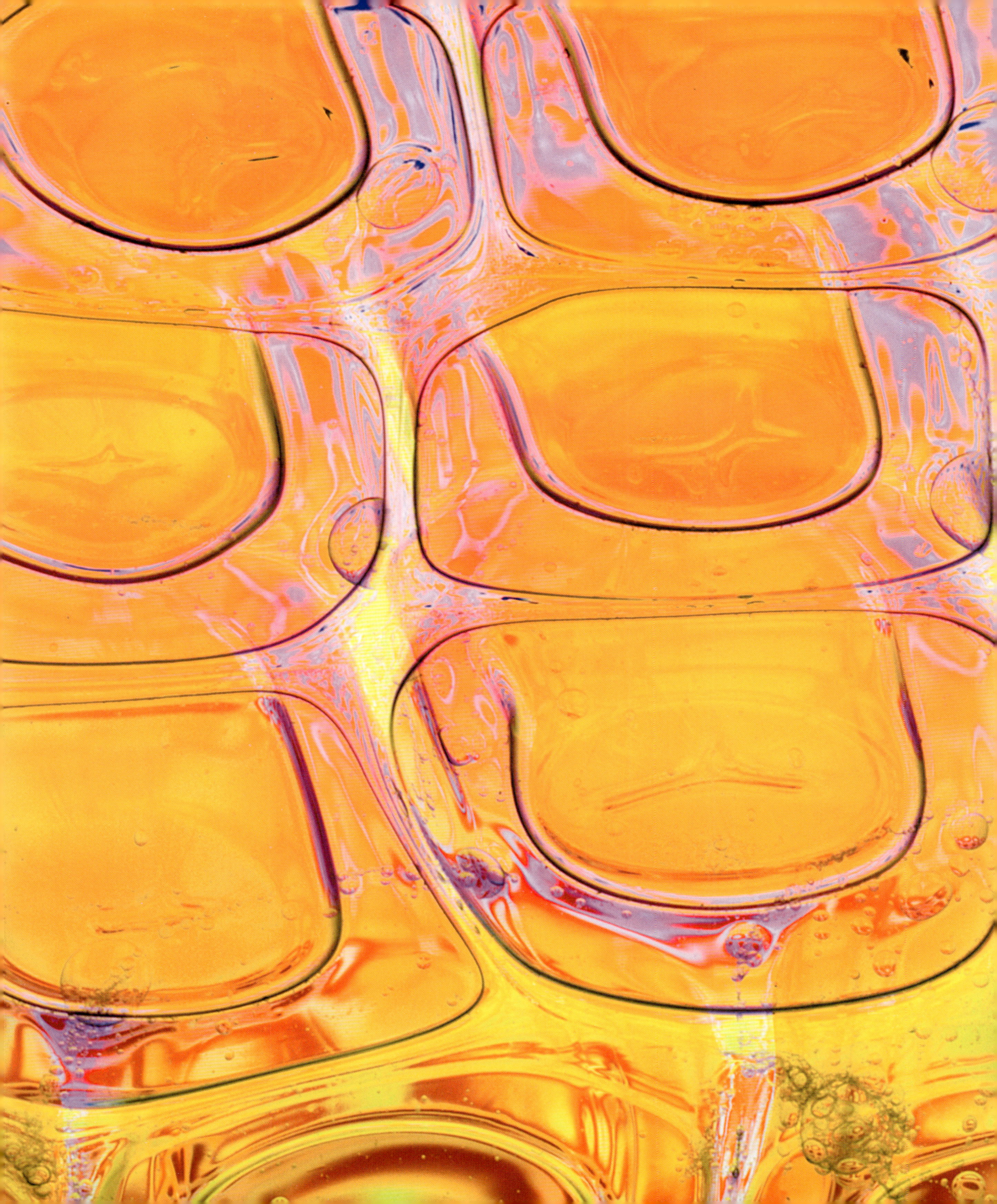

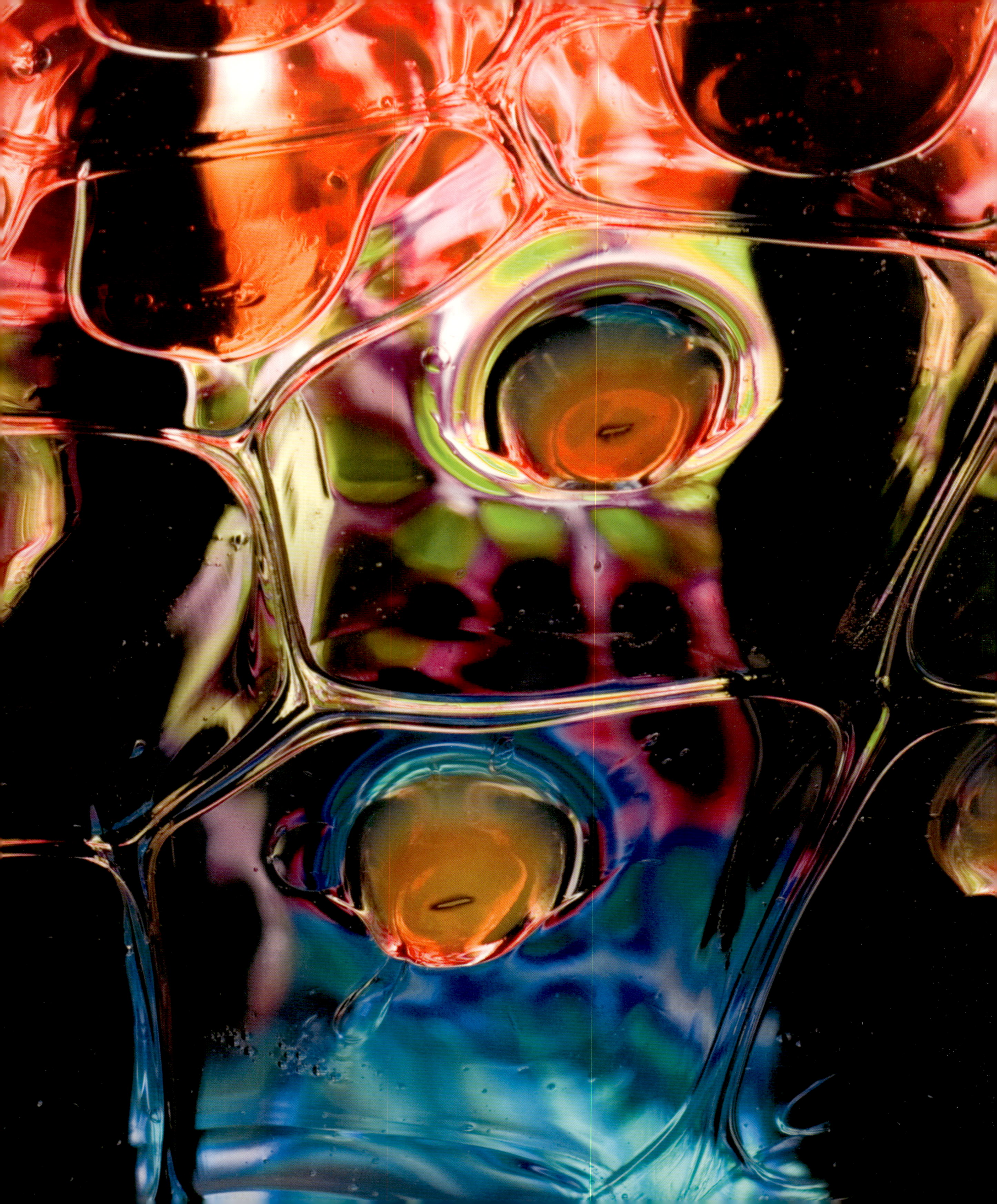

COLLEAGUE AND FRIEND

Professor Stephen Powell is a remarkable member of the Centre College community. While he is known by all as an accomplished, internationally recognized glass artist, we at Centre know him first as an excellent professor. One can only be impressed by Stephen's capacity to have an impact on so many young people—those who major in the visual arts and those who simply want to know about and explore what it means to be an artist. Being a teacher is one of his many extraordinary gifts.

Having spoken of Stephen's competence as a professor, I need to say a word about his dedication to Centre College and his community. So often men and women of high achievement "forget where they live"—and sometimes are reluctant to meet their obligations as citizens in their community. Both Stephen and his wife, Shelly, contribute to their community, their state, and their nation in mighty ways. They understand instinctively and model for others the belief that giving of one's time, talent, and resources for the benefit of others is the rent we pay for occupying space on Earth.

Finally, I note that Stephen Powell might choose to live and share his artistic brilliance in bigger cities or at larger, more complex institutions of higher education. He has made the better choice to remain at Centre College here in central Kentucky. We count it a privilege to call him colleague. We count it a blessing that he and his family are our friends.

John Roush
President, Centre College

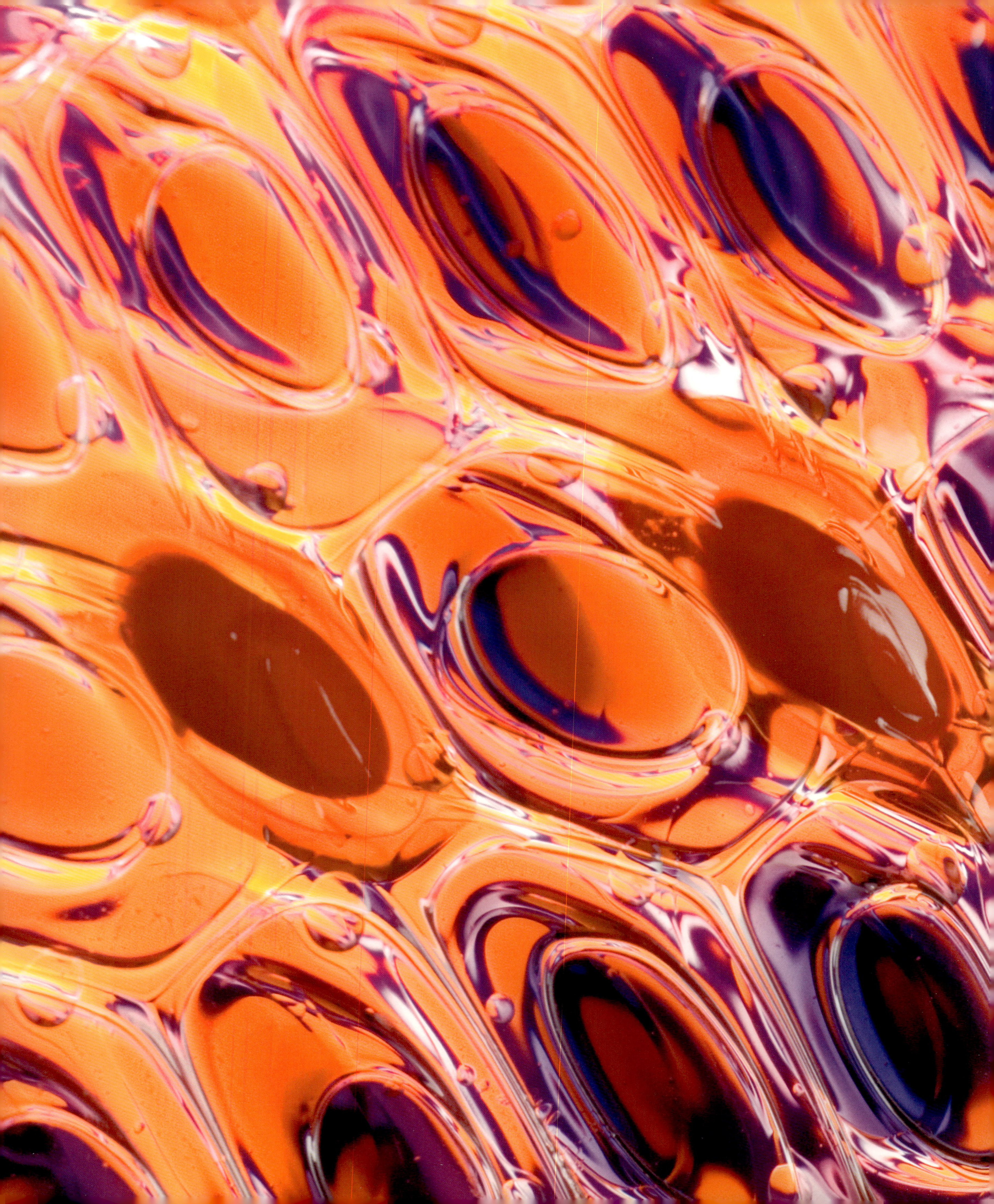

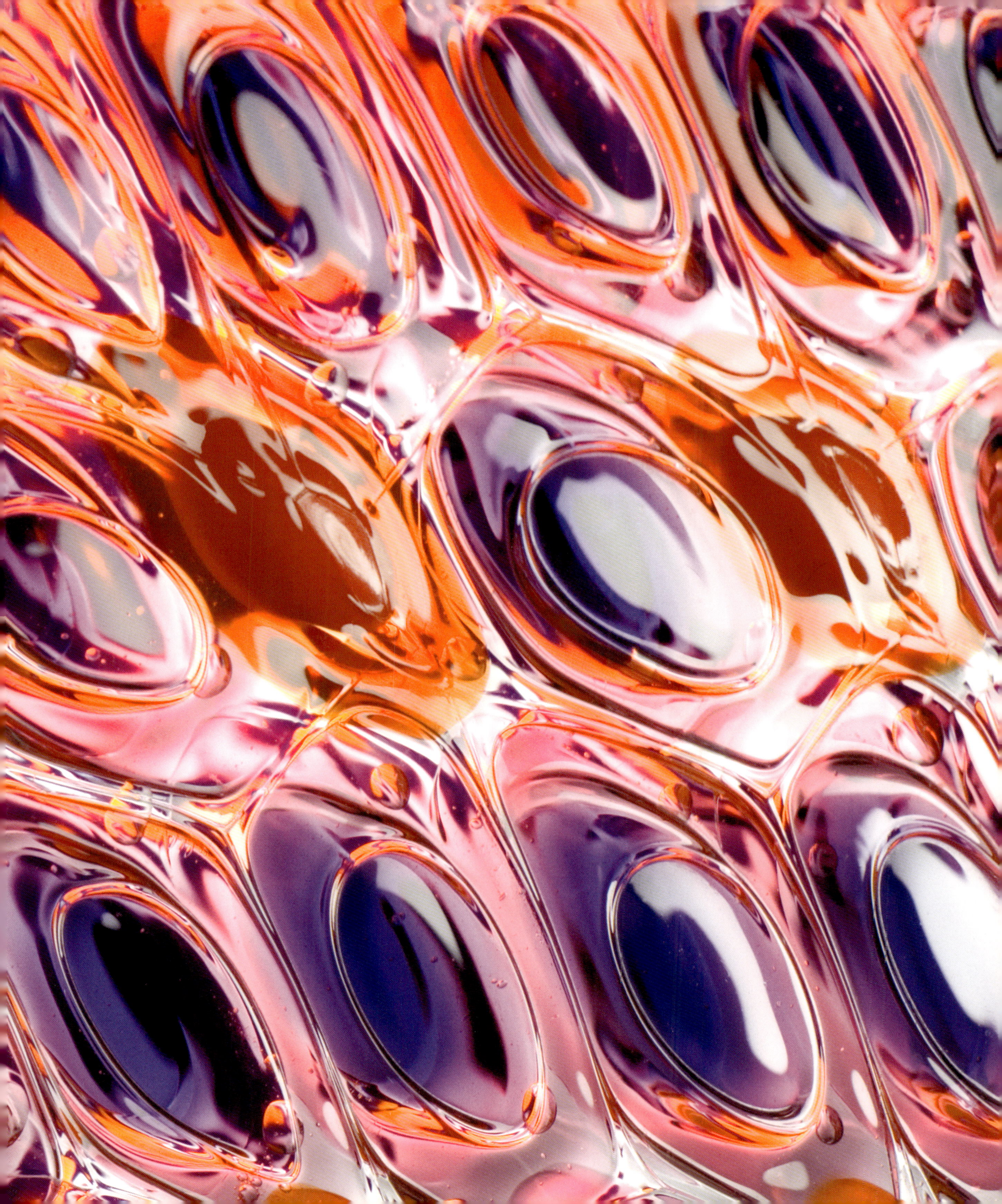

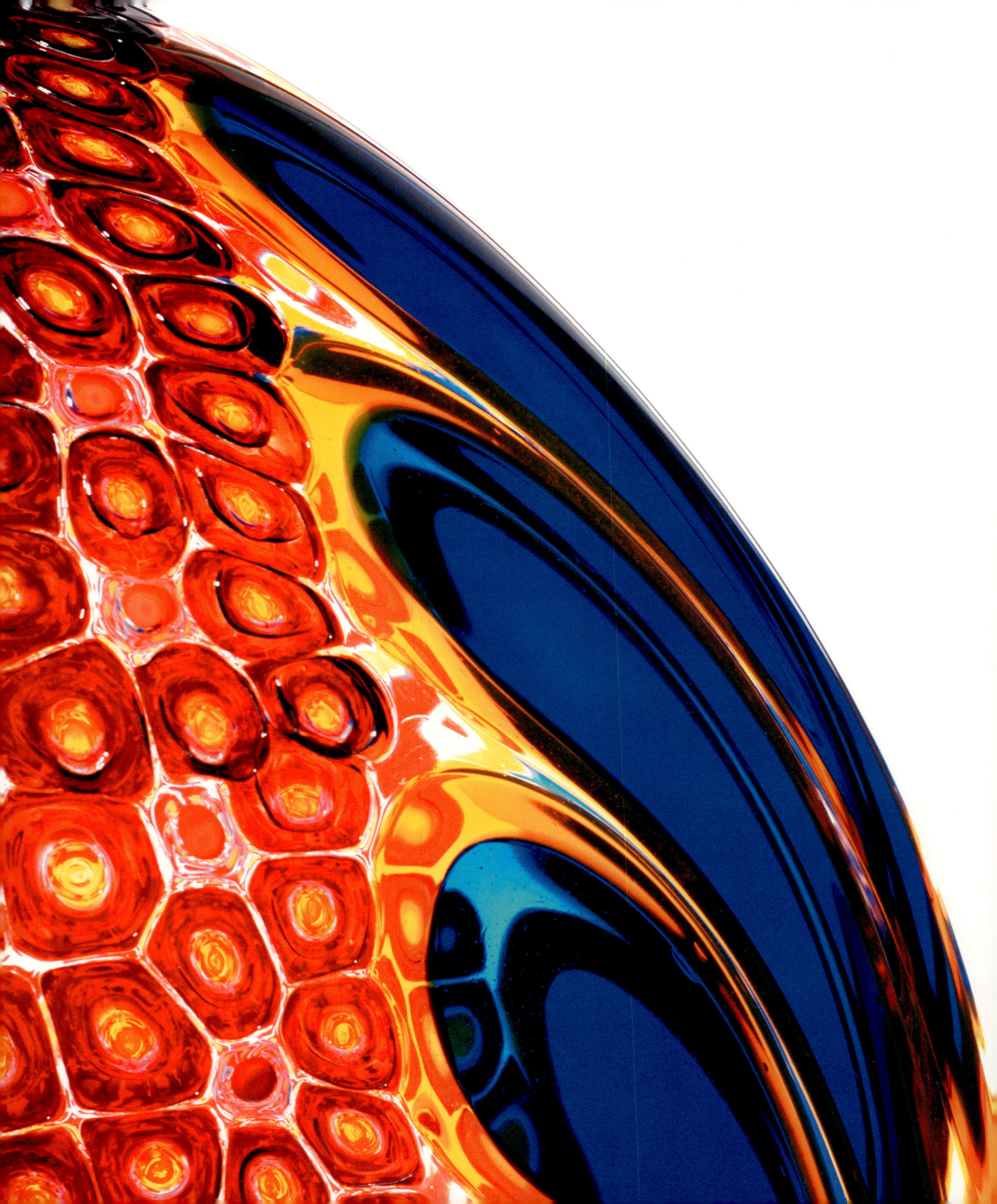

COLOR AND SWEAT: AN ANECDOTAL BIOGRAPHY OF STEPHEN ROLFE POWELL

BEGINNINGS

The first art object Steve Powell ever made was a papier-mâché baseball player. He was eight. He had no idea that art would be his life someday, but he was certain that sports would be. They already were.

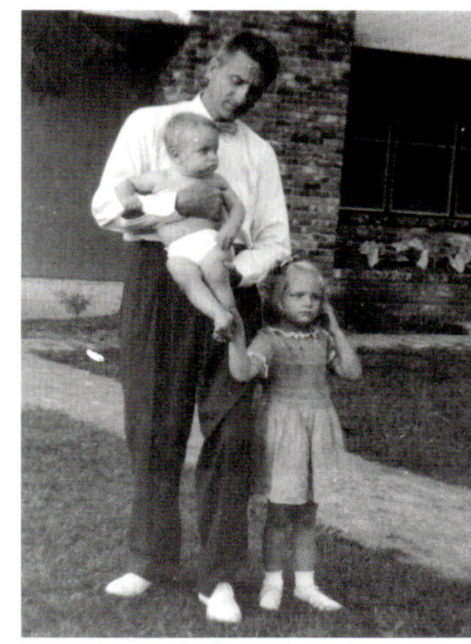

Stephen Powell with his father, Arnie, and sister, Pam, 1952

Growing up on Faculty Row adjacent to Birmingham-Southern College, Steve envied his friend Jim Burch because Jim's dad was the college basketball coach, not a mere professor like Steve's. Steve and Jim played whatever youth sport was in season; they religiously watched the *Bear Bryant Show* on television; they finagled sideline passes for Alabama football games at Legion Field; and they worked as batboys for the Birmingham Barons minor-league team (one of whose players had a name Steve especially liked—Blue Moon Odom). By high school Steve was a local star on tennis and basketball courts, despite the fact that his growth came late and he was only 5'3" and 90 pounds when he got his driver's license.

Steve loved the sweat and competition and spectacle of sports. Interestingly, spectacle was something sports shared with the work of his father, Arnie Powell, who was a playwright, director, and drama professor at Birmingham-Southern. Arnie was a powerful personality ("Dr. God," his students nicknamed him), and he was consumed with his work. To be with him, remembers Steve's sister, she and Steve became "college theatre groupies" while still children. Pam and Steve began to hang out at rehearsals, where they could watch their father at the helm of the bustling teamwork required to pull off a production. Arnie was intense. Steve remembers how the occasional outbreak of temper would electrify the air and bring the whole theatre to focus. Steve loved the scene shop and was allowed to help with set design. He watched plays from the light booth, fascinated by the gels that colored the stage lights. Arnie was fond of the artwork of Modigliani, Miró, and Klee. His avant-garde productions were known for their bold sets and lighting effects. The whole theatre experience was a clinic in color and light and expression whether Steve knew it or not.

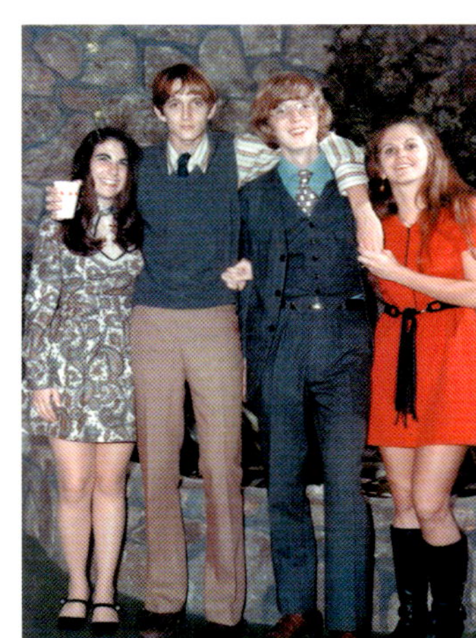

Merry Monsky, Stephen Powell, Hank Long, and Gail Burton at Indian Springs School, 1970

Not all influences, however, were so glittery. There was trouble in the parents' marriage that would lead to divorce by the time Steve was in college. Pam remembers the house as "kind of dark and lonely." At home she and Steve both were "very serious, rather blue." She wonders if it "was partly a desire to break away from those early, drab years that propelled him toward the dazzling color that infuses his work today." The strength of the genie, it has been said, comes from its being confined in the bottle. Another childhood memory is perhaps parallel. Family friend Virginia Rembert, art professor at the college, noticed and cultivated Steve's curiosity about art. He took a summer class for children with her, and she to this day remembers telling his parents that he had a precocious sense of color. Her husband, John, was an artist too, but a stroke had left him almost completely paralyzed. Steve vividly recalls how he was awed by John Rembert's abstract paintings. Despite how locked up the wheelchair-bound artist was, he managed to pour great waves of emotion onto his canvases through the tiny hand movements that the stroke had left him with. It was unforgettable.

EDUCATION

When Steve headed off to Indian Springs School, a private high school outside of Birmingham, it was mainly to play basketball and tennis. Indian Springs turned out to be a place where it was cooler to be smart or creative than to be a star athlete, however, and Steve embraced its free-spirited bohemian ethos. The atmosphere there made everyone want to learn and question and seek. "What is meaning?" "Define life." "Who and what are we?" Those were the kind of 1960s koans that Steve remembers of the charismatic, pipe-smoking headmaster, Doc Armstrong.

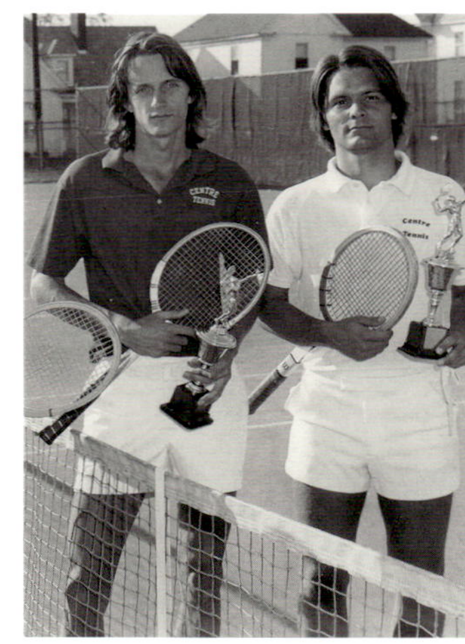

Stephen Powell and Mark Lucas, Centre College, 1973

Indian Springs was good preparation for hippie-era Centre College, the liberal arts school in Kentucky where Steve arrived as a shorthaired basketball recruit in 1970 and graduated as a longhaired artist in 1974. A military draft number of 52 made college (with a student deferment) a doubly wise idea, one his father insisted on. Steve played on the basketball team and seemed headed toward a psychology major at first, but by sophomore year he had dropped basketball rather than obey the coach's no-long-hair rule. Tennis alone was his sports focus now. The coaches were a religion professor and a philosophy professor who built the team as much with wit and laughter as with hard work. Steve's nonconformity suited them fine. He was voted team captain and, to everyone's astonishment, was as dependable a captain as he was a number one player.

Steve also dropped the psychology major and turned toward art, partly under the influence of his summer backpacking trek across Europe after freshman year. Wandering into the Musée Marmottan one afternoon in Paris, he was staggered by the color and glow and unapologetic beauty of the large Impressionist canvases that surrounded him. Back at Centre he studied sculpture, ceramics, and painting now. His senior show at the Norton Center was an extravaganza of 5' x 8' and larger abstract oil paintings, some of the dense clots of color still wet and moving when the work went on the walls.

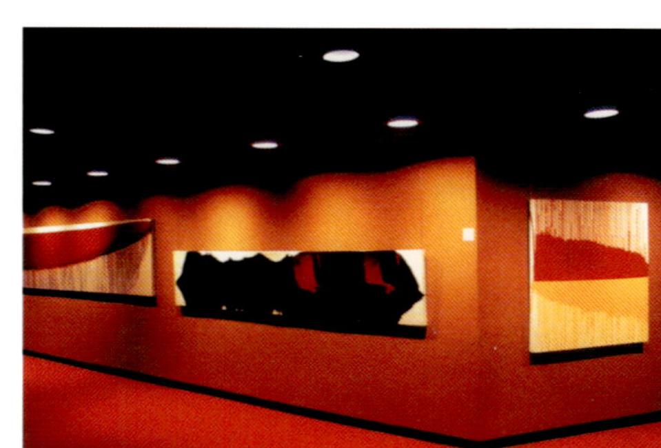

Senior Exhibition, Centre College, 1974

After Centre he outfitted a painting studio in downtown Birmingham where, he laughs now, he was "naïvely waiting to be discovered." A summer (1975) at the Provincetown Painting Workshop showed him most of all that he did not have the discipline to work by himself. It was a hard time of casting about, trying to find his way. The best thing he did was to take on a job teaching art at a maximum-security prison, Draper State in Elmore, Alabama. He was hired to teach painting and drawing to a class of some 15–20 convicts. He had to be escorted to the classroom by armed guards, to the sound of jeers and whistles from each cellblock. One of his best students had killed a girlfriend. Steve could not take turpentine in for cleaning brushes, he was told, because the prisoners would drink it. It was an eye-opening experience, mostly in good ways. These people were hungry for the expression of art and what Steve could teach them. Steve pulled strings, and they put on a successful show in Birmingham. Two cons from the class even began meeting him at the first cellblock entrance for the walk in. The catcalls ceased. There was only one sour note: Steve's name ended up mud with the parole board. Steve wrote the board and helped win work release for one of his students, who proceeded to rob a bank.

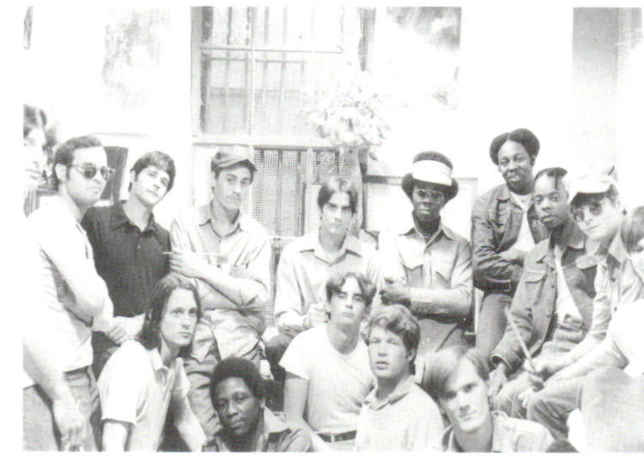

Powell (fourth from left) with his painting class at Draper State Prison, Elmore, Alabama, 1975

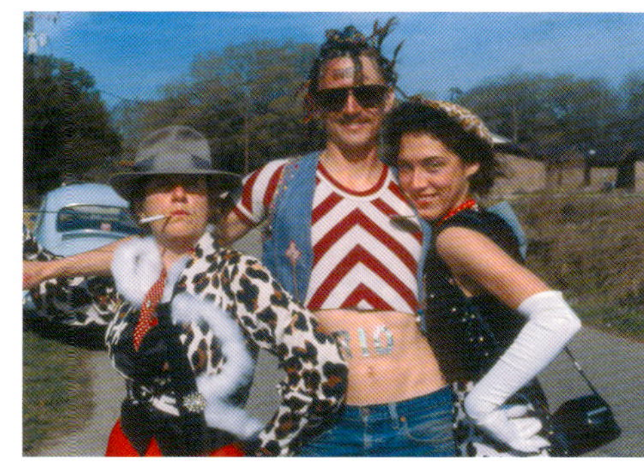

Therese Chabot, Stephen Powell, and Ashley Miller at Mardi Gras, 1980

The prison work built Steve's confidence as a teacher, but he was still in a blind alley as an artist. He got word now that his old school, Indian Springs, needed someone who could teach art and coach basketball and tennis. How many people fit that description? He had fond memories of Indian Springs, he had found that he enjoyed teaching, and the position sounded like a way to get his legs under him. He won the job and taught there four years, his own work focusing on ceramics now. He built a large reduction kiln, recruiting local industry for construction help and materials. He learned darkroom photography and took up serious gardening, skills that would play into his career later.

Then, age 28, he entered the M.F.A. program at Louisiana State University in Baton Rouge and began to grow like corn in the night. The great ceramics teacher there, Joe Bova, told Steve later, "Every year I take one risk student, and you were it." Why did he leave Indian Springs? "Well, I was living in a trailer," he laughs. The LSU graduate program was an exciting place, and Steve was surrounded by serious artists. He was in touch with the big art world now. He paid close attention and, following the style dictates of the time, was "careful not to make anything too pretty." All was going well as big sculptural ceramic pieces became his signature, with funny family names like *Mailbox Jones*.

There was a problem, though. He was being seduced by glass. After the first year of LSU's three-year program, he went to the summer workshops at Haystack Mountain School and the Penland School in ceramic art, but he could not take his eyes away from the extraordinary glass being made there. The prismatic colors were heart-stopping, the vessel forms sensuous and pure. The making process was especially appealing in its drama and athleticism and team spirit, so different from the patient, solitary labor his clay work required. The next summer at Haystack, he assisted Mark Peiser in glass. And back in Louisiana his heart was more and more saying glass and not ceramics. He helped build a new glass studio in Baton Rouge, declared an M.F.A. minor in glass, traveled to New Orleans for time in the Tulane studio, and, while there, watched Gene Koss work large-scale with nontraditional techniques.

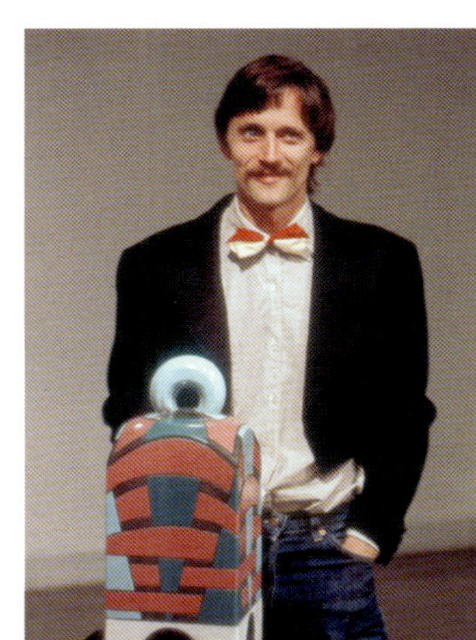

Powell with Mailbox Jones *at his MFA Thesis Exhibition, LSU, 1983*

Steve's mentor in ceramics could see him crossing over to the rival medium. "Glass," he would tease. "It's impossible to make an ugly piece of it." Steve understood the dig but nonetheless found himself thinking, "And what's the matter with that?" By the time he graduated with "M.F.A. in Ceramic Art" on his diploma, he was a determined glass artist.

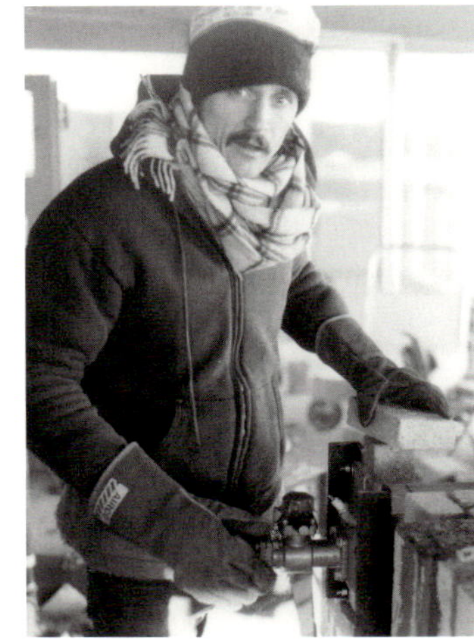

Powell building his first glass furnace at Centre College, 1985

BUILDING A STUDIO AND A CAREER

He was a determined glass artist about to become a professor at a school with no glass studio. There had been an unexpected resignation in the art department at his alma mater. Centre needed someone, fast, to come teach ceramics and sculpture. Steve was the best candidate, but there was one worry. The administrator in charge of the hire was concerned about Steve's reputation as a womanizer. "Would his daughters be safe?" he asked Steve's old doubles partner now on the faculty. The old friend lied, the job came through, and Steve loaded up his blowpipes and pontils and headed off to a school with no glass program.

During his first two years at Centre, Steve had to travel to hot shops in Seattle, Colorado, and Maine to make glass, but he had a plan to remedy that. Just outside the fifth-floor ceramics studio in the Norton Center, there was a large deck that looked to Steve like a glass studio waiting to happen. The plant manager said it could not be done. The administration offered goodwill but not money. Yet by the spring of 1986, Steve had rounded up enough student labor and gratis industrial support to see furnace, glory hole, and ovens all up and running.

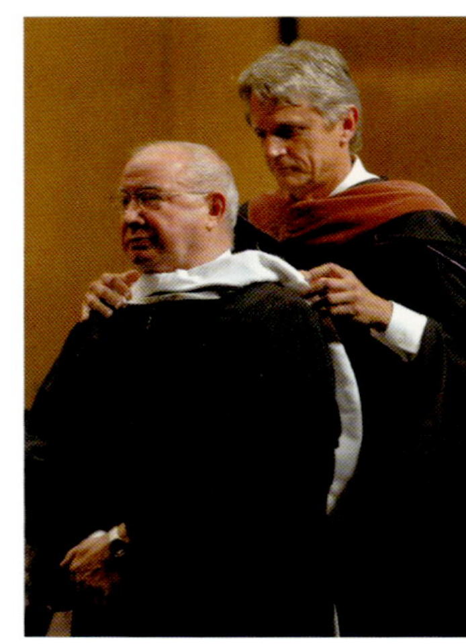

Stephen Powell hooding Lino Tagliapietra at Centre College commencement, 2004

At night the fiery spectacle out on the deck, only half sheltered from the elements by an overhang, drew lots of curious onlookers from both town and gown. The roaring 2,200° furnace vented into the overhang in an especially fascinating way, and people took bets on how long it would be before the whole Norton Center burned down. Meanwhile, what they saw was a lanky, sweating longhair playing with liquid fire. What they did not know was that, from practices as old as ancient Rome and as new as the latest thought in his head, he was working his way toward something unique in the world of glass art.

Steve was now making the earliest of the glass pieces chronicled in this book. At first he stood on a chair for the blow-out. Then came a four-foot wood platform, which evolved into a bigger one of welded steel, which soon needed to be lifted yet higher on concrete blocks. As the work grew in size, so did the glass program at Centre, one consequence of which was a lively competition among students to be selected for Steve's crew. Another consequence was a bigger, better studio somewhere other than the old rooftop where everything started. The state-of-the-art facility in today's Art Barn is in its fourth incarnation now, having been painstakingly adapted and upgraded for residencies by Lino Tagliapietra in 2000, 2004, and 2006.

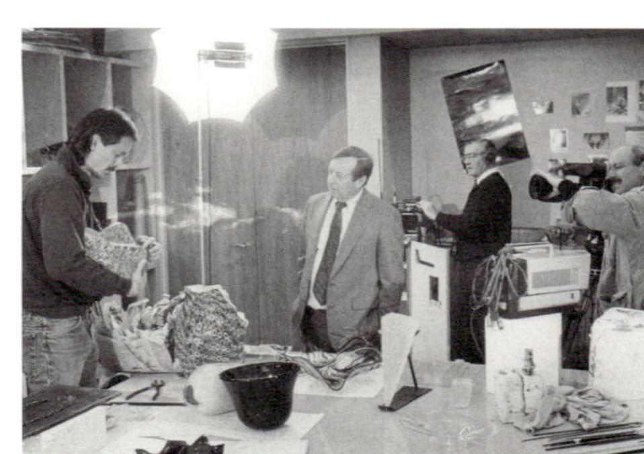

Stephen Powell interviewed by Robert Pierpoint for CBS's Sunday Morning *with Charles Kuralt, 1988*

Steve has international recognition in the glass-art world now (a feature on CBS's *Sunday Morning with Charles Kuralt* among the highlights), but few in that world know that while he was making the work that brought the fame, he was moonlighting at another job: teaching. Or perhaps, to judge from Steve's teaching accomplishments, the glassblowing was the moonlighting. Not once but twice he has been named the state's College Teacher of the Year. Steve describes his way of teaching as "osmotic," and former students agree. Ché Rhodes, who now runs the glass program at the University of Louisville, remembers an undergraduate occasion when Steve complimented his "rigid work ethic." "What he didn't realize," Ché continues, "is that I was only attempting to keep pace with him." Another former student and crew chief, Rich Garvey, says Steve's special gift as a mentor is in conveying the "sense that anything is possible; you truly can achieve anything you desire." Pat Martin, head of the glass program at Emporia State University, cites the pied piper quality that former students repeatedly voice. "In 1986 Steve asked me if I wanted to blow glass, and I said sure, and the next thing I know, I am digging for hardbricks in an industrial dumpster. It is 20 years later, and I find myself still following the same path."

Steve's mature career in glass has been expertly portrayed by such commentators as James Yood and Laurie Winters. What might be added to their analysis is personal background during these years. Four windows into that background are of particular interest: (1) Because teamwork is so critical to Steve's unique making process, a behind-the-scenes description of crew dynamics is illuminating. (2) Because he has been so willing to take his learning and teaching on the road—e.g., demos from Leningrad to Canberra to Salt Lake City during the Winter Olympics—an account of his most unforgettable trip, the 1990 sabbatical sojourn to the old Soviet Union, is perhaps emblematic. (3) Because two freak injuries have deeply affected his work and how he thinks about it, the story of them is revealing. (4) Last, because Steve's inspiration and motivation come more from the *creation* of his work than from the highly prized finished work itself, I offer, to close, a sketch of the strange things that go on in his mind when he makes a piece.

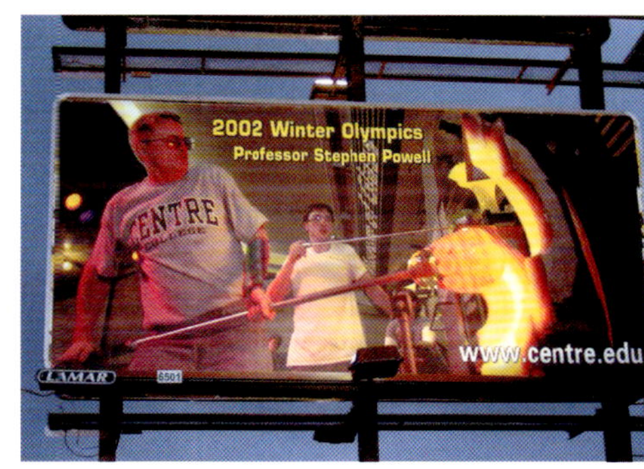

Winter Olympics billboard, 2002

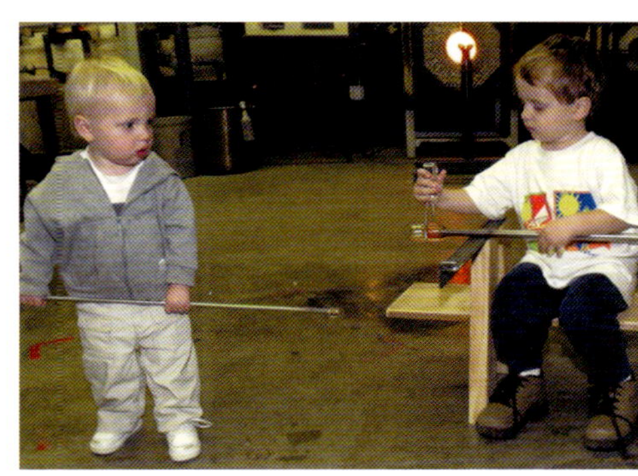
Powell family holiday card with Oliver Blue and Zachary Hawk, 2002

As remarkable as Steve's glass art is, I should inform you that in recent years he has made two works in another medium that are more important to him than *Lemon Jupiter Smith*, *Rattlesnake Johnson*, *Blushing Guppy Jones*, and the rest of their radiant ilk. Their names are Zachary Hawk and Oliver Blue Powell, ages eight and six. He was assisted in this work by his wife, Shelly. Or, rather, he assisted her.

TEAMWORK

An advantage of the team nature of Steve's glassmaking is, he says, the "built-in discipline." The "web of mutual expectations" gives him the structure that he needs. He and his team thrive on it. No matter the turmoil playing out in personal lives or external conditions, the work of "Powell Glass" goes on. "Steve can't not work" is how one crew veteran puts it. For the work to go forward, everyone must come through. In the preparation stages, for instance, one crew member charges the glass; another chops murrini. Steve must stay ahead of the team by defining the color pattern of each piece. A crew member lays out the murrini accordingly. One morning a week for five hours, the whole team, Steve included, pulls the cane that will be chopped into these murrini.

Steve's office at Centre is a collection point for the various stages and ingredients of all this preparatory work. It looks like a mess to the casual observer, but there is order in the places that count—the color bars from Germany and New Zealand all stacked and labeled, the hundreds of buckets full of murrini, the long sticks of cane with their concentric colors, and, most of all, the steel plates holding murrini patterns in vivid grids. A few finished pieces fresh from the annealing oven shine under bright light on a back shelf and furnish inspiration for the next work to come. Most mornings these days, crew veteran Paul Hugues can be found at a back table clipping beads from the skinny rods of cane or patiently filling in the murrini pattern (comprised of as many as 3,000 of these beads) that Steve has indicated with a side row of all the colors. Paul is the all-time master of this work now. An affectionate memory among other veterans, however, is that a standard bit of studio dialogue back when he started was, "Did Paul chop these murrini? Better junk them."

The teamwork intensifies when, twice a week, everyone comes together to "work hot." A complex choreography produces two pieces each session, each crew member responsible for key tasks and operations. Loud rock in the studio sound system provides a soundtrack for these blow sessions, and in the early going there is some joking around among the crew. The music will be silenced when the blow-out nears, however, and everyone will become as serious as a surgeon. All sorts of actions are going on around Steve as, at the bench, he rolls the pipe and hand-works successive gathers of hot glass with fruitwood blocks and a pad of nothing more than newspaper—eight wet sheets, meticulously folded, of the *Wall Street Journal*.

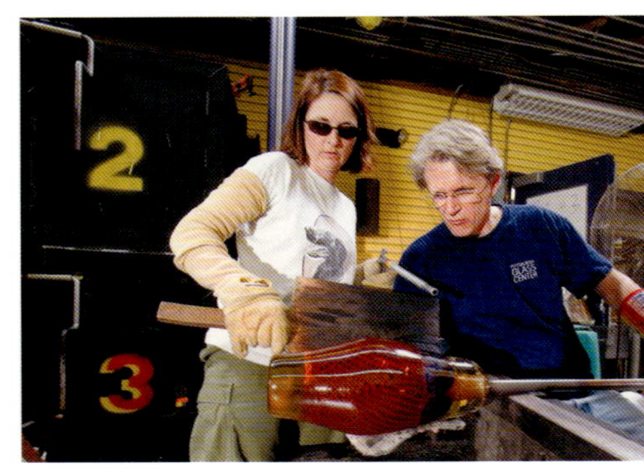
Mitzi Elliott and Stephen Powell, 2006

Among the current crew, Paul, as the most experienced, has ensured that all studio details have been attended to and that the stage has been set for Steve to concentrate entirely on the piece about to be made. There is an unwritten playbook, passed down from crew chief to crew chief, and Paul knows it, as did Chris Bohach, Ché Rhodes, Paul Nelson, Brook White, Pat Martin, Rich Garvey, and Perry Biddle before him. Paul manages the blowpipe during parts of the process and, near the end, he prepares the scorpion torch, a Powell invention, to melt the piece off the pipe. Then he dons the astronaut-looking heat gear to catch the piece in his arms and place it in the annealing oven. Jon Capps handles the pipe some too, most dramatically from the six-foot height of the blow-out platform. He also works a blowtorch, mans the paddles to protect Steve from heat and smoke, and keeps the blocks clean and in the water. He is responsible as well for "waxing the jacks": He heats beeswax and coats the long prongs used to shape the piece's neck, for without wax, the tool sticks and squeals.

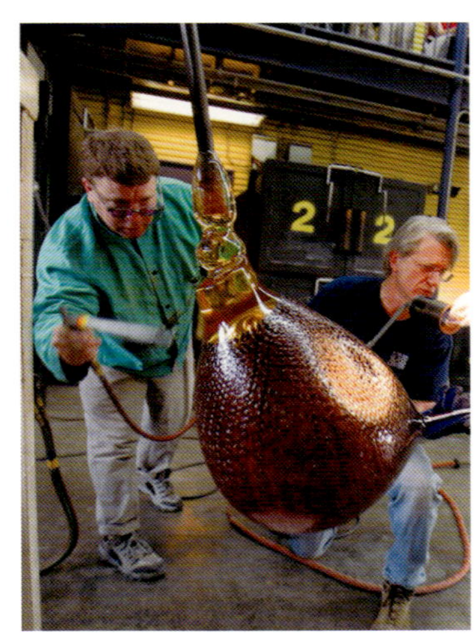
Paul Hugues and Stephen Powell torching a Screamer, 2006

Mitzi Elliott, Steve's business manager when not here sweating with the crew, heats the waiting murrini pattern and does other torch operations. The newest member of the team, she still notices the heat and danger to which the others have become inured. After the first time, she never again wears earrings to a work session; they get too hot. She has a burn scar on her stomach from the snap on a pair of jeans. One of her tasks is holding the blown-out glass on the pontil at the wild-eyed climax of the process. The two people blowtorching the piece at this moment are inevitably blowtorching her, too. Her shoestrings routinely catch fire. When one day her pants do as well, she holds firm on the pontil—as she is expected to—while Steve beats out the flame.

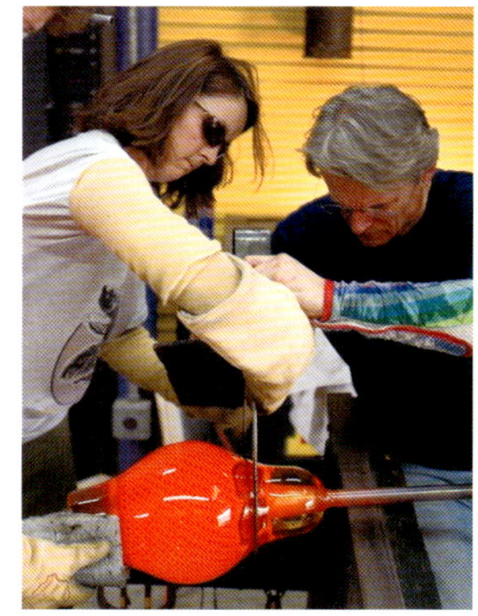
Mitzi Elliott shielding Powell, 2006

When the piece comes out of the oven two days later, Chris Bohach will do cold work, grinding and balancing according to Steve's directions. With water-fed diamond saws and rotary grinders, he will cut to establish the balance of the piece's base, and he will finish the long neck with necessary cutting and polishing.

Everyone on a crew, usually three or four strong, feels a commitment to Steve's professional work as the core of the glass environment at the Centre studio. Like the former coach and team athlete that he is, Steve fosters, feeds on, and returns this loyalty. Steve leads "through example and hard work," says former crew chief Rich Garvey: "Someone once called him the human dynamo—a reflection of his tireless efforts to be the best as an artist, an athlete, and a person." Garvey continues, "Many times you would see assistants exhausted and ready to drop, but they couldn't drag themselves away from the energy and excitement." Ché Rhodes, another former crew head, says he especially admires Steve's "ability to set unrealistic goals—and then meet them." "He's our pied piper," says current crew chief Paul Hugues. "We follow because we can hear the tune." Steve has "amazing drive," Paul continues, and an inspiring commitment to his work: "If you don't believe in yourself, who will?" Of the crew Paul says, "We feel like family, not employees." Then he laughs. "A big dysfunctional family."

Laughter is a constant. Beyond the intense professional teamwork of the studio, there is a lot of joking camaraderie and flat-out monkey business between Steve and the crew that builds esprit. Among crews past and present, tales of the craziness of working with Steve abound: running 5K's at midnight to wind down after blow sessions, donning skimpy leotards to make a parody aerobic-dance video for Shelly, jumping in a baby pool at the old Norton rooftop studio to cool off enough to make the next piece, and watching tools fly off this roof when debris in the polishing slurry ruined a work. A good place to hear these tales is at one of the wolf feasts after a hot-work session—over Bowl-a-Burgers and sweet tea at the bowling alley or, in days gone by, Cluck Clubs and peach shakes at the old Blue Ribbon Deli. The crews all have "Steve stories," in most of which he is cast as a force of nature. He is so driven, nonstop, and full of big ideas that he expects the same of everyone else. They laugh at how they get drawn in, and they laugh at how crew work can turn out to be so widely defined. Paul describes a conversation with Lino

Pho'o by Kate Philips

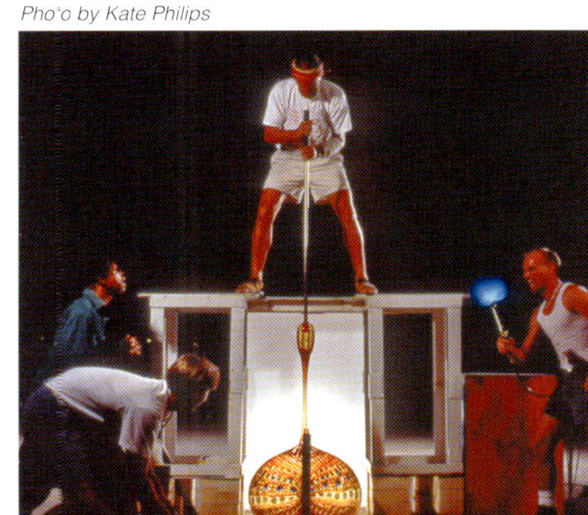
Ché Rhodes, Paul Nelson, Stephen Powell, and Brook Whi'e, 1994

Tagliapietra's crew one time when Lino was doing a residency at Centre. "What are you guys up to tomorrow?" Lino's crew asks, looking forward to the coming rest day. Answer: "Mowing Steve's farm. . . . Don't you guys cut Lino's grass?"

Escapades at Powell Farm are a particular theme. Paul remembers joining Steve in sleet and snow to begin planting 20,000 saplings—the day after Christmas. But then that was no harder than the time they planted 1,000 daffodils, just colder. Brook tells the story of building the beach: One day, swimming in Steve's farm pond, a team member jests, "We should put a beach here." The next day Steve says, "I've got a great idea. Let's put in a beach." And then the next day two 18-wheelers back as far down the hill as they dare with the best sand to be found in the state of Kentucky. "Taking a break from the studio" now becomes, for the crew, long afternoons of shoveling river rock and sand. There is also the story of Steve and the Jet Ski. Ché's version is a well-honed narrative: "It appeared to almost everyone that Steve had crossed the line between enthusiastic genius and insane risk taker when he announced his desire to acquire a high-horsepower Jet Ski for the modest pond at his farm. However, it was only a matter of days before all of the doubters were chronically waterlogged from too many hours zipping, zooming, and sometimes crashing around the pond. But that was not enough. Within a few weeks Steve accessorized the Jet Ski with water skis to be drawn behind. More is always better."

Perhaps the most legendary episode at the pond was the laying of the footbridge. Steve had somehow gotten possession of a 40-foot telephone pole, which he intended to put across the marshy end of the pond to make a bridge. He had a tractor adequate to the pulling task—except that it was not amphibious. There was a way, though. He had an old barn door off its hinges. He, Rich, and Brook would drag it into the pond shallows where they needed it. If Steve could then drive the tractor over this makeshift roadbed fast enough, he could pull the telephone pole into place, swiftly unchain, and then ride away onto dry land on the opposite bank. All was ready. Steve gunned the tractor down the bank, hit the barn door, and promptly sank in muck. When eventually a monster wrecker for hauling semis arrived and, from way up the hill, hooked its cable to the half-submerged tractor, it looked like the water itself was on the end of the towline. This is when the grizzled old one-armed cattleman who raised steers in Steve's back pastures drove up. "Boys," he said, "you all trying to move the pond?" Steve was undaunted, however, and found a way to get the bridge in that afternoon. It is still there.

The teams work very hard, but they feel appreciated. Brook notes how adamant Steve is about his assistants' names being on posters, postcards, and gallery notices. Rare is the glass artist who gives his or her team as much credit. He knows of no other, says Brook. There is "always a payoff," says Paul—in friendship, in the thrill of the medium, in the satisfaction of accomplishment. A case in point is Brook's memory of the next summer blowing season after Steve's arm surgery, perhaps the most intense work season ever. Steve was in "overdrive," says Brook, and the pace was hellish: three pieces a night, three

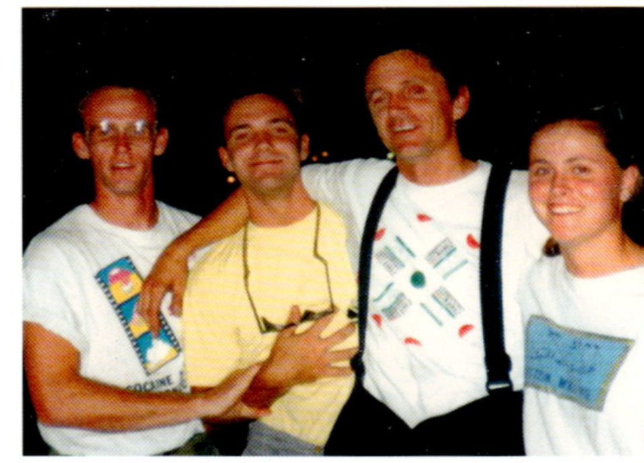

Brook White, Paul Nelson, Stephen Powell, and Alysia Fischer, 1993

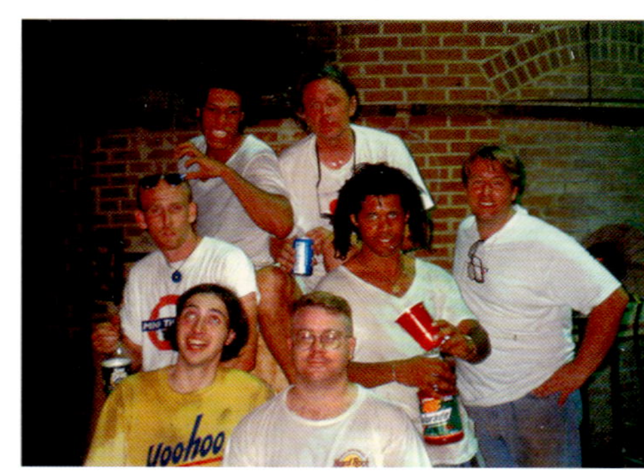

Brook White, Chris Bohach, Nate Watson, Stephen Powell, Paul Hugues, Ché Rhodes, and Doug Ohms at Wheaton Village, 2003

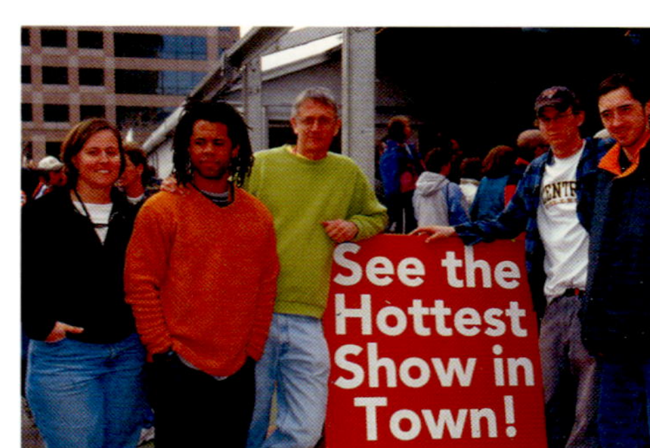

Alysia Fischer, Ché Rhodes, Stephen Powell, D. H. McNabb, and Chris Bohach at the Winter Olympics, Salt Lake City, 2002

nights a week, plus Saturday mornings for experimental works and cane pulling. Then one morning Steve announced, "Let's shave our heads and take a vacation." So for some richly deserved R and R, he flew them all to Isle of Palms where they ate, drank, and swam—and sunburned the scalps they had exposed with their solidarity haircuts.

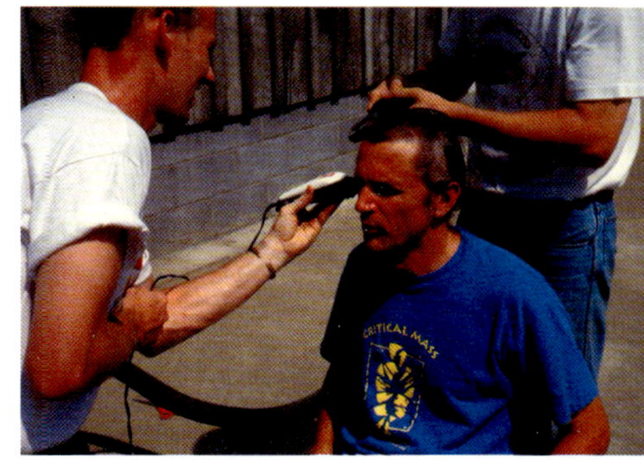

C:ew head shaving, 1992

SABBATICAL IN THE U.S.S.R.

This is the part of the story about the wonderful sabbatical, fall 1990, in the Soviet Union. Except that it was not a wonderful sabbatical. It was an experience in privation and hostility. The long lines and material hardship were to be expected. These were the meltdown days of the old Soviet order, and Leningrad (as it was still called) was suffering. The Mukhina Art Institute there was Steve's base of operations, and his personal host, Valeria Samoshkina, was as hospitable as the language barrier and economic situation would allow. But baffling problems marred a venture on which Steve had set off with the best will in the world. He was in the Soviet Union by invitation but was nonetheless resented as an intruding American. A black-market operation at the Institute confiscated and tried to sell his work at one point. When he had a translator, his freethinking ideas about hands-on glass artistry ruffled feathers. When he did not have a translator, he sometimes went weeks with no conversation. The only way to call home was through the personal intercession of someone at the American Embassy. This was not the pleasure excursion in Venice that his sabbatical might have been if he had been willing to do something typical of an American glass artist with a travel opportunity. He had wanted something different, something original. This was both, but in unexpected ways.

Steve thinks of the experience now as curiously akin to his arm injury. What he learned was to appreciate what he had. He had his own studio; his work was whatever he wanted it to be; he made it himself. This last item may seem like nothing: Don't all artists make their work? In the Soviet Union (as in much of Europe still—with even a version of it in Venice), glass artists were designers only; they made drawings. Workers did the making. "How can you design if you don't know how to make?" Steve found himself wondering everywhere he went.

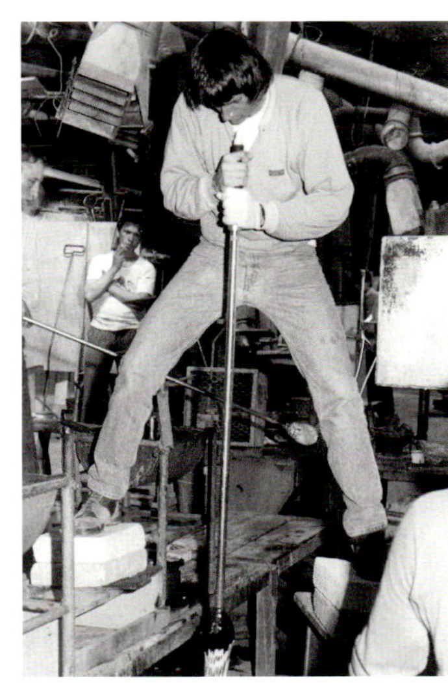

Steve blowing at the Red May Glass Factory in Vishney Volochok, Soviet Union, 1990

He knew about this divide between artist and maker, but he nonetheless felt that he himself could bridge it, at least temporarily. It was rarely to prove so. Part of his frustration, of course, was simply to be chalked up to the leap-before-looking energy that usually worked for him but could not survive the culture barrier in this instance. He had an understanding that he would be allowed to work, but it was hard to get through to people that work, for him, meant shaping the glass himself. When he tried to take the pipe at the Red May Glass Factory, for instance, he was met with plain hostility. His only recourse there, in order to do anything at all, was to stay late after everyone had left, set murrini, and insist on handling the pipe the next day. Late at night he would go back to his isolated room and dole out a few drops each from the two bottles of luxury he was determined to make last all month: a single Coke and a fifth of Jack Daniels.

There were bright spots—the magnificent architecture of Leningrad/St. Petersburg, the presentation of two pieces to the Hermitage Museum, the good work he made at the impressive Art Institute in Lvov, Ukraine—but the undertaking was nonetheless, says Steve, "a long, hard, lonely trip." Coming home, he was never so glad "for wheels to touch down at JFK." When he got back to Kentucky, it was going to be good to get back to work.

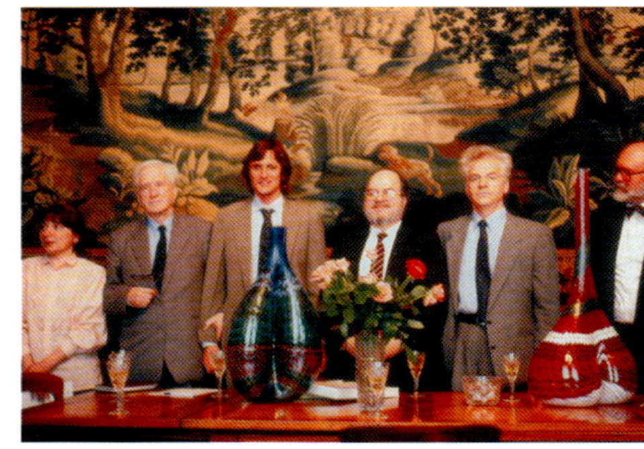

Presentation of Powell pieces to the Hermitage Museum, St. Petersburg, Russia, 1990

TALE OF TWO ACCIDENTS

It was a hot afternoon in the summer of 1991. Steve was in the third-floor studio of East Hall picking colors for the next day's work when he saw a bird fly across the room. A pigeon had gotten in through one of the open windows, old eight-foot, multipane windows on tilt-out hinges. Trying to flush the pigeon, Steve pushed on a window to widen the opening. The pane shattered, Steve's right hand went through, and then, instinctively jerking back, he raked his forearm into a shard that severed nine tendons and the ulnar artery and nerve. Spouting arterial blood, Steve gripped the wound with his left hand and ran down the three flights of stairs and toward an exit, spray-painting the floor with blood at each of the heavy doors along the way. Once outside, he got help from some students who commandeered a professor's car and rushed Steve to the hospital emergency room.

At the Danville hospital, Steve was insisting that his friend the orthopedist Mack Jackson be called. But Mack could not be located until his brother Elmer, head of radiology at the hospital, drove out to Mack's farm and fetched him out of a field. What Steve most remembers about Mack that day, once he arrived and set to work, was that his normally cheerful friend did not smile even once. It was a sign, Steve only realized later, of how serious this injury was. Mack cleaned, clamped, and tagged inside the ugly hole in Steve's arm. Then he said Steve needed to go to Louisville and proceeded to put him in his own Volvo and drive him there himself.

Steve had gotten the best of small-town care. Now the job was up to city doctors. At Suburban Hospital in Louisville, the hand-surgery expert Morton Kasdan examined what Mack already knew was career-threatening damage: all but two flexor tendons severed and critical nerve damage. Steve could not move his hand. Dr. Kasdan prepared for surgery and set to work on Steve in the operating room.

The headline of the front-page article in the *Louisville Courier-Journal* the next day—"Freak Accident Threatens Career of Prominent Glass-Blowing Artist"—was news to Steve too. Not till then had it dawned on him that his glassblowing life now hung in the balance. Dr. Kasdan had skillfully reconnected the sliced tendons and done what could be done for the ulnar nerve, but whether Steve would blow glass again was not a certainty. The doctor compared the nerve reattachment to being like hundreds of tiny strands of sliced spaghetti

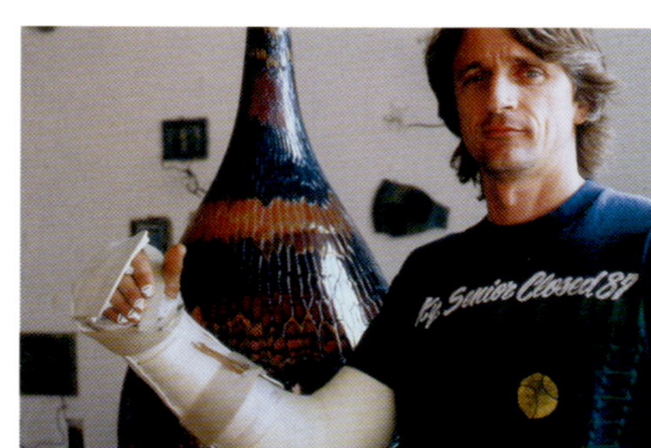

Powell after arm accident, 1991

pushed together in hope that some would realign. Much depended on Steve's commitment to the rigorous rehab discipline now set out for him.

What Steve's friends remember about the next months is that they never saw him when he was not squeezing a rubber ball or working the pulleys, rubber bands, and fishing line of the curious arm-and-hand contraption that had been contrived as both a brace and a rehabilitation tool for him. He lived at the Seelbach Hotel for a week of therapy in Louisville, and then he worked with therapists in both Danville and Louisville. In fact, without telling Dr. Kasdan, Steve engaged three different therapists, instead of the recommended one, to increase the intensity of the rehab. Every day he pinched up and down his arm for signs of returning sensation where the severed nerve had left him numb. He kept steel-spring handgrippers in his car and every room of his house. He tried everything, massage therapy included, that might speed healing as the tendons slowly regained function.

By September he was working glass again, "the best therapy of all," he says. He could make only small pieces for a while, but he was back in the studio, blowpipe in hand. His arm still hurt, and he struggled at first just making cups and little vases. He was having to relearn the use of his hand and even to reeducate his touch. He had a little book of textures—sandpaper, felt, marble, etc.—that he would rub and try to identify. The pain was bearable, however, and he worked through it. The ulnar nerve only partially regenerated—to this day he has limited feeling in the ring and little fingers of his right hand—but come winter he was working large-scale again. Brook White, crew chief at the time, remembers that Dr. Kasdan had said it would be six months before Steve could expect to return to the studio. Four months to the day, however, Steve was doing a special demo in the Danville studio for Dr. Kasdan's entire surgical team. Engraving his signature on the bottoms of these new pieces, he began appending the letters "AA," After Accident.

With the usual sense of invulnerability of the young, Steve had always taken being able to handle glass as a given. Now he saw how swiftly even that could be swept away. What he absorbed from the ordeal, he says now, was a deep sense of how special every good day of good work is. There are a certain number of pieces he can make in a lifetime, he feels, and any missed day in front of the furnace is two or three lost works. The accident also made him more aware of all the people he relied upon, especially his crew. While he was laid up at home on painkillers, this crew pulled cane day after day according to his color directions and made a huge stockpile of murrini. A former crew member came back from out of state to cold-work pre-accident pieces for a show already scheduled. Steve was mellower afterwards, they say, better tempered and more vocal in his support. In a flash of temper the week before the accident, he had called this crew, in the wake of a botched piece one day, "Larry, Curly, and Moe." After the accident, though he would still offer emphatic correction when occasion demanded, he did not say things like that anymore.

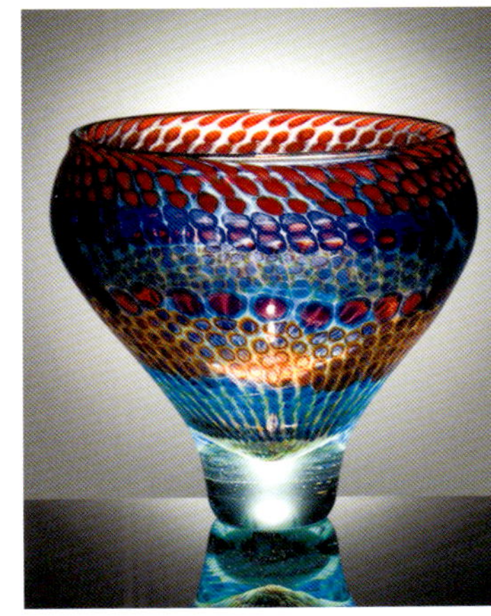

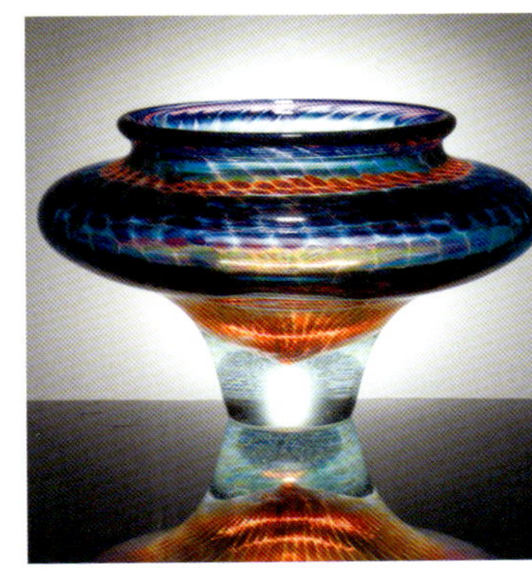

Recovery pieces, 1991

Steve looks back on the crisis now as a crucial passage in his artistic life, equaled in impact only by his trip to the Soviet Union. Glass work was his raison d'être, and to keep working was everything. He may have become gentler with his assistants, but he was more driven than ever. As friends and crew members will testify, Steve's work always goes forward. The first thing Steve said to Brook White when he came to after the operation was, "Did you finish pulling that cane?" His passion is the foundation of the entire enterprise; his drive is something everyone in the crew feels. No matter the complications of equipment, weather, crew, or private life, the cane-pulling and blow sessions proceed with unbreakable discipline.

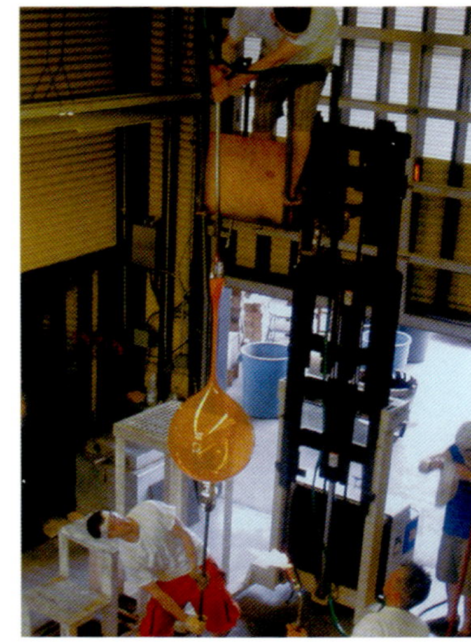

Chris Bohach, Ken Moore, Stephen Powell, and D. H. McNabb experimenting with installation pieces, 2003

Then there was the *other* accident, 13 years later. There was no drama this time—it was just a freak fall while standing on a wobbly stool—but the result was a broken left wrist. And it was very bad timing for a broken wrist: right at the outset of a long, distraction-free summer blowing period with a seasoned crew and everything going full steam. One alternative was that with his wrist temporarily incapacitated and in a cast, he could just close up shop and lose the season. But the broken bone and two other influences converged to create a different and much better result: the new "Whacko" phase of Steve's work.

To keep the work going, Steve saw that his crew would have to handle the pipe, pick up the murrini, and actually blow out the piece, maneuvers that he had always reserved to himself. Surrendering this control now, he discovered that he could control other elements of the process more readily by being freer to move around and thus to better watch and direct.

The changed routine in the studio became a gestation period for a new sculptural form. Steve had long been fascinated with the possibilities suggested by Lino Tagliapietra's asymmetrical shapes, a fascination that was one part of the new idea awakening. He had also been recently at work designing hanging pieces for an installation project at the University of Kentucky. Exploring possible shapes, he had developed large vessels with organ-like contours suggestive of stomachs, livers, and bladders. The installation lost its funding and never came about, but the thought Steve put into it did bear fruit.

Directing the summer work in the studio now with a cast on his broken wrist and a stabilizing boot on an injured Achilles tendon, Steve began to experiment with asymmetrical sculptural forms. He was determined as usual to achieve these forms with some version of his signature nontraditional techniques, techniques that still had the adrenaline rush of his previous work and kept him at a sufficient remove from the feel of Lino's asymmetrical vessels. Swung horizontally during the blow-out, they no longer had a vertical axis. The first 20 or 30 created were made simply to lie on their sides. Then, watching the work evolve from his new perspective away from the pipe and the blow-out platform, Steve had the idea of pulling a tail out of the back part that used to be cut off. Two points could be fashioned from this tail that, in combination with the tip, would create a tripod.

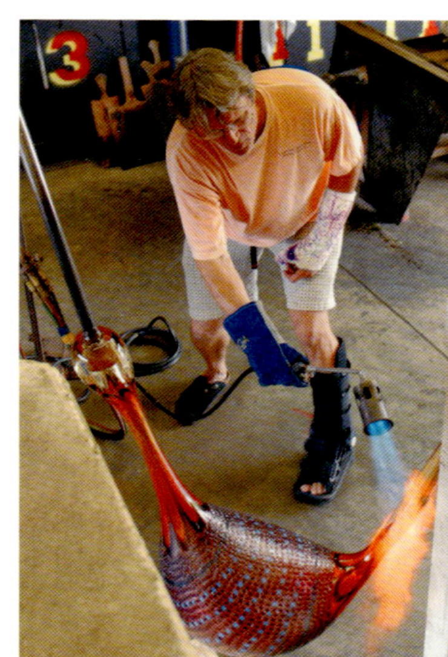

Powell torching a Whacko with broken wrist and torn Achilles tendon, 2004

Steve was pushing the limits of the hot-making process he had developed. With so many split-second maneuvers to perform as the molten glass responded to gravity and centrifugal force, he and his crew found the climactic part of the making process so wild and intense that they began to call the new pieces "Whackos." There was nothing crazy about these beautiful new shapes, but their alignments were a marked departure from the teardrops and lobed symmetry of the past. The asymmetry led to denser patterning of the murrini and new approaches to color. The dynamism of the new work referenced the animal world and nature instead of human forms. Aardvark, anteater, elephant, and armadillo shapes exposed the insides of the pieces and interacted with light in striking new ways. The active postures suggested craning, digging, nudging, sniffing. The name "Whackos" stuck.

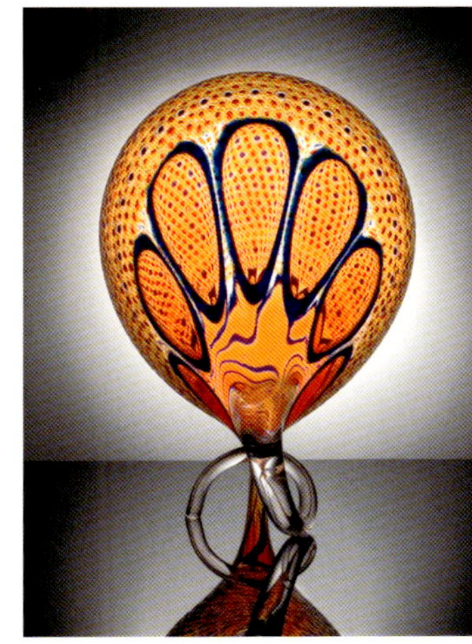

Whacko, Startled Dizzy Snorter, *2005*

THE TRANCE OF CREATION

Steve describes his feeling about the process of making his work as nothing less than "what a drug is to an addict." There is a price to pay, he admits, because he is always thinking about the work; relaxation and normal life come harder than they should. But the addiction has its ecstasy. There is an unmistakable emotional curve to the making of each piece, and it culminates in the climactic intensity of the blow-out, the adrenaline-pumped and dazzling moment near the end of a procedure that is peculiarly Steve's. His nontraditional studio methods are part of the reason he is often described as a "maverick" and as radically "American." They are perhaps relevant as well to his occasional self-description as a "pyromaniac." At any rate, it is telling to hear him express what making one of his pieces is like from the point of view of being inside his skin. One discovers that the making of the work is the big thrill. The energy that runs the whole endeavor is not the beauty of the finished work but the excitement of its creation.

First in the creation process come the decisions Steve makes before even going into the studio. Weeks, sometimes months before, Steve chooses colors which are pulled into canes and later chopped into murrini that will eventually coat the surface of the pieces. Steve says he is constantly thinking of color combinations and "how, weeks later, they will go together." The murrini for particular pieces are often laid out long before their actual use. He is always looking at color blends and contrasts around him, particularly in nature. He even designed his shower with windows to face east so he can look at the colors of the sunrise every morning. And in the evening he watches the sunset from the top of Snow Knob, the big hill at the front of his farm, one of the highest points in the county.

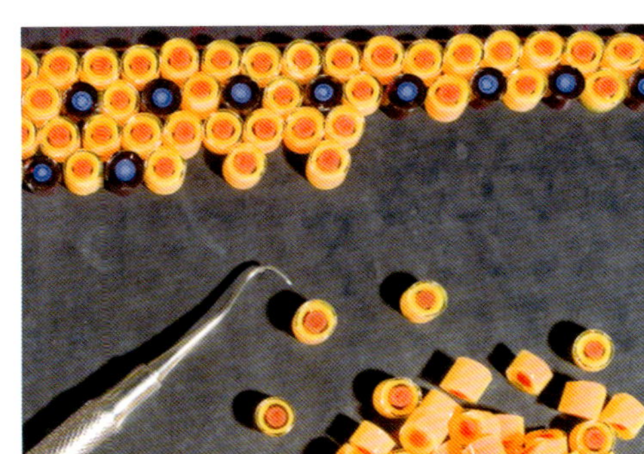

Murrini and dental tool on steel plate, 2005

On the days appointed for working hot, he depends on his crew to have the studio completely ready with no technical problems because he needs to have a clear head when he goes in to begin. He does not mind, however, that "people seem to congregate" in and around glass studios; he has learned how to focus on what he is doing and "tune distractions out." With the first hot gather come the demands of centering the glass, and he is "immediately drawn into the process of making the work." He is aware of the smells in the studio as melted beeswax lubricates the jacks and the molten glass makes contact with the fruitwood blocks. He begins to enter "the zone," a feeling of connection with the glass. This feeling of heightened sensation and hyperfocus is hard to express, but it is like, Steve suggests, when he is "hitting good shots in tennis."

As the successive gathers proceed, building up the clear glass that will be under the skin of color, the intensity in the room builds, and "everyone on the crew becomes more focused." Steve does his best work when he does not have to worry about any of the three or four crew members doing their jobs. They know that, he says, and take pride in making sure he is not distracted. (A favorite anecdote among the crew is about an episode when there was a screw-up and Steve went ballistic: "There's a reason we do exactly the same thing every time," he said, emphatically. "I don't want to have to think!")

The first critical point in the process is the color pickup. If it goes awry, Steve has an expensive lump of lost time and miscarried vision on the end of his pipe. The large scale of his work and his nontraditional method make this moment "a constant challenge," he says. The molten glass cylinder on the end of the hot steel pipe weighs some 30 pounds by now. Rolling this heavy cylinder in a straight line over the murrini is a delicate, easily botched operation. Avoiding a ragged seam at the end of the pickup is even harder. Stationed at various angles around the table, crew members coach Steve's moves to help guide a successful pickup. Once this is accomplished, all feel a momentary relief.

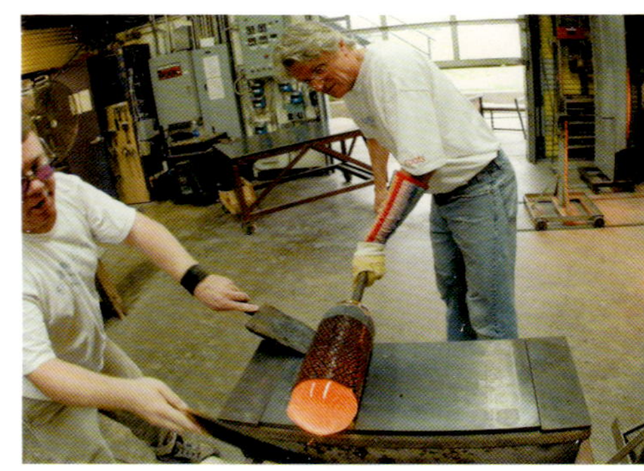

Paul Hugues and Stephen Powell picking up a murrini pattern, 2006

As Steve and crew begin shaping and heating the piece to prepare for the final blow-out, the emotional intensity builds again. You can see it in Steve's face as it contorts in concentration. At the bench he has a curious way of tilting his head and rocking back and forth as he sights down the rolling cylinder, which is fleshed now in a lizard skin of murrini. A crewmember wipes Steve's dripping forehead. Another follows his movements with a wooden paddle that shields his arm from the heat. He shows no awareness of either of them. Smoke rises up out of the wet newspaper Steve is using to work the malleable glass. Every twist and turn, every heating and cooling, now affects the ultimate form.

As he "takes the final heat," he is "mesmerized," he says, "by the piece turning in the glory hole." Anticipation builds. Crew members speak of watching Steve "get through his emotions" as he stares into the glory hole. Staying focused is crucial. The heating must be perfect to achieve a long neck and full body in the piece. The timing now is mostly something he "feels in his body, through his hands." As the glass is brought to life by the 2,300° heat, it becomes "hyper responsive," Steve says, highly reactive to every move "through gravity and the centrifugal force of turning the pipe." As he feels the movement of the piece merge with his visualization of the shape, he knows "the time is right."

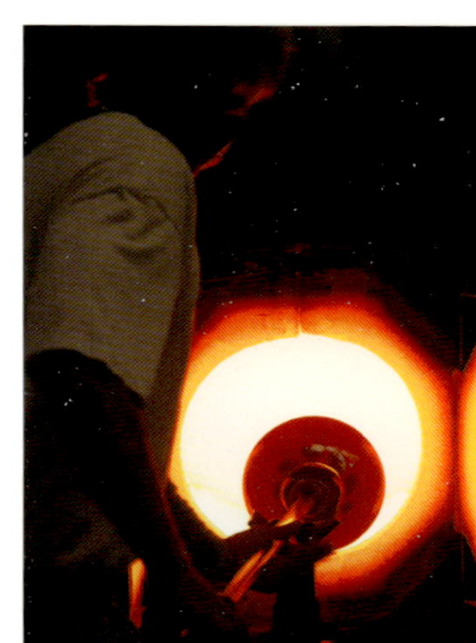

Powell in glory hole, 2006

He is most in the zone now as he "rips the piece out of the glory hole hoping that heat and gravity will pull the neck down enough, but not too much." He passes the piece off to a crew member who in turn passes the pipe up to another who is waiting on top of the six-foot blow-out platform. He then grabs a blowtorch in one hand and an air gun in the other. This is the climactic birthing moment, very different from anything in the slower, more controlled Venetian method that is traditional. Steve describes his way as "everything at once with gravity and centrifugal force." The go-for-broke momentum of it all has a drama and life that Steve loves. Right now, he says, "is like having the 20 years it might take to grow a tree happen in just a few moments before your eyes." This is Steve's last window to work the piece, and he is shouting, shifting, torching, cooling as if a life hangs in the balance. He feels as if he is "out of his mind," yet he is making split-second decisions inside the twisting knot of assistants on and around the blow-out platform. The loud music in the studio is off now. Steve and crew are barking monosyllabic directions over the rumble of the furnace and the hiss of the torches. "Up!" "Down!" "Turn!" "Blow!" "Stop!" "Neck!" Although outsiders have described these moments as frenzied, Steve says they unfold for him in slow motion.

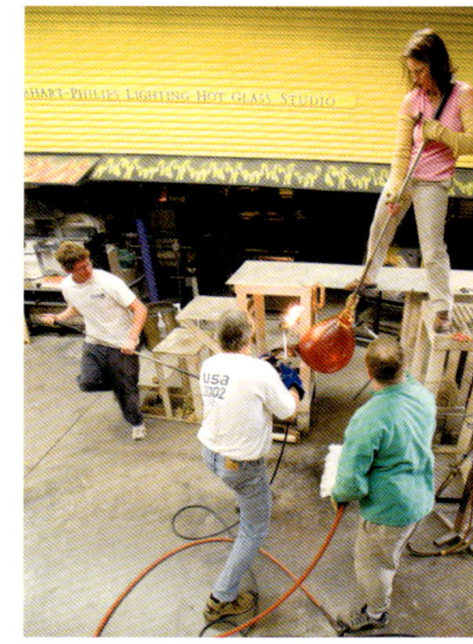

Jon Capps, Stephen Powell, Paul Hugues, and Mitzi Elliott shaping a Screamer, 2006

Once the piece's shape is defined, Steve feels he begins thinking practically again. He and others begin evening up the heat with torches, getting ready to disconnect the piece and put it in the annealing oven. After the scorpion torch is brought out to melt the glass off the blowpipe, the pontil is all that engages the cooling piece. The glass at the bottom of the pontil is chilled and scored, then tapped off with an old hockey stick. The piece falls into the waiting arms of a team member in protective gear. Steve torches it as it goes into its nest in the oven.

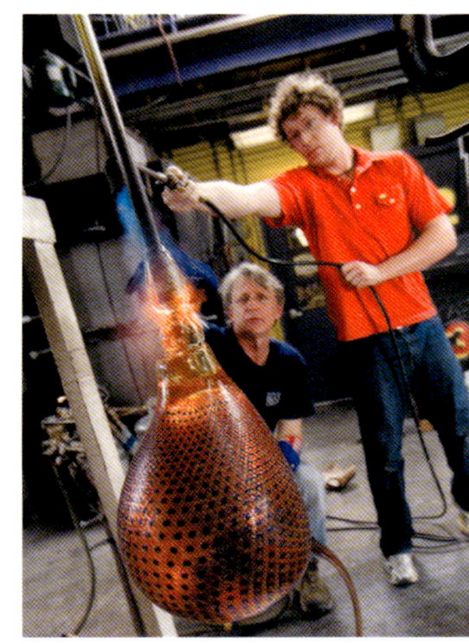

Stephen Powell and Jon Capps finishing a Screamer, 2006

Gradually he has felt himself coming back to normal consciousness. The return is a little reluctant. "Part of me," he says, "wants to stay in that trance of creation." He and the crew look at each other, knowing that they "have just gone through something together." He shakes each crew member's hand. The aura lingers a while, yet "we all know we need to start getting ready for the next piece before the aura is gone." This aura is his addiction.

Afterward, Steve's whole day feels different. He knows he "has done something [he's] supposed to do."

Mark Lucas

Mark Lucas is Jobson Professor of English at Centre College. He writes on Southern literature and culture and is the author of HOME VOICES *and* THE SOUTHERN VISION OF ANDREW LYTLE.

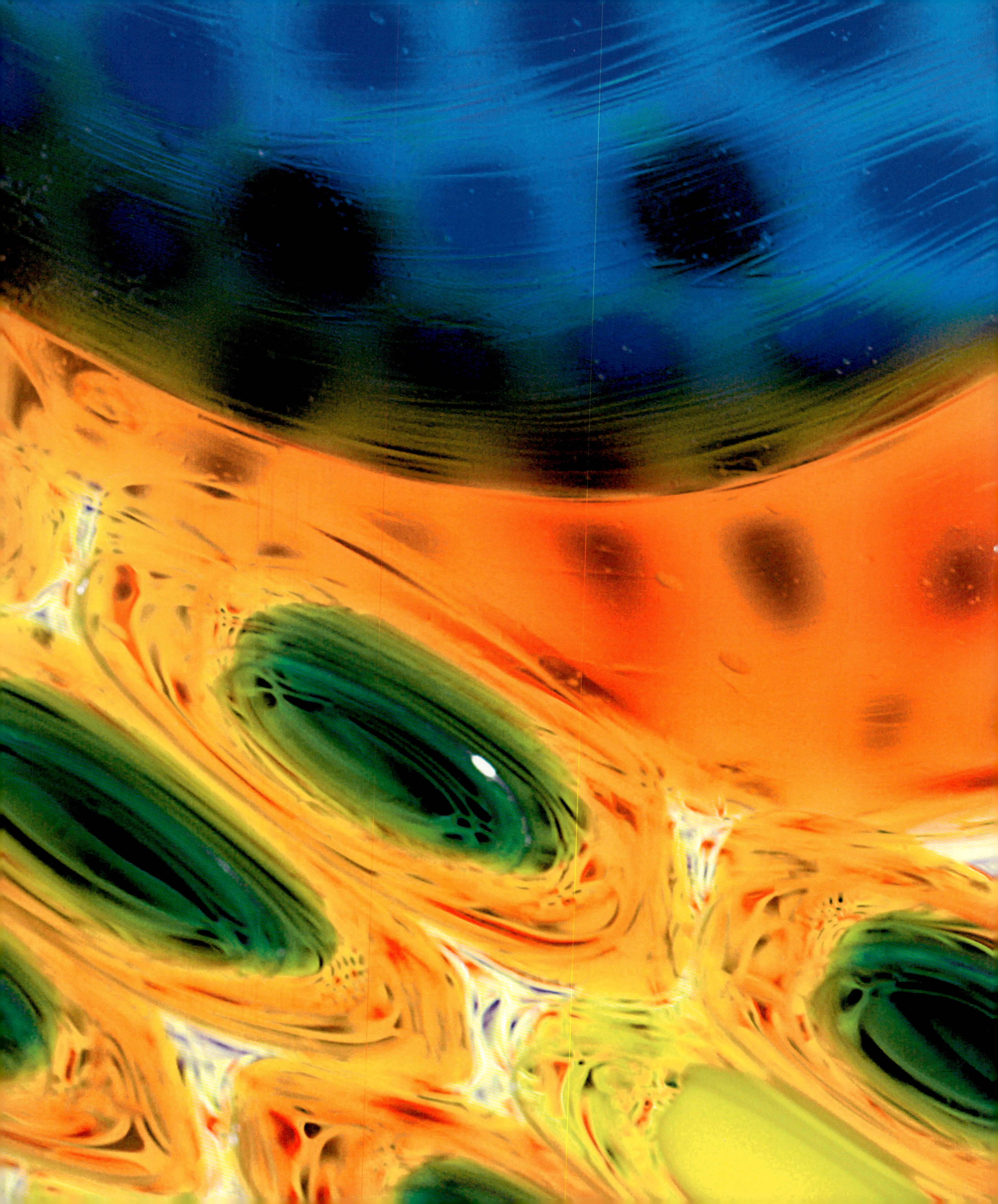

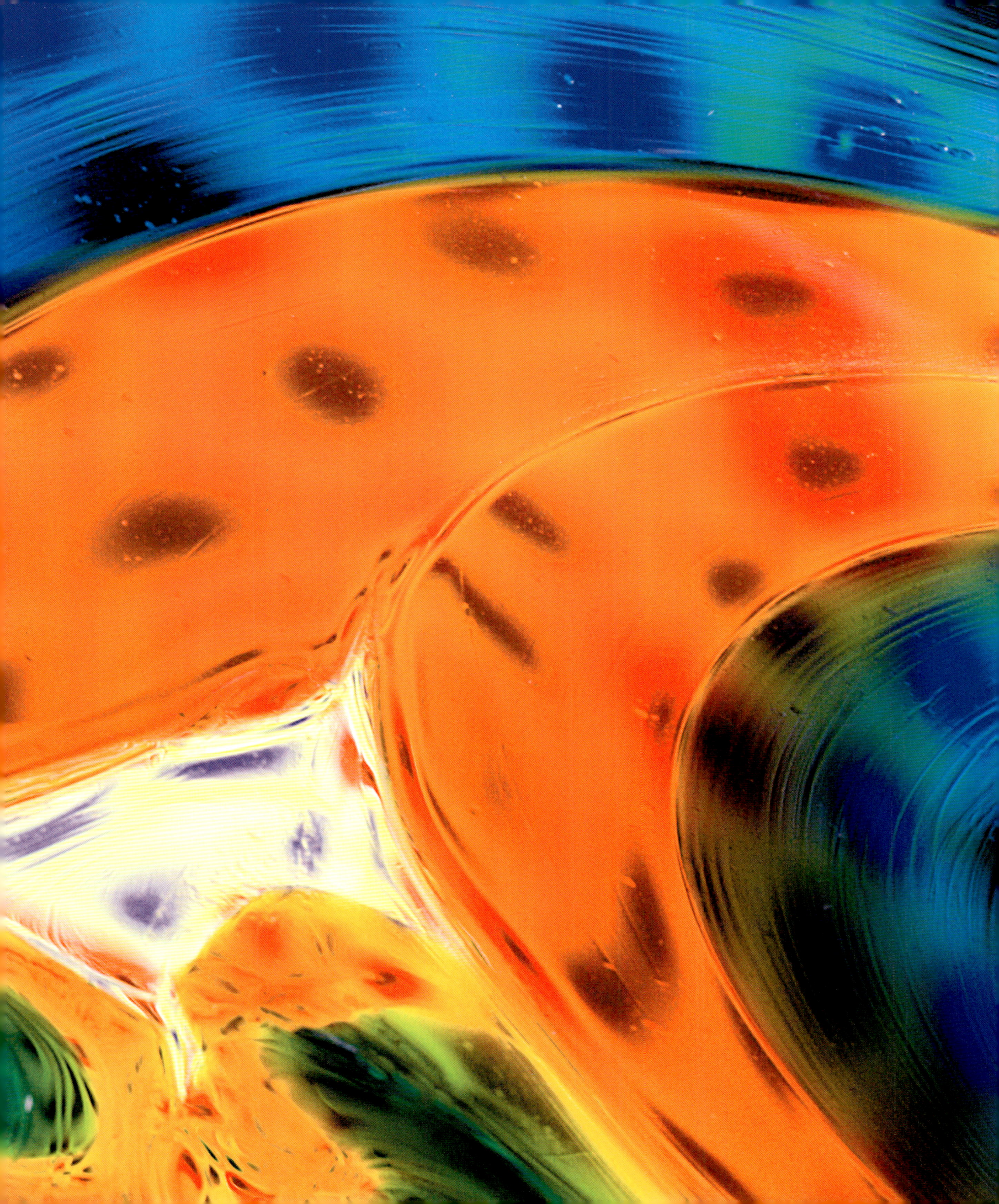

BIOGRAPHY

1951
Born: November 26
Birmingham, Alabama

EDUCATION

1983
Master of Fine Arts in Ceramics
Louisiana State University
Baton Rouge, Louisiana

1975
The Provincetown Painting Workshop
Provincetown, Massachusetts

1974
Bachelor of Arts in Painting and Ceramics, Centre College
Danville, Kentucky

AWARDS

2005
Award of Excellence
Jurors Award–Habatat International Glass Invitational, Sponsored by Toledo Museum of Art
Pontiac, Michigan

2004
Acorn Award
Outstanding Professor at a Kentucky College or University, Kentucky Advocates for Higher Education

2003
Distinguished Alumnus Award
Centre College Alumni Association

2002
Outstanding Alumnus Award
Indian Springs School
Birmingham, Alabama

2001
Sixth Annual Rude Osolnik Award
Kentucky's Most Accomplished Craftsperson

2000/1999
Kentucky Professor of the Year
Council for the Advancement and Support of Teaching/Carnegie Foundation for the Advancement of Teaching

TEACHING EXPERIENCE

1983–Present
H. W. Stodghill Jr. and Adele H. Stodghill Endowed Professor of Art, Centre College
Danville, Kentucky

2007
Instructor
The Pilchuck Glass School
Stanwood, Washington

2005
Instructor
Pittsburgh Glass Center
Pittsburgh, Pennsylvania

2002
Instructor
The Studio at the Corning Museum of Glass
Corning, New York

1997
Instructor
The Studio at the Corning Museum of Glass
Corning, New York

1985
Instructor in Ceramics
Portland School of Art
Portland, Maine

Assistant in Hot Glass
The Pilchuck School
Stanwood, Washington

1976–1980
Art Instructor
Indian Springs School
Birmingham, Alabama

1975
Painting and Drawing Instructor
Alabama Council on the Arts and Humanities, Draper State Prison
Elmore, Alabama

1974
Instructor in Ceramics
Centre College

RELATED PROFESSIONAL EXPERIENCE

2006
Demonstration and Lectures
"Session" Glass Conference
Osaka University
Osaka, Japan

Featured Artist
Melt Down 06
Pittsburgh Glass Center
Pittsburgh, Pennsylvania

2005
Lecture
SOFA Chicago
Chicago, Illinois

Demonstration
Glass Axis Studio
Columbus, Ohio

Juror
Hotglass in the Bluegrass Lecture
Lexington Art League
Lexington, Kentucky

Demonstration and Lecture
Holsten Galleries Weekend
Stockbridge, Massachusetts

Lecture
Muskegon Museum of Art
Muskegon, Michigan

Demonstration and Lecture
University of Miami
Miami, Florida

2004
Demonstration
Third Degree Glass Factory
St. Louis, Missouri

Host for Lino Tagliapietra
Honorary Doctor of Humane Letters
Centre College
Danville, Kentucky

Demonstration
Glass Art Society Conference
New Orleans, Louisiana

2003
Juror, Watertower Annual
Louisville Visual Art Association
Louisville, Kentucky

Panel Discussion
J. B. Speed Art Museum
Louisville, Kentucky

Demonstration and Lecture
Holsten Glass Weekend
Stockbridge, Massachusetts

Demonstration and Lecture
Glassworks, Norton Healthcare
Louisville, Kentucky

2002
Lecture
Headley-Whitney Museum
Lexington, Kentucky

Demonstration
2002 Winter Olympics
Salt Lake City, Utah

Demonstration
Urban Glass
Brooklyn, New York

Panel Discussion
Birmingham Bloomfield Art Center
Bloomfield, Michigan

2001
Panel Discussion
Milwaukee Art Museum
Milwaukee, Wisconsin

Demonstration and Lecture
Cincinnati Art Museum
Cincinnati, Ohio

Panel Discussion
Hunter Museum of American Art
Chattanooga, Tennessee

Demonstration and Lecture
Emporia State University
Emporia, Kansas

Demonstration and Lecture
Center for Creative Studies
Detroit, Michigan

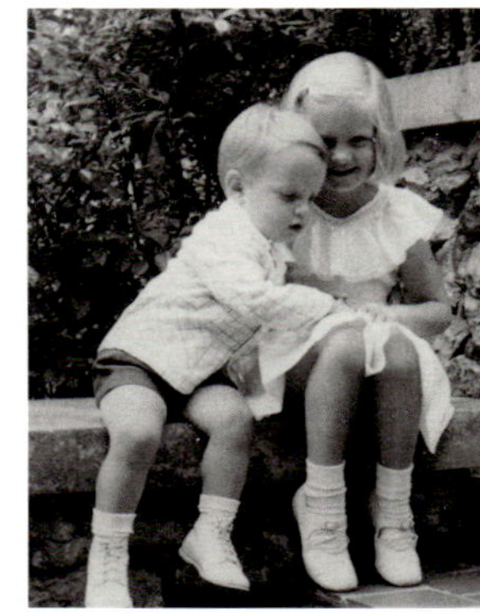

Stephen Powell with sister, Pam. Birmingham, Alabama, 1954

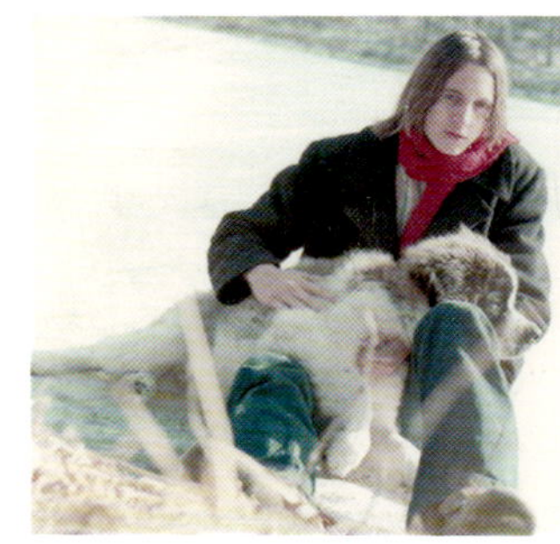

Powell and Leon, Centre College, 1972

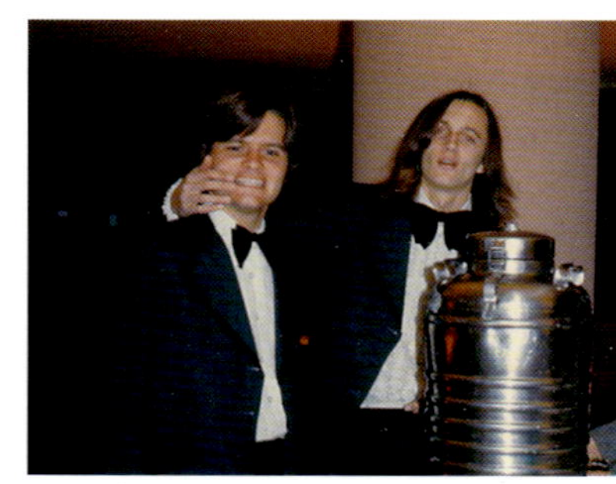

Stephen Powell with Mark "Looney" Lucas at a reception for Senior Exhibition, Centre College, 1974

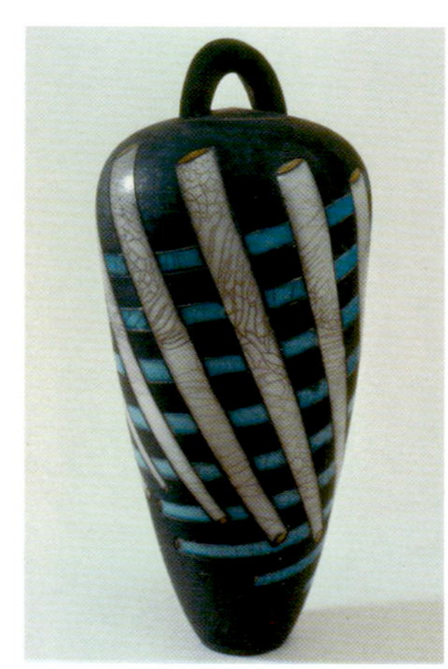

Powell ceramic piece Blue Stripped Smith*. 22" x 10" x 10", raku, 1983*

Demonstration
Habatat Galleries
Pontiac, Michigan

Lecture and Slide Presentation
Montgomery Art Museum
Montgomery, Alabama

Lecture
Kentucky Craft Marketing Program
Louisville, Kentucky

2000
Host
Marvin Lipofsky at Centre College
Danville, Kentucky

Host
Lino Tagliapietra at Centre College
Danville, Kentucky

Co-curator, Millennium
Glass International Invitational
Kentucky Art and Craft Foundation
Louisville, Kentucky

Demonstration and Lecture
Bowling Green University
Bowling Green, Ohio

Demonstration and Studio Tour
Marx-Saunders Gallery
Danville, Kentucky

Lecture and Panel Discussion
Wood Street Galleries
Pittsburgh, Pennsylvania

Lecture
Birmingham Museum of Art
Birmingham, Alabama

1999
Lecture
Southern Illinois University
Carbondale, Illinois

Demonstration
River City Works
Cincinnati, Ohio

Demonstrations
Glass Lovers Weekend
Wheaton Village
Millville, New Jersey

Lecture
Huntsville Art Museum
Huntsville, Alabama

Demonstration
SOFA–Urban Glass
Brooklyn, New York

Lecture
Speed Art Museum
Louisville, Kentucky

1998
Demonstration
Speed Museum Docents
Danville, Kentucky

Demonstration and Lecture
Tyler School of Art
Philadelphia, Pennsylvania

Demonstration and Lecture
Holsten Galleries
Stockbridge, Massachusetts

Demonstration and Lecture
Michigan Contemporary Glass Group
Pontiac, Michigan

1997
Demonstration
Glass Art Society Conference
Tucson, Arizona

Artist in Residence
Sydney College of Art
Sydney, Australia

Visiting Artist
Canberra School of Art
Canberra, Australia

Glass Workshop
Sunbeam Glassworks
Auckland, New Zealand

Lecture
University of Illinois
Champaign Urbana, Illinois

1996
Demonstration
International Glass Invitational
Habatat Galleries
Pontiac, Michigan

Demonstration
Glass Axis
Hawk Gallery
Columbus, Ohio

Demonstration
Cleveland Art Institute
Cleveland, Ohio

Lecture
Ivan Karp Exhibition
Centre College
Danville, Kentucky

Lecture
Riley Hawk Galleries
Cleveland, Ohio

1995
Lecture
Lexington Art League
University of Kentucky
Lexington, Kentucky

Demonstration and Lecture
International Glass Invitational
Pontiac, Michigan

1994
Demonstration
Urban Glass Studio
New York, New York

Workshop and Lectures
Herron School of Art
Indianapolis, Indiana

Lecture
"Glass, History and Process"
University of Kentucky Art Museum
Lexington, Kentucky

Lecture
"Contemporary Glass"
Ashland Area Art Gallery
(for Ashland Oil Corp.)
Ashland, Kentucky

Panel Discussion
River City Glass Works
Cincinnati, Ohio

1993
Demonstration
Glass Art Society Conference
Toledo, Ohio

Demonstration
River City Works
Cincinnati, Ohio

Demonstration and Lecture
200 Years of Craft Conference
Centre College
Danville, Kentucky

Lecture
"Glass Art"
The Kentucky Museum
Bowling Green, Kentucky

Lecture
"Development of My Work"
Texas A&M University
College Station, Texas

Lecture
"The Leight Collection"
J. B. Speed Art Museum
Louisville, Kentucky

Lecture
"Glass Art"
University of Kentucky
Lexington, Kentucky

Lecture
"Development of My Work"
Michigan Glass Collectors
Detroit, Michigan

1991
Lecture
"Glass Art in the Soviet Union"
Eastern Kentucky University
Richmond, Kentucky

Demonstration and Lecture
Toledo Museum of Art
Toledo, Ohio

1990
Demonstration and Lecture
Mukhina Art Institute
St. Petersburg, Russia

Working Trip to Soviet Union
Red May Glass Factory and Lvov Art Institute, Vishny Volochok, Russia, and Lvov, Ukraine

Photo by Kenneth Hayden

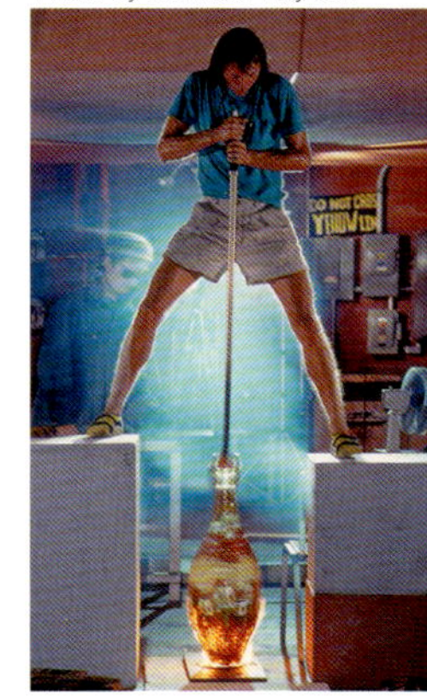

Stephen Powell blowing in the first Centre glass studio; assistant Perry Biddle in background, 1987

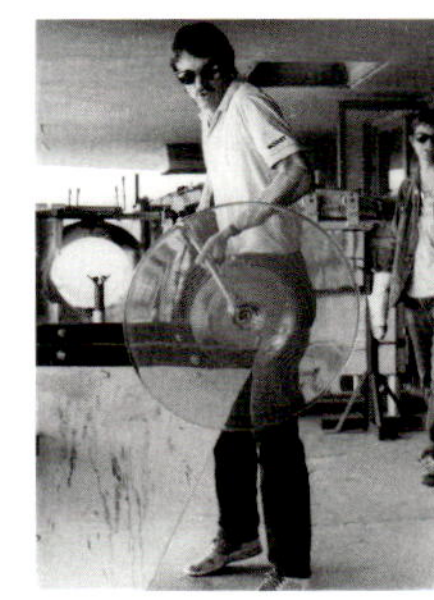

Powell spinning out a rondelle; Biddle in the background. First Centre glass studio built on roof deck of the Norton Center for the Arts, 1985

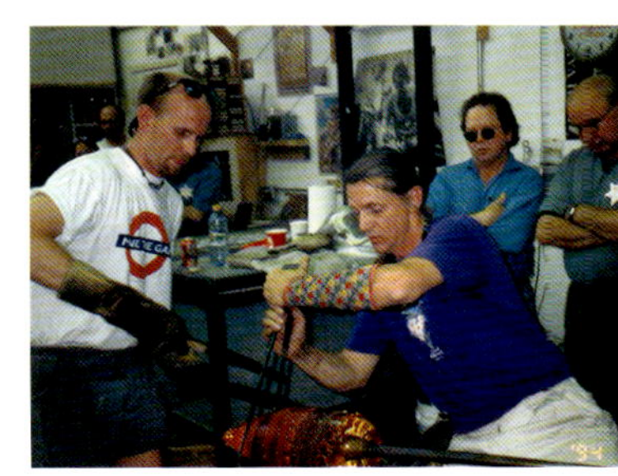

Stephen Powell demonstrating at the Glass Art Society Conference, Tucson, Arizona 1997. Brook White assisting, Richard Marquis and Lino Tagliapietra watching.

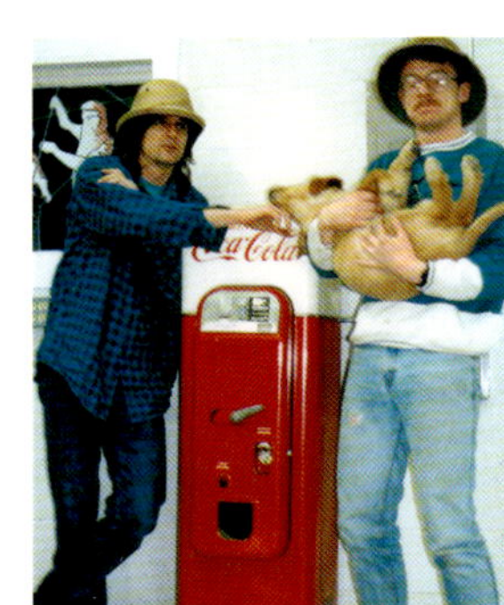

Stephen Powell with Richard Garvey and Pocahontas, 1992

Lecture
"Art and Politics in the Age
of Perestroika"
Kentucky State University
Frankfort, Kentucky

Demonstration and Lecture
The Golden Glass Studio
Cincinnati, Ohio

Demonstration and Lecture
Appalachian Center
Smithville, Tennessee

Demonstration and Lecture
University of South Carolina
Columbia, South Carolina

SELECTED PRINT MEDIA

Glass "Glass Finds a Home in Kentucky," Article by Andrew Page, detail of *Torrid Citrus Nudge*, Fall 2005, number 100, p. 70

DK Collector's Guides 20th Century Glass, by Judith Miller, DK Publishing 2004, featured: *Igniting Lunar Lunacy*, p. 213

American Style, *Audacious Peeking Cleavage*, photo and mention, June 2004, p. 67

International Glass Art, Richard Wilfred Yelle, Schiffer Publishing 2003. Process shot and reproductions of *Gasping Jitter Jones*, *Squirming Zippy Lips*, and *Purple Aloof Cleavage*, pp. 254–255

A Celebration of Glass, Butler Books, 2003. Cover: *Innocent Crying Fire*, reproduction of *Buttery Spanking Breeze*, p. 90

Chicago Life, "Glass," reproduction and mention of *Slippery Tickle Bombcast*, 2003

Contemporary Glass, Guild Publishing, 2001. Reproduction of *Purple Zippy Mania*, p. 41

Object Lessons, Guild Publishing, 2001. Reproduction of *Promiscuous Nubile Jones*, p. 127

American Craft, Stephen Rolfe Powell, Cover, Article by James Yood and reproductions of *Flirting Tangerine Johnson* and *Pyronic Marilyn Monroe*, June/July 2001, pp. 66–69

Glass Art, Richard Wilfred Yelle, Schiffer Publishing, 2000, Reproductions of *Persimmon Jupiter Johnson*, pp. 201–202

GAS News, "Focus on Education," January/February 2000

American Style, "Millennium Glass." Article and mention by Hope Daniels, Number 21, Summer 2000, pp. 34–35

Pittsburgh Tribune Review, "American Glass-Italian Influence." Article by Graham Shearing and reproduction of *Gulping Cheeks Johnson*, September 1, 2000

Profitable Glass, "Stephen Powell Studio." Cover article by Dianne Heilenman, Fall 2000, pp. 4–5 and 15

Black & White, "Exhibitionism." Article by Jane Longshore, November 9, 2000

Arts & Crafts Across Kentucky, "Bluegrass Glass." Cover: reproduction of *Lurid Gasp Johnson*. Article by Nancy Bronner, Fall 1999, pp. 14–15

Kentucky Monthly, "Kentuckians of the Twentieth Century." Article, portrait, and reproductions, September 1999, pp. 22–23

American Style, "Color Fields, Country Home." Cover, article by Lee Lawrence and photography by Linda Hanselman, Summer 1999, pp. 64–71

James Renwick, *Alliance Quarterly*, "An Adventure in Heat and Light." Article by Betty R. Sweren, 1999, p. 4

Neues Glas (Germany), "Venezia Aperto Vetro." Reproduction of *Licking Fire Jones*, Fourth Quarter, 1998, p. 18

Arte (Italy), "Aperto Vetro, Un'altra Biennale a Venezia." Article by Beba Marsano, reproduction of *Tangerine Cheeks Smith* detail, October 1998

Suomen Kuvalehti (Finland), "Lasin Vuodenajat Venetsiassa." Article by Leena Johannsson, Reproduction of *Lemon Jupiter Smith*, October 30, 1998

Glass. Review by James Yood, Spring 1998, Number 70, p. 52

Glass Art. Cover and article "The Color of Beauty: Stephen Powell's Glass Vessels" and reproductions. May/June 1997, pp. 4–10

Craft Arts International, "Genesis and the Vitreous Singularity." Article by Laurie Winters, multiple reproductions, April 1997, pp. 24–27

American Craft. Photo with 1996 Governor's Awards vessels, Craft World, April/May 1997, p. 17

Southwest Art, "Best of the West." Reproduction of *Flaming Cheeks Jones*, detail of *Hesitation Cleavage Smith* and short article, September 1996, p. 38

Ceramics Monthly, "Woodstoke, a Cooperative Anagama Experience." Article by Patsi Barnes Trollinger, October 1996, pp. 35–38

Glass Focus. Interview by Beverly Copeland, Volume 10, March 1996, front page and 16–19

Glass & Art (Japan). Reproduction of *Bodacious Cleavage Johnson*, and mention, Number 11, Autumn 1995, pp. 31–36

Galeries (Paris). Reproduction of *Piranha Sigh Johnson*, Volume 5, Number 1, December 1994–January 1995, front cover

Art News, Marta Hewett Gallery, "Glass Art." Article by Matthew Kangas, reproduction and mention, January 1995, pp. 50, 67

Birmingham News. Article by Susan Strictland, June 4, 1995

Glass. Article and reproduction of *Bosnia Bulb Johnson*, Spring 1994, p. 63

New York Times, "Calendar: Innovative Glasswork," review and reproduction, January 6, 1994, p. C7

Louisville Courier-Journal, "Talent in Jeopardy." Article by Holly Holland, photographs by Keith Williams, July 12, 1991, p. 1

Kentucky Crafts Crown Publishers, Phyllis George, interview with reproductions, Fall 1989, pp. 138–141

Ceramics Monthly, "Raku: Variations on a Theme." Includes picture of *Multi: Cleavage Smith*, June–August 1987, p. 3

Ceramics Monthly, "Stephen Powell." Article with picture of *Mailbox Jones, Jr.*, December 1986, p. 93

The World and I, "A New Renaissance in Glass Art." Robert Kehlman, (picture), September 1986, p. 327

Neues Glas (Dusseldorf, Germany). Reproduction of *Johnson, Smith and Jones*, April/June 1985, p. 125

New Glass Review 6, Corning Museum of Glass, Corning, New York, reproduction of *Johnson, Smith and Jones*, 1985, p. 23

Boston Globe, "Shaping a Movement in Clay." Article by Christine Temine, picture of *Pink Slant Smith*, April 5, 1984

BROADCAST MEDIA

HGTV, "Offbeat America," "Bowling Ball House and More," Episode HOBA-107, August 28, 2005

HGTV, "Modern Masters," Glass Artist, Episode MAS-705, February & November 2002

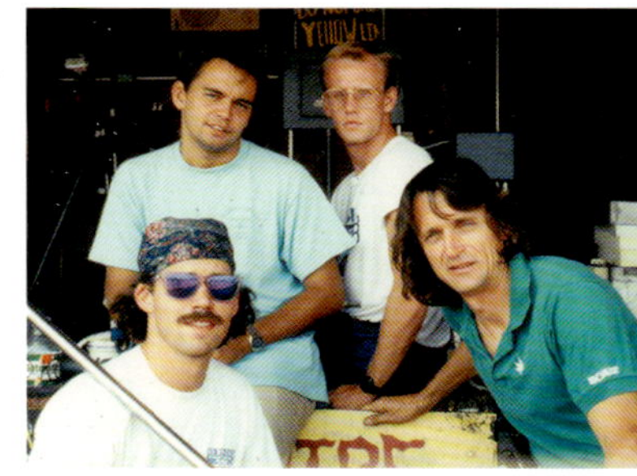

John Stokes, Peter Palmqvist, Brook White, and Stephen Powell. Centre glass studio, 1993

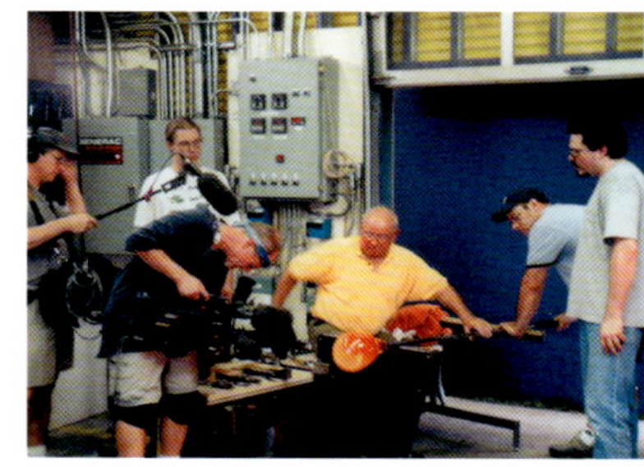

Lino Tagliapietra's first visit to Centre College. Stephen Powell produced an HD video "Lino Tagliapietra: Maestro of Glass." Film crew: Jon McDonald and Marc Pingry. Assisting Tagliapietra are Brent Sommerhauser, Dave "Big Daddy" Walters, and John "Scooter" Kiley, 2000

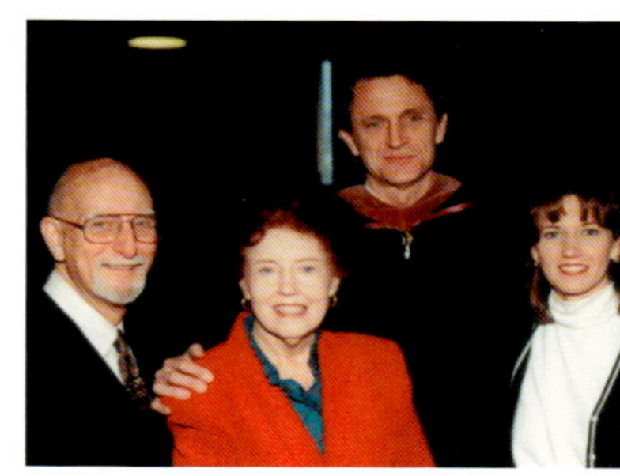

Paul Cantrell, Jacqueline Cantrell, Stephen Powell, and Shelly Powell. Presentation of the Paul L. Cantrell Endowed Professorship to Powell. Centre College, 2000

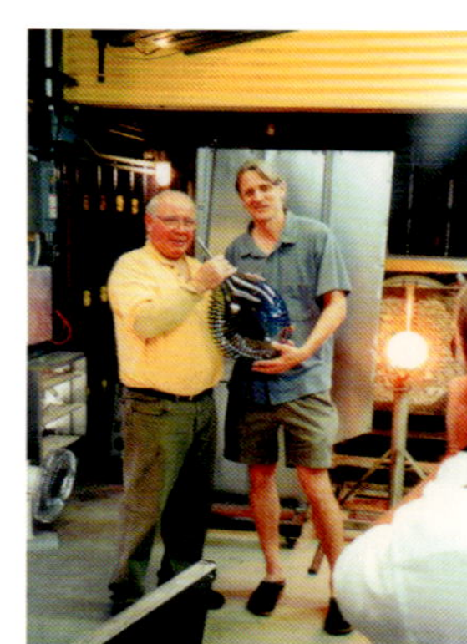

Lino Tagliapietra and Stephen Powell during Tagliapietra's first visit to Centre College, 2000

Video production of Lino Tagliapietra, "Lino Tagliapietra—Maestro of Glass," host and coproducer, May 2000

Kentucky Educational Television, documentary, *Stephen Powell, Glass Artist,* Fall 1993

Soviet television, *600 Seconds with Alexander Nevzorov* (St. Petersburg), May 7, 1990

CBS, *Sunday Morning,* with Charles Kuralt, April 17, 1988

SOLO EXHIBITIONS

2007
Marx-Saunders Gallery
Chicago, Illinois

Kentucky Museum of Art and Craft
Louisville, Kentucky

2006
Foundry Art Centre
St. Charles, Missouri

2005
Concept Art Gallery
Pittsburgh, Pennsylvania

Hawk Gallery
Columbus, Ohio

Muskegon Museum of Art
Muskegon, Michigan

2004
R. Duane Reed Galleries
St. Louis, Missouri

Tobin-Hewett Gallery
Louisville, Kentucky

2003
Marx-Saunders Gallery
Chicago, Illinois

2001
Marta Hewett Gallery
Louisville, Kentucky

2000
Marx-Saunders Gallery
Chicago, Illinois

Gallerie Alegria
Birmingham, Alabama

1999
Blue Spiral 1
Asheville, North Carolina

Marta Hewett Gallery
Cincinnati, Ohio

Compositions Gallery
San Francisco, California

Nantucket Glass Works
Nantucket, Massachusetts

Riley Hawk Gallery
Columbus, Ohio

1998
Habatat Galleries
Pontiac, Michigan

1997
Marx-Saunders Gallery
Chicago, Illinois

Suzanne Brown Gallery
Scottsdale, Arizona

Glass Artists' Gallery
Sydney, Australia

Masterworks Gallery
Auckland, New Zealand

1996
Marta Hewett Gallery
Cincinnati, Ohio

Riley Hawk Gallery
Columbus, Ohio

Riley Hawk Gallery
Cleveland, Ohio

Suzanne Brown Gallery
Scottsdale, Arizona

1995
Habatat Galleries
Boca Raton, Florida

Blue Spiral 1
Asheville, North Carolina

Linda Schwartz Gallery
Lexington, Kentucky

1994
Marx-Saunders Gallery
Chicago, Illinois

Galerie L
Hamburg, Germany

Habatat Galleries
Aspen, Colorado

Bell Gallery
Memphis, Tennessee

1993
Habatat Galleries
Farmington Hills, Michigan

Marta Hewett Gallery
Cincinnati, Ohio

Kentucky Art and Craft Foundation
Louisville, Kentucky

1992
Habatat Galleries
Boca Raton, Florida

Kimzey Miller Gallery
Seattle, Washington

Harris Gallery
Houston, Texas

Kirvan Bartoszewicz Gallery
Palm Springs, California

1991
Habatat Galleries
Farmington Hills, Michigan

Habatat Galleries
Boca Raton, Florida

Kirvan Bartoszewicz Gallery
Palm Springs, California

1990
Kimzey Miller Gallery
Seattle, Washington

Kirvan Bartoszewicz Gallery
Palm Springs, California

Sarah Squeri Gallery
Cincinnati, Ohio

1989
Harris Gallery
Houston, Texas

1988
Swanson Cralle Gallery
Louisville, Kentucky

SELECTED GROUP EXHIBITIONS

2007
International Glass Invitational
Habatat Galleries
Boca Raton, Florida

International Glass Invitational
Habatat Galleries
Royal Oak, Michigan

Art Miami
Marx-Saunders Gallery
Miami Beach, Florida

Palm Beach
Marx-Saunders Gallery
Palm Beach, Florida

SOFA New York
Marx-Saunders Gallery
New York, New York

Glass Weekend
Marx-Saunders Gallery
Millville, New Jersey

SOFA Chicago
Marx-Saunders Gallery
Chicago, Illinois

2006
SOFA New York
Marx-Saunders Gallery
New York, New York

Stockbridge Glass Invitational
Holsten Galleries
Stockbridge, Massachusetts

2nd Invitational Glass Exhibition
Venice Art Center
Venice, Florida

Clear Impact
Tobin-Hewett Gallery
Louisville, Kentucky

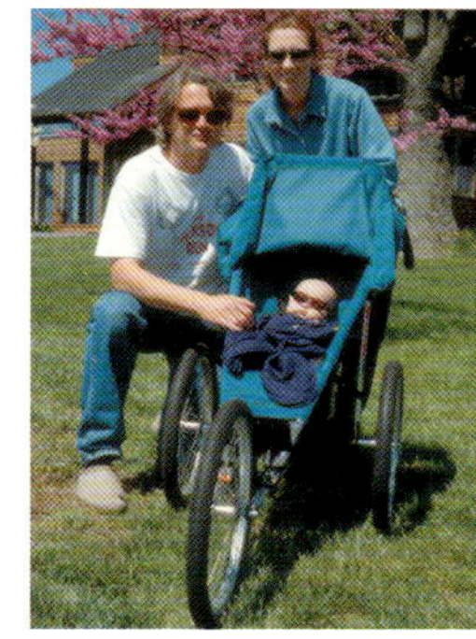

Powell family in front of their new house outside Danville, 1999

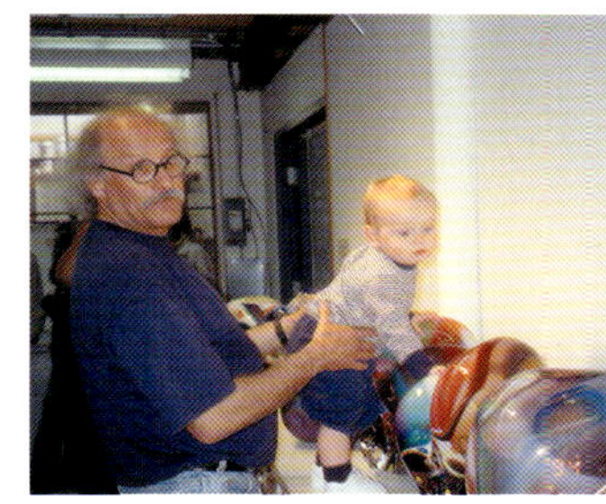

Marvin Lipofsky visits Centre College, makes his "Kentucky Series," pictured with Zachary Hawk Powell, 2000

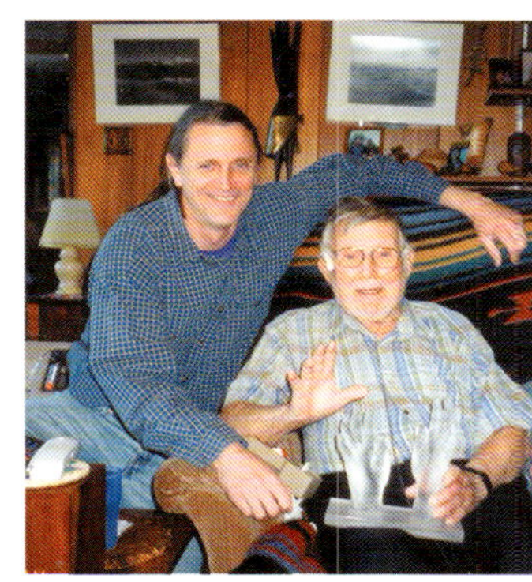

Stephen Powell and Rude Osolnik. Powell received the Osolnik Award for Kentucky's most accomplished craftsperson. He made a glass casting of Osolnik's hands.

Glass Art Society demonstration at Rosetree Studio in New Orleans. Left to right: Paul Hugues, Patrick Kolten, Chris Bohach, Stephen Powell, Brian Pavloff, Mark Rosenbaum, Jon Capps, and Dante Marioni.

Masters of Reflection
Everhart Museum
Scranton, Pennsylvania

34th International Glass Invitational
Habatat Galleries
Royal Oak, Michigan

Eccentric Vessel
Habatat Galleries
Royal Oak, Michigan

Art Miami
Marx-Saunders Gallery
Miami Beach, Florida

Palm Beach 3
Marx-Saunders Gallery
West Palm Beach, Florida

2005
26 from the World of Glass
Dennos Museum Center
Traverse City, Michigan

Sculpting in Glass
Mary & Leigh Block
Museum of Art
Evanston, Illinois

Invitational Glass Exhibition
Dubuque Museum of Art
Dubuque, Iowa

23rd International Glass Invitational
Habatat Galleries
Boca Raton, Florida

SOFA Chicago
Marx-Saunders Gallery
Chicago, Illinois

Art Chicago in the Park
Marx-Saunders Gallery
Chicago, Illinois

Chicago Contemporary
& Classic
Marx-Saunders Gallery
Chicago, Illinois

Master Craftworks: Kentucky
College of Mount St. Joseph
Cincinnati, Ohio

33rd International Glass Invitational
Habatat Galleries
Royal Oak, Michigan

2004
Traditions Transformed: Murrini Glass
Craft Alliance
St. Louis, Missouri

SOFA Chicago
Marx-Saunders Gallery
Chicago, Illinois

International Glass Invitational
Habatat Galleries
Boca Raton, Florida

2004
SOFA, New York
Holsten Galleries
New York, New York

Centred on Glass
Flamerun Gallery and Studio
Louisville, Kentucky

The Haverty Collection
Mobile Museum of Art
Mobile, Alabama

Palm Beach Contemporary Art Fair
Marx-Saunders Gallery
Palm Beach, Florida

International Glass Invitational
Habatat Galleries
Royal Oak, Michigan

2003
Glass Weekend '03
Wheaton Village
Millville, New Jersey

Masters of Contemporary Glass Art
Berkshire Museum
Pittsfield, Massachusetts

SOFA Chicago
Marx-Saunders Gallery
Chicago, Illinois

Corporal Identity: Body Language
Museum für Angewandte Kunst
Frankfurt, Germany

The Light Within
J. B. Speed Museum
Louisville, Kentucky

The Glass Vessel,
An International Invitational
Kentucky Museum
of Arts & Design
Louisville, Kentucky

Light Works
West Valley Art Museum
Surprise, Arizona

Trial by Fire,
Contemporary Glass
Florida State University
Museum of Fine Arts
Tallahassee, Florida

Art Form
Marx-Saunders Gallery
Palm Beach, Florida

Art Palm Beach
Marx-Saunders Gallery
Palm Beach, Florida

International Glass Invitational
Habatat Galleries
Royal Oak, Michigan

International Glass Invitational
Habatat Galleries
Boca Raton, Florida

2002
Contemporary Reflections
of Venetian Glass,
Cantor Center for Visual Arts
Stanford, California

International Glass Invitational
Habatat Galleries
Boca Raton, Florida

SOFA Chicago
Marx-Saunders Gallery
Chicago, Illinois

Italian Influence of
Contemporary American Glass
Habatat Galleries
Royal Oak, Michigan

Classical Glass / Modern Forms
SPACE
Atlanta, Georgia

From Functional to Fine
Headley-Whitney Museum
Lexington, Kentucky

SOFA New York
Marx-Saunders Gallery
New York, New York

International Glass Invitational
Habatat Galleries
Royal Oak, Michigan

Clearly Kentucky:
Contemporary Studio Glass
The Carnegie
Covington, Kentucky

2001
Contemporary Glass
Naples Museum of Art
Naples, Florida

SOFA Chicago
Marx-Saunders Gallery
Chicago, Illinois

Glass Weekend '01
Marx-Saunders Gallery
Millville, New Jersey

SOFA New York
Marx-Saunders Gallery
New York, New York

Celebration in Glass
Marx-Saunders Gallery
Munster, Indiana

International Glass Invitational
Habatat Galleries
Boca Raton, Florida

Colors
Suzanne Brown Gallery
Scottsdale, Arizona

International Glass Invitational
Habatat Galleries
Pontiac, Michigan

2000
International Glass Invitational
Habatat Galleries
Boca Raton, Florida

1999
SOFA Chicago
Marx-Saunders Gallery
Chicago, Illinois

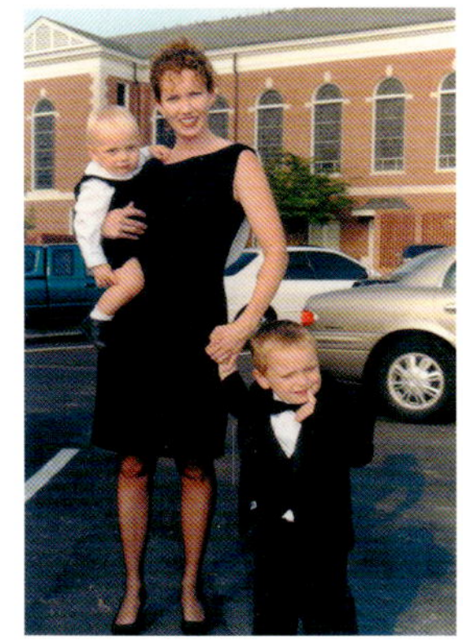

Oliver Blue, Shelly, and Zachary Hawk, 2001

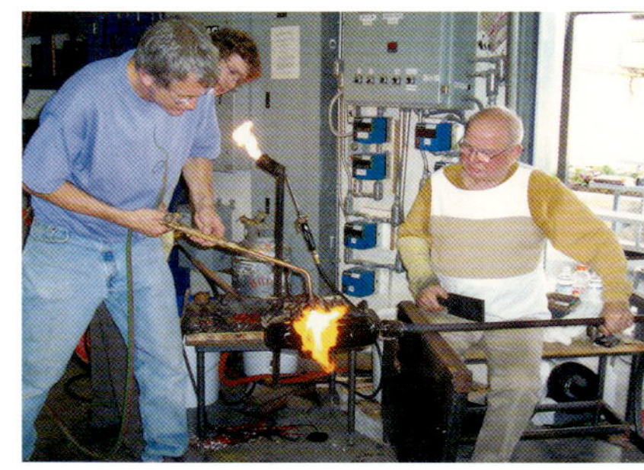

Powell torching for Lino Tagliapietra during his 2004 visit to Centre College. Tagliapietra, along with Sandra Day O'Connor, was given an honorary doctoral degree from Centre.

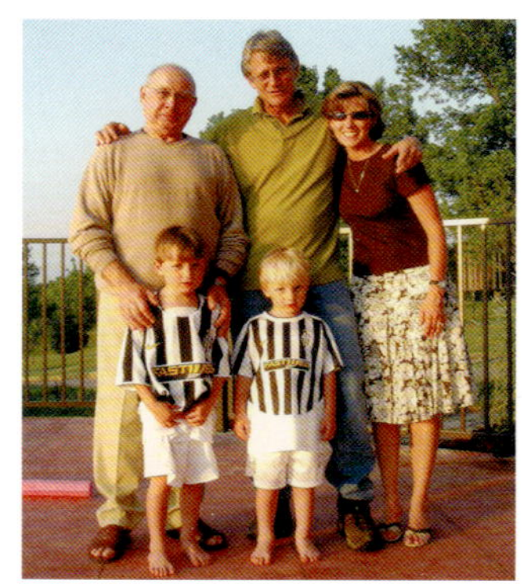

Lino Tagliapietra with Stephen, Shelly, Zachary Hawk, and Oliver Blue. Shot during 2004 visit to Kentucky.

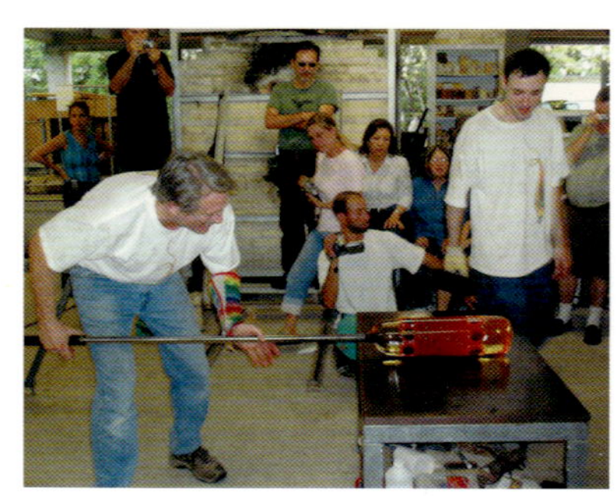

Powell demonstrating at the University of Miami, Florida. Chris Bohach assisting, 2005

The Italian Influence:
Contemporary Glass
Wood Street Galleries
Pittsburgh, Pennsylvania

Southeastern Glass Invitational
Blue Spiral 1
Asheville, North Carolina

Glass America
Heller Gallery
New York, New York

Glass Invitational
Holsten Galleries
Stockbridge, Massachusetts

SOFA New York
Riley Hawk Galleries
New York, New York

Millennium Glass Invitational
Kentucky Art and Craft Foundation
Louisville, Kentucky

International Glass Invitational
Habatat Galleries
Pontiac, Michigan

Hidden Talents
Kentucky Art and Craft Foundation
Louisville, Kentucky

Two for 2000
Blue Spiral 1
Asheville, North Carolina

1999
International Glass Invitational
Habatat Galleries
Boca Raton, Florida

SOFA Chicago
Marx-Saunders Gallery
Chicago, Illinois

15 Years on Main Street
Kentucky Art and Craft Foundation
Louisville, Kentucky

Glass Weekend '99
Wheaton Village
Millville, New Jersey

Kentucky's Best:
New Works from Old Friends
Kentucky Art and Craft Foundation
Louisville, Kentucky

Vessels: A National Glass
Invitational
Ellen Noël Art Museum
Odessa, Texas

SOFA New York
Marx-Saunders Gallery
New York, New York

Southern Glass Now!
d'Art Center
Norfolk, Virginia

International Glass Invitational
Habatat Gallery
Pontiac, Michigan

1998
Venezia Aperto Vetro
Palazzo Ducale
Venice, Italy

SOFA Chicago
Marx-Saunders Gallery
Chicago, Illinois

20th Anniversary Glass Invitational
Holsten Galleries
Stockbridge, Massachusetts

International Glass Invitational
Habatat Gallery
Pontiac, Michigan

Glass America '98
Heller Gallery
New York, New York

SOFA New York
Marx-Saunders Gallery
New York, New York

International Glass Invitational
Habatat Galleries
Boca Raton, Florida

1997
Glorious Glass
Owensboro Museum of Fine Art
Owensboro, Kentucky

Blowing Hot, Cutting Cold
Lakeview Museum of Arts
and Sciences
Peoria, Illinois

35th Anniversary of
Studio Glass Movement
Cleveland Museum of Art
Cleveland, Ohio

Arte en Vidrio
Museo del Vidrio
Monterrey, Mexico

Currents in Contemporary Glass
Woodstreet Gallery/
Concept Art Gallery
Pittsburgh, Pennsylvania

Art Glass '97
Hanson Gallery
Knoxville, Tennessee

25th International Glass Invitational
Habatat Gallery
Pontiac, Michigan

A Marriage of Earth and Fire
Kentucky Art and Craft Foundation
Louisville, Kentucky

SOFA Florida
Mark-Saunders Gallery
Miami, Florida

Art Festival
Temple Beth-El
St. Petersburg, Florida

Glass America '97
Heller Gallery
New York, New York

1996
Master Works in Contemporary Glass
TriArt Gallery
Louisville, Kentucky

A Museum in the Making:
The Scottsdale Center for the Arts
Scottsdale, Arizona

SOFA Chicago
Marx-Saunders Gallery
Chicago, Illinois

Glass Focus II:
The Vessel and Related Forms
Blue Spiral 1
Asheville, North Carolina

International Glass Invitational
Habatat Gallery
Pontiac, Michigan

SOFA Florida
Coconut Grove
Convention Center
Miami, Florida

International Glass Invitational
Habatat Galleries
Boca Raton, Florida

Glass America '96
Heller Gallery
New York, New York

Art Glass '96
Hanson's Artsource Inc.
Knoxville, Tennessee

1995
Group Show
Riley Hawk Gallery
Columbus, Ohio

SOFA Chicago
Navy Pier
Chicago, Illinois

Glass America '95
Heller Gallery
New York, New York

International Glass Invitational
Habatat Galleries
Pontiac, Michigan

International Glass Invitational
Habatat Galleries
Boca Raton, Florida

Alabama Impact
Museum of the South
Mobile, Alabama

Alabama Impact
Huntsville Museum of Art
Huntsville, Alabama

International Survey of Contemporary
Art Glass
Concept Art Gallery
Pittsburgh, Pennsylvania

Contemporary Class
Craft Alliance Gallery
St. Louis, Missouri

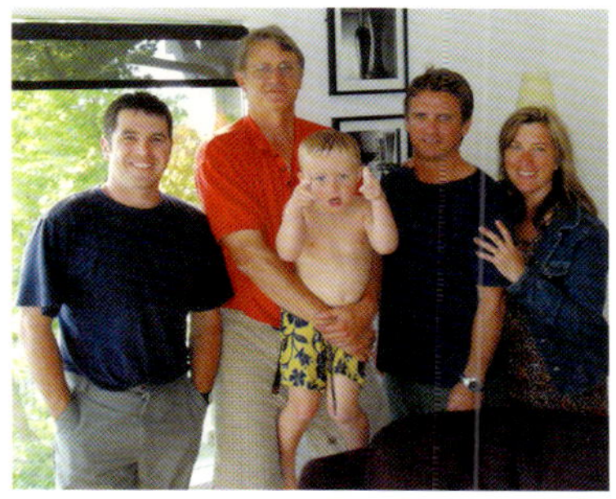

Ben Edols, Stephen Powell, Lino Marioni, Dante Marioni, and Alison Marioni. Marioni home in Seattle, 2003 (shot by Russell Johnson)

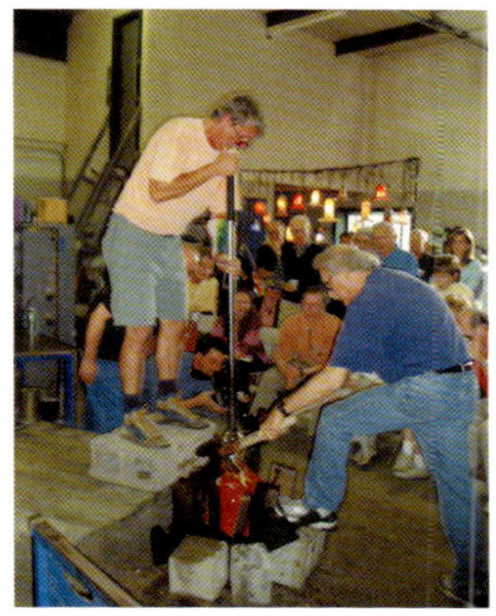

Stephen Powell working with Marvin Lipofsky at Holsten Glass Weekend, Stockbridge, Massachusetts, 2003

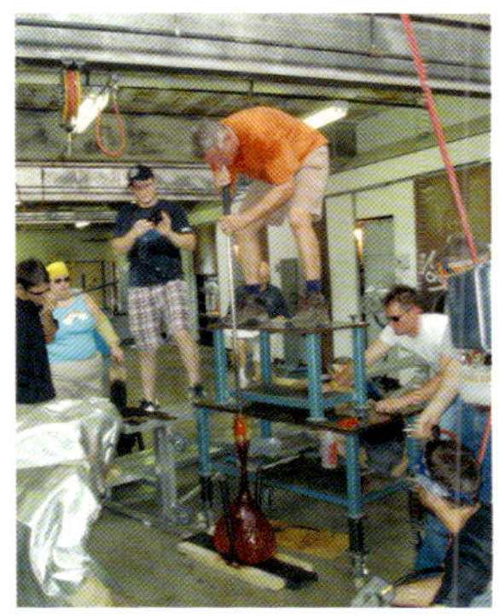

Powell blowing at the Pittsburgh Glass Center, 2005

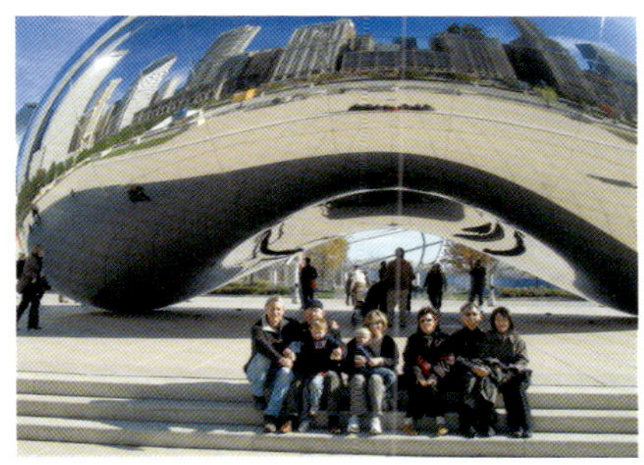

SOFA Chicago 2005, in front of "Cloud Gates," by Anish Kapoor in Millennium Park, Chicago. Left to right: Stephen Powell, Lino Tagliapietra, Zachary Hawk, Oliver Blue, and Shelly Powell, Lina Tagliapietra, Tony Leung, and Cecilia Chung.

1994
Contemporary Art Cincinnati
Contemporary Arts Center
Cincinnati, Ohio

Glass Invitational
Hodgell Gallery
Sarasota, Florida

Contemporary Glass Invitational
Concept Art Gallery
Pittsburgh, Pennsylvania

Glass America '94
Heller Gallery
New York, New York

Transitions '94
Paramount Art Center
Ashland, Kentucky

Transitions '94
Southeast Community College
Cumberland, Kentucky

Transitions '94
Yeiser Art Center
Paducah, Kentucky

International Glass Invitational
Habatat Gallery
Farmington Hills, Michigan

Centre Glass
Elizabethtown Community College
Elizabethtown, Kentucky

1993
Harmony in Glass
Marx Gallery
Chicago, Illinois

Glass America '93
Heller Gallery
New York, New York

Contemporary Glass
Museum of Art
Fort Lauderdale, Florida

Leight Collection
J. B. Speed Art Museum
Louisville, Kentucky

Contemporary Traditions
The Kentucky Museum
Bowling Green, Kentucky

New Art Forms
Marx-Saunders Gallery
Chicago, Illinois

International Glass Invitational
Habatat Galleries
Farmington Hills, Michigan

1992
Cristalomancia
Rufino Tamayo Museum
Mexico City, Mexico

Cristalomancia
Museo de Arte Contemporaneo
Monterrey, Mexico

Europ' Art
Genve-Palexpo
Geneva, Switzerland

Glass America '92
Heller Gallery
New York, New York

International Glass Invitational
Habatat Gallery
Farmington Hills, Michigan

Group Show
Marta Hewett Gallery
Cincinnati, Ohio

200 Years of Kentucky Craft (touring)
Owensboro Museum and the
Kentucky Art and Craft Foundation
Owensboro and Louisville, Kentucky

1991
International Glass Invitational
Habatat Galleries
Farmington Hills, Michigan

Glass America '91
Heller Gallery
New York, New York

Exhibitor
New Art Form Exposition, Navy Pier
Chicago, Illinois

Group Show
Lane Gallery
San Diego, California

1990
Contemporary Glass
Contemporary Crafts Gallery
Portland, Oregon

Two-Person Show
Kimzey Miller Gallery
Seattle, Washington

Group Show
National Glass Invitational,
Kidd Gallery
Birmingham, Michigan

Centre Glass
The Parthenon,
Centennial Park
Nashville, Tennessee

1989
Kentucky Glass
Central Library
Exhibition Gallery
Lexington, Kentucky

Southeastern Glass
The Pavilion,
Atlanta Arts Festival
Atlanta, Georgia

1988
Focus on Kentucky
Glass Capitol Arts Center
Bowling Green, Kentucky

Gallery 15 Collection
(Best of Show)
Stairways Gallery
Louisville, Kentucky

1987
Four-Person Show
Joan Robey Gallery
Denver, Colorado

Works in Clay and Glass
Harris Gallery
Houston, Texas

Exhibition 280:
Works off Walls
Huntington Museum
Huntington, West Virginia

Gallery 15 Collection
(Best of Show)
Stairways Gallery
Louisville, Kentucky

1986
Glass Art National
Downey Museum of Art
Downey, California

Spotlight '86
University Gallery
University of Florida
Gainesville, Florida

Put the Lid On
Joan Robey Gallery
Denver, Colorado

Raku Invitational
Artworks Gallery
Seattle, Washington

1985
A Clear Vision
Sara Squeri Gallery
Cincinnati, Ohio

Art of Five
Morlan Gallery/
Transylvania University
Lexington, Kentucky

Summer Faculty Show
Baxter Gallery/Portland School of Art
Portland, Maine

Ceramics: The Oriental Influence
The Arts Council of Wilson
Wilson, North Carolina

The Regionalists
Owensboro Museum of Fine Art
Owensboro, Kentucky

LaGrange National
(Purchase Award)
Lamar Dodd Art Center
LaGrange, Georgia

1984
Introduction '84
Harris Gallery
Houston, Texas

Spotlight '84
University of Kentucky
Lexington, Kentucky

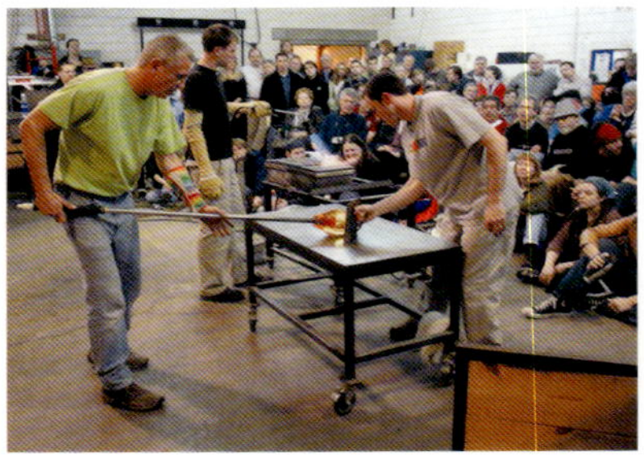
Stephen Powell demonstrating at the Glass Axis Studio in Columbus, Ohio. Matt Cummings torching and Chris Bohach assisting, 2005

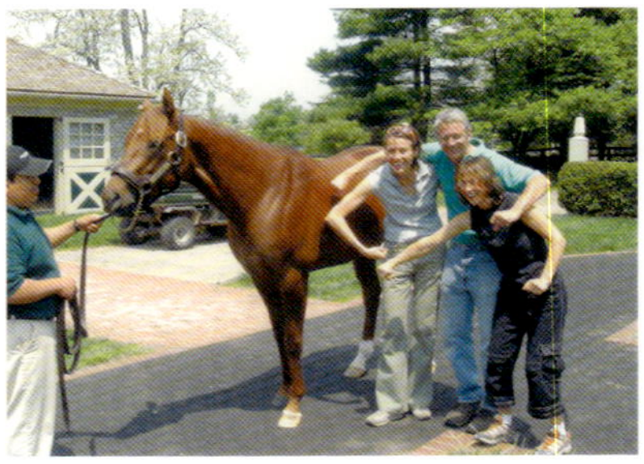
Smarty Jones, Katherine Gray, Stephen Powell, and Nancy Callan at Three Chimneys Horse Farm, Midway, Kentucky, while Nancy and Katherine were visiting artists at Centre, 2005

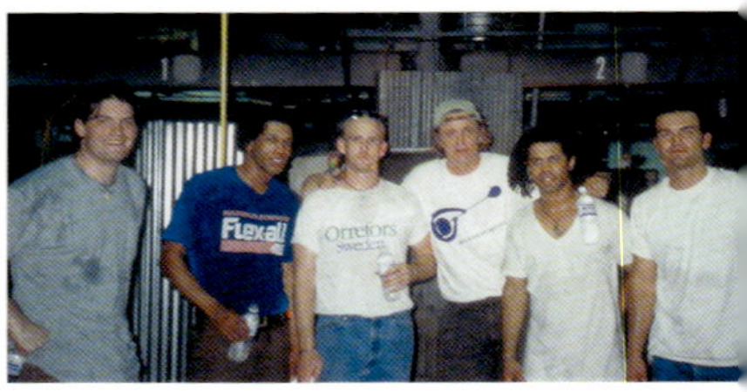
Powell and crew invited to demonstrate at Urban Glass in New York City. Left to right: Bill Couig, Nate Watson, Brook White, Stephen Powell, Ché Rhodes, and Adam Kenney, 2002

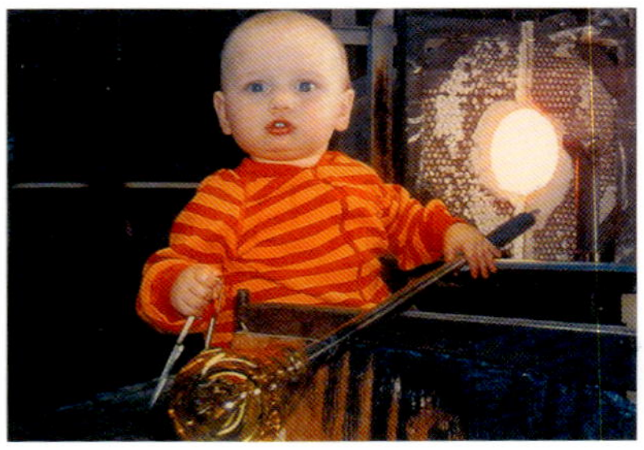
Zachary Hawk Powell blowing glass, Powell family holiday card, 1999

SELECT PERMANENT COLLECTIONS

Adele and Leonard Leight Collection, Louisville, Kentucky

Auckland Museum, Auckland, New Zealand

Baptist Memorial Hospital-Desoto, Southhaven, Mississippi

Birmingham Museum of Art, Birmingham, Alabama

Centre College, Danville, Kentucky

Cincinnati Art Museum, Cincinnati, Ohio

The Cleveland Museum of Art, Cleveland, Ohio

Corning Museum of Glass, Corning, New York

The Detroit Institute of Arts, Detroit, Michigan

Donnelley Printing Corporation, Chicago, Illinois

Grounds for Sculpture, Hamilton, New Jersey

H.E. Sheikh Hamad Bin Jassim Bin Jabor Al-Thani, Foreign Minister, Doha, Qatar

Haystack Mountain School of Crafts, Deer Isle, Maine

Hermitage Museum, St. Petersburg, Russia

Humana Corporation, Louisville, Kentucky

Huntsville Museum of Art, Huntsville, Alabama

Jewish Hospital, Louisville, Kentucky

Lamar Dodd Art Center, LaGrange, Georgia

Lvov Art Institute, Lvov, Ukraine

Mobile Museum of Art, Mobile, Alabama

Montgomery Museum of Fine Arts, Montgomery, Alabama

Muskegon Museum of Art, Muskegon, Michigan

Providian Corporation, Louisville, Kentucky

Red May Glass Museum, Vishny Volochok, Russia

The Regent Hotel, Le Plume, Hong Kong

Sydney College of the Arts, Sydney, Australia

Tropicana Corporation, St. Petersburg, Florida

Wagga Wagga Art Gallery, Wagga Wagga, Australia

Wustum Museum of Fine Arts, Racine, Wisconsin

EARLY WORK

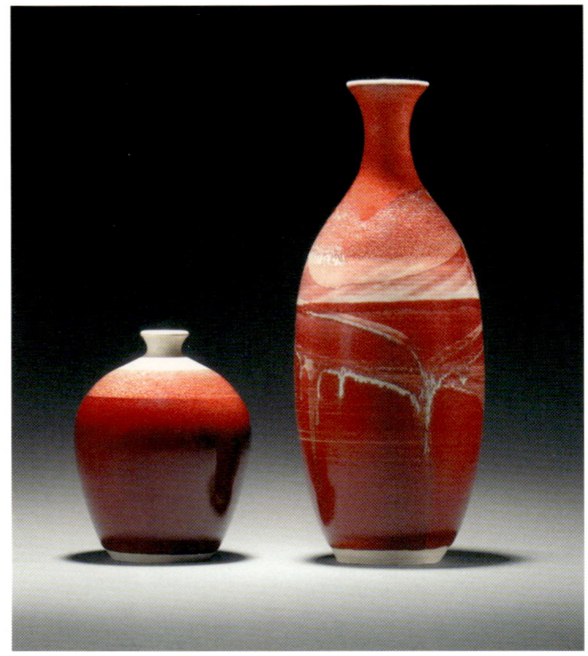

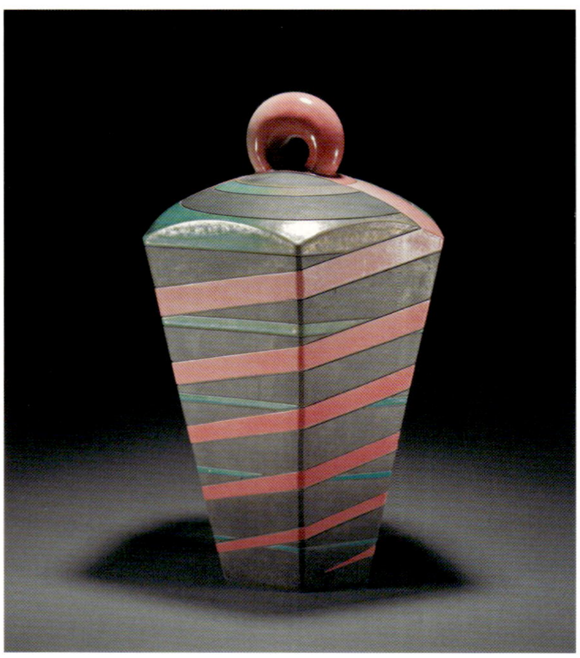

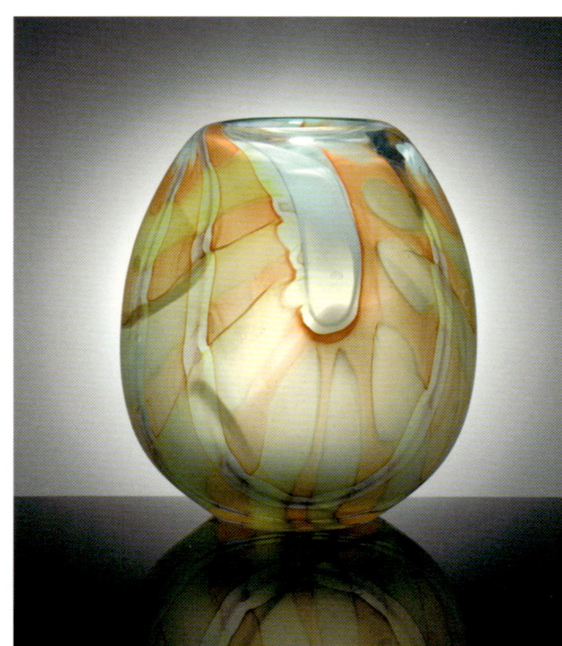

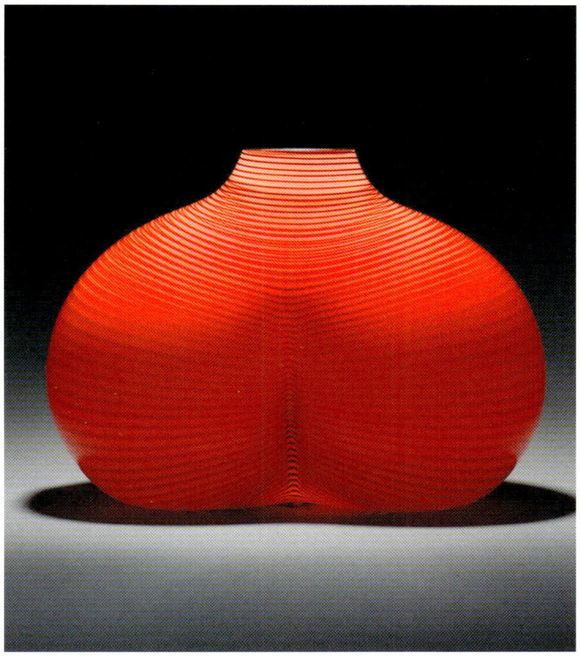

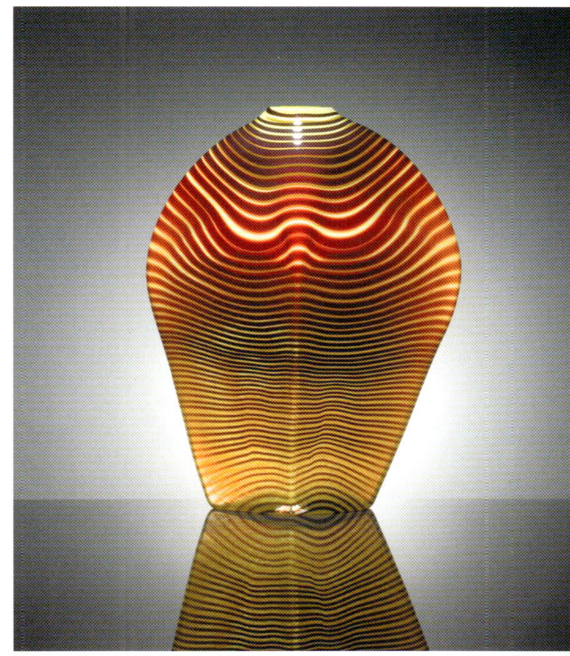

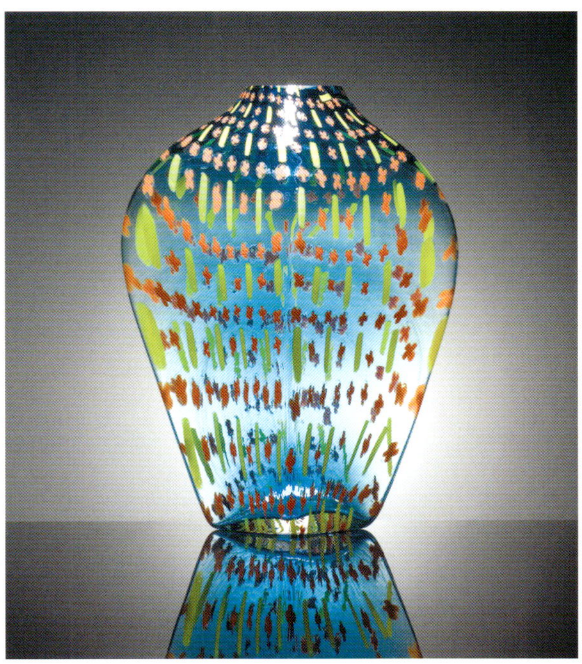

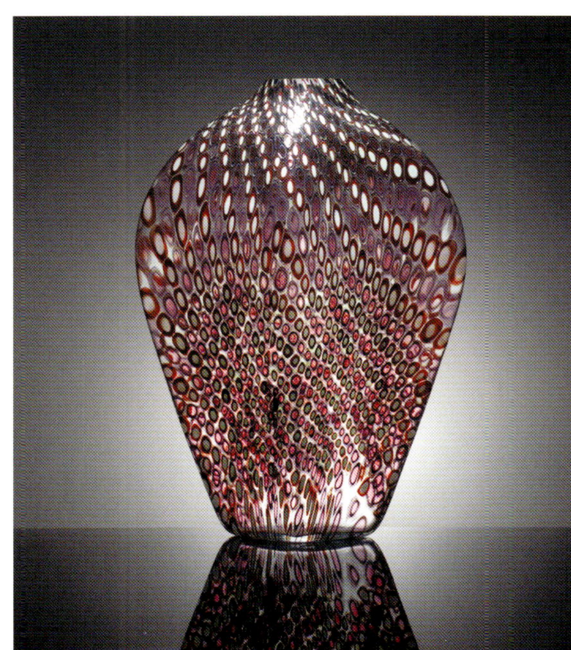

CHECKLIST

All dimensions are in inches.

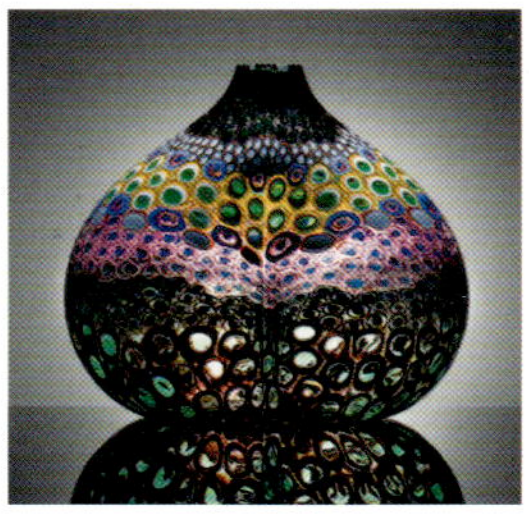

Peacock Cheeks Johnson
18 x 20 x 12
1988
page 19

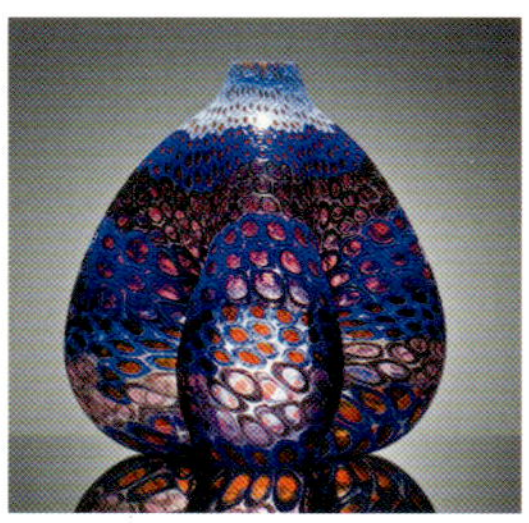

Blue Saggy Smith
18.5 x 18 x 17.5
1988
page 20

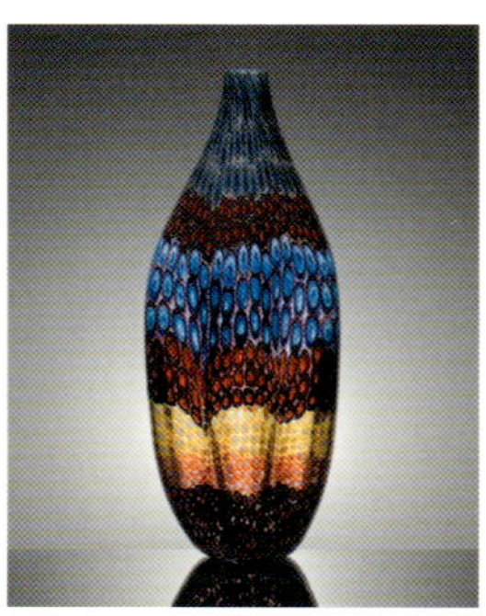

Praying Okra Smith
27 x 11.5 x 11.75
1989
page 22

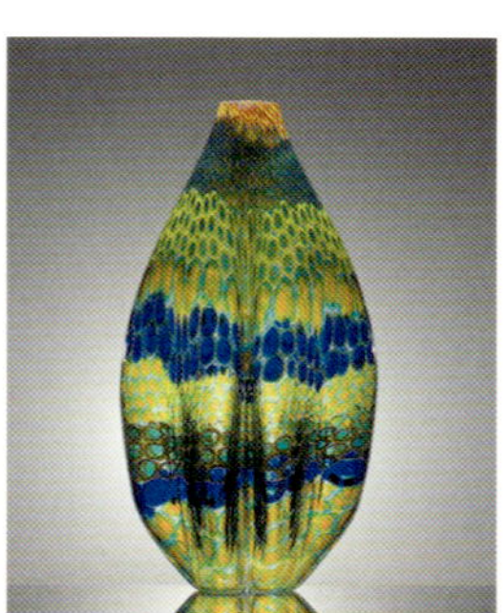

Green Accordion Jones
26.5 x 13.75 x 8.5
1989
page 25

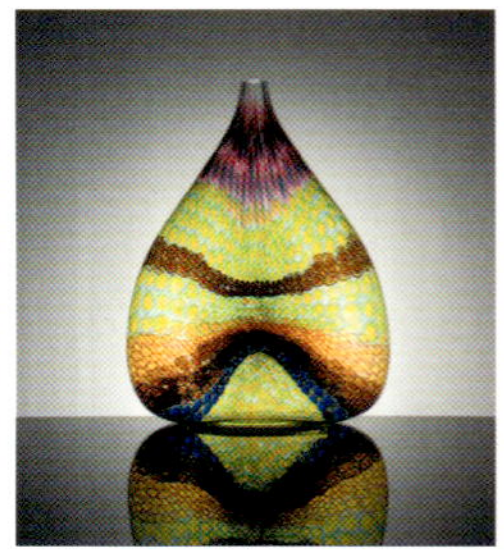

Acid Gasp Johnson
27.5 x 20.5 x 6
1990
page 26

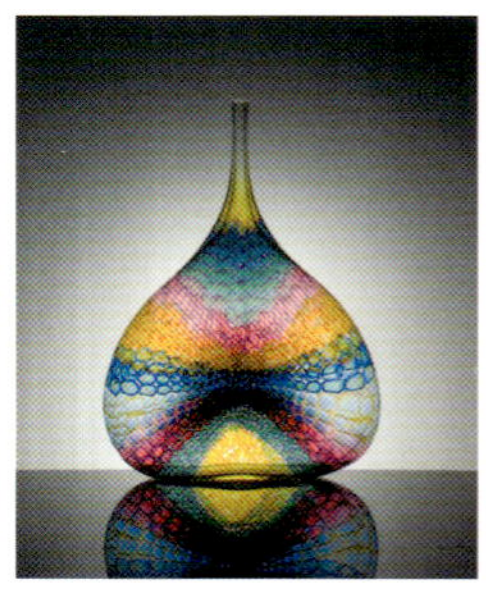

Gasping Manic Johnson
31.25 x 22.5 x 6.5
1993
page 27

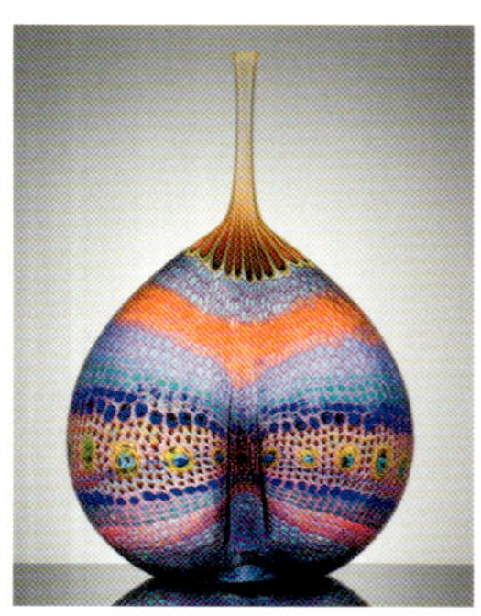

Jitter Buns Johnson
28.25 x 21.75 x 13
1998
page 28

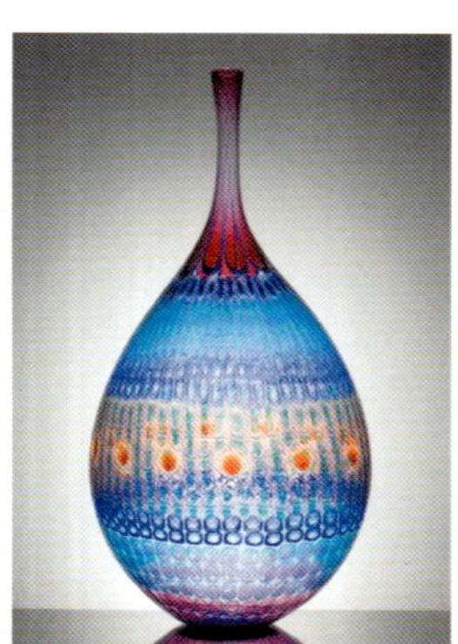

Red Eye Hawk
40 x 20.25 x 20.25
2001
page 31

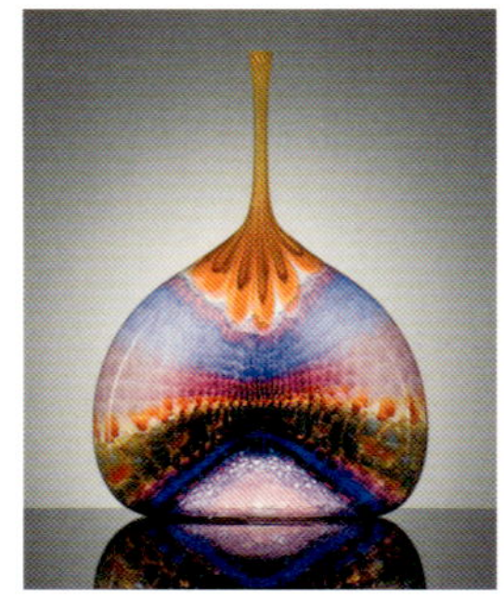

Nostalgic Gasping Dusk
35.625 x 24.75 x 6
2001
page 32

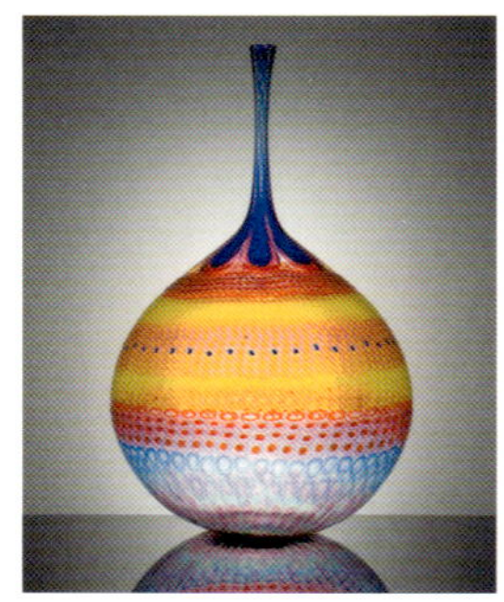

Winking Tangy Orb
36.5 x 26 x 26
2003
page 35

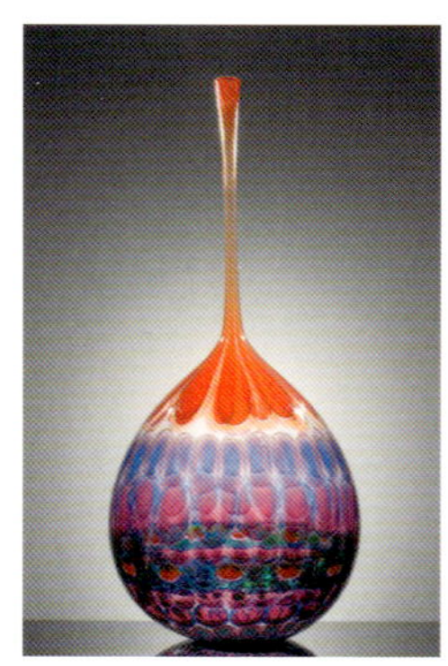

Sticky Fingers Smith
46 x 19.5 x 19.5
1999
page 36

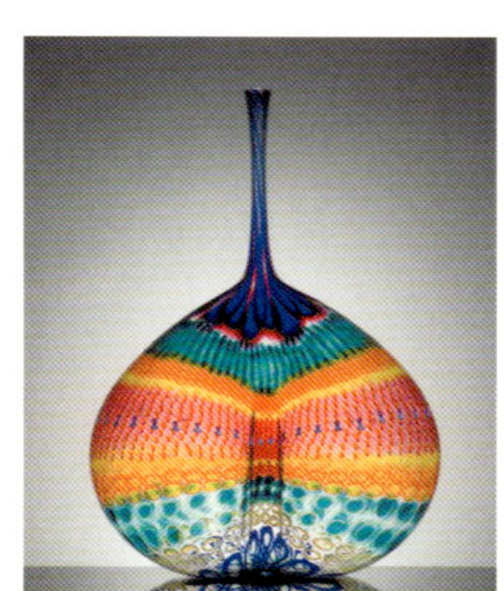

Tropical Sarcastic Cleavage
33.75 x 23.75 x 13.25
2002
page 39

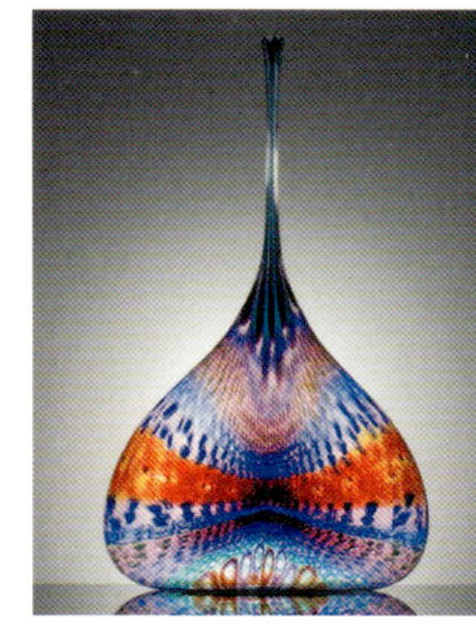

Gasping Arnie Index
49.75 x 25.75 x 6.5
2000
page 40

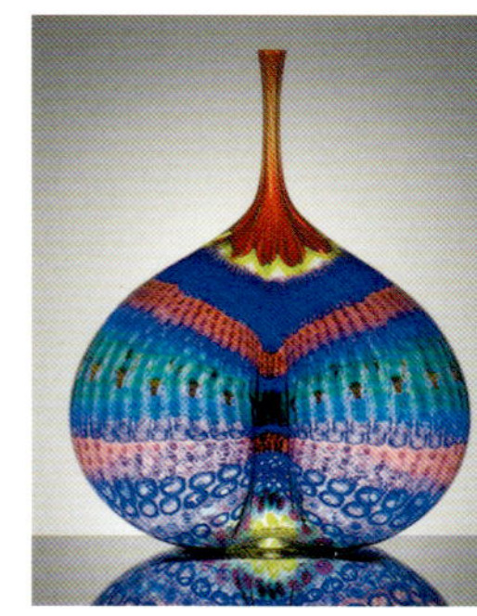

Audacious Scuba Mania
30.25 x 24 x 13.25
2002
page 43

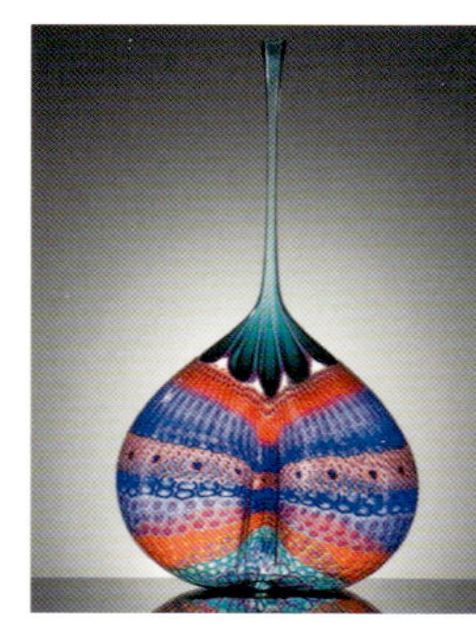

Insatiable Giverny Cheeks
42.75 x 23.25 x 13
2001
page 44

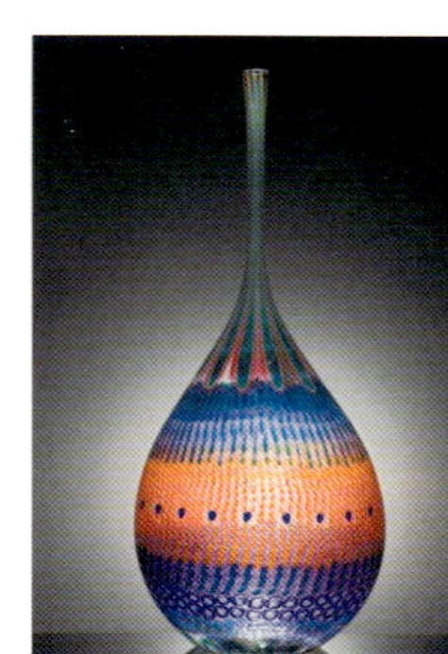

Lurking Innocent Fig
46.5 x 20 x 20
2001
page 47

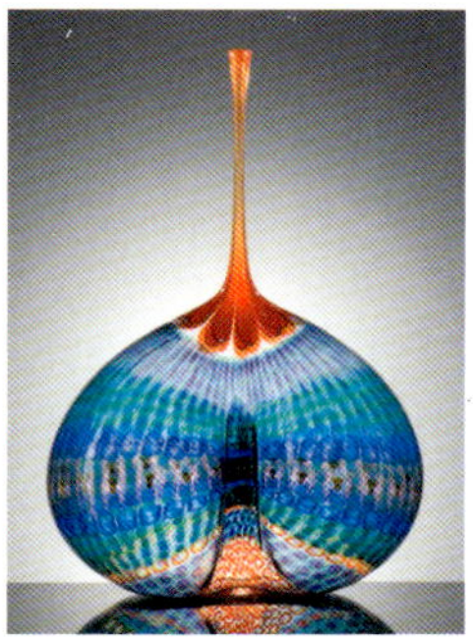

Insatiable Ardent Leer
36.75 x 24.75 x 14
2003
page 48

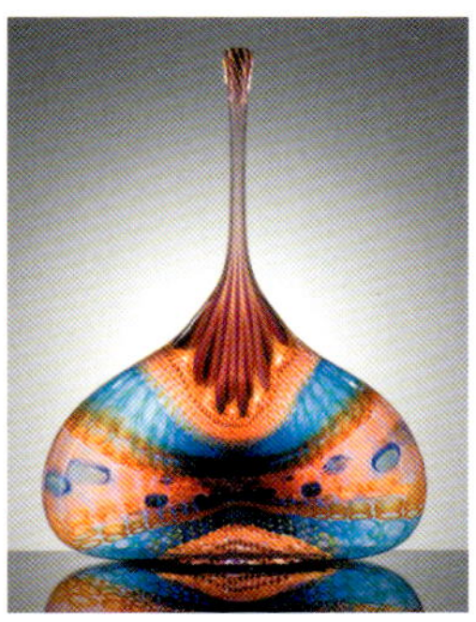

Licking Purple Manic
35.625 x 26 x 6.5
2001
page 51

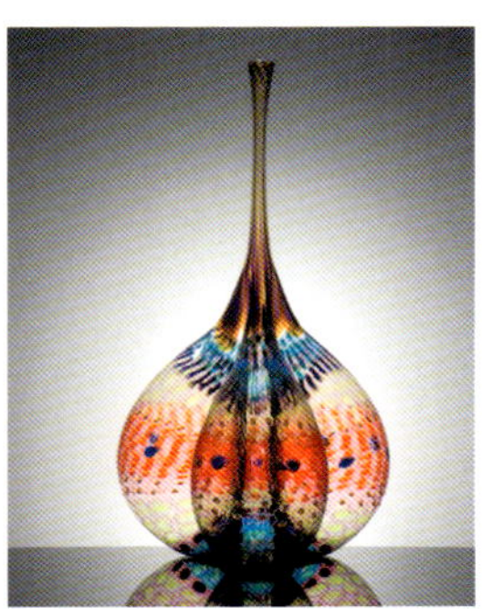

Igniting Buxom Tenacity
39.75 x 20.25 x 20.25
2003
page 53

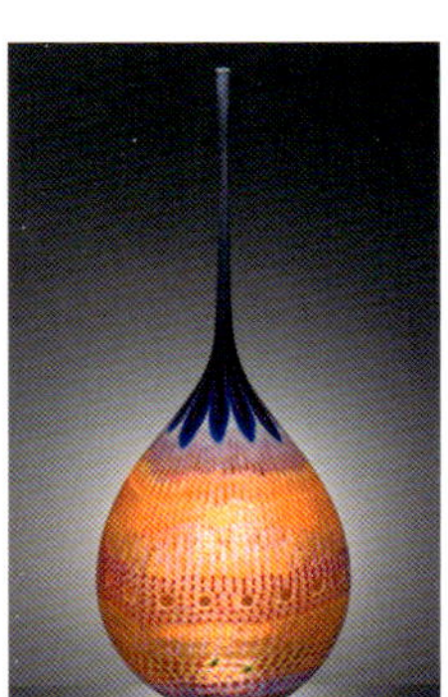

Lemon Marilyn Monroe
48 x 19 x 19
1999
page 54

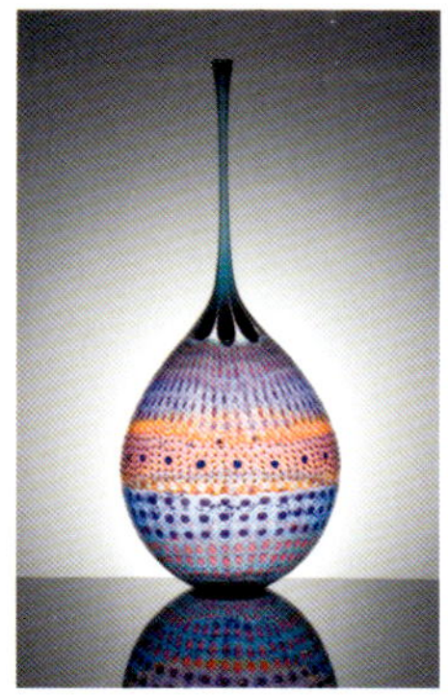

Whispering Purple Infatuation
50.25 x 20.25 x 20.25
2003
page 57

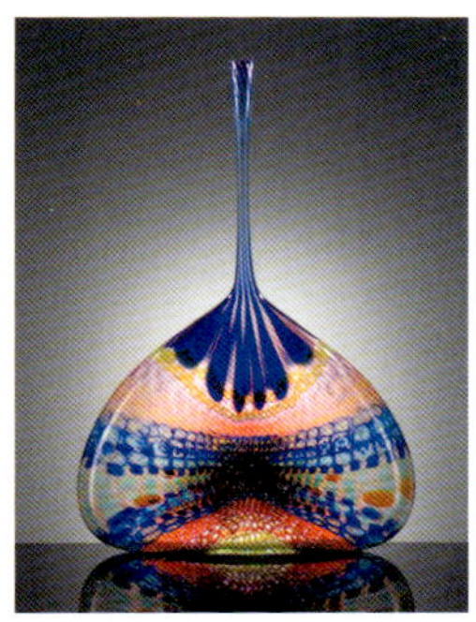

Hypnotic Sigh Smith
39 x 26.5 x 6.5
1999
page 58

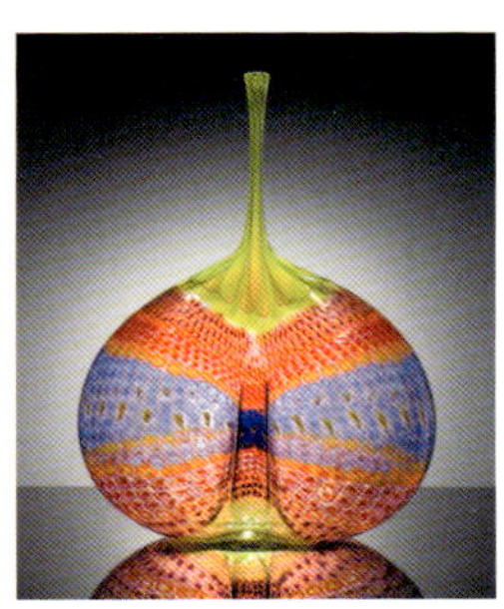

Frazzled Yellow Lick
33 x 24 x 13
2003
page 59

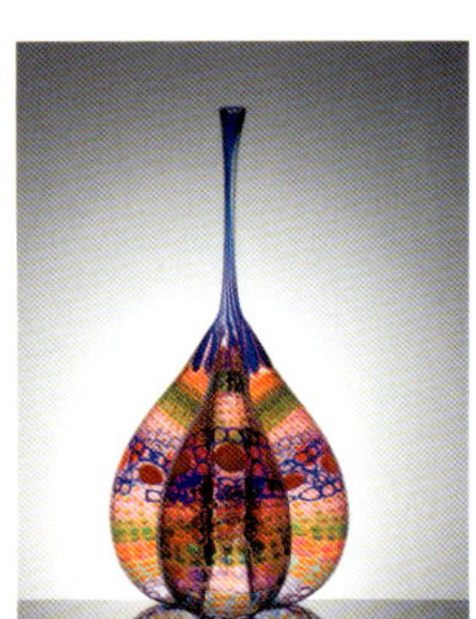

Autumn Jealous Cleavage
38 x 18 x 18
1988
page 60

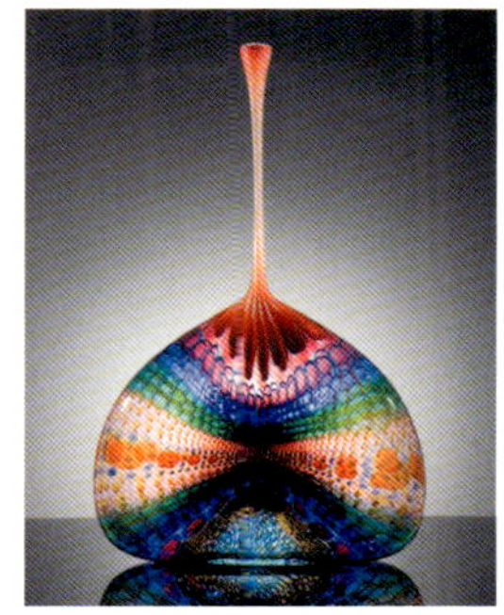

Vanishing Naïve Mania
39 x 24.5 x 6.5
2002
page 63

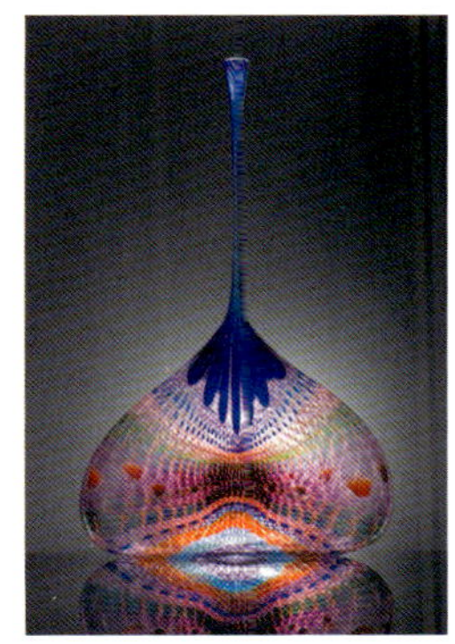

Spanky Squeeze Johnson
43.75 x 27 x 6.5
1999
page 64

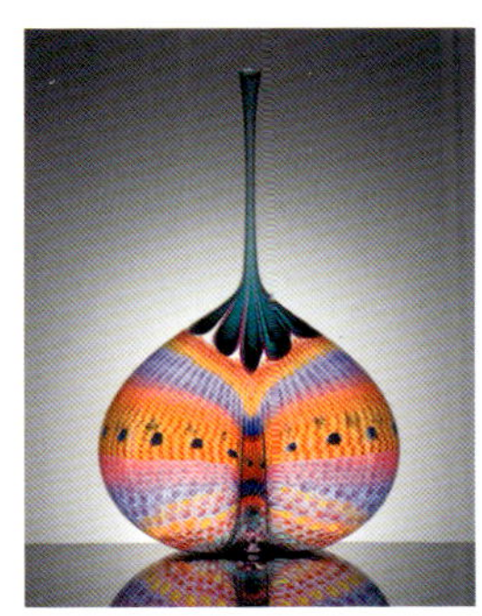

Lascivious Torrid Cleavage
41.25 x 25.25 x 14.5
2003
page 67

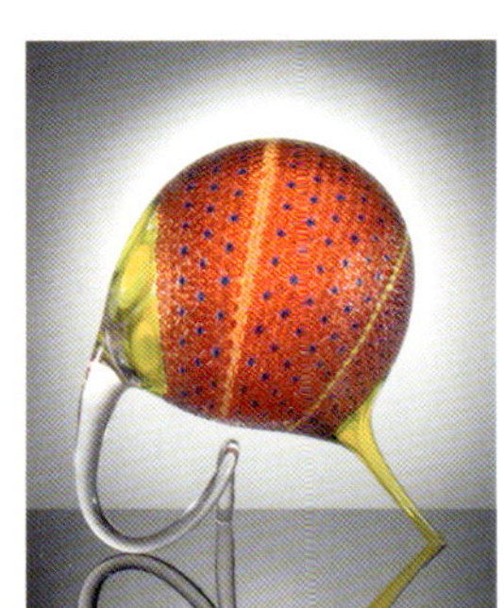

Lemon Lurching Mania
27.5 x 24.5 x 18.5
2005
page 78

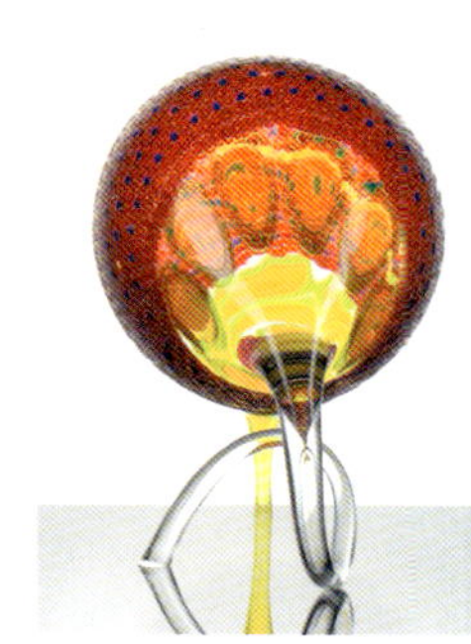

Lemon Lurching Mania
27.5 x 24.5 x 18.5
2005
page 81

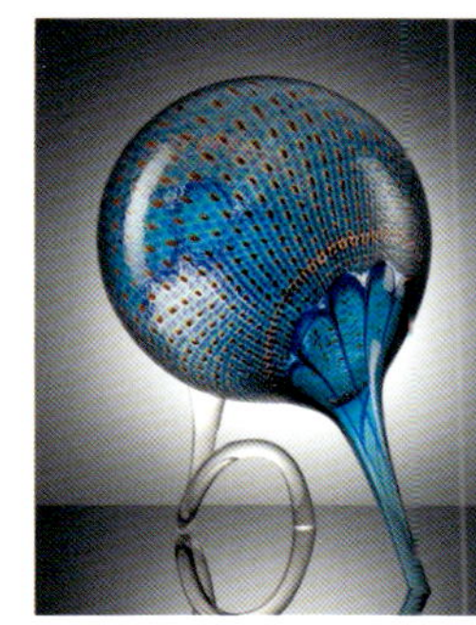

Pushy Violet Throb
29 x 24 x 19.25
2005
page 83

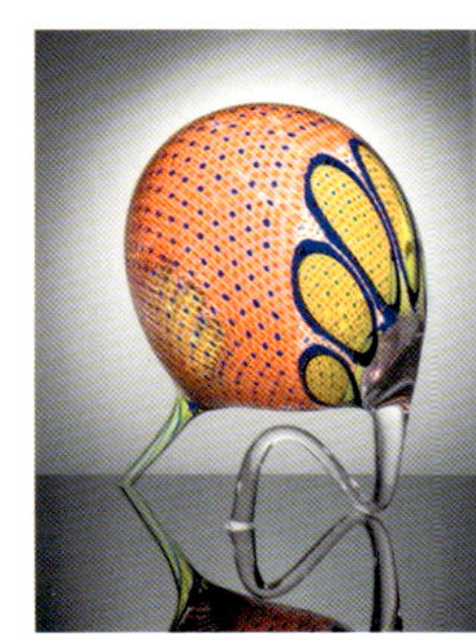

Acid Puffy Snoop
28 x 23.5 x 20
2005
page 84

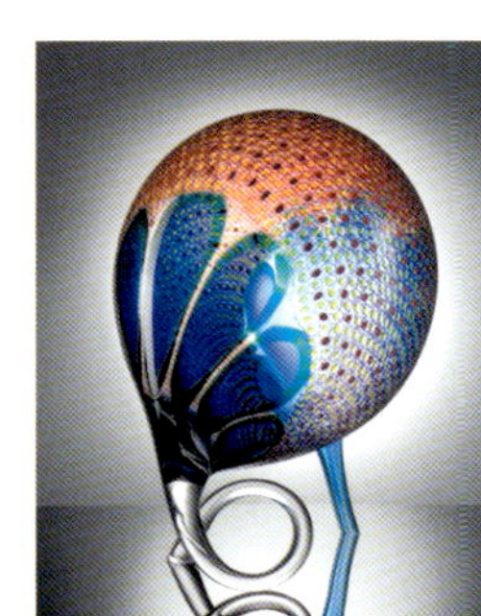

Lurking Tangy Puffer
27.75 x 22.75 x 18.75
2005
page 86

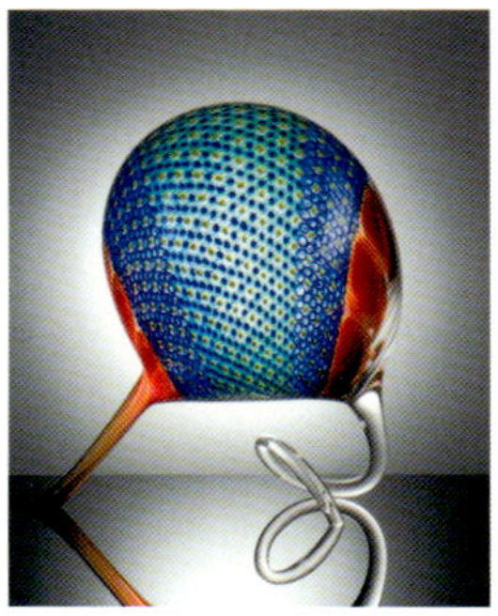

Sniffing Snoop Pooch
28.125 x 25 x 19
2005
page 88

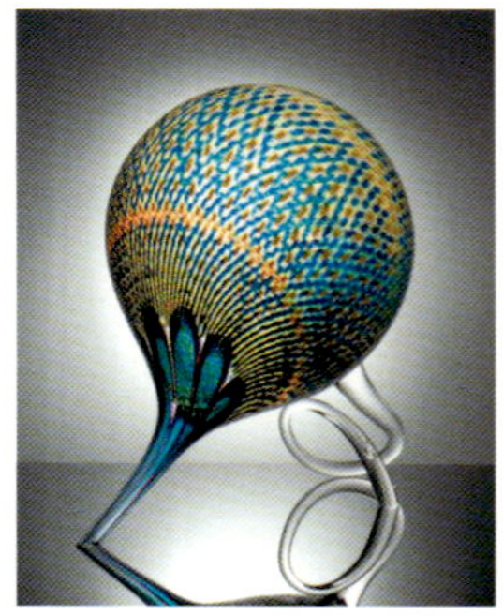

Brainy Voracious Thrust
26.5 x 30.5 x 18.5
2005
page 97

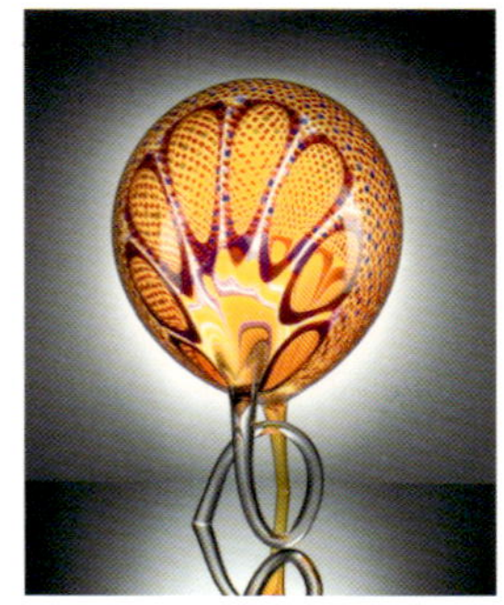

Frenetic Leering Sniffer
30.5 x 24 x 19.5
2005
page 105

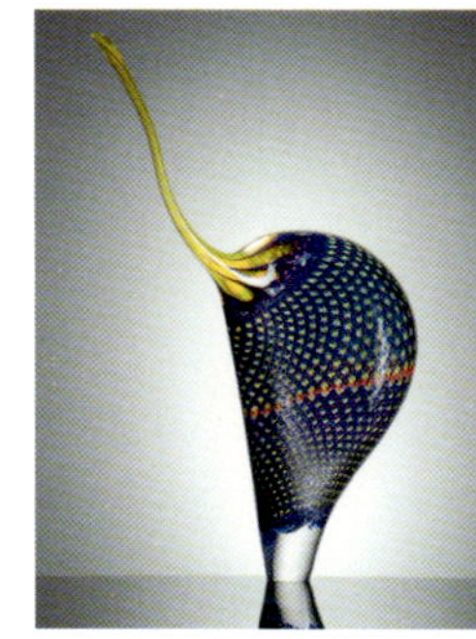

Gulping Enigmatic Swish
38 x 30.5 x 13.25
2006
page 124

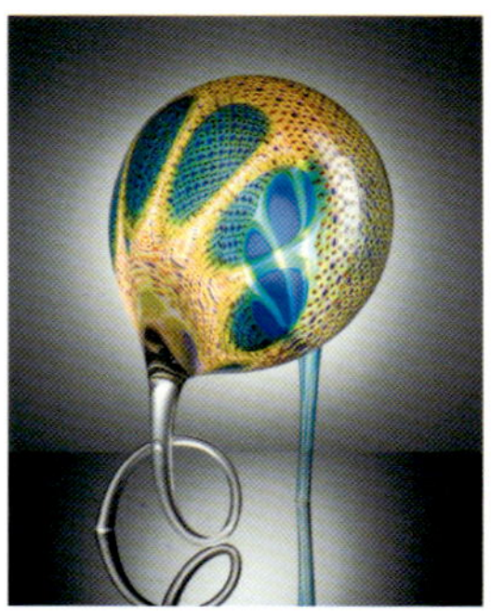

Teasing Frantic Lurch
31.5 x 20 x 19.5
2005
page 91

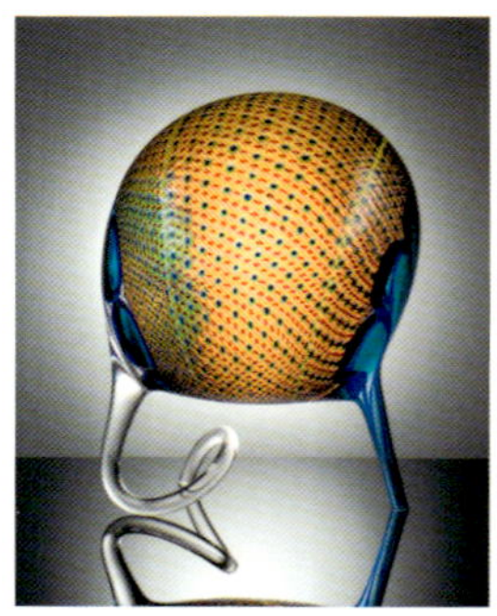

Sultry Zealous Pulse
27 x 20.25 x 19
2005
page 98

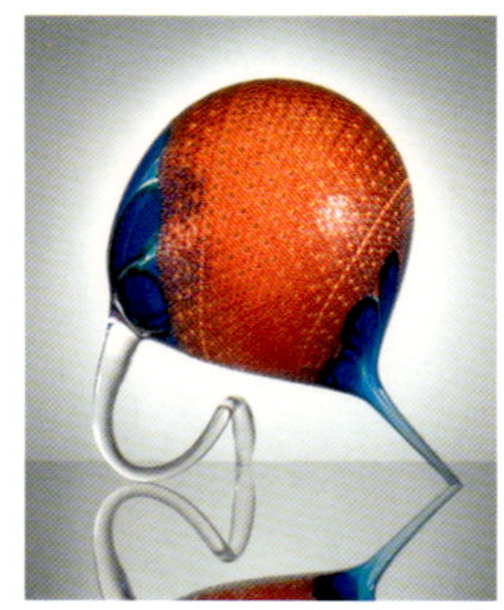

Nudging Lemon Snoop
28.5 x 25.5 x 21
2005
page 106

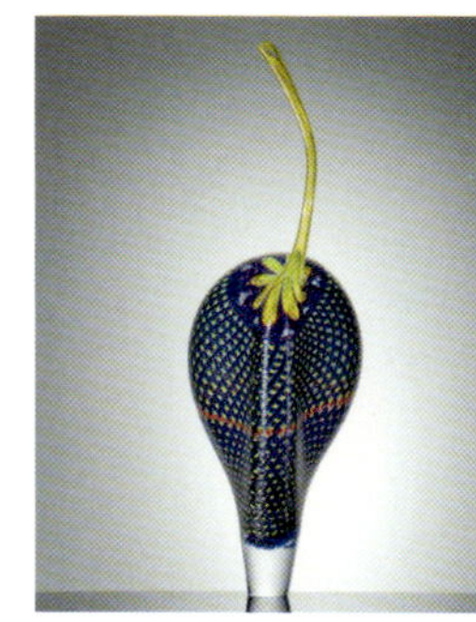

Gulping Enigmatic Swish
38 x 30.5 x 13.25
2006
page 125

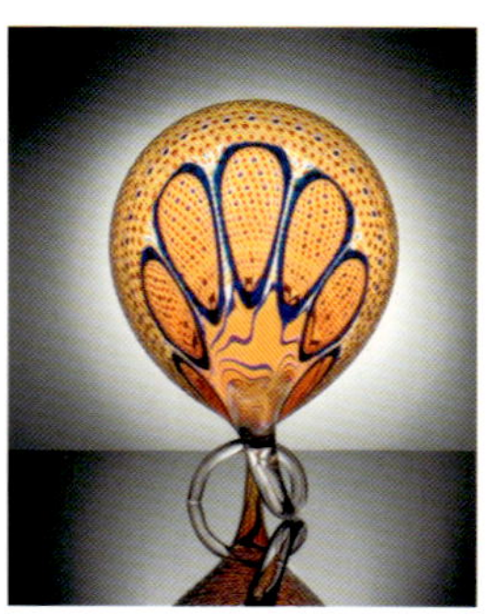

Startled Dizzy Snorter
27.75 x 23 x 18.75
2005
page 92

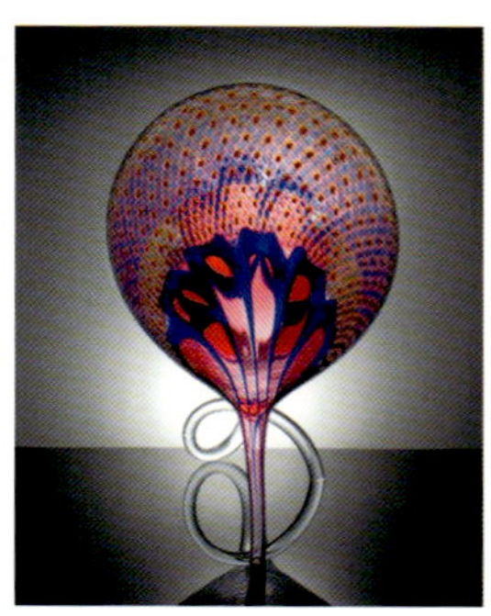

Hurricane Lemon Puffer
29 x 26.25 x 19.75
2005
page 101

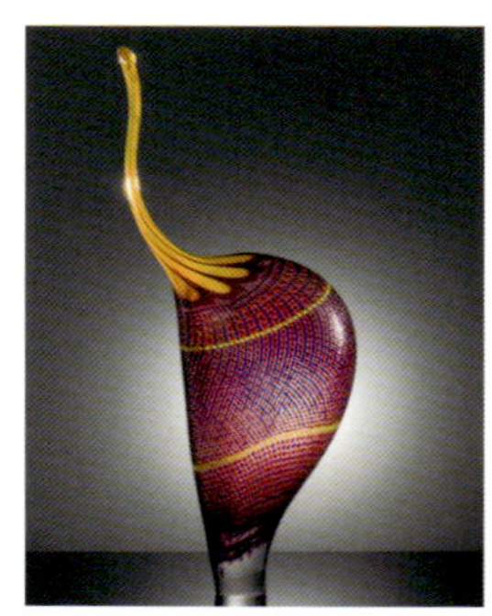

Craning Frenetic Phobia
37.75 x 20 x 8.5
2006
page 121

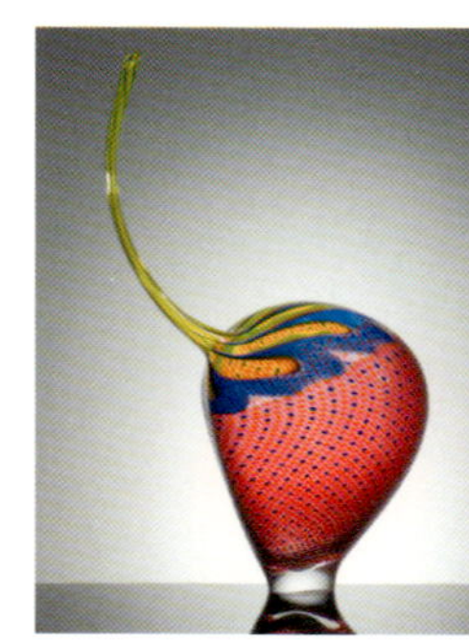

Winking Torrid Zeal
32 x 22.5 x 14
2006
page 127

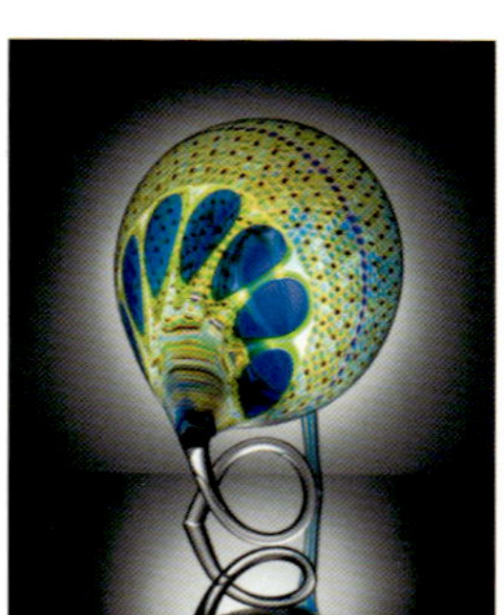

Innocent Emerald Sniffer
27.5 x 22.25 x 19.25
2005
page 95

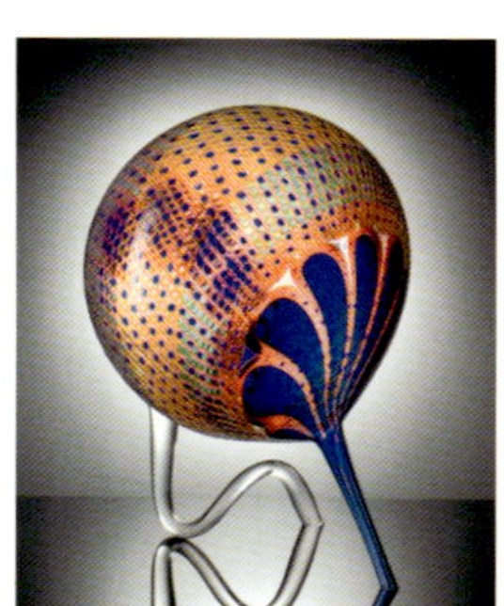

Wheezy Snooper Nudge
27.25 x 21.5 x 20
2005
page 102

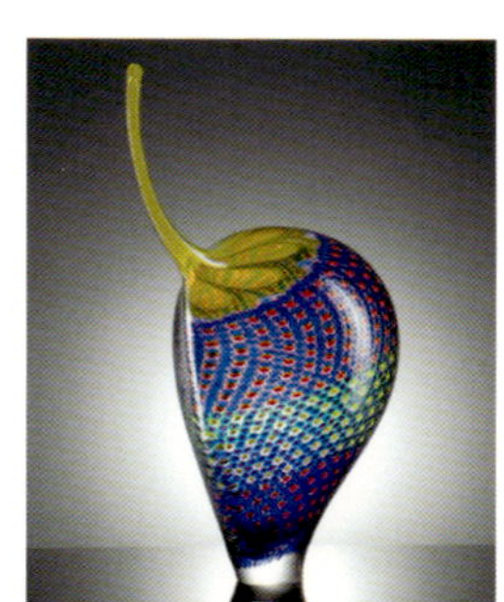

Manic Trumpeting Pooch
30.625 x 21.5 x 14
2006
page 122

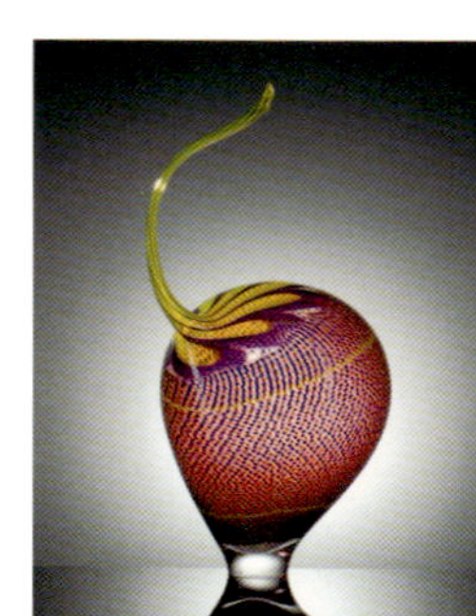

Frenetic Bayou Pouncer
33.5 x 20.25 x 15.25
2006
page 128

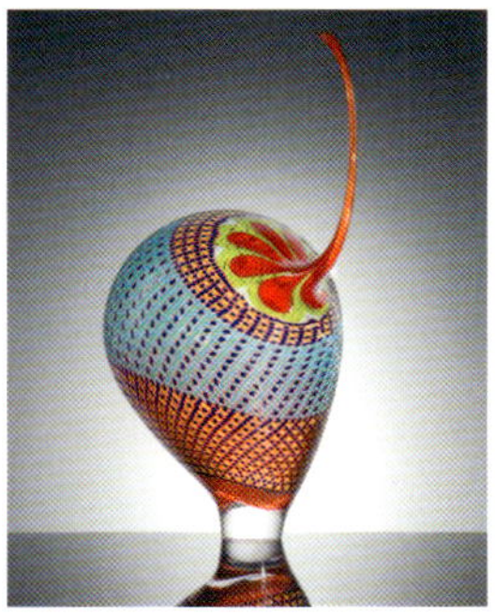

Nubile Pulsing Snort
32.5 x 23 x 15.5
2006
page 131

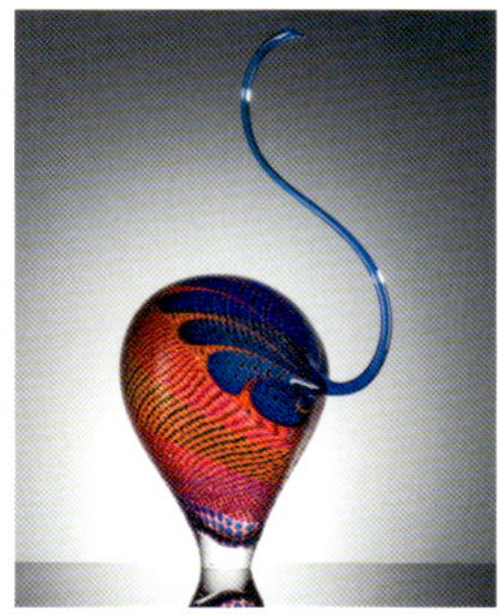

Lascivious Vertigo Sniffer
41 x 27.75 x 15.75
2006
page 138

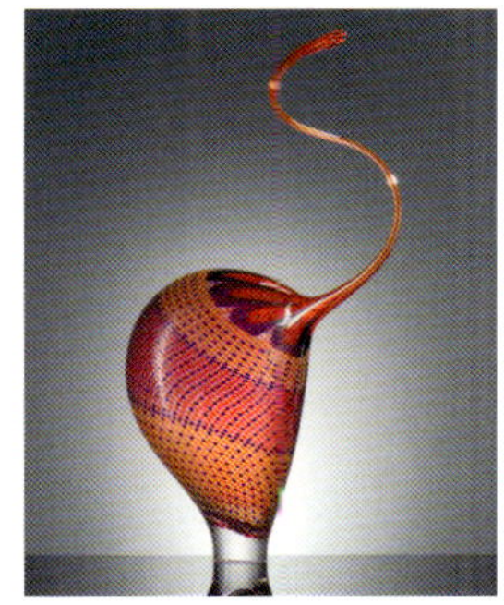

Torrid Nippled Viper
41.5 x 26 x 13.25
2006
page 145

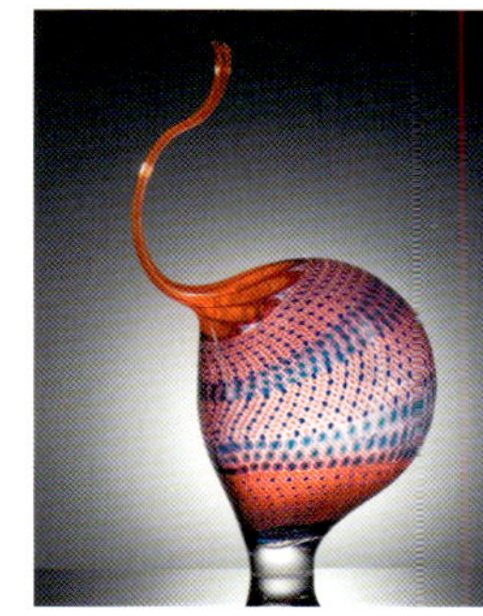

Sassy Poochy Meander
36.5 x 23.25 x 15.75
2006
page 153

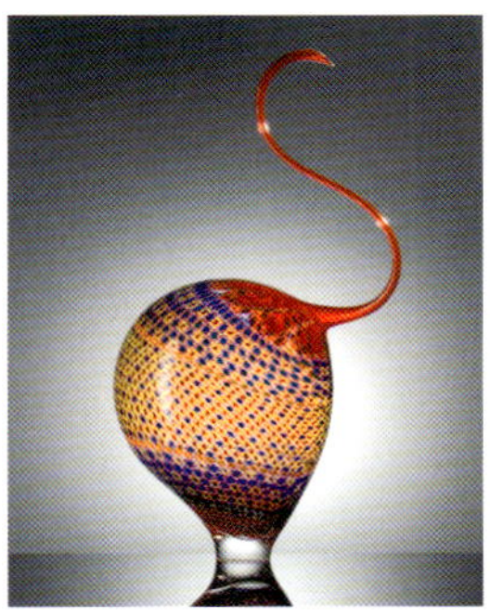

Lurid Pulsing Meander
38.75 x 24.25 x 16.25
2006
page 132

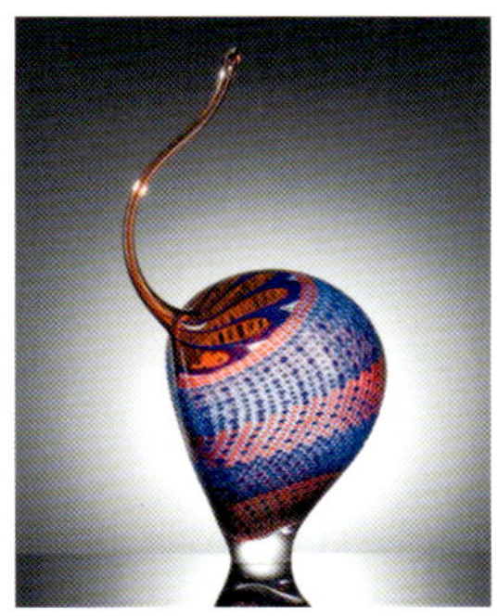

Drizzling Sultry Craner
34.75 x 22.25 x 14.75
2006
page 141

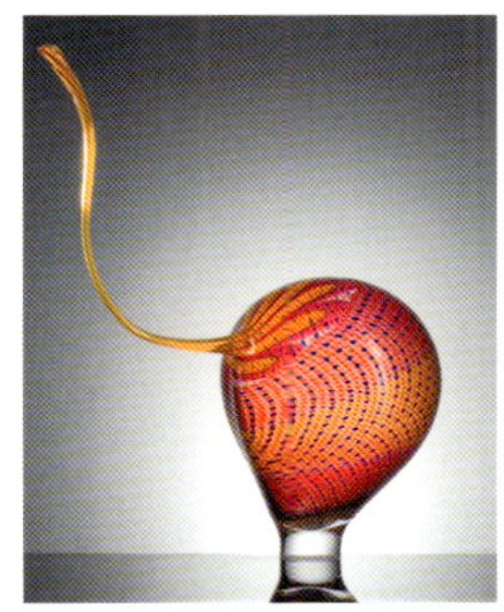

Copious Solar Spank
37 x 31.5 x 16.25
2006
page 146

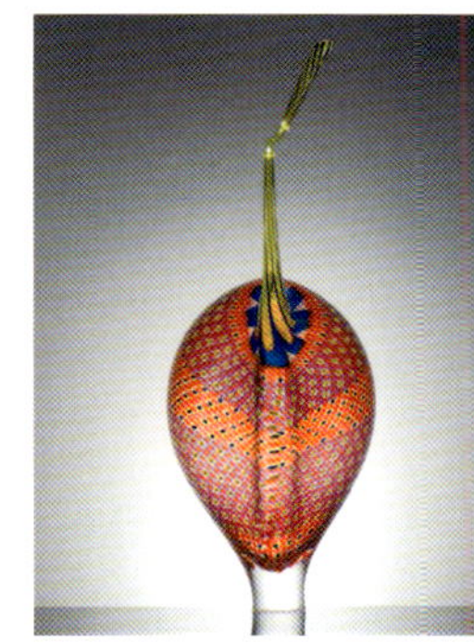

Sultry Lemon Jitter
42.5 x 24.25 x 15.5
2006
page 154

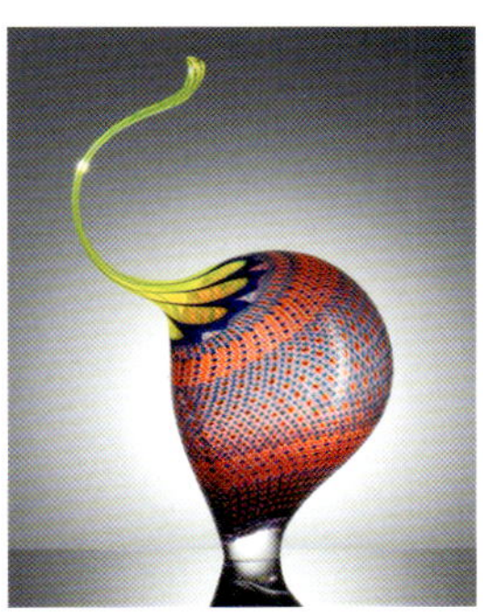

Glancing Naive Swooper
36.5 x 24 x 15.75
2006
page 135

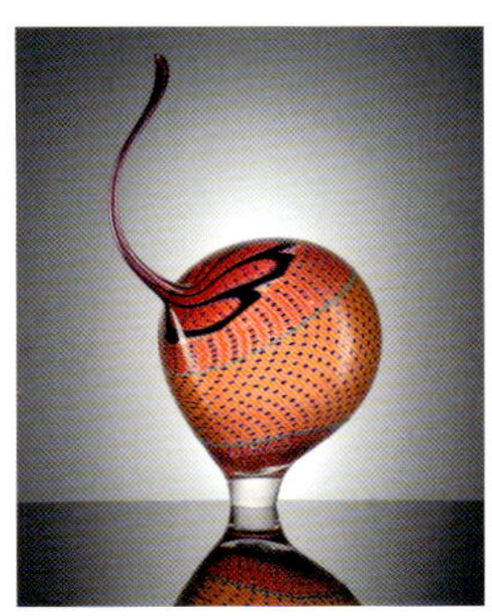

Craning Nubile Pouncer
34.25 x 24.25 x 16
2006
page 142

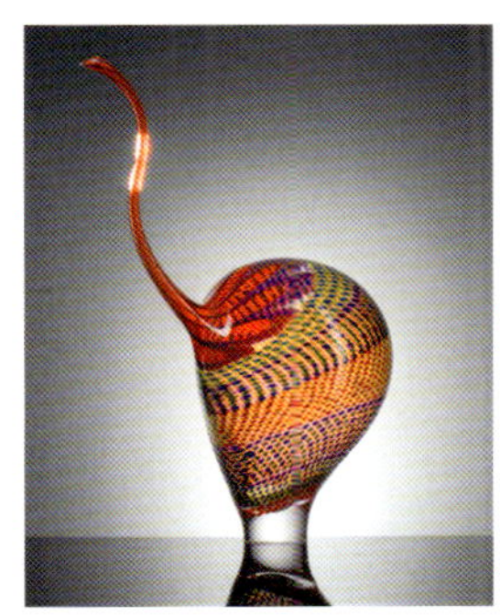

Meander Kissy Quiver
34.5 x 24 x 14.5
2006
page 149

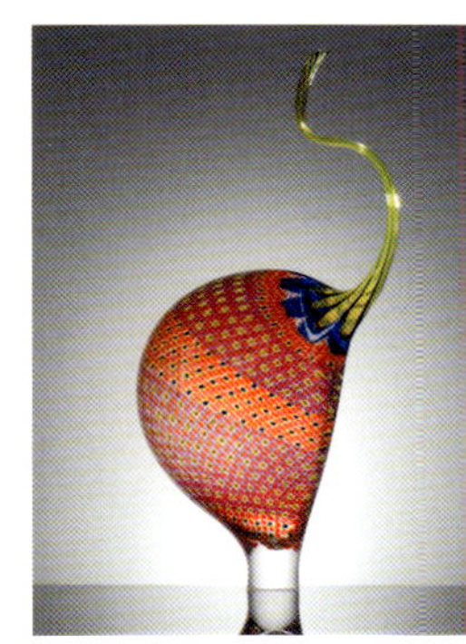

Sultry Lemon Jitter
42.5 x 24.25 x 15.5
2006
page 155

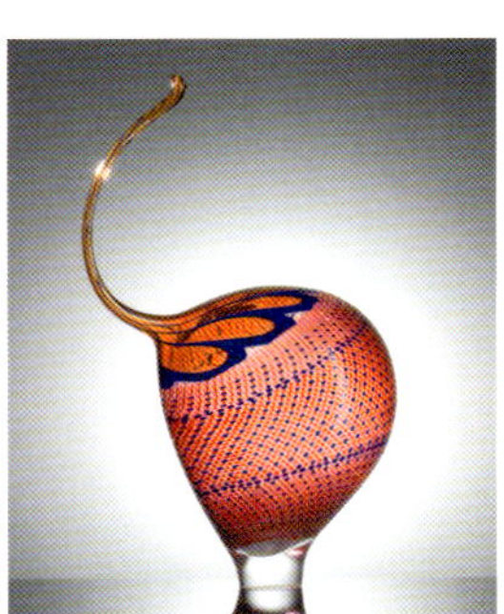

Lunar Nippled Mania
33.25 x 22 x 14.5
2006
page 136

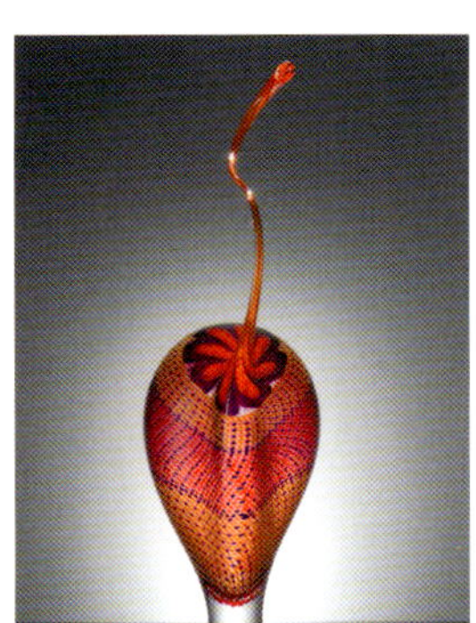

Torrid Nippled Viper
41.5 x 26 x 13.25
2006
page 144

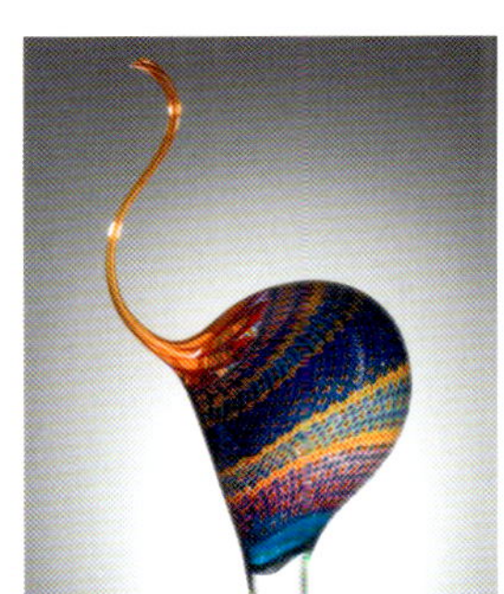

Intrepid Yearning Gaze
40.75 x 26.5 x 14.25
2006
page 150

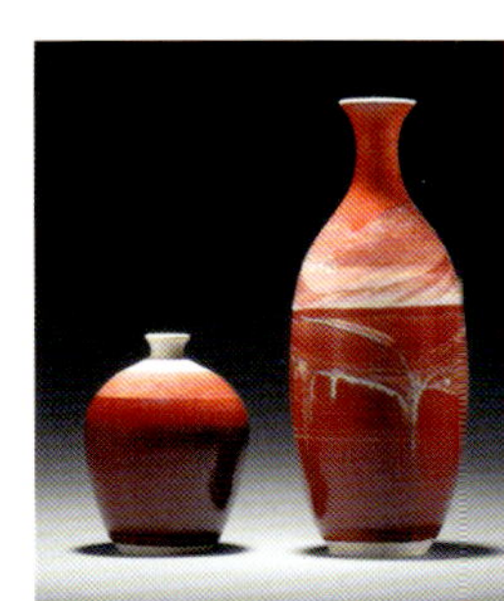

Untitled (Porcelain)
6 x 4.5 x 4.5
1978
page 206

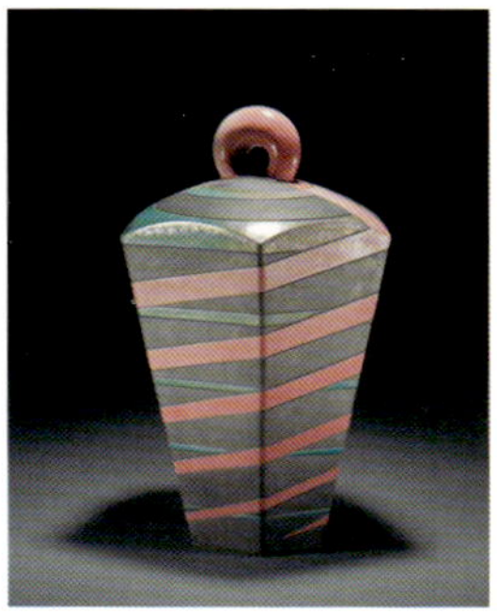

Pink Slant Smith (Raku)
21.25 x 12 x 11
1983
page 206

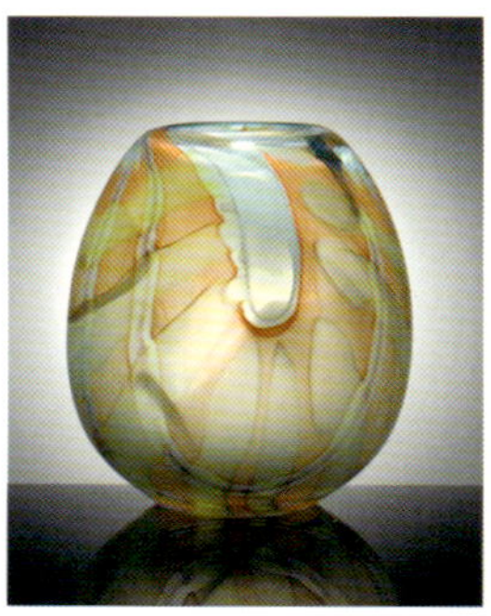

Untitled
7.75 x 7 x 7
1982
page 206

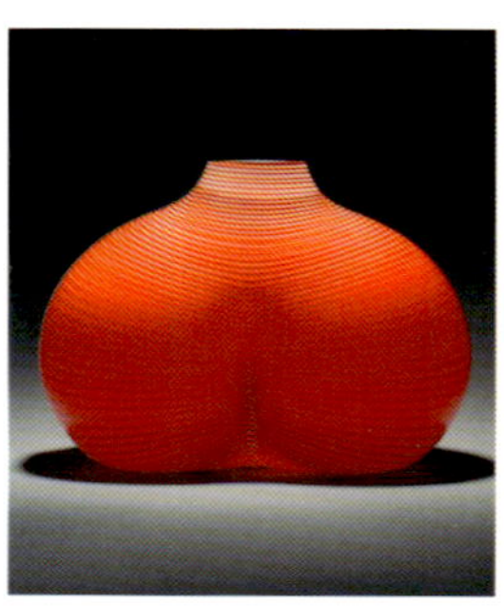

Red Cheeks Johnson
12 x 16.5 x 10.75
1986
page 207

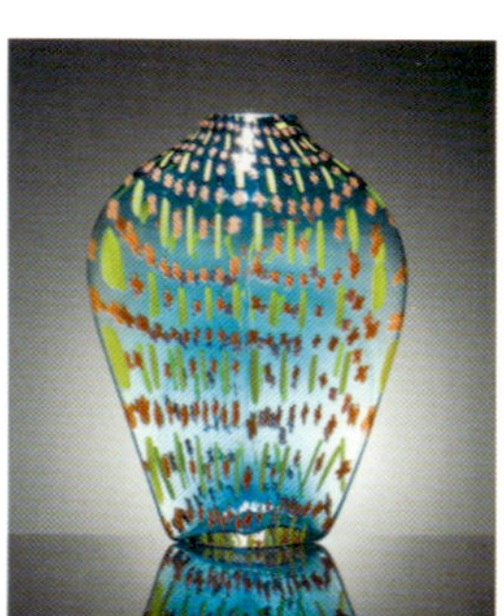

Nova Mummy Smith
17.25 x 12.75 x 8.25
1987
page 207

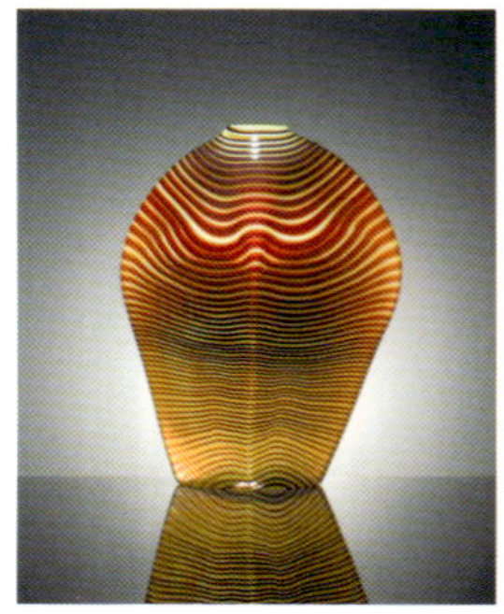

Maroon Zebra Jones
15.75 x 12 x 7.5
1987
page 207

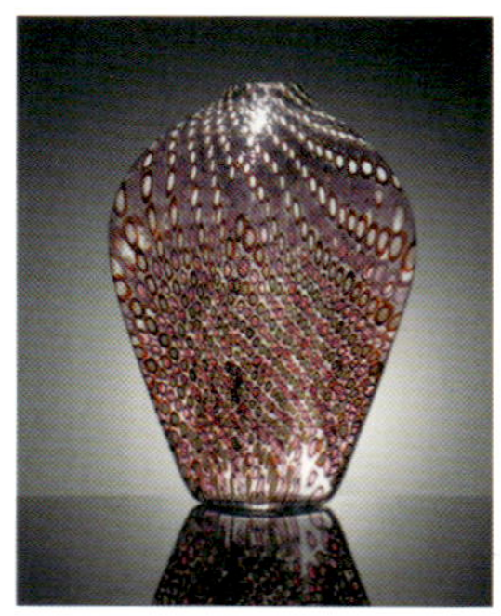

Rattlesnake Johnson
17.5 x 12.5 x 8.25
1987
page 207

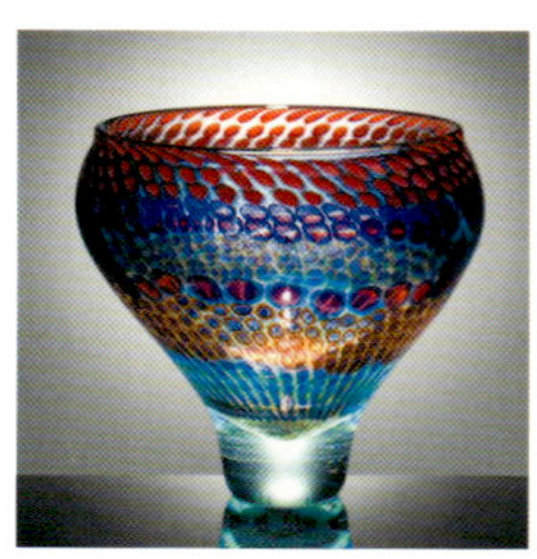

After Accident Bowl #1
9 x 9.5 x 9.5
1991
page 191

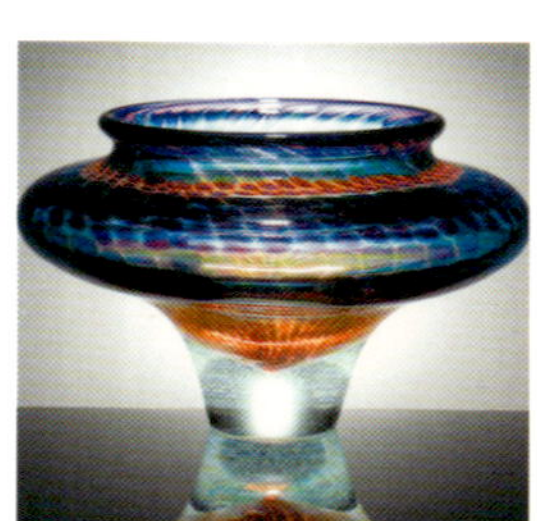

After Accident Bowl #2
7 x 10.5 x 10.5
1991
page 191

CONTRIBUTORS

Mark Lucas is Jobson Professor of English at Centre College. He writes on southern literature and culture and is the author of *Home Voices* and *The Southern Vision of Andrew Lytle*.

Laurie Winters is curator of European art at the Milwaukee Art Museum. She has written widely on the decorative arts and has organized several major international exhibitions on diverse topics.

James Yood teaches contemporary art history and criticism at the School of the Art Institute of Chicago and is a contributing editor to *Glass* magazine. He is the author of many books, including studies of the work of William Morris and Jon Kuhn.

David Harpe is a photographer/artist working in Louisville, Kentucky. His unique photographs of glass artwork have appeared in numerous books and publications.

Julius Friedman is a graphic designer and owner of Images, a design studio specializing in corporate and cultural design. His work is included in the permanent collections of the Museum of Modern Art, New York; National Gallery of Art, Washington, D.C.; Dansk Plakat Museum, Denmark; and the National Museum of Poster Art, Warsaw, Poland.

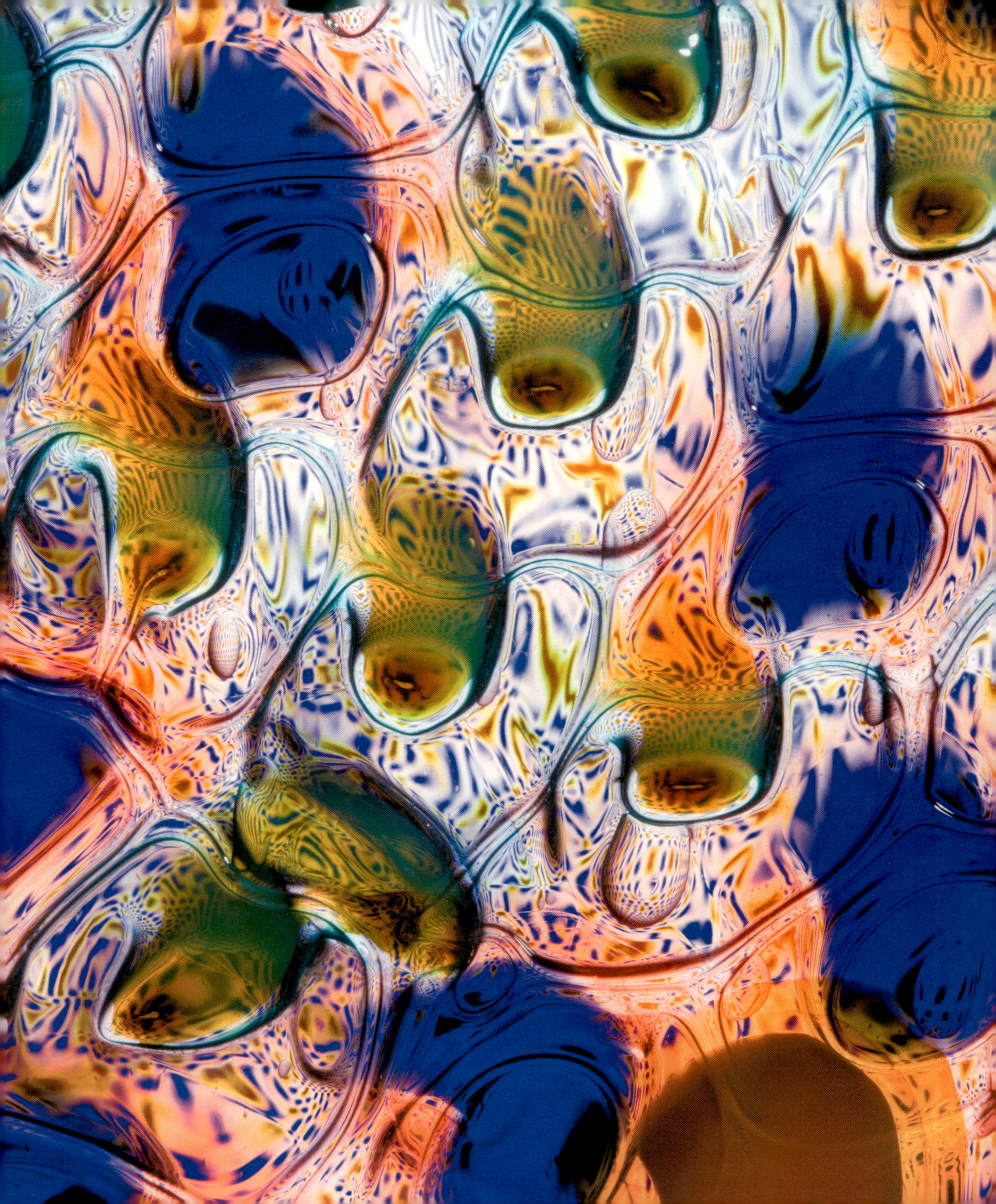

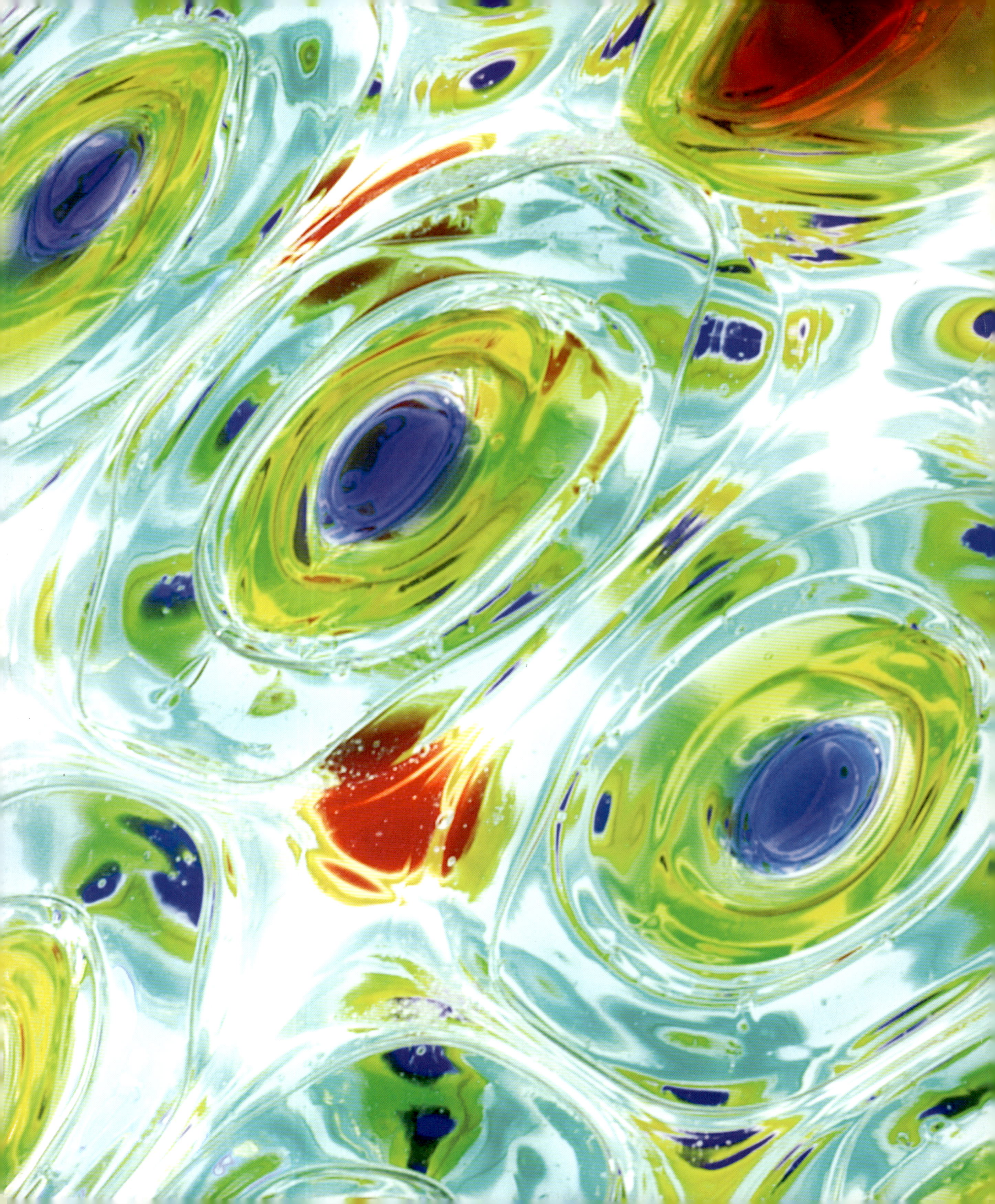